COPING WITH THE FINAL TRAGEDY:

Cultural Variation in Dying and Grieving

Editors
DAVID R. COUNTS
DOROTHY A. COUNTS

PERSPECTIVES ON DEATH AND DYING Series
RICHARD A. KALISH, Series Editor

D1550805

Baywood Publishing Company, Inc.
AMITYVILLE, NEW YORK

Library of Congress Catalog Number: 90-27920
ISBN: 0-89503-081-0 (Paper)
ISBN: 0-89503-082-9 (Cloth)

Library of Congress Cataloging-in-Publication Data

Coping with the final tragedy : cultural variation in dying and
    grieving / edited by David R. Counts, Dorothy A. Counts.
        p. cm. -- (Perspectives on death and dying series)
        Includes bibliographical references (p.) and index.
        ISBN 0-89503-082-9 (cloth) . -- ISBN 0-89503-081-0 (paper)
        1. Death--Social aspects--Cross-cultural studies. 2. Grief--Cross
    -cultural studies. 3. Bereavement--Cross-cultural studies.
    4. Funeral rites and ceremonies--Cross-cultural studies.
    5. Indians--Mortuary customs. I. Counts, David R. II. Counts,
    Dorothy Ayers. III. Series
    HQ1073.C68 1991   90-27920
    306.9--dc20   CIP

DEDICATION

This book is dedicated to Richard Kalish who inspired this book
and whose untimely death lent immediacy to it.
And for Kolia, Sigi, and Ngaloko whose deaths have touched us
and for whom we have grieved but not yet mourned.

Preface

This volume was conceived in January 1986 when Richard Kalish, an editor for Baywood Publishing Co., Inc., asked us to prepare a collection of cross-cultural studies of the processes of dying and grieving directed to students, hospice workers and others concerned with dying people and their families, as well as to anthropologists. To be useful, the volume's chapters should address both the common concerns shared by all people and the experiences unique to specific cultures. While anthropologists emphasize cultural diversity, we also concentrate on experiences common to all humanity. Thus it is with dying and grief. Each of the cultures in this volume has a distinctive understanding of the meaning of death. The people of each society express grief in their own, singular way. Nevertheless, dying, the loss of loved ones, and the pain of grief are common to all humans.

To assist us in providing a forum in which our contributors could address common themes, the Social Science and Humanities Research Council of Canada and McMaster University generously granted funding for a conference on the cross-cultural experience of grieving and dying, held in May 1988. All but two of the chapters in this book were presented in draft form and discussed during the three days of that symposium. S. M. Mead was unable to join us, but had agreed early on to provide a chapter, and William Simeone, just back from his doctoral field research, attended and participated in the symposium, but had not had time to prepare a paper for presentation.

We were pleased and excited that Dick Kalish had agreed to serve as our discussant and to write a concluding chapter for the volume. However, in tragic and poignant irony, he discovered in March, 1988 that he was terminally ill. He died on April 22, 1988, less than two weeks before our conference began. This volume is dedicated to him.

Although no one could replace Dick Kalish, we felt that we needed the perspective of an outsider—a non-anthropologist—with practical experience in dealing with dying persons and their families. At the last minute we asked John O'Connor, who is Director of Chaplaincy Services at McMaster University Medical Centre, to attend our conference and comment on our work from a practitioner's point of view. His remarks constitute Chapter 15 of this volume. Perhaps his most valuable observation is that there is no really exotic expression of grief: there is no response to death in our accounts that he has not seen at least once in his office. He asks anthropologists for insights and tools he can use to help make people's lives better. Implicit in his request is a paradox that underlies the relationship between social scientist and clinician.

We have been demanding of our contributors as they and we have exchanged drafts of the chapters that form this book. We thank them for their cooperation and for their patience. We also thank them for the time they have given to this project, for at our request each took responsibility for providing written critical comment to at least two of their fellow participants. This work is an integrated set of approaches rather than a disparate collection of papers in large part because they took the task of addressing each other's work seriously.

The symposium was an emotional high for those taking part. We hope that our readers are pleased with the book that gives it final form.

Dorothy and David Counts
Dundas, Ontario, Canada
July, 1990

Contents

CHAPTER
1

Introduction

David R. Counts
and
Dorothy A. Counts

Most of the chapters in this book you are about to read have been written by anthropologists and are a sampler of the variety of ways in which the people of many cultures experience death, express grief, and approach the problem of repairing the gap left by the death of one of their members. Not all of the contributors are anthropologists, however. One chapter is authored by a scholar of religious studies, who shares with anthropologists the experience of working in an exotic society. Another is by a clinician who spends much of his time counselling dying and grieving people in a hospital in a major Canadian city. His chapter emphasizes our common humanity and the degree to which we all respond to death and experience grief in similar ways. Despite sometimes profound cultural differences, we all must experience the loss of loved ones, the pain of grief, and our own dying. And, as Mandelbaum reminds us, all human groups must dispose of the bodies of the dead, help their bereaved members reorient themselves to society, and adjust to the loss of one of their members (Mandelbaum, 1976:344). All of our chapters focus on the importance of culture in understanding the process of death, grief, and mourning. Each society represented here approaches these processes uniquely: each has its own explanation for the universal human fact of death; each has rules decreeing how its members may express grief when death strikes; and each has a prescription for its members to follow when, through public mourning ritual, they begin the process of healing. The chapters in this volume thus address both the concerns common to all people and the experiences that are special to each culture.

ANTHROPOLOGICAL PERSPECTIVES

Although most of the contributors are anthropologists, the chapters approach death and grief from a number of perspectives. The variety of approaches is almost as great as the variety of societies whose customs we seek to understand. Some of us present ethnographic studies of small-scale societies whose understanding of death and grief may be considered exotic by members of modern Western society. One examines the reaction to death across a number of species of the primate order. Others illustrate the ways that traditional societies or ethnic minorities accommodate to the pressures of belief, law and technology imposed on them by a dominant majority. All these kinds of study are important because, as Eisenbruch has pointed out, the Western obliteration of traditional ways of confronting death and expressing grief may result in increased vulnerability to illness for the peoples whose traditions have been eradicated (Eisenbruch, 1984b:340–341). At the same time—as O'Connor reminds us—there is compelling evidence that thanatologists and clinicians could learn from the people of other cultures ways to help Westerners mourn more successfully and avoid pathological grief. When we force others to behave as we think proper we are doing harm to ourselves as well. We may well be eliminating traditions from which we could learn how to cope with the final tragedy.

Anthropologists working with exotic societies—whether they be European, Pacific Island, or even, at the furthest reach, non-human—can contribute ideas to clinicians who counsel grieving North Americans. The work of anthropologists is almost always (at least implicitly) comparative with modern Western society. Comparison with our own society provides a kind of reflecting pool. What we see in others may tell us something about ourselves. We as anthropologists follow a tradition of field work among people of other cultures in part because we believe it is important to translate the exotic into terms that are familiar in our own society. We also do it because it is useful—especially to clinicians who try to help people whose expressions of grief are interpreted as being 'abnormal'—to see the strangeness, the cultural construction, and the artifice in the too familiar and taken-for-granted rules of our own society.

The contributors to this book present their work from a variety of perspectives. Although the mix of participation and observation varies, all anthropologists are participant-observers. The chapters in the volume represent the wide range of approaches to fieldwork that is characteristic of anthropology. We move from Chapter 2, written from the perspective of the researcher who is almost entirely an observer (the physical anthropologist watching non-human primates), to final ones that are intimately participatory.

The chapter by Zeller examining grief in monkeys and apes, is the most nearly 'scientific' and the least participatory one in this volume. Zeller cannot speak with her informants to ask them how they feel or what they are thinking. She can only observe their behavior and the clinical changes they undergo when they are separated from an infant, parent, or other individual who is important to them. Comparing these data, which are measurable and quantifiable—as the data in most of the other chapters are not—with similar data on grieving humans, she infers what the animals are experiencing. She, and we, assume that the data are comparable. We assume that an infant primate, whether human or non-human, who responds to the death of its mother by withdrawing from social contact, refusing to eat, and clutching itself while rocking back and forth is experiencing grief. We assume but, because we are unable to ask, we can never know for sure.

Ramsden is an archaeologist who works with artifacts left by the Huron. His work is necessarily focussed on the dead and on what the remains of Huron society can tell us about their culture, including how they understood and dealt with death. Ramsden's chapter is the 'scientific' account of an observer in that he works with data that he can measure and count, but it is also participatory. Combining the perspective of an archaeologist with his own experience as a British-Canadian, Ramsden explicitly compares the death practices of these two cultures separated in both space and time—British Canadian and prehistoric Huron—and gains insight into the meaning of death for both.

Mead also writes from a dual perspective. He is an anthropologist as well as a New Zealand Maori elder. As an elder he has participated in Maori ceremonies that respond to death and channel grief. There is, as he notes, a difference between a participant-observer and a member of the in-group. Mead both understands the Maori way as an insider and analyzes it as a professional.

Waugh and Morris have spent considerable time living with and studying communities that are defined by their religious commitment. Waugh focuses on the death of an Islamic Sufi religious leader, a saint, and the responses of his followers. Morris writes about Russian ethnic religious communities that are tiny encapsulated isolates, self-consciously preserving an ancestral past against the onslaught of modernity.

The chapters by Badone and Wellenkamp stand out because they are the only contributors whose field research was specifically concentrated on death, grief, and mourning practices. This makes their chapters on the Breton French and the Toraja of Indonesia particularly rich in focused ethnographic detail. Toraja society places unusual cultural emphasis on death and mourning and is well-known in anthropological literature.

Badone's chapter exemplifies self-conscious, reflexive anthropology. Not only is her chapter focussed on a rural European people with a long historical tradition on which students may draw, but the account embodies an interpretive style in which the ethnographer becomes part of the ethnography.

Simeone, the Prestons, the Weigands, Lieber and the two of us have prepared chapters that are derived from long-term association with small communities. While none of us will ever be 'insiders' in the communities we discuss, our decades of ongoing association with the people permit us to analyze the *process* of grief in action, for we have mourned with them and shared their grief at the death of friends.

Kaufert and O'Neil write from the perspective of anthropologist-clinicians working in an urban setting to apply anthropological knowledge. Their research has been with Cree and Ojibway mediators who work in Winnipeg hospitals to translate and intercede between the medical staff and Indian people. Their chapter makes an important transition in the volume. Most of the other chapters revolve around conflict of some sort: the conflict that death itself brings by providing evidence of the rupture of social relations or the potential conflict arising from the danger of unrestricted emotional storms that follow death. Kaufert and O'Neil, too, structure their chapter around conflict, but it is the conflict derived from cultural contradictions. People are caught between the values and organizational imperatives of a large urban health care system and those of small encapsulated groups of naive people whose terminally ill members are brought to hospital to die. There they may undergo autopsies or other invasive procedures that neither they nor their bereaved kin understand or approve. The chapter is transitional because it suggests what can be accomplished when the potential for conflict is recognized and measures are taken to allow for informed intervention and advocacy on behalf of those with recognized cultural differences.

O'Connor's chapter brings us to the immediacy of grief in our own complex and imperfect society. His is the voice of the clinician denied the luxury of the calm and distanced analytical view of the academic because he must *do something* to help his clients deal with their pain and loss. He must respond without the benefit of informed knowledge to help people whose values, sexual orientation, or personal history may add the stigma of 'abnormality' to the trauma of dying or grieving. His chapter is a plea for anthropologists and practitioners to speak to one another.

There are two recurring themes that run through the book. One is that it is important to note whether a society's focus of concern is the *death* that has taken place or the *grief* that it triggers. For some societies as for some persons, the grief may pose a greater threat than death itself. The other theme is the distinction that many societies make and the disjuncture that may exist between physical death and social death—a phenomenon that occurs in a great variety of forms.

In the concluding chapter of the volume we direct the reader's attention to the special contribution of each chapter and summarize the ideas that this volume offers to scholars trying to understand—and clinicians trying to help—people who must cope with the final tragedy.

CHAPTER 2

The Grieving Process in Non-human Primates

Anne Zeller

Grief is the common human response to the loss of a cared-for person, often referred to as an attachment figure. Humans communicate their grief to others both verbally and by body posture, weeping, breathing patterns, lethargy and other responses indicating depression. In her studies of communication patterns in monkeys it has become clear to Zeller, and to others such as Jane Goodall who has studied chimpanzees for nearly thirty years, that primates experiencing the loss of an attachment figure send non-verbal cues similar to those of grieving humans. They moan or shriek, clasp themselves, rock back and forth, refuse to respond to others, and in some cases die. In order to establish whether these behaviors are truly similar to grief in humans, intensive studies of the behavioral and physiological responses to separation of closely bonded primates (usually mothers and infants) have been undertaken over the last twenty years. The marked similarity in causes of the behavior, stages of grief, nature and pattern of physiological changes, immunochemical responses, and response to reunion clearly suggest that the outward manifestations of behavioral similarity between human and non-human primates reflect an underlying similarity of causation, physiological patterning, and potential biological function for grief. Non-human primates respond to loss on an individual rather than a cultural plane, but that does not make the loss any less painful for them, as is indicated by the numbers of both experimental and wild animals who die, simply as a consequence of the loss of their parent or offspring.

*   *   *

Ever since Darwin revealed that human origins lie in a non-human past, studies of the similarities between us and the other members of the primate order—the monkeys and apes—have been undertaken by zoologists, psychologists, and anthropologists. Simply stated, zoologists are interested in similarities of structure and ecology while psychologists focus on similarities of perception and problem solving. Anthropologists are concerned with the origins and patterning of both individual and group behaviors in primates.

These are all broad fields of study since there are nearly 200 species of primates, some only recently discovered and others on the verge of extinction. Humans are most closely related to apes, particularly to gorillas and chimpanzees. Immuno-chemical evidence suggests that human and chimpanzee evolutionary lines separated between five and eight million years ago—a mere moment in evolutionary time. Humans share more than 98 percent of the DNA, which is the genetic blueprint of life, with chimpanzees. We have the same number of hairs per square inch of skin (although ours are finer), the same blood groups, and if necessary we can receive blood transfusions from chimpanzees.

Humans are less closely related to gorillas and orangutans—the other two types of great apes—but all four of these primates share similar stages of infancy, childhood, adolescence, and adulthood with similar timing. The major difference is the long dependency of ape infants who are not usually weaned until four or five years of age. Apes usually begin to reproduce at about twelve years old (females) or sixteen years old (males) and can live to forty or fifty years in the wild. Since this age span is so similar to humans it is difficult for a researcher to conduct longitudinal studies on apes. Monkeys, who are social primates with complex behavior patterns, do not live as long and are more frequently used as research subjects. Monkey infants are usually weaned at six to eight months of age and are sexually mature at four to six years.

There are more species of monkeys than apes, but I will only mention those that have been the subjects of studies referred to in this chapter. A number of different macaque species are included: rhesus, bonnet, pigtail, barbary, and Japanese. All belong to the genus Macaca. These are group-living animals who are fairly easy to keep in captivity and therefore are popular research subjects. Baboons are closely related to macaques, but are larger and stronger and are infrequently utilized in experiments. Since they are mainly terrestrial they are often observed in the wild. Langurs are another type of monkey found in India and Southeast Asia that have been observed both in the wild and in captivity. These monkeys are all more similar to each other than they are to any of the species living in South America. The South American, or New World monkeys, have had an independent evolutionary history for about 35 million years, but derive from the same ancestors as Old World monkeys and apes, and show similar behavior patterns. They include squirrel monkeys and titi or Callicebus forms.

Thus morphology, immunochemistry, life stages, and evolutionary relationship are indicators of the close ties humans have to the rest of the primate order. Current research on communication, socialization patterns and group interaction (e.g., Goodall, 1986) is revealing even more striking similarities between the mental and emotional lives of primates and humans than have previously been suspected.

This volume is mainly concerned with the dying, grieving and mourning process as it occurs in human beings. But since humans evolved from a non-human past, we study the basis of many of our behaviors by examining the responses primates make to similar life situations. Arguments about whether these behavioral similarities are analogous (having a different underlying cause but similar appearance) or homologous (arising from the same underlying cause although the function may differ) will affect how we interpret such behavior. A major characteristic of a homology is the occurrence of the phenomenon across populations living under many difference conditions. The presence of the grief response in humans seems to be universal. It is also very similar in appearance and physiological correlates to the behavior seen as a response in a wide variety of primates. The closeness of primates to humans in the evolutionary record, and the nature of social phenomena as well as the marked similarities in the grief process, suggests a similar system underlies the grief response across the membership of the order Primates.

This is not to suggest that the processes of grief and mourning are identical in humans and primates. Human society is much more developed, much richer and more symbolic than animal society. Therefore the level of complexity in expression will certainly differ. A major factor distinguishing human and primate responses to loss is the occurrence of mourning. Since mourning is the culturally constructed social and public response to the loss of an individual, it rests in a social and symbolic context which is not available to primates. Humans exist as both physical and social personae. The ritual, religious and theoretical understanding of the meaning of death which gives order and shape to the human expression of loss, and allows the laying to rest of the social person, is beyond the level of primate social responses. Primates do not mourn, nor is grief a group activity. It occurs as an individual response to loss, although the death of one may be responded to by several animals. A researcher can investigate human grief and mourning by asking survivors how they feel, what they will do, what the normative patterns and standards of mourning are, and how other people are likely to react, as well as by observing them. Of this whole array of methodologies, a primate researcher can use only observation to study the loss of an attachment figure in primates. Also, the subject of research cannot be the whole social nexus surrounding death; rather it can only be the loss of an attachment figure. Because of the nature of attachment, I have also included some data on primate loss of a human foster parent and a few words on the reciprocal case of humans losing a primate they have fostered. One other area with relevant but sparse levels of information is the response of primates to the loss of a non-conspecific animal with whom they had a strong bond.

Three types of limitations make this study difficult.

- First, only observations are available as data. Observation of behavioral response to loss occurs in free ranging situations as well as in captivity, but most of the data come from arranged separations of animals. These behavioral observations are supplemented and extended by recording and comparing the physiological endocrinological and hormonal correlates of separation with the ensuing behavioral responses. This work suggests a substantial level of endogenous response, but is not matched by an equivalent level of data from humans. The few cases of actually being able to ask signing apes about their response to loss do not add substantially different types of information to that gained by observation.

- The second limitation derives from the experimental nature of most research on primate loss. Most of the work involves manipulation of variables, such as length of separation, comparisons of removal of infant versus removal of mother, and infant responses to seeing but not having access to the mother. These studies are concerned with ascertaining which environmental and social factors elicit the reaction to loss and only provide indirect information about the response to death.

- The third problem stems from the vocabulary which we use to refer to the subject under discussion. In studying humans, even if we do not know their language we use the label "grief" to refer to similar behaviors occurring in the same context in which we would experience grief. The attribution of human emotional responses to animals is often called anthropomorphism. For many years it has been an unacceptable way to refer to animal behavior. Anthropomorphism has a variable history, however.

Darwin, in *The Expression of the Emotions in Man and Animals* (1872) referred to such terms as anger, happiness, jealousy, cunning and sadness when referring to both the cause and manifestation of animal behaviors. Robert Yerkes, the major founder of American primate behavior studies, used the same types of terms when referring to apes and monkeys. He also attributed complex emotion driven behaviors such as revenge and deception to them (Yerkes, 1925). The behaviorist school turned away from such language to the extent that it was no longer permissible to assign gender to the "research animal." Jane Goodall (1986) noted that in her first publication on free ranging chimpanzees, a reviewer had changed all the "hes" and "shes" to "its." For an animal as social as a chimpanzee and with the level of sex based differences observable in their lifestyle, this change would have obscured, rather than clarified, discussions of behavior.

Within the last decade the realization that human observation is influenced by an underlying assumption of the causes of behavior, has led to a reexamination of anthropomorphism. Asquith separates the term into two different levels. She calls general anthropomorphism the "ascription of purposefulness to higher animals" (1984:140). In other words primates are aware of what they are doing, although this does not imply that their psychological experiences are necessarily identical to ours. Specific anthropomorphism, on the other hand, is the "ascription of particular or specific mental and emotional states like those of humans to animals" (1984:140). One of the major difficulties in distinguishing between these levels is the types of terms which are frequently utilized in primate studies.

Does the term "dominance" imply a purposefulness or intention to be higher ranking than another, or does it imply something that a primate feels about him (or her) self? Smuts (1985) and de Waal (1982) both extend acceptable terminology of behavior classification to embrace such concepts as friendship, trust, affection and grief, based on the social consequences of repeatedly observed constellations of behavior. In other words, these concepts are once again permissible subjects of inquiry, if they can be supported by replicable observations of underlying behavior patterns. The level at which these behavior patterns occur and can be observed may be extremely fine grained, and I have argued that this may be the basis for what is considered an intuitive understanding of primate behavior (Zeller, 1985). Many of the research reports on separation depression in primates begin with a discussion of the similarity in effect of human "object loss" and a primate infant's separation from its mother (see, for example, McGinnis, 1980; Mineka, 1982; Suomi, 1982; Reite and Capitano, 1985). I used the term "object loss" above when referring to humans, to indicate how the affective content of language does influence our perception of the situation. The term "object loss" comes from Suomi who was referring to "human depression . . . centered on object loss, that is, separation from or loss of a loved one (or possession)" (Suomi, 1982:192). He is in fact referring to bereavement in humans and comparing the depression that can arise with the "severe (sometimes fatal) depression [which] is a common reaction of infant and juvenile primates to the loss of their mothers in the wild" (Suomi, 1982:192).

DEPRESSION STUDIES

The National Institute of Mental Health report on depression research (Teuting and Koslow, 1966) suggests that humans experiencing grief due to the loss of an attachment figure show many signs of clinical depression—crying, withdrawal, apathy, sleeplessness, loss of appetite and weight—on a temporary basis, but do eventually return to the normal life patterns. The human list of depressive symptoms is quite long but not very exclusive. It is divided into five aspects (Mineka, 1982).

affective: feelings of sadness, helplessness, hopelessness and depression.
cognitive: negative cognitions about self, world and future.
behavioral: lethargy, paralysis of will, lack of overt aggressiveness.
somatic: decreased appetite, libido, sleep disturbance, some disturbance of certain brain neurotransmitters.
loss of self esteem

There do not seem to be any necessary defining features of depression in adults, so Mineka questions the need for requiring specific indicators of depression in children and primates. It is recognized that the cognitive aspects of adult human grief and depression may be much more complex than in the case of children and primates, but the affective and somatic aspects are quite similar. Increased mortality and morbidity accompany grief and bereavement, even in adult humans (Reite et al., 1981). This type of response is paralleled by Lee's statement that in primates . . . "the most frequent consequence of the loss of a mother is the death of the infant" (1983:73). This statement refers to animals who have reached the age where they can be nutritionally self-supporting and might be expected to survive. Very young infants might be expected to die since few unweaned young can find a substitute caregiver who will adopt and nurse them, although it has been known to happen (e.g., Dolhinow, 1980).

The three foci of attention in depression studies which are relevant to an understanding of grief are: the type of trauma which induces the response, the behavioral somatic and physiological manifestations of the condition, and the outcome or recovery phase of grieving. I have briefly sketched these for the human condition above and will now turn to both experimental and wild primate research to examine the parallels in these three areas. As mentioned in the introduction, I will conclude with narrative accounts of responses to other situations of loss.

Type of Trauma

Since the instigating event of grief is the loss of an important attachment figure, it is necessary to understand the characteristics of such a relationship. Gubernick (1981) suggests several criteria of attachment. These include:

1. Preference for the (presumed) attachment figure.
2. Maintenance of proximity to that figure (also used as an indicator of preference).
3. Response to brief separation from that figure.
4. Response to extended periods of separation.
5. Response to reunion with attachment figure.
6. Use of the attachment figure as a secure base to explore the world.

He generalizes these points into the following statement (Gubernick, 1981:244):

> Typically attachment is defined as a special affectional relationship between two individuals that is specific in its focus and endures over time.

The evidence that not just any female who provides mothering care will relieve separation distress is found in studies of adoption among monkeys. Thierry and Anderson (1986) have noted that infant monkeys may have a continued aversive reaction to mother loss and not respond or become attached to available substitute care givers. In spite of being carried and groomed they can exhibit physiological signs of depression such as decreased body temperature and disrupted sleep and activity patterns. One langur female, who already had an infant, adopted a seven-month-old orphan. In spite of this, the orphan rarely played, became increasingly isolated and indifferent to the adoptive female, engaged in more self directed activities and died after two months (Thierry and Anderson, 1986). Rowell's study of six-month-old baboon infants is a particularly clear case. The mothers were removed when the infants were six months of age, and when the mothers were returned six months later they were anesthetized so they could provide no cues to the infant. Nonetheless, all but one rushed to its own mother and clung to her, giving infant lost calls and resumed relations with her while ignoring their substitute care givers. In the one case in which an infant did not return to its mother, the substitute mother had lost her own infant and a close attachment bond appeared to have developed between the substitute and adopted infant (Rowell, 1972).

Responses to loss of the attachment figure can range from death to redirection of the attachment bond even within one species. Gubernick (1981) noted that five of eleven langur infants remained attached to alternate care givers even after their mothers' return. In contrast, Dolhinow and Murphy noted that three of twelve of their langur infants died within four days of losing their mother, although they were of comparable ages and in similar social situations (Dolhinow, 1980; Dolhinow and Murphy, 1983). The influence of social situations is also seen in the response of a bonnet macaque infant (which is a species where infants are frequently adopted) left in a group of familiar pigtail macaque females who would not respond to its solicitations for mothering. This bonnet macaque infant exhibited all the symptoms of despair usually found in pigtail infants and not usually found in separated bonnet infants because of the more supportive social system (Reite and Snyder, 1982). The conclusions that can be drawn from this data are that the attachment figure is a specific individual rather than a source of food, warmth, and support. The physiological benefits are important to an infant, but the psychological comfort provided by the bonded individual is even more important.

> Attachment bonds are central to the development of many higher organisms . . . and their disruption may be closely linked to the development of serious psychopathology (Reite et al., 1978:370).

Behavior and Physiology of Grief

Coe and Levine (1981) report that the disruption of the mother infant relationship is one of the most potent stimulators of behavioral agitation and stress in animals. When human infants and children are separated from their mothers (as in hospitalization) they undergo a very marked stage of agitation and protest. Then a reaction sets in and children and most primates decline into a despair or depressive state. These are two parts of a three-stage separation syndrome defined for humans. The stages are labeled protest, despair and detachment (Bowlby, 1973). The third or detachment phase, in which children take some time to respond to their mothers in the reunion stage, is only rarely seen in primates.

The protest stage is a time of agitated searching, crying, and calling. It is accompanied by increased levels of heart rate, body temperature, plasma cortisol and adrenal catecholamine. This precedes the despair stage, which is more closely correlated with grief (Mineka, 1982). Much of this experimental work has been done with macaques, but it is supported by experiments on separation and adoption in infant langur monkeys conducted by Dolhinow and her co-worker. In their studies, mothers of six- to eight-month-old infants (who should be able to feed themselves) were removed, but the infants were left in a known social group. The variability of langur infant response was extreme, with some young dying in response to separation and others finding adoptive mothers to nurture them. The protest phase began during day one of separation, after the langur infants noticed that their mothers were gone. Protest was characterized by increased vocalization, locomotion, and searching, concomitant with reduced play and grooming which lasted for the initial twenty-four to forty-eight hours.

The despair stage then ensued with reduced activity, play, grooming, approaches to and by others, object manipulation and other social behaviors (Dolhinow, 1980). By day three, play had almost ceased and, although vocalization and locomotion were still higher than baseline levels, they had reduced from day one and two. The other adults did not respond to the visible and auditory distress of the separated infants by approaches or grooming, but some infants began to approach adult females and attempt to elicit care, holding, and some nursing (Dolhinow, 1980). None of the infants chose females who were closely related to them, although there were six cases where this would have been possible (Dolhinow and Krusko, 1984). Some females responded to these searching infants with increased threat levels, but seven of nine infants managed to elicit adoptive mothering. When their own mothers were returned, five of these seven remained with their adoptive caregivers. Only four—two who were adopted and two who were not—went back to their mothers. The mothers did not generally attempt to rejoin their infants or interact with them. If the infant returned, the mother accepted it, but if it did not, she did not pursue it. Most of the mothers spent their time and attention re-establishing their social relationships with the group rather than focusing on their infants. When compared to these langur infants, human children in the despair phase also withdraw socially, are lethargic, lose their appetites and experience sleep disturbance. These types of behavior are indicators of depression by adult diagnostic standards (Suomi, 1982). Young macaques in the despair stage frequently show loss of exploration and play, reduced locomotion and calling, increased self clasping, a hunched posture and social withdrawal (Tenting and Koslow, 1966; Coe and Levine, 1981; Mineka, 1982).

Additional information is derived from some pigtail and bonnet infants who have been telemetrically implanted in order to measure physiological responses to separation (Reite et al., 1978; Reite et al., 1981; Suomi, 1982). Pigtail infants, who are not normally adopted by substitute caregivers, show a very marked depressive reaction. During the agitation/protest phase the heart rate and body temperature increased as the infants moved and vocalized. As despair developed the first night and subsequent nights there was a significant drop in body temperature and heart rate, frequent sleep disturbances and decreased REM sleep (Rosenblum and Plimpton, 1981). The bonnet infants seem to have their behavioral response to separation attenuated by the willingness of other females to adopt them. However they still show behavioral agitation, increased vocalization and active searching—coupled with increased heart rate and body temperature—the first day of separation. The second day they begin the behavioral aspects of despair: slouched posture, slow locomotion, distress vocalization, sad facial expression. Their nocturnal heart rates fell from a mean of 182 beats per minute to a mean of 120 beats per minute, and the number of cardiac arrhythmias increased. Nocturnal body temperature was down one degree Celsius and there was an increase in time awake at night and a decrease in REM sleep (Reite and Snyder, 1982).

Much of the endocrinological and hormonal work on separation responses has been done with rhesus macaques and squirrel monkeys—two very different types of primate, behaviorally and evolutionarily speaking. I will, therefore, finish the discussion of macaque separation experiences by using rhesus examples and discuss squirrel and other New World monkey responses below.

The physiological systems which have been studied in response to separation include:

- changes in hypothalamic serotonin (5HT)
- adrenal gland catecholamine (CA)
- synthesizing enzymes
- plasma cortisol
- these systems are in addition to work on sleep patterns, heart rate and body temperature.

Rhesus infants show the same series of behavior symptoms to separation as are generally seen in other macaques and human children. The physiological responses accompanying protest include elevation of heart rate, blood pressure, body temperature and blood cortisol levels, indicating a major activation of the sympathetic nervous system (Suomi, 1982). The physiology of despair in rhesus includes sleep disturbance, lowered body temperature, elevated levels of 5HT in the hypothalamus, and higher levels of adrenal catecholamine and plasma cortisol. These reactions occurred when rhesus were separated from peers, and from their family units as well as in the context of mother-infant separations. Peer reared animals were more severely affected by peer separation than were mother reared ones. After a period of time the behavioral changes induced by separation reduced, but hormonal and physiological changes continued (Gubernick, 1981). Rhesus show some individual variability in the degree and length of their separation response, but animals who have a severe response when young seem to retain this pattern in their future lives (Suomi, 1983). Suomi argues that this difference may be related to differences in autonomic reactivity and be largely of genetic origin (Suomi, 1982). This viewpoint contrasts with the idea that levels of attachment bonding and the nature of the social group affect the despair phase of separation, but both factors may well have some impact. Rhesus mothers respond behaviorally to separation, but if they can see their infants they do not show the marked levels of plasma cortisol elevation seen in infants. It seems probable that psychic conflict, fear, and frustration elicit many of the stress responses seen in macaques. These could easily be underlying aspects of grief.

I have separated the discussion of New World monkeys from the Old World ones because of the 35 million year divergence in evolutionary history and the fact that some factors in their responses differ from those found in Old World forms. However, many aspects of the pattern are quite similar, and a number of researchers use the squirrel monkey and other New World forms as models for assessing human separation responses.

Among squirrel monkeys the attachment process solidifies within a few days of birth. Within the first year infants present an agitated response to separation from their mothers (Coe et al., 1985). The pattern is very similar to the macaques, with the initial protest phase showing vocalization (isolation peeps) and agitated locomotor activity. Thirty minutes after separation the infant's pituitary adrenal activity levels are elevated to 120 percent over basal values. If they are left separated for six hours the plasma cortisol levels continue to rise, but the rate of agitated calling reduces after the first hour (Coe et al., 1985). The despair phase usually occurs before twenty-four hours have passed. Activity levels are lowered, play and object exploration decrease, and the infant withdraws from the social group and exhibits self clasping (Coe and Levine, 198). Repeated separations will result in reduced calling levels, but the adreno-corticoid response continues to occur. If the squirrel monkey infant is left in its home cage with other known individuals, the rate of plasma cortisol rise is not as great, especially if it is able to contact other animals. It is not the home cage alone which provides the ameliorative effects because if the monkey is left alone in the home cage its plasma cortisol levels rise sharply. The most stressful type of separation assessed by plasma cortisol levels is isolation in a strange environment. This does not correlate with overt behavior, however, since agitation and calling responses subside more quickly in isolation than they do when the animals are separated from their mothers but can still see them.

If females are available who will act as allomothers and carry the infants, no overt behavioral distress is evident. The infant will cling to the substitute mother and not engage in active calling. Nevertheless, endocrinological data still show high plasma cortisol levels, indicating that the infant is responding physiologically to the loss of its own mother. Mothers also show elevated plasma cortisol rates after separation, but these fall much more rapidly after reunion than do infants' rates. The infant's behavior is not agitated after reunion, but the high level of endocrine activity indicates disassociation of behavioral distress markers and internal indicators of arousal (Coe and Levine, 1981).

An interesting alternative pattern to that found in squirrel monkeys is demonstrated in Callicebus, the titi, which is a monogamous New World form (Mendoza and Mason, 1986a; 1986b). The members of a number of family groups were tested for elevation of plasma cortisol levels in situations in which they were separated from their mates or from their offspring. The separation from their mates resulted in significant elevations in plasma cortisol levels as well as agitation and distress in both sexes. Neither sex showed this response to offspring separation, in spite of the fact that the male shows a lot of offspring care. When these animals were tested in a Y maze, adults of both sexes preferred to approach their mates rather than the infant. If the choice was infant or empty cage, adults would approach the infant. In situations in which the infant was removed from the cage and then returned to the cage floor, both sexes would approach to retrieve it at about equal rates. When the infant had the choice of which parent to approach it frequently chose the father, indicating that attachment bonding in titis has a different pattern than is found in most other primates (Mendoza and Mason, 1986a, 1986b). Mendoza and Mason compared squirrel monkey response to mate loss with mate loss in Callicebus and found that squirrel monkeys, who are not usually monogamous, did not seem to respond to separation from their mates with distress.

Another major class of primates are the apes. Ape responses to separation are even more similar to human responses than are those of monkeys. In addition to showing protest and despair, in some cases they also show a brief detachment phase (Codner and Nadler, 1984). The length of time that young apes continue in each phase is longer than occurs in monkeys, an additional similarity to the human pattern. Gorilla, chimpanzee and orangutan infants were separated from their mothers at ages ranging from thirteen to thirty months. They all immediately showed protest responses, with high levels of vocalization and active locomotion. The chimpanzee and orangutan showed persistent agitation over a number of days, while the gorilla's response was not as marked. On the other hand, the gorilla was the oldest and was adopted by his adult sister (Codner and Nadler, 1984). In Maple and Hoff's (1982) study of three infant gorillas aged twenty-seven months, the protest phase of loud screaming and active agitation lasted two days. This was followed by a one-month despair stage in which infant-infant contact, peer play, object examination and solitary play dropped to low levels. The next five months of separation produced a gradual return to more active social interaction. In chimpanzees who have been peer raised rather than mother raised (Snyder et al., 1984), separation and isolation in a strange environment at 7.5 to 10.5 months of age produced a very severe agitation, alternating with despair.

These infants cried, screamed, rocked and increased self directed behaviors such as self clasping. Their levels of self play diminished and they exhibited the cry face, whimper face, and pout face—all indicators of distress. By day three their behavior had become more violent. They banged, rocked and threw themselves against the walls alternatively with depressive behaviors such as frequent sleeping, staring into space, loss of the clinging response, and holding a limb out rigid for several minutes—floating limb phenomenon (Snyder et al., 1984). In the wild, such young animals would have no hope of surviving since, even with adoption, those who lose their mothers before they are four years of age almost always die.

The evidence for detachment at the third stage of separation comes from Maple and Hoff's (1982) gorillas who, when they were returned to their mothers after six months absence, spent the first few days in closer contact with their peers and only gradually resumed their relationship with their mothers. However, within a few weeks their patterns of behavior were similar to their pre-separation levels.

Chimpanzee and gorilla mothers also seem to show distress at the death of their young offspring. A chimpanzee at the Arnhem Zoo consistently lost her infants because she had no milk. Every time this happened, "she would go into a kind of depression. For weeks on end she would sit huddled into a corner without reacting at all to the goings-on about her. Some times she would start screaming and yelping of her own accord" (de Waal, 1982:70). The gorilla keeper at the Metro Toronto Zoo reported that one female gorilla was seen to carry, pat and gently encourage nursing in a stillborn infant for four days before she put the by then smelly corpse down and allowed them to remove it (Cole, 1986:394). This same female lost her next infant at age twenty days and became very lethargic. She sat leaning her head against the wall with a "facial expression resembling a grieving human" (Cole, 1986:395).

Recovery Phase

The third aspect of depression studies is the outcome or recovery phase of the grieving process. As is undoubtedly clear by now, the course and severity of the separation syndrome is dependent on many factors. These include the species of primate, the social conditions it lives in, the nature of separation, who is separated from whom, the presence of substitute caregivers, and the age at which separation occurs, as well as individual differences in susceptibility to distress. Thus the outcomes of the reunion process may well be expected to vary in relation to these factors. However, to summarize the material, if the infant survives the separation process there are several possible results which may ensue. Reite et al. (1981) commented that researchers saw no real evidence of recovery after thirteen days of separation in the pigtail macaque. This supported Hinde and Spencer-Booth's (1970) findings with rhesus monkeys. During separation other familiar animals may approach the infant in its depressive state and invite it to play (Rosenblum and Plimpton, 1981). This type of interaction may gradually calm the infant and recovery may occur. The separated young macaque may achieve affective stability, age normal activity levels, body maintenance activity, exploration, and play—but not usually before thirteen or more days of separation have passed. The infant will still respond very strongly to the mother's return, but many were able to overcome severe grief before reunion (Rosenblum and Plimpton, 1981). Older peer raised rhesus who are repeatedly separated may become more and more disturbed, showing increases in stereotypy, self clasping, huddling, pacing, and restless agitation (Mineka, 1982). It seems plausible to argue that even in the peer raised condition these animals are under a considerable level of stress and are not very well equipped to cope with instability in their living situation, let alone loss of their social companions. Peer raised rhesus monkeys do not become less agitated over time even when they undergo as many as twenty repeated separations (McKinney, 1985). Even older (five-year-old) rhesus, who are repeatedly separated from their family group and put into isolation or with strangers, have an increasing level of depressive response. Younger animals (six-month-old), who are separated from their mothers but are still able to see them, have a marked depressive response but recover rapidly at reunion. If the separations are repeated frequently enough the young animals may suffer from slowed or arrested growth (Reite et al., 1981). Deprivation dwarfism also sometimes happens in human children who have no attachment figure. Another long-term result of repeated and stressful separations in some rhesus is the observation that infants who lost their mothers still showed "insecurity" up to one year after reunion. These animals cling tenaciously to their mothers and spend very little time at a distance from them (Hinde and Spencer-Booth, 1970; Mineka, 1982; Spencer-Booth and Hinde, 1971). The level of heart rate increase above base line seems to correlate with the amount of peer contact and the maintenance of some social interaction during the despair phase of separation (Caine and Reite, 1981). Those infants who showed a precipitous drop in heart rate during the depression stage also were less interactive and playful. They therefore missed the psychological and physiological benefits of contact (Caine and Reite, 1981).

One of the most interesting aspects of examining both behavior and physiology is the realization that in the grief response there may be considerable disassociation between the two indicators of stress. This is evident in adult humans (Mineka, 1982) as well as rhesus and squirrel monkeys. Behavioral agitation can decrease but levels of pituitary adrenal activity can remain high, even when the infant is being carried by a female and it seems not to be in distress (Vogt and Hennessy, 1982). Repeated separations in squirrel monkeys can reduce calling levels, but elevated adreno-corticoid response still occurs (Coe et al., 1985). The length of separation also influences the response of infants to reunion. Among pigtail macaque infants, after three days of separation all the infants returned quickly to their mothers when they were reintroduced. However, after thirty days of separation ten infants jumped away from their mothers for a period of several minutes to several hours. This is much like the detachment phase seen in children. The mothers frequently followed their infants and maintained visual contact and, unlike the situation with the langurs, eventually all of the infants returned to them (Baldwin, 1985).

Effect on Immune System

Another type of data emphasizing the similarities of grief physiology in humans and primates are the alterations in the immune system accompanying bereavement (Reite and Capitano, 1985). In macaques, prolonged cortisol elevations induced by sustained separations can adversely affect the immune system (Coe et al., 1985). An eleven-day separation in macaques affected immune function measured by the proliferative response of lymphocytes to mitogen stimulation (Reite, Harbeck and Hoffman, 1981; Coe et al., 1985). This compares very closely to studies by Bartrop et al. (1977) indicating that humans who lose a spouse have a similar mitogen response (Coe et al., 1985). Stressful events and a sense of loneliness can interact with the immune system and affect natural killer cell activity in humans (Kiecolt-Glaser et al., 1984; Coe et al., 1985). Separation experiments with squirrel monkeys indicate a decrease in complement proteins C3 and C4 thereby reducing immune responses to bacteria, serum levels of immuno-globins, and the formation of antigen-antibody complexes. Decreased levels of C3 and C4 proteins are found in a number of human disorders such as systemic lupus erythematosus, rheumatoid arthritis, and chronic liver disease.

To summarize the material on depression studies, attachment is an important aspect of primate life which may be a neurobiologically based and mediated bio-behavioral system (Reite and Capitano, 1985). Separation creates pronounced stress, accompanied in adult humans by a constant set of somatic symptoms: disturbances in appetite, cardiovascular and respiratory function, mobility, and sleep. In children and primates, distress is usually expressed in a two or three phase syndrome. It begins with agitated protest, showing high levels of activity, searching, vocalization and heart rate. Then it moves to a despair stage of disturbed sleep and reduced activity, play, body temperature, and heart rate. The response to reunion is variable. Children frequently are reluctant to interact with the mother. Primate response ranges from intense clinging to refusal to rejoin the mother due to the formation of a new attachment bond. Evidence that these systems operate in similar fashions in humans and primates comes from the similarities in cause of onset, behavior patterns, and physiological consequences, as well as the influence of separation distress on the immune system.

FIELD DATA

Most of the information presented here has been about mother-infant separation and death in captive situations because, in most cases, this is the primary focus of separation research. However, in free ranging groups both adult males and females are often involved in interacting with infants and juveniles after the loss of their mothers. In *Macaca sylvanus*, the barbary macaque, males often have individual relationships with particular infants whom they sometimes use in interactions with other adult males in a pattern known as "agonistic buffering." Here a male carries an infant up to another male, and both males respond to the infant with appropriate infant-directed gestures, such as teeth chattering and grooming. Having established friendly relations, the males can then interact with each other. Males who interact with a living infant also interact with it after death. A mother frequently carries a dead baby for the first few days. When she leaves it, males will pick it up and continue to carry it for several days, smelling it, chasing the flies, and lip smacking to any perceived movement of the corpse. Other members of the matriline may also carry a dead infant, although juveniles tend to be rougher with the corpse than they are with living infants. In contrast to this high level of continued care, two stillborn infants, with whom no animal had social relations, were left immediately by the mother and all the other animals (Merz, 1978).

In some Japanese macaque troops, males commonly show caregiving behavior to yearlings whose mothers are having another infant. However, after the death of a mother, only some males adopt young. Hasegawa and Hiraiwa (1980) observed thirty-four Japanese macaque orphans of whom seven out of nine under one year of age died, three of eight juveniles died and two out of fifteen older animals died, leaving two infants, five juveniles and thirteen older juveniles alive. These orphans spent time with adult males, immature siblings, and peers to a greater extent than with non-kin adult females. The males groomed and carried infants, and the high ranking male took care of four orphans at once. Females may embrace and groom orphans but they do not protect them from attacks by others as the males do. Other types of macaques tend to show less male care of orphans. One very young (eleven week) rhesus macaque infant was orphaned and showed a day of agitated searching. He then went into a depressive phase and underwent several weeks of decreased activity, hunched posture, and frequent whoo-calling. He was cared for by adult males for the first ten days and then began to spend more time with his three-year-old sister who carried and held him. When she left him and went out of sight, the infant showed distress but did not follow her (Berman, 1983). I observed a three-year-old Barbary macaque female who cared for a younger sister who was only a few months old when her mother was shot. This young female provided as much protection as she could and carried, groomed and slept with the infant, successfully raising her. She was also noticeably proficient with her own first infant.

Baboon males who have special relationships with infants may also carry or sit with a dead infant for up to several days (Smuts, 1985). Rhine et al. (1980) reported on a free ranging baboon group in which Sikio, a past prime male, cared for a four-month-old female orphan. He waited for the infant when the troop moved, remained within 15 metres of her, retrieved her over 200 metres, and carried her over 2 kilometers eighteen times. He was attacked several times by other adult males while carrying the infant and when it was finally killed, he was seen grooming the corpse. Another recently orphaned baboon infant about five and one-half months old was seen to be distressed—moaning, calling and not following the group. He became less alert, sat with his head bowed, cradled a tree trunk as an infant does its mother, and finally lay down and stopped breathing. He did not join other troop members who were around him, and may have died from dehydration lying in the hot sun (Rhine et al., 1980).

Infant langurs whose mothers die in the wild may find another female to adopt them (Lee, 1983), but in most cases the infant will die. Mohnot (1980; Box, 1984) described the responses of a young wild langur infant to its mother's corpse. The infant showed agitation, tried to nurse, vocalized, watched the corpse, and returned to it intermittently. The orphan was prevented from touching the body by three other females who approached the corpse and then attempted to hold the infant. Other juveniles and infants also approached and attempted to hold the distressed orphan. The adult male of the group was unresponsive at first but later became quite agitated and led the group away (Mohnot, 1980). The next day as humans picked up the corpses, the infant screamed loudly and followed the body. When Jay was studying wild langurs in India, one group had three dead brown infants who were carried, groomed and inspected by other females for several days before they were finally left behind (Jay, 1963).

Chimpanzees show a very strong aversive response to dead conspecifics. Teleki (1973; Box, 1984) observed the responses of a group of wild chimpanzees to the sudden death of an adult male who broke his neck. The rest of the group seemed disturbed although they did not attempt to move or touch the corpse. Adult males responded quickly and intensely, whereas adolescents showed less interest at first but maintained their interest longer (Box, 1984). Chimpanzee mothers with dead infants carry them as monkeys do, but seem more distressed. A Gombe chimp named Olly carried her four-week-old infant for several days after it died. She seemed dazed and sat staring into space, just brushing away the flies. She ate very little and moved slowly, resting frequently (Goodall, 1971). Unfortunately, in most cases the process of infant loss is not observed in wild chimpanzees. However, number of young chimpanzees have been observed after their mothers died. Goodall (1986) has reported that their symptoms usually include huddled posture, a typical "sad" facial expression, listlessness, withdrawal from social activity (especially play), and impaired coordination. Some of these young die and show no apparent cause of death when autopsied. Of thirteen orphans at Gombe, the three youngest starved and six older but not fully weaned ones were adopted, but two of these died within two years. Of the four who remained, two showed marked retardation of physical development—psychosocial dwarfism (Goodall, 1986). The four older orphans had the physical skills required to survive but one of them, Flint, age eight and one-half years, died twenty-nine days after his mother.

He sat by her body in a very lethargic state, became increasingly withdrawn, and stopped eating. His sister groomed him and waited for him, and he did spend some time with his older brothers, but the loss of psychological and social support represented by his mother's death was something he could not survive (Pusey, 1983).

Even being separated from her mother overnight made a young chimpanzee female very agitated. She whimpered, screamed, climbed trees searching, rushed up and down paths, cried out in her sleep, and the next day eventually found her brother and later her mother. Another young chimpanzee survived the loss of his mother at age three because he was adopted by his six-year-old sister. However, he was in very poor shape physically, pulled out his hair, regressed socially and in his ability to use tools, and died of polio within a few years. This pattern was repeated by another young animal, Beatle. Beatle survived longer, however, because her nine-year-old sister was strong enough to carry her, and perhaps provided a more secure base of psychological support. Although she was depressed and emaciated for several years after her mother's death, she did recover by age six. Other young animals were adopted by their immature siblings but, unless the siblings were over eight years of age, the profound depression in the young animal could not usually be overcome by the level of security offered by an immature foster parent.

CAPTIVE APES AND HUMAN RESPONSE

Human-reared captive apes seem to require the same type of psychological support and constant presence from their caregivers that young apes require of their mothers in the wild. When Yerkes was writing about ape care in 1925, he realized that constant companionship was extremely important, commenting that "Miss Alyse Cunningham's gorilla died only a few months after she parted with it, apparently because of lonesomeness" (Yerkes, 1925:73). Goma, a young gorilla being reared in captivity, immediately became sick with diarrhea and refused her food when her foster mother wet away on a trip for just a few days. She (Goma) recovered on Mrs. Lang's return, but needed a lot of extra cuddling for some time (Reynolds, 1971). Chimpanzees are just as sensitive as gorillas to separation from their human foster mothers, even when they are three to four years old.

> He (the chimpanzee) eventually died when the mother was away on a trip, in my opinion from an acute agitated depression which produced sufficient stress, so an infection which would normally have been of little consequence did him in (Temerlin, 1975:198).

These deaths do not usually have observable cause, other than weakening of the immune system, a shut down of the physiologist system, and a general lack of the will to live.

Researchers have deduced the level of distress that chimpanzees feel at the loss of their attachment figures by observing them and noting their extreme responses to loss. One other source of information comes from the writing of Roger Fouts who recorded his sign language conversation with Washoe when he had to tell her that her baby, who had been removed for pediatric care, had died.

> . . . her first question was:*"Baby?* Fout's response to Washoe's question was to sign to her: *"Baby dead, baby gone, baby finished."* Washoe who had been holding the sign in the questioning position then dropped her arms that had been cradled in the *baby* sign position to her lap and she broke eye contact and slowly moved away to a corner of the cage. . . . She continued for the next several days to isolate herself from any interaction with the humans and her signing dropped off to almost nothing. Her eyes appeared to be vacant or distant. For the next three days when R. Fouts would arrive, she asked the same question: *"Baby?" Fouts gave her his same response and she reacted in the same way* (Fouts et al., 1982:169-170).

In this reaction to loss the linguistic and behavioral evidence reinforce each other in assessing Washoe's emotional response to the loss of her infant.

Captive great apes also respond with distress to the loss of their pets. Lucy, who was a family raised chimpanzee, had a pet cat who she played with and carried up and down trees. One day the cat died in Lucy's presence. Her human caretaker reported that Lucy screamed loudly when this happened, stared at the body and reached out a forefinger as if to touch it, but did not.

She did not search for the cat after that. However, about three months later when she saw a picture of herself in a magazine with her cat she signed "Lucy's cat, Lucy's cat" repeatedly and stared at the picture for about fifteen minutes. Lucy was not friendly towards other cats after hers died (Temerlin, 1975). This is in contrast to Koko, the gorilla who had a tailless kitten for a pet. When it was run over by a car she was very upset and asked for another one (Patterson, 1985).

Human caretakers are also often very attached to their great ape charges, especially when they live in the same household. Robert Yerkes, one of the founders of American primatology, had several chimpanzees but was particularly fond of a young pygmy chimp called Prince Chim. Yerkes reported his death in a paragraph beginning. "Finally the tragic day dawned . . ." (Yerkes, 1925:254). Yerkes's daughter said that when Prince Chim died her father commented "The heart went with him from my anthropoid research" (Yerkes-Blanshard, 1977), and "We were all grieved by the loss of Chim" (Yerkes, 1925:254).

Another researcher who has had to watch her chimpanzees die is Jane Goodall. Quite early during her research a polio epidemic struck the part of Africa she was working in and fifteen chimps were afflicted. Of these fifteen, six died, four of the disease and two who were shot by the researchers because they were completely incapacitated and suffering badly. One of these had lost the use of both legs and was rubbed raw by dragging himself along the ground. Goodall mentions how difficult it was for the researchers to watch the animals suffer and how much she missed the ones who had died (1971). Fossey (1983) was very distressed by the deaths of her gorilla population due to poaching, both because of the threat of extinction and because of her feelings about them as individuals. Neither of those researchers, who had spent years in habituating their study animals to human approach and who had won their acceptance and trust, was prepared to take a non-interventionist stand after some of the study population had died, in spite of whatever criticisms they may have received from their colleagues.

SIMILARITIES IN HUMAN AND PRIMATE GRIEF

I would like to reemphasize some of the similarities and differences in the grieving process as seen in humans and non-human primates. The basic cause of grieving seems to be very similar: the loss of a highly valued attachment figure. Even rhesus raised on surrogate cloth mothers show similar types of response to its loss as rhesus infants do to the loss of their real mothers, although not as strongly (Hennessy et al., 1979). The second similarity lies in the patterning and types of behavior seen during the course of a grieving episode. Young children respond to initial separation from their mothers with agitation and protest which often includes screaming fits (Suomi, 1982; Thunberg, 1981). After a few days of protest many children drop into the despair stage characterized by depressive behavior, social withdrawal, loss of appetite, lethargy, and sleep disturbance. The only difference between monkey and human young in these patterns is that many monkeys continue to eat adequately, although Dolhinow and Murphy (1983) said that it was their opinion that one of the separated langur young had starved to death. Also, in Rasmussen and Reite's 1982 study, an older separated depressed rhesus female cut down radically on her food intake and began to look emaciated. An orphaned wild monkey infant is in a worse state because it loses access to its mother's milk, which is important nutritionally long after solid food is a large part of the infant's diet. Withdrawal, lethargy, and disrupted sleep patterns are experienced by many primates under conditions of separation. In addition to these behavioral transformations are the physiological effects of changes in heart rate and body temperature. It has been suggested that the adrenal mobilizing stage with elevated levels of plasma cortisol is an adaptation to permit a lost infant to attract as much attention as possible and perhaps be found by its mother. On the other hand, the depressive phase of slowed heart rate and lowered body temperature is either part of the burnout of the activation system, or a way for the infant to shut down its attention getting behaviors and act in the conservation-withdrawal mode proposed by Kaufman (1977; Rosenblum and Plimpton, 1981).

The outcome phase of grief responses shows similar behaviors over a similar range for both human and non-human primates. The most severe response to loss is death of the afflicted individual. This is a fairly common response to loss in young free ranging animals and also happens in captivity, sometimes even after the mother has been returned (Dolhinow and Murphy, 1983). The next level of response is physical distress severe enough to affect the individual's state of health. Several primatologists (Goodall, 1986) have noted the very retarded physical development in some bereaved animals. This has been compared to the phenomenon of deprivation dwarfism in humans.

This response is caused in humans by lack of stimulation and attachment bonds. If a young primate loses its major attachment and cannot replace it, it may slow or cease its growth process, probably due to the neurobiological feedback between levels of brain serotonin, catecholamines and inefficient metabolism. Another type of physical response is development of a particular physical malady. Ally, one of the signing chimpanzees, developed hysterical paralysis when separated from his first human foster mother (Linden, 1985). Presumably he had already been separated from his own mother, but researchers almost never take the effects of that experience into consideration when they study home-raised apes.

The young separated primate may not be severely enough affected to show physical defects, but in some cases of long or repeated separations the young animal shows behavioral retardation or excessive levels of mother approach and clinging for periods up to one year. Human children can also show excessive clinging and dependence, as well as regression from physical and social levels of achievement such as toilet training and speech (Thunberg, 1981). However, usually children in supportive environments regain their pre-separation levels of development within a few weeks of reunion. Recovery to fairly normal levels of activity and physiological functioning can occur in monkeys if they are able to maintain sufficient food intake and establish social relations with other members of their troop. This process is much faster in species that have supportive environments for separated young, for example bonnet macaques and langurs who show extensive allomothering (Caine and Reite, 1981). These infants usually recover pre-separation levels of activity fairly quickly, and may not return to their own mothers on reunion (Dolhinow and DeMay, 1982). The argument that bonnet macaques are genetically buffered against separation distress is dispelled by studies in which a bonnet infant was left with known pigtail mothers who were not accepting. This infant showed despair behavior and physiology as acute as that in separated pigtail macaques (Reite and Snyder, 1982).

The differences in manifestations of separation-induced grief are related to some extent to the different speeds of development seen in monkeys and humans. Every day represents a larger fraction of an infant a monkey's life, so the transition from protest to despair tends to occur more quickly than it does in children. In apes, whose initial developmental stages are much more humanlike, the periods of response tend to be longer than in monkeys, and more like that of humans. Another difference is the generally noticed lack of a detachment phase in monkeys, although the monkey's perception of being forcibly separated from its mother may well be different from the child's perception of being left behind by its mother. If the separation is long, or the infant monkey has found a new attachment figure, detachment may also occur, and ape infants may show a fairly human pattern of detachment.

Figure 1. Merlin: A young chimpanzee whose mother had died.

CONCLUSION

The question of whether the levels of similarities observed represents analogous or homologous systems of behavior and response depends to some extent on the theoretical understanding of what system underlies the grief phenomenon. If the systems are analogous, their operation and functions are different between primates and humans even though the results appear similar. If the process is homologous, the same system underlies separation and grieving in humans and primates, thus accounting for the similarities. Cairns (1977) is quoted by Rosenblum and Plimpton as saying that "distress induced by separation may indeed be a homology across related mammalian forms" (Rosenblum and Plimpton, 1981:236). If separation distress and grief are processes that have an adaptive advantage, it seems probable that they would be homologous between closely related forms, such as higher primates and humans. The similarities in physiology, behavior, and probable adaptive function are very marked. The protest response is long and loud and may enable the infant to relocate its mother or find an adoptive care giver. The quiet despair stage may allow an exhausted infant to re-coup its resources [conservation-withdrawal (Kaufman, 1977)], or it may be a physiological backlash from the tremendous outpouring of adrenal hormones and activity occurring in the protest stage [opponent-process theory (Rosenblum and Plimpton, 1981)]. The despair stage is a very dangerous one for young primates because they can lose the group through inattention or exhaustion, or they may not be able to escape from predators. Due to the nature of the mother-infant attachment bond, infants require one major attachment figure as the psychological basis of well-being. If they lose that individual, the consequences can be life threatening even if they actually are physically well enough developed to carry on. Often negative psychic influences weaken the body's physiological response to infection, and animals die due to inability to cope with the relatively minor infections that would not kill a happy, secure, well attached youngster. As Goodall noted about the young chimpanzee Merlin:

> Hunched up with his arms around his knees he often sat rocking from side to side with wide open eyes that seemed to stare into the far distance. . . . By this time Merlin was so thin that every bone showed. . . . Often he lay stretched flat on the ground while other youngsters played, as though he were constantly exhausted (van, Lawick-Goodall, 1971:230-234).

Merlin did not survive the loss of his mother.

ACKNOWLEDGMENT

Bibliographic material provided by the Primate Information Centre. Research supported in part by SSHRC supporting grant N1H RR00166.

CHAPTER 3

Alice in the Afterlife:
A Glimpse in the Mirror

Peter G. Ramsden

Peter Ramsden is an anthropological archaeologist whose primary research has been focussed on the culture of the Huron of Ontario. In the spirit of the new developments in archaeological interpretation, he takes on here the task of making sense of death practices of the Huron. He finds, on introspection, that understanding the structure of Huron death and dying helps him to understand his own culture's attitude toward death. In this chapter, Ramsden proposes an analytical model of the relation between life/death and living/dying that may have very wide aplication.

*   *   *

I'll tell you all my ideas about Looking-glass House. First, there's the room you can see through the glass—that's just the same as our drawing room only the things go the other way.

— Alice, in *Through the Looking Glass*

There are two traditional axioms in the archaeology of mortuary ritual: one is that mortuary rituals reflect attitudes towards the afterlife, and the second is that they reflect attitudes towards this life. These are derived from the observation, or assumption, that the ritual that accompanies a person's burial in some way embodies the roles he or she played in life, or in some way anticipates the roles he or she is expected to play after death.

More recently, archaeological approaches to the interpretation of mortuary practices have focussed less on what burials tell about people's attitudes towards such things as the afterlife, and have explored instead the ways in which variations in mortuary patterns may, consciously or unconsciously, embody elements of a society's social structure (Ucko, 1969; Binford, 1971; Tainter, 1978; Chapman et al., 1981; Spence, Pihl and Molto, 1984). The assumption here is that the network of social relations and obligations that surrounds a person in life finds expression in the kinds of social rituals that attend his or her burial. The further assumption, of course, is that variations in these rituals should produce analogous, and discernable, variations in the surviving archaeological record of the burial.

The point of this chapter is to suggest that whatever else mortuary customs do, they reflect attitudes towards death itself: what death is, the relationship between life and death, and the nature of the transition between the two. All societies in some way distinguish between those who are living and those who are dead, although not necessarily in simple dichotomous terms, and construct some notion of what it is that happens when a person makes the transition from one category to the other. My contention is that mortuary customs, what you do with somebody who is changing their status from living to dead, must be profoundly affected by what it is you believe is happening to them. Similarly, although it may be difficult archaeologically to detect such things as grief or mourning, the nature of grief must also be structured in part by a notion of just what death is. So mortuary customs and grieving are parts of a single phenomenon: an appropriately and socially constructed reaction to a person who is experiencing death, however that is perceived.

Since perceptions of the nature of death are societally constructed, and necessarily embody notions of the nature of life and of the afterlife, mortuary customs probably do subsume all of the traditional issues mentioned above. A notion of what death is cannot be separated from a notion of what life is, and it necessarily implies some concept of what follows death, even if that concept is that nothing follows death. It is also probably impossible to separate a perception of death from a perception of society, insofar as it is probably impossible to dream up a notion of *anything* that is entirely independent of one's experience of social relations.

What I propose to do in this chapter is to explore the ways in which mortuary customs in two different societies reflect entirely different views of living and dying. I will begin with a description of the mortuary customs and attendant attitudes of the 17th century Hurons of southern Ontario, based on ethnohistorical and archaeological evidence. I will contrast this with a general characterization of the customs and attitudes in a Western European-Canadian culture with which I am most familiar, and I apologize beforehand for the necessarily anecdotal nature of some of this discussion. I will proceed to argue that while the perceptions of death are entirely different in these two societies, there is a common underlying structure in the perception of the relationship between life and death, and that this perception is reflected in mortuary customs.

The title of this chapter suggests that death and its attendant customs are a mirror (Aries, 1974:51). This is intended to express my central contention that societies construct a notion of what comes after death as a mirror image of what precedes it. The ways in which a society divides up or constructs a person's life are also the ways in which it constructs or divides up a person's career after death, but as a mirror or reverse image. Thus, while perceptions of the nature of life and the nature of death may vary widely, the one will consistently be reflected in the other.

One approaches death, obviously, as a living person, and leaves it as a dead one. The social definition of death shapes the way in which one approaches it, and also the way in which one leaves it. The approach to death is expressed through social categorizations of the 'dying' person and appropriate forms of behavior (Kalish, 1985:130). The departure from death recapitulates this in reverse, and is also expressed through social categorization and appropriate behavior. The behavior in this case includes mortuary customs, and part of it survives archaeologically in the form of burial patterns. It should, therefore, be possible to interpret archaeological burial patterns as indicative of the way in which a past society categorized and behaved towards the dead, and to speculate on that basis about its perception of the nature of death itself.

17th CENTURY HURON MORTUARY CUSTOMS AND DEATH ATTITUDES

The Hurons were a confederacy of Iroquoian-speaking tribes who inhabited south-central Ontario. In the 17th century they were visited there by several French chroniclers including Sagard, Champlain and the Jesuit missionaries (Wrong, 1968; Giguere, 1973; Thwaites, 1896-1901). They lived in palisaded villages, and subsisted by a combination of horticulture, fishing, gathering and hunting. Ethnohistoric information about Huron social structure is sketchy and often unreliable, partly because people like the Jesuits were unfamiliar with what they were observing, and not very interested in such things in any case. Fortunately, however, the Jesuits were vitally interested in Huron religious matters, including death and burial, and described them in some detail. The following summary of Huron burial customs and beliefs is based largely on Tooker (1964) and Trigger (1976). For further information, the reader is referred to these and other sources listed in the references.

The Hurons did not view death as a single, momentary event, but as a process with different stages. The ideal death in this society was an expected one, due to old age, illness or injury, which gave the dying person and his relatives time to prepare for the eventual death of the body. Ideally, the last stage of life was that of 'dying': winding down life in preparation for death. During this period, the dying person would pick out the clothes in which he or she would be buried, and would make other plans for the burial ceremony. Relatives and friends would come and visit and discuss the impending death, say goodbyes, and in many ways 'wrap up' the loose ends of the dying person's life. So in this society, there was a well-recognized category of 'dying person,' with well-established behaviors and attitudes, for the dying person and for others.

Huron life, then can be seen as consisting of a stage of being 'alive,' followed by a period of 'dying,' ending in what we would recognize as physical death. At this point, behavior and attitudes towards the individual changed, and a third stage was initiated. This third stage can be labelled the state of being 'just dead.' In this period, the individual's soul was considered to stay in the village, and was believed to continue to take part in the activities of the living. At some feasts, food was provided for consumption by these spirits. How long this stage lasted is somewhat ambiguous, or more probably, it was variable in accordance with a number of circumstances.

Periodically, Huron villages were moved to new locations because of depletion of firewood or corn field fertility, or threat from enemies. The spirits of the departed did not move with the village. Instead, they entered a final stage of death by travelling *en masse* to the village of souls where they remained for eternity. In this village they 'lived' in every respect as living people did in their villages. This is the Huron stage of being 'fully dead,' in which no change is expected, and is the mirror image of the stage of being 'fully alive.'

What sort of mortuary system might we expect to grow out of this set of attitudes towards death? I would expect that some preparation for burial might be carried out prior to 'death,' and we have already noted that this was the case. Second, I would predict that the 'temporary' state of being 'just dead' might be reflected in a temporary primary burial, situated so that the deceased's soul had access to the activities of the living. Following this I would predict a more 'permanent' burial, in which the body is permanently and irretrievably disposed of, in a special location removed from the living.

Our knowledge of Huron mortuary customs comes from two sources. We have the first hand accounts of early French chroniclers who happened to witness portions of the mortuary system. In addition, we have information from archaeology which both corroborates and expands their testimony. What the chroniclers tell us is that once an individual was defined as 'dead,' he or she was placed on a scaffold in a village cemetery or, in rare instances, buried in the ground. The cemetery is recorded as being very near the village. There are also suggestions that occasionally people kept (or buried) the bodies of deceased relatives in the house. The French commentators are quite explicit that this disposal of the body following death was temporary, and coincided with the phase in which the soul of the departed was still active in the affairs of the living.

The French observers also state that when the time came to move the village, the bodies of the village dead were removed from their temporary graves, and buried in a communal grave some distance removed from the village. In preparation for this burial, bodies which were not already reduced to skeletons were stripped of soft tissue, and the bones of the dead individuals were purposely mixed together, so that they travelled to the village of souls as a group.

Two important features of this secondary burial are, first, that the bodies had to be reduced to skeletons prior to final burial; and second, that their bones had to be mingled together. The importance of skeletonization prior to final burial is also noted by Hertz (1960:32) in the two stage burial system of the Dayaks of Borneo, and suggests to me that the stages of corpse decay are regarded as part of the process of dying. When the corpse is reduced to a skeleton (i.e., when the dying process is finished), then the individual is finally and permanently dead, or, as we would say, not only dead, but "dead and gone;" no further change will take place.

The mingling together of bones in the ossuary is clearly a political statement of transcendent solidarity among a group of people who from time to time found themselves in conflict (Trigger, 1976:87). It also reinforces the solidarity among the deceased who henceforth would have to live together in the village of souls. I wonder whether it also symbolizes the fact that in the final stage of death, a person's living individuality and identity are lost; with the reduction of a recognizable corpse to a skeleton that looks much like any other, the living personality is finally gone, and the involvement of the living with that individual will cease.

From eye-witness accounts, and from archaeological evidence, we know that these communal final graves (ossuaries) were large, deep pits, lined and covered with layers of hides, bark or wood (e.g., Kidd, 1953). Some mourning apparently took place in conjunction with the primary burial, and women in particular made a habit of frequenting the cemetery and mourning at the graves of departed relatives. Of interest here, however, is the fact that the Jesuit Brebeuf was impressed with the intensity of mourning that occurred in conjunction with the secondary burial, even for people who had been 'dead' for a decade or more.

What is clear from this description is that the mortuary system reflects the Huron view of physical death as a two stage process. In the first stage, a person is only 'partly dead,' and through physical decomposition 'continues' to die. The living and the dead are placed so as to have easy access to each other, and mourning at this stage presumably reflects the disruption of some, but not all, of the social relations of the deceased. In the second stage, final or permanent death occurs, as indicated by the reduction of the corpse to a skeleton, and the dead are physically removed from the living, and placed beyond reach. At this point, more mourning takes place, in some cases apparently quite intensely, and would seem to reflect the severing of all social ties to the deceased person, who finally leaves the living village and goes to stay for ever in a separate, distant village of dead souls. It also reflects the departure of the living to a new village site, and "the regrettable necessity for the living and the dead, who had remained near to each other as long as the village lasted, to part company" (Trigger, 1976:85).

The picture I have given above of 17th century Huron burial patterns represents the 'normal' or ideal death. The departures from this ideal pattern provide some of the most convincing evidence of the role of Huron attitudes towards the process of death in structuring mortuary customs. The French themselves noted some exceptions. Very young infants are reported to have been given special treatment in that they were apparently not placed in the village cemetery, or in the final ossuary, but were instead *buried* on paths. We might suggest a correlation of this with high rates of infant mortality, and the belief common in pre-industrial societies like the Huron, that fully human, or fully 'alive,' status was not achieved until some time after birth, presumably when it became clear that the infant had a good chance of surviving to adulthood. From the perspective of this chapter, that the structure of death and its attendant mortuary customs are mirror images of the structure of life, this seems to make eminent logical sense. An infant who has never been 'alive' obviously cannot 'die' (Hertz, 1960:84): one cannot go through any of the stages of death if one has never gone through any of the stages of life, since one can only reach death, the surface of the mirror, through life. So an individual who never appears in the real world will obviously not be in the mirror either. Thus, very young infants are not eligible for any stage of death; they simply return to 'Go' and start again. Archaeological corroboration of this takes the form of the very low representation of young infants in ossuaries, and the abundance of infant skeletons that remained buried in houses (Kapches, 1980; Knight and Melbye, 1983; Fitzgerald, 1979). Frequently, these infants are not buried in specially dug pits, but are intruded into ash or refuse pits; alternatively, the infant's grave pit is often subsequently re-used for the disposal of ash or refuse (Ramsden and Saunders, 1986).

The French also recorded that those who died violently, such as suicides and warriors, were disposed of differently from others, and were immediately interred away from the village. This again seems consistent if we remember that in order to reach the point of death, the plane of the mirror, one ought to go through a stage of 'dying,' of being on the way to death. From here one gets into the looking-glass stage of being 'just dead,' and from there to 'permanently dead.' If one dies in the state of being fully alive, should one go directly to the state of being permanently dead? If so, how would this be expressed in the mortuary system? We might speculate that it would take the form of being permanently buried away from the village immediately following death, which is what the records seem to describe. It is also noteworthy that over the graves of the violently dead were built huts similar to the one built over the site of the ossuary, perhaps signifying that this was a final burial (Trigger, 1976:90).

Archaeological corroboration, and embellishment, of the burial of the violently dead is probably to be found in the Van Oordt cemetery in southwestern Ontario (Molto, Spence and Fox, 1986) which, although it relates to the neighboring Neutral Iroquois, probably reflects a set of beliefs very similar to those of the Hurons. At this site, thirteen young adult males were interred separately, at some distance from the nearest village. The burials appear to have been made very shortly after death, but it is clear from damage to the bones that the bodies were dismembered and perhaps *defleshed* prior to burial. The age and sex profiles, as well as the presence of traumatic injury, strongly hint that these individuals were warriors killed in battle.

A similar case may be observed in one of the Draper site burials (Williamson, 1976:119) which shows clear evidence of violent death, and these bones also had been *defleshed* prior to a permanent burial within the village.

These 'warrior' burials have features in common which bear on the notion that the stages of their deaths mirror the stages of their lives. Obviously they were not interred in the village cemetery, nor were they ever removed to an ossuary. The evidence of dismemberment or defleshing, however, shows that they were reduced, immediately after death, to a physical state approximating that of those who were sent to their final destination through ossuary burial. In the terms used here, the burial treatment of these individuals places them *immediately* in their permanently dead condition. The absence of the 'dying' stage in life is mirrored by the absence of the 'just dead' stage in death.

In a similar way, people who drowned or froze to death (i.e., who died 'sudden' or 'unanticipated' deaths) were *buried* in the cemetery, after having the *soft tissue stripped from their bodies*, and were *not moved to the ossuary* for re-burial (Tooker, 1964:132). Here again, the absence of the stage of 'about to die' from life is mirrored by the absence of the stage of 'just dead' from death.

Archaeologists have encountered other burial modes on Huron sites. Of most interest are interments of adults of various ages and both sexes buried in graves either in houses, in open spaces between houses within a village, or outside of villages in what may have been the village cemetery. A large proportion of these appear to be individuals who suffered from disabling diseases, some of them congenital, and who would have been visibly handicapped (e.g., Garrad, 1970; Shropshire, 1970; Melbye, 1983; Melbye and Knight, 1982; Saunders, 1986). A striking ethnographic hint of this is found in the case of a Huron hunchback, deformed from birth, who asked to be buried in the ground when he died, so that the spirit of which he felt himself to be an incarnation could return directly to the underground world whence it came (Tooker, 1964:99-100).

What has happened to these archaeologically known people is that following death, they have been placed in something analogous to the conventional 'temporary' burial (i.e., the body has been left intact), but have never been removed from there to the final, permanent burial of the ossuary. Why? My suggestion is that these people, being visibly disabled, in at least some cases from birth, were always in the 'dying' or 'not fully alive' category, as in the case of the hunchback cited above who was told he was the incarnation of a non-human spirit, and therefore not quite human. Their career after death mirrors this, insofar as they are permanently in the 'not fully dead' category, and having never been classed as 'fully alive' they cannot proceed to being 'fully dead.' In describing analogous 'special treatment' for certain categories of deceased among the Dayak of Borneo (who also practice communal secondary burial), Hertz (1960:85) arrives at a very similar interpretation by observing that their exclusion from the 'final' burial means " . . . that the transitory period extends indefinitely for these victims of a special malediction and that their death has no end."

Huron burial customs, then, serve as an illustration of how one society constructs the relationship between physical death and social death through its perception of what death is. The Huron explicitly recognize that the body does not, usually, die suddenly, but gradually declines from a state of health through a series of stages including what we recognize as 'clinical death' to a final state of inert bones. The position of a person on this life-to-death continuum is one of the variables of social categorization. There is a way of categorizing a 'dying' person, and a set of appropriate behaviors. Just as the Hurons perceive that 'clinical death' does not mark the end of the physical process of dying, so they perceive that it does not end the social roles of the dying person, and there is also an appropriate set of behaviors and attitudes to those who are in the 'post-death' stage of dying.

One might view the Huron structure of life and death as a three-stage process, life—dying—death, in which the dying phase begins with the onset of illness or old age, and ends with the reduction of the corpse to a skeleton. Alternatively, one might wish to separate analytically physical life and death from the social persona. In this case, the social life of the individual can be seen as outlasting the physical life defined in Western terms.

I suggest that it is analytically more useful to view the Huron structure of life and death as being symmetrical, with 'clinical death' (the cessation of heartbeat, breathing, voluntary physical activity) as the pivotal point. This pivotal point serves as a mirror, so that what comes after it in terms of life stages is an accurate but reversed image of what went before.

The structure of death as a mirror image of life is particularly evident in the cases of those Hurons whose lives were atypical. I have shown that stages omitted from life were also omitted from death, so as to preserve the fidelity of the reflection. Neither the three-stage model, or the social vs physical life model, can adequately explain these departures from the typical practice. Moreover, the model of death as a mirror is also applicable, although initially in less obvious ways, to quite different conceptions and structures of death, such as the Anglo-Canadian example to which I turn now.

ANGLO-CANADIAN MORTUARY CUSTOMS
AND DEATH ATTITUDES

What I am calling an Anglo-Canadian culture refers specifically to the social milieu in which I grew up: working class to middle class Anglo-Saxon society in suburban London, England and emigrants from that society in Toronto.

My characterization of Anglo-Canadian attitudes and customs will be in part introspective, but since I do not claim for this characterization any validity beyond the sub-culture in which I grew up, it seems fair to use it as an ethnographic example, particularly since I can provide insight into the emotional as well as the behavioral content of the mortuary system.

I should also caution those raised in a North American cultural tradition to resist the temptation to presume that death attitudes and customs are similar throughout the English-speaking world and that therefore I must be mistaken in some parts of my characterization. On the contrary, there really are critical differences in attitudes and behaviors, particularly with regard to avoidance of the corpse, reflecting the "entirely different evolutionary path" followed by mortuary customs on the other side of the Atlantic in the 20th century (Cannadine, 1981:193).

In my Anglo-Canadian example, the event of death is perceived as an instantaneous occurrence, and marks a sharp boundary between a state of being alive, and a state of being dead (Hertz, 1960:28). In general, although life certainly has different stages, these are "weakly marked," and there are not considered to be different degrees of being alive once an individual is successfully born and has survived his or her first hour or so (Hertz, 1960:81). Life is viewed as a straight line from birth to death. Death itself is considered to be a sudden termination of life, and the ideal is that until the moment of death, one is fully alive (Kalish, 1985:26). The perception of what it means to be dead is a mirror image of this on the other side of death: immediately following death, one is fully dead, and remains fully dead for the duration. Just what constitutes the duration can vary according to religious conviction, but the point is that the nature of death is fairly well agreed upon in this culture: death is an instantaneous and irreversible change from one ideally constant state, life, to another, being dead. The most important elements of this view are: 1) life and death are profoundly different and completely unrelated states; 2) once born, one maintains a constant state of life until the moment of death, and once dead one maintains a constant state of being dead; and 3) the event of death is an instantaneous leap from one state to the other: there is no transitional state, no grey or ambiguous area.

Ironically, this view of death as a sudden leap from one steady state to another is most clearly reflected in behavior and attitudes in situations of classificatory ambiguity. In this subculture, there are two common forms of behavior towards those who are clearly 'dying,' usually due to advanced age or illness. One, in keeping with the ideal conception of death, is to dismiss the idea of approaching death, and to attempt to maintain as much as possible a 'normal' pattern of behavior towards the dying person by being cheerful or 'positive,' and helping the individual as much as possible to continue a 'normal' round of activities (Kalish, 1985:147). It is traditionally bad form for either the dying person or anyone else to mention the approach of death, and all those involved, including the principal, conspire to maintain the fiction that he or she is as fully alive as ever, albeit temporarily bed-ridden. In this pattern, then, the person in the potentially ambiguous status is steadfastly kept in the alive category through the stalwart continuation of behaviors appropriate to those fully alive, until the actual cessation of heartbeat allows their reclassification as clearly dead. It may be of interest to note that in cases of prolonged ambiguity, such as a lengthy terminal illness or greatly advanced age and senility, the 'moment' of death, and the resultant ability to reclassify the person in a category in which, finally, they clearly belong, is often greeted with expressions, and feelings, of relief.

The second common approach to the dying person is, in a sense, to reclassify them as dead as soon as their status becomes ambiguous (Kalish, 1985:26, 130, 131). This is done by experiencing grief when their 'dying' state becomes apparent, and thereafter avoiding contact with them entirely and more-or-less dismissing them from mind, as one might more appropriately do with a 'dead' person. This option would probably not be seen as particularly admirable behavior in this culture, but it is fairly common, particularly in cases in which the relationship with the dying person is not close.

Just as people approaching death can present situations of ambiguity, and emotional discomfort, so too can those just leaving death. One of the most persistent themes in 'horror' literature and films of this subculture is that of ghosts, and the 'living dead' (Gorer, 1965:114). Even the phrase 'living dead' is emotionally laden, reflecting the fact that it presents a severe linguistic and classificatory contradiction. It denotes a category of things that cannot exist, since the unbridgeable gulf between living and dead is one of the most profound dichotomies in this culture.

As a further illustration of the degree to which members of this culture deny any contact or relationship between life and death, some of the most serious *faux pas* that one can commit involve behaving towards a person in one category as though he or she were in the other. As indicated above, even mentioning the approaching death of a dying person is a serious embarrassment. Also in this category would be making preparations for burial, or disposing of a person's property, before they were labelled as dead. On the other side of the coin, of course, behaving towards a dead person ('dead body' or 'corpse' would be the term used, since one cannot be dead *and* a person) as though he or she were alive is not only considered inappropriate or even disgusting, but in all 'Anglo-Saxon' jurisdictions many such behaviors are serious criminal offenses.

In what ways do the mortuary customs of this society reflect the above-described view of death? My expectation as an archaeologist would be that no burial preparations would occur before the recognition of death, that burial would occur as soon as practicable after death, that the disposal of the body would be in a place separate from living space, and that the body would be disposed of permanently and irretrievably. Needless to say, with the benefit of my fore-knowledge, this is precisely the structure of the mortuary system. As I have already indicated, it is generally considered highly inappropriate to make funeral preparations prior to death, and even long-range planning like purchasing a prepaid burial scheme for oneself while still in the prime of life is usually regarded with some embarrassment or awkwardness. Certainly, going out and selling one's dying mother's car in order to purchase her a coffin would be the height of vulgarity.

Once death has occurred, the corpse is always handled only by professional corpse handlers, and, in my subculture, contact with or proximity to the deceased on the part of the relatives is brief or non-existent. Ideally, again in my subculture, the relatives never actually see the dead person after death. Disposal of the body is done by one of two means: interment or cremation. Again, both are carried out by professionals, and both are done in specially designated disposal areas. In the case of cremation, the corpse is obviously disposed of permanently and irretrievably. In the case of interment, the corpse is securely fastened into a strong box which is finally buried several feet below the ground. Once the brief burial ceremony is over, it is unusual for anyone to visit the interment site again.

Feelings and expressions of grief are a part of people's reaction to death, and may be visible during burial ceremonies. Anticipated deaths usually give rise to less intense feelings of grief than do sudden ones, probably due to the fact that grieving takes place before the actual death. The feelings of grief in the case of an 'inappropriate' (i.e., completely unexpected or very untimely) death may be very intense, and often include feelings of disorientation and hopelessness. However, expressions of grief before, during and after the burial ceremony, are expected to be 'low key,' and dramatic or flamboyant expressions are causes of concern and embarrassment. Women and children are permitted to cry at funerals, while men are expected to be stoical but solemn. This is in keeping with the general expectations of 'emotionality' for different ages and sexes in all situations, and it should be noted in this context that the tears of women and children are not necessarily taken as indications of intense feelings, since it is felt that these classes of people cry 'easily.'

The emotion surrounding death and burial in this culture reflects, first, the fact that all social ties are irreparably severed by death, and second, the fact that no preparation for a change in relations with the deceased is allowed prior to the actual death. Relations with the living person are expected to remain unchanged until death, at which time they ideally should change instantly to a different set of attitudes and behaviors more appropriate to somebody who is dead. Since such an instantaneous shift in attitudes is practically impossible, the preparation for the funeral and the funeral itself, which may span a total of two or three days, provides an occasion to practice the newly appropriate postures: to shift gears from 'X is a living person' to 'X is a dead person.' In spite of the belief in this society that death, and the change in status of the deceased, is instantaneous, a ritualized period of a few days is allowed in which to assimilate the new relationship (or lack of relationship) and the new status. This is accomplished through a period of social interaction among the mourners, *in the absence of the deceased*, during which there is expected to be emotional behavior and reorientation. I would suggest that the intensity of emotions during this period, and the social interaction among the survivors, is a means of 'unlearning' the previous attitudes and behaviors that were appropriate towards the living person, and, in a sense, taking a 'crash course' in the new attitudes and behaviors that are appropriate now that the person is 'gone.'

To summarize, this society views being alive and being dead as two entirely separate states, and death as an instantaneous leap from one to the other. Both states are viewed as being unchanging, in that there are no culturally recognized degrees of being alive, nor of being dead: one must be either alive or dead; 'alive but almost dead' and 'dead but almost alive' are not legitimate social categories.

The mortuary system reflects both the static view of life and death, and the notion that the change is instantaneous. The social rituals surrounding disposal of a corpse provide opportunities for the living to reorient social and emotional attitudes as quickly as possible, and indeed provide social rewards for those who appear to have done this most successfully. The actual patterns of corpse disposal clearly reflect the belief that death is an event, and that once dead, one enters a state, completely separate from life, from which there is no return, and in which there is no anticipated change or evolution. Immediately following death the corpse is removed from the company of the living, and never seen by them again. It is disposed of as quickly as practicable in a manner that precludes any suggestion of further involvement with the deceased. The complete avoidance of the corpse also precludes any opportunity to detect changes in the individual following death, reinforcing the perception that death is a static state. The message is that the dead are, physically and socially, immediately 'gone.' From the moment of death, the physical condition of the body is of no consequence, with the exception that it must be permanently removed from the world of the living just as the dead person must be banished from social relations. The growing popularity of cremation in Britain is an expression of this conviction that physical death brings an immediate end to social existence.

Here again, then, the structure given to death by grieving and mortuary rituals can be seen as a mirrored reflection of the structure of life. Life is a constant, unvarying state. It begins in an instant, continues on a steady and even plane for about eighty years, and ends equally instantaneously. Death is constructed similarly: it begins abruptly at the instant that life ends, and continues uninterrupted and unchanging on a level, although very different plane, towards some destination that is beyond our knowledge.

The expected behaviors and attitudes surrounding death serve, on the one hand, to maintain a perception of unwavering life up to the moment of death, and, on the other, to construct a reality of unchanging 'deadness' after it. The usual mourning and burial customs also reinforce the notion that the dead move to their new state instantly, and that this new state is entirely beyond the realm of the living.

In the Huron case, departures from the ideal provided insight into the role of the death trajectory as a reflection of the life trajectory. Similar insight into the Anglo-Canadian case is difficult to provide, inasmuch as there are no stages of living or dying which can be omitted, and the very nature of the beliefs virtually precludes exceptions. One could, therefore, argue that the treatment of the dead and dying in this culture reflects only the desire to distance death-related things from the living as much as possible (Gorer, 1965), and that the apparent reflection of the life trajectory in death is coincidental.

In response to this, I would argue, first, that this theory cannot explain why the death trajectory is perceived as it is. The notion that death, and all dead things, are completely removed from the living, does not predispose one to a perception of a death trajectory that mimics that of life. In fact, the mere wish to separate life from death would seem more effectively expressed by viewing the two states as having very different structures.

Second, while it may not be easy to find exceptions to the ideal life and death trajectory in England, we might consider the partly derivative North American customs, which are somewhat different, to be an analog of such an exception. Does the different treatment of the dead in America reflect only a different way of coping with bereavement, or does it, as my model would suggest, reflect a different view of life and dying?

Compared to British practices, mourning and mortuary customs in America typically entail more overt, more prolonged and more elaborate mourning; more elaborate and social burial rituals; and more elaborate treatment of the corpse, in the form of embalming, restoration, application of cosmetics and display. In the American mourning ritual, the deceased, although acknowledged by the mourners to be dead, is made to appear 'alive' through the manipulations of professional specialists, and during the period of display, social interaction takes place between the mourners and the corpse. This is part of the state of the "living dead" (Kalish, 1985:47-48), defined as a state following physical death in which the person nonetheless still 'exists' socially. This is an 'in between' phase in the American structure of dying, in which the deceased is really considered to be only partly dead inasmuch as it is still possible to interact with the corpse and through it with the social persona.

Is there any hint of a corresponding in-between stage preceding death in the American system? I suggest that increasingly there is. The American conception of death is that it takes place in a hospital where the dying person is cared for during the final hours by doctors and nurses. The life status of such a dying person is ambiguous inasmuch as he or she may be avoided, regarded as dangerous and transformed into a "non-person" (Kalish, 1985:130-131). In other words, there is a brief period prior to death when the individual is labelled as 'already partly dead.' Correspondingly, for a brief period following death, the individual may be regarded as 'not yet completely dead,' or 'not yet gone.' My unsystematic observation of North American mortuary customs is that those who die sudden deaths, particularly violent ones, are not afforded the full 'partly dead' treatment after death, and are more likely to be buried quickly, with little or no corpse preparation or display: the partly dead stage did not occur in life, and is therefore omitted from death.

My contention would be that on an attitude continuum from the British example to the Huron example, North America would be near, but not at, the British end. There is a more marked tendency in North America to view dying as a process, albeit a short one, in which an individual 'passes' across the threshold of physical death, rather than leaping instantly to a different plane of existence. There is reason to suspect, however, that, as in the Huron case, a suddenly terminated physical life is likely to be reflected in a suddenly terminated social life.

British death customs have been characterized by Gorer (1965) as representing a refusal to recognize or 'accept' death, and this has been popularized in the phrase "the denial of death" (Becker, 1973; Kalish, 1985:84) or "the denial of mourning" (Gorer, 1965:113). Gorer's analysis maintains that death has become a taboo subject, hedged about with prudery and mechanisms of denial, and has replaced sex as the facet of human life which must not be acknowledged. Now Gorer's contrasting of Victorian England (lots of death, no sex) with modern England (lots of sex, no death) may be structurally elegant, but in the end it fails to characterize accurately either sex or death in either era. What it adds to an understanding of either subject is somewhat obscure.

The assertion that "the majority of British people today are without adequate guidance as to how to treat death and bereavement" (Gorer, 1965:110) is at best an over-generalization. The pattern of death behavior I have outlined above is structured and predictable. There is no doubt in my mind about how to treat death and bereavement: I 'treat' death by pretending that it will not happen to me or my loved ones until one day when we are all ready for it; I treat bereavement by making it very low key, and *private*.

A contrary analysis to that of Gorer's is presented by Cannadine (1981) who suggests that far from indicating an inability to deal satisfactorily with death, the virtual lack of mourning behavior in Britain reflects an easy facility to accept the deaths of others. In contrast to the horrors of the first half of the 20th century, during which mourning rituals were exposed as entirely inadequate to deal with such things as the death of one-third of the young adult male population between 1914 and 1918, the realities of death since 1945 have been relatively easy to accept. Death *now* is experienced predominantly by the elderly (i.e., it is usually 'appropriate'), and medical care can make it relatively painless (i.e., it is not so frightening to watch). That same medical care, and many other benefits of late 20th century life, make it possible to live 'fully' until an advanced age when death can 'overtake' us in our sleep at home. What this adds up to is that increasingly, our experience of death conforms to our ideal notion of how death is supposed to be.

As I have argued above, from my perspective that the structure of death mirrors the perceptions of life and of dying, and given the nature of these perceptions in modern Britain, the feelings and behaviors surrounding death, burial and mourning are entirely predictable, and could hardly be structured in any other way.

SUMMARY AND CONCLUSION

The basic point of this chapter has been that mortuary customs, grief and mourning are structured expressions of a society's beliefs about what death is. I have suggested that however death is conceived, there is some point at which a person changes from being alive to being dead, and that this point can be viewed as though it were the surface of a mirror. The approach to death, to the mirror, is structured by the way in which a society visualizes the nature of life and death. Once through the glass, the path followed by a person, now dead, is a reflection of the path followed in approaching it, in reverse as a mirrored reflection would be.

Mortuary customs are the means whereby society structures or traces the progress of the deceased person along the mirrored path of his or her life. In the Huron case, life before death is divided into stages, and life after death recapitulates these in reverse. If any of the stages before death is omitted, it is also omitted from life after death. In the Anglo-Canadian case, there is a strong conviction that life before death is constant, and not divisible into stages or 'degrees' of being alive, and life after death is correspondingly static.

In view of the fact that both of these societies view, and label, an individual's career after death as a 'life,' it should not be surprising that the life before death should be used as a model of the life after it. Perhaps the reversal of life history following death provides a measure of security in considering one's own mortality or in grieving over the death of another. If the dead are in a sense retracing or repeating their steps, they may be seen as 'returning' to somewhere familiar, rather than as striking out alone into an unknown, and unknowable, other universe, where not even our thoughts can follow.

CHAPTER
4

Sleep, Sleep, Sleep; Farewell, Farewell, Farewell. Maori Ideas About Death

Hirini Moko Mead

In Chapter 4 Hirini Mead discusses the Maori way of death and mourning. Writing from the dual perspective of an active Maori Elder and an anthropologist, Mead places Maori practice in the context of New Zealand society, dominated by British settlers since the 19th century. While most Maori are Christian today, many traditional attitudes toward death and the spirits of the departed remain strong, as do the old ways of containing and resolving the grief that death brings. These beliefs often run counter to those of the church, but they are so deeply ingrained a part of being Maori that they seem impervious to change.

*   *   *

Although trained as a anthropologist and currently Professor of Maori Studies at Victoria University, I am as well an active participant in my own culture. This chapter springs largely from direct experience in attending many *tangihanga* ('mourning ceremonies'), both as a member of the bereaved family and as a visitor. I write also as one who has had to play the role of elder and speaker on many of these occasions. There is a considerable difference between being a participant observer and being an actual in-group member.

PROVERBIAL SAYINGS

It is a truism that human life is but a brief moment in the stream of history, that life is transitory, is measured and, being limited in duration, is highly valued. The wise men of the Maori world had many proverbial sayings about the nature of life and death. An example is the following:

Rarangi maunga tu te po, tu te ao: rarangi tangata ka ngaro, ka ngaro, ka ngaro
(A range of mountains remains standing night and day but a group of people is lost, is lost, is lost).

Sayings such as this one continue to have an important place in the mourning ceremony called *tangihanga* ('the weeping') because people want to know what their ancestors thought about death and what wisdom and good advice there is for them. Although proverbial commentaries on death might be repeated again and again, members of a Maori community do not tire of hearing them. Likewise, the story of Maui's attempt to seek immortality for us humans can be told many times without boring the audience. This is because the stories have a spiritual and mystical dimension to them which is additional to the knowledge carried by the words.

SIGNIFICANCE OF TRADITIONS

There is, in fact, more to the so-called myths of tribal society than scientifically trained educators realize. Moreover, the explanations for death given by scientists or by Christian teachers are not inherently superior to those that belong to indigenous cultures, nor are they more comforting to the bereaved. For the Maori people of New Zealand it was their culture hero Maui-tikitiki-a-Taranga (Maui the topknot of Taranga) who provided the model of death. He was the first to die and since he died we must all follow him. There is no escape from the path prepared by Maui.

How he died provides one cultural model of behavior for the modern-day Maori. He attempted to expand the frontiers of immortality by challenging the Goddess of Death. The theory the sages proposed for the confrontation was that death is the opposite of birth, that the spark of life lies in the womb of woman and that the way to secure immortality was to reverse the process of birth, grasp the spark of life and remove it from the Goddess, Hine-nui-te-po (Maid of the Great Night). Maui failed. His accomplice, the twittering fantail, laughed at the spectacle of the man-god Maui re-entering the womb. Consequently the Goddess woke up with a fright and crushed Maui and that was how he died. He did not wait for death to claim him. Rather he tried to outwit the Goddess but failed in his attempt. Thus life can be viewed as an active pursuit of the spark of life. To give up this struggle is to succumb to the Goddess of Death.

EXPLANATIONS OF DEATH

During a *tangihanga* a lot of talking and explaining is done. Usually lasting three days, formal speech-making (*whai korero*) is a standard requirement of the ceremony, and it is during these speeches that people remember and talk about Maui. Explanations of death are of paramount importance to the mourners, to the relatives of the deceased, to the friends who are touched by the sense of tragedy which death always causes and to those who are summoned together to attend the *tangihanga*. The tragedy of the situation affects the immediate family perhaps more than others, and they especially want to hear the explanations, the proverbs and the comforting words of the ancestors. This is not to denigrate other explanations such as Christian ones, which are frequently heard at *tangihanga* in New Zealand today. It is also fair to say that not all modern Maori families are attuned to and trained in their culture. Many are not familiar with Maui's deeds and their association with the *tangihanga* ceremony. This is due to the nature of the New Zealand society, dominated by an English speaking, largely British-oriented majority and their values and customs. Some Maori families are persuaded to follow the mourning customs of the *Pakeha* 'non-Maori descendants of the settlers' and not their own. Nonetheless, there is a strong ethic among Maori people to conduct the ceremonies of mourning properly and in the proper cultural context.

PUBLIC AND PRIVATE GRIEVING

There are some obvious reasons for people wanting to talk about death. First is the human need to share the tragedy and draw support around the immediate kin. The next is to express grief through tears and talk and by these means to come to accept the death of their relative.

Maori practice favors open grieving but, as happens in other cultures, there are patterns to this apparent free-for-all weeping. The culture does not expect mourners to weep copiously for three or four days. Rather there are public and private moments for grieving. The public times are signalled either by the arrival of visiting mourners or by significant changes in the ceremony. In the former case the *manuhiri* 'visitors' and the *tangata whenua* ('people of the land') or the home side engaged in loud wailing sometimes exacerbated by the presence among the visitors of a close relative. Such concentrated wailing and weeping among the women may last about five minutes.

It stops when the home orator gets up to make his formal oration. The wailing may start again half an hour or more later when the visitors come to meet the *tangata whenua* and the *kiri mate* ('dead skin') or the immediate family. In between the arrival of visitors and late at night there are comparatively private times for the family. They are free to weep on their own, and many do.

POINTS OF INTENSITY IN MOURNING

Other times when weeping is likely to become intense are, as mentioned already, when some irreversible stage is reached in the ceremony. The arrival of the corpse onto the *marae* 'courtyard' to lie in state is one of those moments. Another is when the coffin is finally closed and the face of the deceased is never seen by human eyes again. Yet another moment is when the body leaves the *marae* for the cemetery. Often the most dramatic and poignant occasion for the mourners is when the coffin is finally lowered into the ground. At this point, all physical signs of the deceased are lost and this is the final farewell, the final closure on a life. The words *"haere, haere, haere"* 'depart, depart, depart' take on a special finality.

A year later, when the memorial stone is unveiled, the kin gather again at the *marae* to go through an abbreviated form of the *tangihanga* ceremony. Weeping is less intense at this time but, as before, custom allows loud weeping at set times—at the very beginning of the unveiling ceremony and again beside the grave at the cemetery. Outside of these prescribed times the bereaved family is free to weep privately in their own way.

THE LEADING ROLE OF WOMEN

What characterizes the *tangihanga* ceremony is the respect paid to those who are weeping and the care taken not to stem the flow of tears. The mourners have the right to weep in public. There are no limits set on age or sex, but there is a clear expectation that it is the old women who lead the mourning and who set the cultural standards for the occasion. The British value placed on the stiff upper lip in the face of adversity has no place in the *tangihanga* ceremony. Instead, grief is given expression in tears, wailing, and talking. In former times women used to cut themselves with obsidian, but this is no longer done. What remains from the past is a form of weeping which is like a dance. The mourner employs the quivering hand movements of dance and weeps to a sort of dirge. It is a very beautiful form of mourning which is becoming less common.

REVIEWING THE LIFE OF THE DECEASED

There is no shame in tears and there is great comfort in words. Visitors tell of their memories of the deceased, and sometimes recount their shared experiences. At times the life's work of the deceased is subject to criticism or praise. Often an orator draws attention to the loss to the community as well as to the family. A person is lauded for the activities they performed for the common good, for the tribe *iwi* or for Maori society generally. Or the deceased might be condemned for not doing enough. But it is a time which can be used to bury the hatchet and allow conflicts to be resolved.

SHARING TRADITIONAL KNOWLEDGE

During the formal speeches, speakers frequently allude to traditional Maori knowledge. This occurs when the exploits of Maui are interpreted to make them relevant to the bereaved. People talk about Maui as though his encounter with the Goddess of Death occurred only yesterday. The speaker mentions those already departed and may talk about the journey of the deceased to Te Reinga in the northern tip of the country and the ocean journey to Hawaiki-nui (Big Hawaiki, Hawaiki-roa (Long Hawaiki) and Hawaiki pamamao (Distant Hawaiki) to the mythical homeland of the Maori (Oppenheim, 1973:94). We share with many other Pacific cultures the idea of the spirit going on a journey to a land of peace and plenty. In the Maori case, heaven is in Hawaiki far out into the Pacific Ocean.

CONTEST BETWEEN LIFE AND DEATH

Death is often described as a struggle between life and the forces which conspire to terminate it. These forces include the ill will of adversaries, ritual errors committed innocently or deliberately, sickness, accident, willful violence and so on. For example, some ceremonial handles are decorated with the powerful image of a human figure contending mouth to mouth with a lizard which is regarded as the symbol of death (Barrow, 1972; Fig. 296, p. 166). Here the message is easy to read. Life is a continuous struggle to prevent the lizard from entering the stomach of a victim and then slowly eating away its body. The idea of a lizard being the cause of sickness is part of the belief system of the Maori (Best, 1941; 1:107). Ill health was not caused by a germ caught without design from the atmosphere. Rather the germ is in the form of a lizard, and someone maliciously directed it to a victim. In other words, one does not 'catch' a sickness such as a cold from another person. A person actually *gives* a sickness. There is usually a reason for this sort of giving.

In other art work the image might be of a human figure biting the tail of a lizard. In this case, the message is that rather than accept philosophically that we must all die and so wait for it to come, one should tease the tail of death and lead an adventurous life. In other words, people should follow the example of Maui.

NON-MATERIAL ASPECTS OF LIFE

Each living person has several non-material aspects. *Mauri* and *hau* are both regarded as principles of life. *Mauri* is translated as the life principle (the thymus) and *hau* is the vitality or vital essence of a person (Williams, 1957:197). Both are delicate, and an attack on one affects the other. Sorcerers were apt to focus especially upon the *hau* 'vital essence' when they worked their arts of black magic known as *makutu* (Oppenheim, 1973:81-86). The expected result of *makutu* 'sorcery' was that the state of being well, *hau-ora*, would change to a state of near death or *hau-mate*. Thus the role of the sorcerer was to negate *ora* 'life' and convince victims that their life principles had been destroyed. If not halted, the *mauri* weakens, the spark of life loses its vitality and warmth, and the victim dies.

MAKUTU (SORCERY)

In traditional times accusations of *makutu* 'sorcery' were quite frequent and many of the suspected sorcerers were identified and killed (Oppenheim, 1973:85).

The frequency with which sorcerers were killed suggests that the homicides were justified on the grounds that the sorcerers had caused death. In other words a person, not the gods, had killed out of malice. The family had to establish who exhibited the greatest malice towards them.

Sometimes the reason for a person becoming ill and dying was diagnosed as being due to the victim committing a ritual transgression. For example, an error in the public performance of a *waiata* 'song' or in the recitation of a genealogy would be regarded as a serious ritual error. Similarly, mistakes in the visual arts including carving, painting, lattice work and weaving would result in some expected *utu* 'reciprocal answer.'

RITUAL ERRORS

Another source of trouble was the violation of an important ritual rule such as desecrating a *wahi tapu* 'sacred area.' Any ritual transgression gave cause for some reprisal. Sometimes these took the form of a chain of disasters which befell a family. For example, members of the victim family might all die in strange and horrible ways—by murder, by road accidents, by their own hands, and so on. People usually explained such a tragedy as being due entirely to some ritual transgression. There was no other explanation acceptable to Maori elders.

In modern terms the cause is described as a *whiu* 'curse.' A *whiu* is 'caused' by committing ritual errors and is a consequence of them. While some *whiu* have very serious consequences, others have comparatively mild ones. In some cases a family is described as a *whare ngaro* 'lost house' because it is believed that a curse was put upon it that resulted in death after death among the children. Only one child may survive the curse, and then only to provide a means by which the family can continue. While Maori elders can cite case after case of *whiu* operating in modern society, people believe that most such curses can be averted. The solution is *karakia* 'traditional prayers.' It is necessary for the gods to intervene. Today this intervention often requires people to appeal both to the Christian god and to the gods of traditional Maori society.

ROLE OF TOHUNGA (PRIESTS)

The more important appeal is to the traditional gods of the Maori using *karakia* 'traditional prayers.' These must be recited by an acknowledged priest or *tohunga*. Even physicians in hospital occasionally find it necessary to appeal to *tohunga* 'priests' to help save their patients from illnesses which are described as *mate Maori* 'Maori sickness.' I have also heard of big companies requiring the services of a *tohunga* to convince factory workers that the proper rituals for their protection in the work place were indeed carried out and hence their families were not in danger.

PROGRESSION TOWARDS FINAL DEATH

Death itself is seen to be progressive; that is, a person goes through a transformation from a state of good health to a state of *hau mate* 'vital essence is dying or dead.' When a person becomes very ill, as for example in a case of cancer, the body is described as beginning to *whakaheke* or 'descend.' There is weight loss and the person's vital essence now lacks spark. The metaphors of descending and sinking are used to describe this state of dying and refer to the belief that the dead go into the care of the Goddess of Death in the underworld.

TRANSITION FROM PERSON TO CORPSE

Just before a person dies there is a ceremony called *tuku wairua* which sends the spirit of the dying away while the person is still alive and conscious of what is happening. Once the spirit has departed, the person may be medically dead but, in a Maori sense, he or she is not wholly dead yet. An important transformation has occurred: the person is now a *tupapaku* 'standing shallow,' a corpse. The ceremonies collectively called the *tangihanga* commence and the *tupapaku* is given a space in the meeting house or house of mourning. The corpse lies in an open coffin so that the face can be plainly seen. It is dressed up and prepared nowadays by professional undertakers, but this used to be a task performed by the extended family.

THE FICTION OF SLEEPING

Ornaments, weapons or traditional Maori cloaks may be placed over the corpse who is now ready to 'participate' in the ceremonies. At this stage all the orators address the corpse in the first person. Participants act as though the corpse can hear and is merely sleeping. In fact, orators move from statements of "sleep, sleep, sleep" to "depart, depart, depart" as though the status of the corpse is ambiguous. What is clear, however, is that all orators address the deceased. To this extent there is a general belief that the deceased is sleeping and still able to hear.

Three days later when the *tupapaku* is buried, a further stage of death is reached. The person's face is now out of sight and the person is gone for good (see Figure 1). Mourning is still not complete until a year later when the memorial stone is erected and the relatives come together once again to confirm that the mourning ceremonies were completed properly. At this stage the spirit of the deceased is summoned back to the courtyard to witness the event and one may hear again the words "sleep, sleep, sleep." Now the message of farewell is much stronger and so the words "*haere, haere, haere*" have a ring of finality about them. They mean 'farewell, farewell, farewell.' After this, death is final. Restrictions upon widows or widowers are lifted and they are free to re-marry.

Figure 1. The chief of Ngati Pahipoto, Dr. Eruera Manuera, is carried to
the cemetery by his sons on 19 June 1990, at Te Teko, Bay of Plenty.
The coffin is closed and his face is seen no more by
his whanau (extended family).

OBLIGATIONS OF KIN

The assembly of the relatives is an important part of the mourning process.
Maori clearly understand that near relatives must attend while more distant relatives should do so. Close relatives are obliged to stay for the whole ceremony
because their support is needed. It is a time of social renewal, of ensuring that
one's face is seen, of re-emphasizing the importance of the social unit, the *hapu*
'sub-tribe' or the *whanau* 'extended family,' and of getting to know younger
members of the unit and the in-laws. This group of relatives is assembled twice, at
the beginning of the mourning cycle and at the end. The more important the
deceased, however, the more likely it is that the 'kin' group would be required to
assemble more often than the two occasions mentioned here. There is another
series of ceremonies called *kawe mate* which entail taking the death to other kin
groups at different places in the country. The obligations upon the kin can be quite
demanding in terms of time, and some people have difficulty obtaining leave from
their jobs. The coming together emphasizes the importance of the *hapu* in helping
its members through crisis.

THE METAPHORS OF DEATH

There are many ways of expressing the often devastating effects of death. Occasionally, as in the case of a long illness, death is really a great relief for the whole family. Often, however, death comes unexpectedly or quickly and the family is not ready for it. In Maori society the effect is variously referred to as the shattering of a canoe, as whales cast upon the shore, as a house destroyed, as a mountain covered by dark clouds, or as a rough cloak which has to be worn. The portents of death are the flashing of lightning, the peals of thunder, the shaking of the earth by earthquakes and the darkening of the sky.

THE FLAX BUSH

For some, warnings of impending death within the family come in the form of dreams which are then analyzed for the message. It is a point of comfort for Maori that the deceased leave behind a *pa harakeke* or a 'flax bush.' This is a family of children to become the living faces of the departed, to become their hands and their feet, and to continue the work they did not finish. There is a strong sense of continuity down a line of descent to children who in turn will grow up and do their part in the chain of continuity. There is, as well, a strong belief that the ancestors do live and find expression in their descendants. This might be manifest in voice, in appearance, in mannerisms or in some qualities which remind the members of the group of relatives no longer to be seen. Reflections of them are, however, seen in their descendants.

Thus, while death causes closure on one individual life, in the normal scheme of things there is continuity in the descent line. One lives on in one's children. This is the only way in which death can be overcome.

CHAPTER
5

Death and Mourning Among the Huicholes of Western Mexico

Celia García de Weigand
and
Phil C. Weigand

In the following chapter the authors, Celia and Philip Weigand, consider an encapsulated minority, the Huichol of Mexico. In their mountainous region the Huichol have maintained their cultural distinctiveness and resisted the forces of assimilation. As with the Maori of the preceding chapter, the Huichol beliefs and practices often form a counterpoint to the precepts of the "folk Catholicism" practiced by most. Unlike the Maori, though, Huichol death and grief practice stresses the continuing relations that spirits and living humans share. The authors call our attention to the component of anger in Huichol grief—a point that will be made in a number of subsequent chapters.

*   *   *

The Huichol Indians of Nayarit and Jalisco, Mexico, occupy the mountain and canyon vastness of the southern edge of the Sierra Madre Occidental in the Chapalagana and Camotlán drainages. The extremely marginal quality of their environment allowed them to maintain a strong degree of political independence from the Spanish colonial system for the first 200 years of its existence. This isolation is broken today, but it continues with enough effect to allow a great deal of cultural independence.

The traditional Huicholes are organized into five *gobernancias* (large districts dominated by a colonial-style politico-religious, or *cargo*, hierarchy), which in turn are grouped into three *comunidades indígenas* (crown-chartered, communal land-holding units which are inalienable). The *comunidad* Huicholes number about 8,000-10,000, many of whom are monolingual Huichollan (Uzo-Aztecan) speakers and are culturally very conservative. They were formed into their contemporary groupings by processes of response to outside pressures, beginning with their long period of resistance to the Spanish. These responses, summarized more fully in Weigand (1985a), included:

1. the acceptance of many refugees from the surrounding areas;
2. the adoption of raiding as a major political and economic underpinning of their post-contact but pre-conquest society;
3. the successful introduction of cattle and sheep herding into the area prior to conquest; and
4. the intensification of their political system around the kings of Tonati.

Contemporary Huichol culture, hence, is composite in historical character. Demographically, as well as culturally, it was fed by traditions from runaway African slaves, other Indian groups—both neighboring and in service as Spanish auxiliaries—and a cast of failed revolutionaries and general misfits from all over western and northwestern Mexico. The area was, and is today, a *región de refugio* (zone of refuge, *cf.* Aguírre Beltrán, 1967, Crumrine and Weigand, 1987). Catholic missionization has been sporadic, and while never highly intensive the *cargo* system of governance, mayordomos, and saints was introduced.

Amid the themes of response and compositiveness, however, are cultural patterns basically different from neighboring Indian and mestizo populations. The social patterns of flexibility entailed in response and compositiveness are, nonetheless, woven into an articulate series of ideologies concerning life-ways, governance, and social organization. The basic historical sources and ethnographies for the *comunidad* Huicholes are: Ortega (1944), Saavedra (1899), Lumholtz (1973), Preuss (1982), Fábila (1959), Zingg (1938), Benítez (1968), Fikes (1985), and Weigand (1972). Ortega and Saavedra were chroniclers of the Colonial period. The field work of Preuss and Lumholtz was accomplished in the 1890s (see Weigand, 1985a for a treatment of the archaeology and ethnohistory of the region under consideration).

While many Huicholes (perhaps as many as 50,000—Valdés and Menéndez, 1987) live in the cities, dependent suburb villages, and coastal plantations of western Mexico, they will not be considered in this chapter. Most of the observations presented here, unless otherwise noted, are drawn from three years of field work, which began in 1966 and continues today, among the Chapalagana Huicholes of the Comunidad Indígena de San Sebastián Teponahuastlán.

ATTITUDES TOWARD DEATH AND DYING

Huichol attitudes toward death (defined as passing from the community of Huichol *living humans*) clearly reflect their historical situation: Roman Catholic and Native American ideas from multiple sources are woven into a common interpretative fabric. A person may 'die' in one of seven different ways.

1. by sorcery (the worst way);
2. by exile, or 'social' death (the second worst);
3. by accident (defined as violent murder, falls, lightning, etc.);

4. by natural causes (defined almost exclusively as the noticeable progression and result of old age);
5. by religious sacrifice;
6. by *nahualismo* (or transformation into animals); and,
7. by execution by the ancestors.

There are ambiguities between the boundaries of some of these categories, especially regarding sickness, diseases, degenerative illnesses, certain types of accidents, sudden and mortal swoons, etc., which, for the same victim, some might regard as natural and others as sorcery, depending on their origins. Since the society's religious system is characterized by ancestor worship/veneration, especially along the agnatic line, the physical death of a strong male is felt differently from that of a child, young person, or most women (see below). Ancestors eligible for veneration are called upon to perform a wide variety of tasks in service to the living: preventative curing ceremonies, which are petitions for a healthful balance to be maintained at the lineage level; field fertility rites; and alleviating curing ceremonies, just to name a few, are among the most common. The presence of these ancestors among the living is real, and their physical death does not impinge upon their continued social life and functions. These ancestors, if they are purified and hence eligible for veneration, are regarded as 'living' *ancestor humans,* in a continuity with, rather than separate from, the *living humans.* This point will be discussed in greater detail below. The ancestor humans are feared, loved, and respected all in the same breath.

At the opposite end of the spectrum are those that are socially dead but physically still alive. These individuals, too, are usually males, exiled for violent behavior, incest, bestiality, sorcery, or ceremonial violations beyond the pale of acceptability. Their passing from the community of the living is viewed with relief, despite the fear that they continue to inspire among their survivors. They are not treated with ceremonial respect.

Cross-cutting some of the aforementioned categories is the seventh cause of death listed above which is provoked by the ancestors themselves. When human misconduct has been so great that the individual is not considered to be worthy of continued life, the ancestors may execute, or kill, him/her. While some of these individuals may be 'socially dead' prior to their physical deaths, the misconduct of others may be invisible to the living but completely visible to the ancestors. Ritual offenses or ritual neglect are the main categories of misconduct that can provoke this type of execution (Fikes, 1988). The first category can include disrespect, the second simply carelessness.

One result of the ancestor veneration complex is that the Huicholes are geopious. Geopiety is, in the most basic sense, reverence for one's land and the gods/spirits that protect it (*cf.* Wright, 1966). Reciprocity lies at the core of geopiety. It is a tightly woven interrelationship between people and place which is cemented by the strong sense of communality of living humans and ancestor humans. Thus, exile is a powerful punishment; not having one's spirit reunited with the ancestors is the most potent form of exile because it can be forever. The proper fate for the immoral and impious is exile, either as social death for the still living, or spiritual isolation for the deceased. No bonds are more important than the religious ones which link an individual to his/her lineage, and that lineage to its ancestor humans. These bonds can be expressed only in place. The ancestor houses are the lineage altars; they are inextricably tied to agricultural fields and to holy springs and caves, from which these particular ancestors first emerged. To break this linkage is to stop being Huichol, living or dead. Another material link to the ancestors in general is the fire hearth, especially at night and/or during ceremonies of almost any type. The bond between individual/lineage and place is biological in intensity.

Sacrifice is another way to die. Human sacrifice, once common throughout all of Mesoamerica, has not been documented for the Huichol area in recent years. A persistent rumor discusses the sacrifice of a young girl during the peak of the 1948 famine. Non-Huicholes are certain that it was the Huicholes who sacrificed the youngster. Huicholes say that it was done among the Cora. Since the topic was so sensitive, we never felt it should be pursued to the detriment of our other interests.

The following observations about sacrifice should be made, however, in order to balance the discussion; human sacrifice was an important way of dying in the past (cf. the 1550 Mapa del Obispado de Compostela). The sacrifice of children commonly was regarded as a feature of the agricultural cycle. It was not part of the better known cycle of political sacrifices so well documented elsewhere in Mesoamerica (cf. Sahagùn, 1981; Nicholson, 1971; Carrasco, 1981; 1982). As a 'first month' rite, child sacrifice was dedicated to the themes of fertility, renewal, and water. In this cycle, deer are common motifs, and they serve as sacrificial animals in these renewal ceremonies among the Huicholes. Deer are equated with the ancestors, in addition. As deer have been hunted into regional extinction, young bulls are now substituted. These types of sacrifices are directed toward the gods, especially those with Quetzalcoatl-like attributes, and the ancestors directly partake of them. The distance between the most ancient ancestors, like the *tsévi* who inhabit some of the great archaeological sites of the region, and the gods *per se* is not an absolute distance nor a difference in kind. Rather, there is a gradation, a difference in degree. Living humans, ancestor humans, ancient ancestors, and gods interact in a common society that is cosmic in nature, and appreciable and immediate in scope.

A kind of death may also occur by transformation, whereby a human in this world is metamorphosed into another dimension that, at the same time, is and is not quite of this world. These transformations, called *nahualismo,* are discussed for the Huicholes by Fikes (1985). They involve what seem to be godly abilities to begin with, as seen in the creation stories. *Nahualismo* involves humans changing back and forth into dogs, among other things. Aside from these abilities, some *nahualismo* involves sorcery, at times in consort with demons. Some transformation stories clearly reflect folk-Catholic input. During those times when *nahualismo* occurs, raw power is dangerously loose, and malign forces can introduce all sorts of evils into the living human/ancestor human community: plague, invasion, and drought, to name a few. A person who has undergone a *nahuatl* transformation and has returned to the living human community is forever suspect of sorcery, and is an object of fear among the living humans and ancestor humans.

At this point, we should detail how sorcerers work in connection with Huichol ideas about living human health and, hence, death. *Chaos* is the natural state of things, and ceremonialism in its broadest context is the only means by which *order* can be achieved and maintained; nonetheless evil is external to most humans. A corollary of this premise is that if things go wrong it is most often the fault of others. In daily life, for the most part, these 'others' are sorcerers who court evil and chaos as part of their power. Fertility (in reproduction, water, land) is the expression of order at the grand scale; an individual's health is that expression at the smallest scale. Therefore, an inordinate amount of ceremonial time is spent on the fertility/health continuum. In these fashions, 'evil' and 'chaos' (as the natural state of cosmos) are linked, just as 'order' (the unnatural state of the cosmos) and fertility/health are linked. Ceremonialism brings order from chaos, while sorcery brings chaos from order; or, better said, sorcery attempts to reestablish the natural state of the cosmos, which has its own set of rules, using an individual or a lineage as the microcosmic step to that grander goal.

The sorcerer reestablishes evil/chaos by interrupting the delicate balance, ceremonially maintained, that living humans and ancestor humans alike regard as health. The Huichol body contains three centers and forces of life: the brain/skull, the heart, and the liver.

1. The brain/skull is the center of reason and the conscience. It is the link between living humans and the gods, especially the sun, since it is infused into the unborn by them, directly. Its realm is the heavens.
2. The heart is the center of mental vitality, memory, emotion, will, and knowledge. It is the entity which goes to the world of the ancestors, after death. The heart is vulnerable as it can be damaged by one's own actions, such as immoral behavior, ceremonial neglect, or acculturation. It is also vulnerable to the actions of sorcerers. The realm of the heart is the sun.
3. The liver is the center of physical vitality and affection. It can emit a bad air if one is acting immorally or in a ceremonially careless manner. Sorcerers, however, can emit this bad air on purpose, and use it as part of their repertoire to spread evil and chaos. The realm of the liver is the earth.

This brief discussion of the centers of the body does not do justice to this aspect of Huichol thought, nor do we pretend fully to understand this ethno-medical system. However, it is obvious that if one is to be healthy, the three vital centers and forces of life must be in balance—a disturbance in one would be reflected immediately in the other two. This ethno-medical symbolism, thus, unites living humans with ancestor humans, with ancient ancestors, and with the gods. A sorcerer, in order to succeed, must try to break this linkage by unsettling the orderly balance of health.

Acts of sorcery are also dangerous to the sorcerer's well-being. Powers too great to be contained can be loosened and turn upon the sorcerer's persona. In addition, if discovered, acts of sorcery are dramatically punished, for a sorcerer's act is an attack on the entire community's ceremonially maintained order, fertility, and health. Since these acts are so dangerous to all concerned, they are performed in deepest secret and solitude. This fact makes verification of sorcery hard to prove to the authorities that represent the community, and to the community *per se* (see below).

A death may be tainted by suspicions of sorcery if there are motives such as vengeance, material gain, lust, envy, etc., or dreams may reveal the act of sorcery and, often, the actual identity of the sorcerer. There may be, as well, inspirational revelations about sorcery; these are: 1) signs in nature; 2) messages received while under the ceremonial influence of peyote; 3) voices from the crystals during a ceremony (see below); and 4) dreams. Revelations often come from ancestor humans, and these ancestors expect to be honored and obeyed. Dreams and other revelations are, therefore, taken very seriously by everyone in the community. A revelation identifying a sorcerer can damage that person's standing in the community even without other proof. In self-defense a person may maintain that an accusation of sorcery is inspired for other, base reasons; the worst of these other reasons may be sorcery itself. Because of the reciprocal nature of vengeance, such counter-accusations of sorcery occur; one person's *mara'akáme* 'singer/curer' may be another person's sorcerer.

There is a vague feeling among many Huicholes that it takes a sorcerer, or at least a person who is potentially one, to identify another one. Therefore, although they are charged with maintaining balance and order, almost all singers/curers are regarded as at least potentially malevolent. The singers/curers cultivate this image of highly differential access to all sorts of power, but must not overdo it. Maintenance of the image is a delicate balancing act in itself, and helps to explain why so many singers/curers try to develop extremely loyal, quasi-political followings.

Ancestor humans play a major role in Huichol understanding of health and death. Without them, and without their link to the ancient ancestors and the gods, there would be no order, no fertility, no health.

Huicholes have a pervasive fear of ghosts, especially of the ghosts of those who died from sorcery and are seeking vengeance, and of the ghosts of sinners who cannot be ritually purified. Sorcery victims may wreak vengeance on their own kin if they feel that the survivors are not avenging them appropriately. Vengeful ghosts can murder living humans by sending sickness and disease, or by causing accidents. If a victim of sorcery is avenged, and if the person is capable of ritual purification, then the spirit may become part of the ancestor human world.

There are very rare accounts of a person who has been killed but refuses to die. The account we recorded concerns the decapitation of a singer/curer during a period of regional violence. The setting appears to have been either the 1910 Revolution or the Lozada Insurrection of the 1870s. The head of the deceased was placed in the top branches of four different trees, but it kept on talking and singing, to everyone's dismay. Finally, another singer/curer approached the head and asked him what he wanted. He wanted to join his ancestors and rest in peace, but first his death had to be avenged and then his head placed in the crown of a brasil tree. The vengeance was performed and the head placed in the fifth tree. Thus the spirit was thus finally released from its ghostly head. Incidentally, this is why the brasil tree has red wood, being stained by the blood of the talking head. This last mythic element undoubtedly means that the story is very old and is updated at times to fit new events.

Sorcery accusations, especially those involving deaths, are pursued with incredible vigor and perseverance. When such accusations are pursued outside the supervision of the governance hierarchy, long-lived blood feuds are engendered. The feuding cycle often can be broken only by imposing social death on the most aggressive protagonists. Deadly sorcery is practiced by both males and females, usually those of middle or old age. Once identified to the community at large, such persons lose many of their human qualities, and their deaths produce vengeful ghosts that are often of fearful proportions.

All sorcery-related death, social death, and accidental death is considered the result of chaos and is, therefore, far worse than natural death. Natural deaths have an element of the positive in them, as they are viewed as part of a cycle of renewal upon which all human destinies ultimately rest. A natural death can be defined unequivocally as such only in those cases of observably advancing old age, best bolstered by foretelling one's own death to others. All accidental deaths or deaths due to illness are, by definition, open to sorcery suspicions. Such deaths are always investigated scrupulously by the *gobernancia* hierarchy. This hierarchy is appointed by rotation from among the eligible, older male population. The organized efforts to distinguish between deaths attributable to sorcery or to other causes can consume a great deal of time. Members of the *gobernancia* listen, sometimes for days, to testimony and speculation until everyone has had an opportunity to speak, no matter how inane the contribution. The lengthy process of reaching a decision about the ultimate cause of a death requires community consensus. Any survivors not reconciled to the decision are often suspects in future sorcery accusations. The only deaths that are regarded as clearly accidental are those that involve the godly forces of nature, such as lightning, or the agencies of outsiders, such as murder by mestizo cattlemen or army patrols.

THE DEAD *PER SE*

The great public rituals celebrating the deaths of high leaders are things of the past (*cf.* Saavedra, 1899; Ortega, 1944). The mummification and public display of high status corpses for prolonged periods of time apparently ended with the Spanish destruction of the huge temple/palace complex at Tonati in 1722. The mummies of the Nayarita kings were destroyed because they were rallying points for the Cora and Huichol resistance to the Spanish colonial order. More powerful than simple ancestor humans, they represented the polity's continuity as well as the royal lineage's right to rule. How widespread the practice of mummy display was, away from the centers of political power, is hard to evaluate. A super-surface style of burial, called 'tipi' burials (Weigand, 1985a), which were lightly constructed and easily re-enterable, dot the area but are no longer in use. Certainly, mummies guarded in caves and the *shiríki*, or ancestor houses—the latter are found in the main compound of every rancheria complex—are no longer on view. Body parts, especially hair, *may be* in these ancestor houses, but the bodies themselves are now either buried or left permanently in distant caves, away from view. Since the hair of dead humans and the hair of ritually killed deer are regarded as the same substance (both being ancestors), it is not possible for us to make a distinction or determination.

Ancestor houses, regardless of their actual contents, are the spiritual homes for specific generations of purified ancestor humans that are organized around agnatic lineage figures of high prestige. An ancient compound may have five or six active ancestor houses being maintained, and several others in ruins. The spirits that reside in these houses normally are not feared as they protect, help, cure, and enable.

The voices of the ancestor humans most often come to their descendants through rock crystals, preferably quartz crystals of high, or optical, quality. Not everyone can hear these voices equally well, and one of the major functions of the singers/curers is to hear and interpret the voices. They bring instructions, responses to questions, advice, threats, warnings, information about lost cattle or items of value, revelations, etc. Informants differ as to whether the ancestor humans actually inhabit the crystal while communicating with living humans; that is, whether they return as rock crystals, or the crystal is a medium through which they communicate. Fikes (1988) prefers the first possibility, but our information suggests the second. It is possible that this disagreement represents another instance of regional differences in Huichol religion.

Quartz crystals, as artifacts, are one of the many important continuities with the archaeological cultures of the general region. Optical quality quartz crystals are found in the prestigious shaft-tomb burials of the Formative period in the lake zones to the south of the Huichol area, and thus may have a 2,500 to 3,000 year history. A great obsidian and quartz workshop at Las Cuevas still has ceremonial connotations for the Huicholes (Weigand and Spence, 1982). Another continuity of importance with the archaeological cultures is the portrayal of the physical closeness of the living humans and the ancestor humans. These portraits are seen in the architectural group figurines of the Formative and Classic periods, and show human-like figures sitting underneath the residential platforms of the living (Weigand, 1985a; 1985b; von Winning and Hammer, 1972).

Not all of the dead are eligible to become ancestor humans. Those executed by the ancestors and social misfits in general are joined by others who, for a variety of reasons, are not purified by ritual just after their deaths. Persons often die away from home while working as wage laborers in the cities or on coastal plantations, and cannot be buried with appropriate ritual. Often, too, they are simply not treated correctly, in the ritual sense, by their survivors. While the spirits of such people are often benign, they are incapable of becoming ancestor humans and thus are lost to the community of the living humans and ancestors. They cannot help their living relatives with curing, protection, or revelation. Those dead who sinned unforgivably during life also cannot help living humans. By some accounts, these spirits are confined to an underworld and continue a dim version of life on earth; others suggest that they carry on a nebulous existence in the Pacific Ocean. Yet other accounts have most spirits (even purified ones) confined for part of their time after death to a strange region up above, guarded by a great eagle. Purified ancestor humans may leave this place periodically in service to the living humans. Through a doorway in this region is a land that superficially resembles the earth, with trees, mountains, caves, rocks, streams, and grass. As they did on earth, spirits live in ranchos. Aside from these resemblances, everything else is the opposite of normal earth. Passing through the door is equated with looking through a mirror. Such reversal symbolism is widespread in Mesoamerica (cf. Nicholson, 1971): one leaves order for chaos, light for dark, life for death, etc. in a precise dualism that is remarkably symmetrical. In the region of the great eagle, spirits must adapt to the fact that meat becomes excrement, maize becomes hay, clear water becomes con-taminated, and simple pleasures become painful ordeals. Aspects of chaos (which has its own rules and logic) reign, and confinement to this region is regarded to a degree as a punishment. Between our work and that of Fikes (1985), Lumholtz (1973), and Zingg (1938), regional and temporal differences apparently are at play. It is also true that there are many highly individualized versions of myths and religious accounts.

The journeys that the eligible spirits take prior to their purification and just after death (where many of the ancestors are reunited temporarily), are discussed in Lumholtz (1973), Zingg (1938), and Benítez (1968). The emphasis on a separate place for many of the spirits is counter-balanced by the Huichol insistence that ancestor humans also are close at hand. What seems in Western terms to be a contradiction does not concern the Huicholes.

Spirits travel and interact with the gods, and most gods have kinship prefixes to their names (e.g., Grandfather, Father, Grandmother). Spirits undergo privation and trials in their after-life, but when ceremonially purified ancestor humans are needed, and the appropriate conditions have been established, they are with the living humans in community. The situation is more complicated than this suggests, though, for ancestor humans on their own or at the demand of the gods, can pay unsolicited visits to their living human relatives, even at nonceremonial times. They can inhabit the ancestor houses, and ranchos in general, without living humans being aware of them. Ancestor humans are active in their after-life; they are not simply waiting on call for the needs of living humans, though these needs are of primary importance to them. The continuing social role of ancestor humans is barely mentioned by Benítez (1968), and, from the perspective of our fieldwork, is inadequately described by Lumholtz (1973) and Zingg (1938). It remains a largely unexplored avenue for understanding the interrelationships of social organization, religion, and ceremonialism among the Huicholes. Fikes' work (1985) has the most promise in this regard.

RESPONSE TO DEATH

Corpses of individuals, especially those who are to be featured in ancestor veneration, are handled with a great deal of respect and care. This is done under the leadership and supervision of a singer/curer who is usually closely related to the deceased. As the body is prepared for the rites, and for burial or placement in a cave, the attributes of the deceased are recited, clothing changed or added to the body, personal items arranged to accompany the body, and the person's hands and face are washed with water from the lineage's holy spring(s). Most adults aid in this preparation of the body, unless deep animosity or emotional collapse prevents such activity. Most people are relatively calm during these preparations.

The actual moment of death, or discovery of the death, provokes a great deal of crying and wailing. This subsides during the preparations, but resumes again at the funeral site. The dead are visible for all to see for the several hours that precede burial or placement in a cave. Rarely is a burial postponed even until the next day. There are strong feelings about where the final resting place should be. In general, caves are favored by traditionalists and burials by Catholics, but that distinction obscures great differences among the semi-Catholic population about what constitutes proper burial. Some insist that proper burial can only be accomplished within atrium grounds. For example, the atrium of the *capilla* at the pueblo of San Sebastián is full of unmarked burials, to the point where every new excavation turns over the bones of older burials. There have been no collections of bones into ossuaries, as in the atrium grounds of Azqueltán, a neighboring Tepecano *comunidad indígena*. Others believe that burial grounds near the home site are adequate. The site of burial can be influenced by the personality of the dead person; a contentious and angry adult is better off in the atrium while an innocent child can be close to home.[1] Attendance at the grave site rituals reflects the status and age-set of the individual involved. A baby may have only three or four persons present, while a *kawitéro* ('a man who knows everything'—the highest status and position to which Huichol males may ascribe) may have hundreds.[2]

The names of burial sites are of interest (*cf.* Zelinsky, 1975). The *capilla* atrium burial ground is called the *Campo Santo*. Other burial grounds are either unnamed or given the lineage name, usually using the toponymn or family name that normally applies to the rancho or the major rancho of the rancheria as the designative. Alternatively, toponymns are used for cave burial sites if they are located some distance from the rancheria (*e.g.,* Mesa Hueca). These toponymns, however, can reflect the site's use as a repository for the dead (*e.g.,* Cuesta de los Huesos). Of the categories of place-names listed in Zelinsky (1975:174), the 'descriptive' and 'possessive' classes seem to be the only ones in use among the Huicholes. An occasional, unelaborated natural stone may mark the head of a burial, which is almost always placed to the west. Most burials, however, are completely unmarked with commemorative features.

Piles of stones to keep dogs, coy-dogs, and coyotes from excavating the fresh bodies, are common. These stones are frequently reused for newer graves once their purpose if fulfilled, but otherwise most graves are unmarked. The fear of having one's body eaten by dogs or coyotes is a major theme when Huicholes discuss dying. These fears are cited by many as the reason for their preference for burial rather than cave placement. The fear is realistic, for some of the cave placements that we saw were disturbed by animals, with the bodies disarticulated and parts missing. Heavy rocks are stacked up to block the entrances to caves, but they are seldom successful. The fear expressed is beyond that of just being eaten or disarticulated by animals, although that would be horrible enough. Worse is the possibility that one of these animals might be a transformed *nahual*—a sorcerer— and no-one knows what evils might transpire with that.

Cannibalism is regarded as repugnant nowadays despite the likelihood that some ritual consumption of human flesh was sanctioned in prehistoric times (*cf.* Carrasco, 1981; 1982; Nicholson, 1971, de Leyva, 1579:28). The consumption of human flesh by a transformed *nahual* is particularly repulsive, for the purpose is not to enhance health or fertility, but rather the destruction of health by evil. While today the ritual consumption of human flesh is no longer conceivable among the Huicholes, its consumption by *nahuales* is. Whereas the first is simply repugnant, impossible, and against the grain of the folk-Catholicism which they all practice, the second is believed to be entirely possible and horribly frightening.

[1]Babies and the very young may return again to life on earth as new children. Babies are often called *angelitos* ('little angles' in Spanish), and they can return because they were totally innocent when they died. If a mother dies in childbirth, or is already dead when a youngster dies, then the child should stay with her as otherwise she would miss him/her.

[2]The Catholic ceremony of Regreso de los Muertos (Return of the Dead, held during early November) is present among the neighboring Cora Indians, but is not observed among the Huicholes.

After burial or cave placement a new spirit may either start its journey immediately or hover about the site for three to five days, feeding from the offerings of milk, cheese, and tortillas left in nearby trees. Those spirits who stay close-by are thought to be confused about their status. Once they are convinced that they are physically dead, *i.e.,* when the body begins to putrefy, they seek the company of other human ancestors and the gods. Their quest requires the ceremonial aid of their survivors and takes them to several places in search of ancient ancestor homes and symbols. During the spirit's search, the survivors prepare for the ceremony befitting the dead person's new status. There are singing and chanting ceremonies during which the survivors tell the spirit of the newly deceased how much he/she is missed and introduce it to the ancestor humans. This transference is the responsibility of the survivors. These ceremonies may be very simple and may even forego animal sacrifice and the brewing of maize beer (*nahúa*), but they must be done properly or the spirit may become an unhappy and vengeful ghost. Through the singer/curer, the spirit may make demands on the survivors. The funeral rituals, called *hutairmari*, are accompanied by the recitation of texts. Fikes (1988) has collected three such texts and fragments of several are published by Benítez (1968).

Once purified, the dead are viewed as capable of residing among the living humans where they use the power of the ancestor house ceremonialism to work for their communal benefit on a different plane. For the most part, the Catholic idea of Heaven as a permanent residential site for all the spirits is contrary to the ancestor house ceremonial cycle. Permanently removing the purified ancestor humans from the presence of living humans is not regarded as rational by most Huichol. A permanent heavenly site is the same as exile for all of the spirits—the positive, the benign, and the evil ones all grouped together forever.

The contrast between Huichol ideas about the dead and those of Catholic Christianity is profound. The Christian intent is to *loosen* ties to place so that the newly dead might enter Heaven more easily. No grave could hold the body of Christ and no one place could hold His spirit. Similarly, spirits of the Catholic dead should not be space-bound here on earth. While the pre-Conquest Nayarita defined a particular heaven-like place, called *mucchita* 'the place of the dead' (Ortega, 1944), for spirits whose deaths were natural, the relationship of *mucchita* to the ancestor humans' communality of interests with living humans is unknown. Today, the Huicholes are folk-Catholics, but they are highly selective about the aspects of Christianity which they accept. The Christian notion of a permanent heaven is not acceptable. On the other hand, Psalm 65:9-14 is known by heart by some Huicholes, who find its message about God and natural forces almost completely compatible with traditional beliefs. There are many other Christian concepts, both philosophical and organizational, which are structurally integrated into the Huichol cosmos. But the Christian concept of Heaven is akin to spiritual exile. Indeed, Ortega (1944) reports the unhappiness of survivors with *mucchita*.

Spiritual exile is proper only for the immoral and the impious, and completely incorrect for purified ancestor humans. The Huichol passion for place persists into the afterlife, with ancestor humans being as strongly anchored as are living humans. A recent study of the Huicholes, which used urban informants (Myerhoff, 1974), postulated an incomplete transition to agriculture. The reality of life in the *comunidades* is a thorough dedication to agriculture in virtually every feature of religious life. The dedication to place is a corollary of that type of economic structure.

MOURNING

Since the spirits of ancestor humans are ideally near to living humans and exert positive influences on the course of daily events for their mutual benefit, the outward expressions of mourning are often brief. Women who have suffered the death of a mother or a child often express their grief and loss by suicidal gestures; the stated goal of such behavior is to accompany the deceased. However, these gestures seldom result in suicide.

It is very important that the immediate survivors understand and agree upon the cause of death. They must be willing to convey their thoughts in a convincing manner to the rest of the community. The cause of death affects the subsequent pattern of bereavement. If survivors are convinced that the cause was natural or accidental (*i.e.,* completely untainted by sorcery), mourning takes the course of wailing and crying, sorrow, expressions of suicide, and—later during lineage ceremonies—chants accompanied by animal sacrifice. If the cause of death is tainted by sorcery, then in addition to wailing, crying, and sorrow, fierce anger and vengeful behavior can surface. But whatever the cause of death, most spirits eventually become part of the living community as ancestor humans, and are integrated into the ancestor house ceremonial cycle.

Ideally, individual mourning should be limited to the period during which the spirit is not yet reintegrated into the lineage as symbolized by the ancestor house. Mourning is expected to be brief and public, or at least potentially public. Ideally, it is open and highly visible behavior. Private expressions of grief on the other hand, often involve withdrawal and isolation and may last for varying periods, sometimes for life. Normally, the bereaved person is expected to resume normal economic and social functions very quickly. The marginality of Huichol subsistence agriculture and herding do not allow inactivity, for whatever reason, to be prolonged.

An exception is made if an individual is perceived as dying from grief. This is viewed as a natural death that under some unfortunate circumstances cannot be avoided. Huicholes assume that the *distance* between the state of death and the state of life is shortest when the survivors are actually grieving. Thus, it is easiest to travel that short distance if grief is very intense, and it is not unnatural to want to do so. Yet actual suicide is regarded as an abnormal expression of grief. It is avoided by mutual companionship among the survivors who constantly accompany each other, and by their joint participation in ceremonialism. A slow death from grief is simply fate. The dead can 'call' the living to join them, and the living can choose to follow.

Mourning varies with the 'value' that the individual had to the lineage or, to a lesser degree, to the community. Old people, especially old men with singing and recitation abilities who retained their mental powers until death, are deeply mourned. The ceremonial importance that these individuals had, and the direct contacts with the ancestors that they cultivated over a life-time of religious dedication cannot be matched. As each generation dies off it pushes prior generations further toward obscurity. The most ancient ascending generations become more generalized and god-like, gradually losing touch with any specific lineage of living humans. The number of generations of ancestors recognized as human by a particular lineage remains at five or six. Every generation humans pushed toward obscurity and into the category of ancient ancestors is vaguely missed and their loss is viewed as a loss of power. Just as ancestor humans are more closely linked with living humans, ancient ancestors are more closely linked to gods.

Young people, male and female, of working and reproductive age are also of high value to the lineage, and thus are often mourned with considerable intensity. Aside from the emotional attachments survivors may have had to such persons, the economic impact of deaths in this age-set is openly acknowledged. Least 'valued' of all, and most lightly mourned, are small children, especially females. The attachments here are entirely emotional. Table 1 summarizes lineage 'values' for deceased persons organized by age-sets. Table 2 does the same from the perspective of the *gobernancia* or *comunidad indígena*. It is important to note that these tables are the constructs of the authors, and only in a general fashion reflect the range of emotions, feelings, love and heartbreak that death brings.

Table 1. "Value" Expressed in the Lineage

	Age Set				
Value	Very old	Old	Mature	Youth	Child
Ceremonial	XX	X	0	—	—
Economic	—	X	XX	X	—
Emotional	X	X	X	X	XX

Note: XX, very positive; X, positive; 0, becoming positive; —, none.

Table 2. "Value" Expressed in the *Comunidad Indígena*

Value	Age Set				
	Very old	Old	Mature	Youth	Child
Ceremonial	XX	X	0	—	—
Political	X	XX	X	0	—
Economic	—	X	X	X	—
Emotional	X	X	0	—	—

Note: XX, very positive; X, positive; 0, becoming positive; —, none.

CONCLUSIONS

The Huicholes view death from a variety of perspectives that are largely governed by the deceased's age, economic productiveness, ceremonial knowledge, and sex. The cause of death is a major concern, not only for the immediate survivors, but for the entire community. While death separates lineage members physically, a unity exists between living humans and purified spirits who eventually become ancestor humans. Ancestor humans, venerated in ancestor houses, are continuing and productive members of their lineages. Ghosts, on the other hand, can be produced by ritual neglect, sinful behavior, and/or sorcery. They can be angry and vengeful, and hence are feared. The difference between a beneficent spirit and a vengeful ghost is often the cause of death or the behavior of the survivors regarding that cause. Invariably, it is sorcery that produces ghosts, and accidents, illness, and disease are often thought to be caused by sorcery. Only gradual and noticeably advancing old age is regarded as a clear instance of natural death. Ancestors themselves may execute a particularly sinful or disrespectful individual. Unpurified spirits/ghosts are not regarded as ancestor humans, and hence do not participate in the ancestor house ceremonialism.

Mourning is meant to join living humans with ancestor humans in a new level of lineage life, whereby these spirits will protect, cure, and work for the benefit of the living, and the living will venerate the spirits during the many ceremonies involving fertility and health and ancestor houses. Ancestor humans are linked with the ancient ancestors and the gods. The ceremonialism directed toward them all is meant to insure order, by which is meant fertility and health. Since living humans and ancestor humans share a communality of productive goals and interests, an individual's grief is expected to be short and his or her mourning formalized and brief.

ACKNOWLEDGMENTS

This research has been supported by the National Science Foundation, the Wenner-Gren Foundation, the Mesoamerican Cooperative Research Fund of Southern Illinois University Museum, and the Instituto Nacional Indígenista. We wish to thank Jay C. Fikes for his most helpful critique of the first draft of this manuscript. Further critiques by members of the symposium, to which this research was presented, and by James Officer, substantially strengthened our presentation.

CHAPTER
6

Saintly Death:
Coping with Grief through
Human Transformation

Earle Waugh

Chapters 6 and 7 turn from ethnic isolates to the consideration of death and grief in communities defined by their religious practice. In the following chapter, Earle Waugh examines the response of a particular sect of Sufi Muslims, the Burhanis, to the death of their leader. The beliefs of the Sufi permit them to transform their deep grief over the leader's death into joy in his continued participation in their lives. The deaths of ordinary members of the sect allow no such transformation, and so the chapter calls our attention to the special nature of the death of charismatic persons.

*   *   *

"We were heart-broken," she sobbed. "The shaikh was so beautiful. He was so powerful. Then he died." She paused, biting her lip and drying her eyes. She smiled, brightening. "But he began to send us songs. Now I see he can be with all believers everywhere. Our Shaikh is greater than he ever was!" She looked uncomfortable for a moment, then added, "It seems strange. But I guess he had to die to be greater."

This statement from a follower of Shaikh Muhammad Uthman Abd al-Burhani was the catalyst for this study. The grief had apparently been very profound and heart-wrenching; even a year after his death, sadness crept into conversation. Yet I could tell there was a new confidence and a certain strengthening, a quality hard to pinpoint. I was intrigued that the Islamic tradition, with its strict line of demarcation between the living and the dead, should spawn a group that went so far as to claim communications from beyond the pale; mindful of the abhorrence of any exaltation of the human such as had allegedly occurred in Christianity, I was drawn to explore the extraordinary devotion accorded the Shaikh. Even if the group belonged to that famous movement in Islam called Sufism, whose well-known mystical propensities made it more attune to unusual phenomena, this seemed unique. Since I was to be in Egypt for almost a year on Sufi-related research, I set out to follow as many strands as possible to determine the significance of what I had heard.

What became clear was that the death of the Shaikh had freed him to be transformed into a spiritual 'presence,' especially during the special rituals, so that he was available universally wherever people gathered to perform the remembrance rituals designed by him. In effect the Shaikh became available through a ritual structure in a way that, during his life on earth, had been limited to one locale. What I seemed to be seeing was a valuable grief-control process, that transformed the loss into new hope and renewed human potential. This chapter will concern itself with elucidating this process.

It is important to underline the processual nature of this death, for it has similarities to other studies in this book. Thus, like death among the Toraja of Wellenkamps' investigation (Chapter 8), the death itself may have come as an 'end of physical life,' but the meaning of death was such that it required a gradual process of disengagement and rearrangement. In the Indonesian case, this activity centered on the presence of the body. Among the followers of the Shaikh, a special turban-topped lamp chimney, lighted by a candle, provided the physical metaphor of the Shaikh's real presence during the rituals. This, however, was extinguished at the end of the rituals. How then could the Shaikh be said to be permanently 'alive?' As in the Wellenkamp study, the soul lives on with the intent of providing spiritual blessings. But among the Sufis generally, and the Burhanis particularly, the Shaikh comes to function as a very powerful mediator. So when the believer is held to interact with the Shaikh in dramatic personal ways during the rituals themselves, the follower is assured that intercession is taking place on his behalf. Thus whatever personal loss one might feel, it is overcome by the continuous 'good' rituals which provide the adept with the conviction that his concerns are being presented by the Shaikh to higher powers in the heavenly realm. Yet these rituals are fundamentally social and corporate. We have to conclude, then, that a procedure is provided by which individual loss is subsumed into and transformed by corporate worship. Loss is continuously acknowledged (i.e., a symbol is present, not the human Shaikh) but just as continuously overcome when the group has a 'good' ritual. Such a procedure would appear to make the Sufi case distinctive when compared to either Wellenkamp's experience among the Toraja or the Counts' findings among the people of Kaliai (Chapter 12), despite the similar underlying conception of process.

BACKGROUND

The Shaikh was born in the Sudan in 1902. His parents were members of the Mahas, of Nubian-Arabic stock, dominant in the extreme northern section of the country. The Burhani family were from Wadi Halfa, a town with a long connection to Egypt immediately north, both in terms of trade and language. The area had been Arabized early in the 1700s by migrants from Mecca (Trimingham, 1965). Around the same time, Northern Sudan came under the influence of Sufi orders or brotherhoods especially that led by Hamad ibn al-Mujdhub (1693-1776), which had a marked effect on the region.

Sufism is the mystical tradition in Islam. Its followers contend it was founded by the Prophet, but its distinctive forms derive from a movement begun early in the 8th century. Its most primitive forms appear to have stressed asceticism and self-denial, along with a rejection of the courtly extravagances of the official Islamic government. It spread among a wide range of classes and peoples until it reached from the scholars and judges to the humblest laborer. Eventually the movement was to be organized into orders, centered upon the discipline designed by a founding spiritual leader. The founder might be called a Shaikh, as a measure of respect, and some Shaikhs became so powerful that, after death they were perceived as saints.

Each order developed its own form of *dhikr* or ritual form of meditational dance, with the ultimate goal being an encounter with God in an experience believed to be mystical union. Critics held the goal ran counter to the distinction between things human and divine; they objected to the implicit depreciation of the law which, to the ordinary layman, defined Islam and they were repelled by Sufism's sense of mission that had little to do with the achievements of state or military power. In the conflicts that erupted, officialdom tried to kill the leading proponents of the mystical movement. The purges did not deter the Sufis, and the movement prospered. By the middle of the 11th century, mystical practices had been regularized around a holy man, with an institutional structure based at a *zawiya* (meeting place of the movement, usually attached to a mosque). The earliest founder of an order is said to have been Abd al-Qadir al-Jilani (1077-1166) whose group, the Qadiri spread rapidly throughout the Muslim world.

It was to an institutional Sufism that al-Mujdhub belonged when he went on the pilgrimage to Mecca some five centuries later. By this time, Sufism had become widely acknowledged and respected, and its influence touched every aspect of Muslim life. Reform was in the air, and al-Mujdhub was drawn to a dynamic reformist group called the Shadhilis. While the order traced its history back to Abu'l Hasan Ali Ash-Shadili (d. 1258) it was far more forceful than the Qadiris, and it attracted reform-minded people like al-Mujdhub. He joined and took the Shadhili discipline back to the Wadi Halfa area, where the order attracted a wide range of members. The Shadhili order has had considerable success in Egypt and the Sudan, much of it through reformist organizations within the larger body, and it was through one of these, the Disukiya, that the hero of our story's family became involved in Sufism.

The Disukiya order was introduced into the Sudan late in the 1800s by followers of Ibrahim al-Disuki, a holy man from a small town in the upper Delta region of Egypt. Every year hundreds of thousands of pilgrims journey to Tanta where the shrine of Ibrahim is located, and Muhammad Uthman's family made that journey several times.

Great diversity marks the orders in the Sudan, with a spectrum of orientations from extremely conservative and literalist to popular, liberal or folk in style. The Shadhilis are usually known for their orthodoxy and learning, with concern for the purity of their teaching. This image has attracted members from a wide range of social levels and particularly appeals to the educated and business classes. The reputation of the Shadhilis and the attractiveness of the group to the Sudanese middle class accounts for Muhammad al-Burhani's group being established among the immigrants to Europe, according to Jamal al-Sinhoury, the leader of the Burhanis in Cairo. During the time of my research, the Burhanis hosted an international gathering in Cairo attended by a number of European converts of both sexes, representing sister organizations in Munich, Zurich, and Berlin. According to my informants, the Burhanis are making every effort to adapt to the European context, even to the point of allowing participation of women in the *dhikr*, an activity officially forbidden in Muslim countries. The Burhanis also have sister orders in the United States and Canada.

The Burhanis fit the 'cellular' style of order which Trimingham identified (Trimingham, 1965); the style is well-known in the Sudan. Such groups maintain a great deal of autonomy, allowing for the development of local leaders, and this characteristic was important for the growth of Muhammad Uthman, who as a *khalifa* (second in command in the order) rapidly attracted devoted followers.

Little is known about the early life of the Shaikh. He attended a traditional Muslim school, learning *Qur'an* and studying the traditions associated with the Prophet. At a young age he became an active member of the Disukiya and, since he was a good singer, his talents were immediately recognized. Followers say his later name derives from an honorific title accorded to Ibrahim al-Disuki, that is Burhan ad-din (proof of religion), and attached to Muhammad when his spiritual prowess began to be recognized. Shortly after receiving a dream from the Prophet, he established his own group, based on a reformulated Disuki discipline. So powerful were his spiritual gifts that he was said to have been an acceptable guide for four other orders: Rifa'i, Gilani, Qadiri and Ahmadi. Muhammad was sensitive to the criticisms of Sufism, especially to those that regarded the ritual practices of the orders as 'too folk,' and he rejected the use of musical instruments and drums, replacing them with a choir of male voices and the hand clap to regulate the swing of the *dhikr* (Waugh, 1989).

In the last years of life, Muhammad al-Burhani began laying the groundwork for an international center in Khartoum which would serve as a teaching and outreach facility. He had already begun plans for his mausoleum in 1979 and a headquarters in honor of Ali, the son-in-law of the Prophet who is regarded by the Burhanis to be the first Sufi. Donations from all over the world were being received. The Shaikh died in April 1983, and the mausoleum was not completed until the following year. Despite this, devotees visited the site to pray at the shrine and to implore his special assistance and guidance. Thus, what began as a minor sister order in a remote area of the Sudan has now become an international network of remarkable extension, with an international center that serves as the focal point for Burhani devotion around the world.

THE DEVOTION OF SUFI ADHERENTS TO THE SAINTS AFTER DEATH

All Sufi adherents participate in a special world of meaning; central to that world is the saint. The saint is usually understood to be the founder of the order, but sometimes a Shaikh will be held to be particularly powerful and may be referred to by the honorific term. Regardless of where the holy person stands in the historical framework, he is held to be unified with the original founder by the spiritual power and authority present in his life. This power includes the ability to intercede on the adherent's behalf with God or the denizens of heaven, as well as give special guidance and assistance in the adherent's life.

It is beyond the scope of this chapter to deal with the many facets of belief that have contributed to the conception of the saint (Trimingham, 1965); rather I have chosen four different selections from among those garnered during my research to indicate some of the perceptions accorded to the saint.

Facets of Belief

I. The first is related by Dr. Magda Andil, a music researcher from Ain Shams University, who has been working for several years in folk and Sufi music.

> In the villages they praise the *wali* (literally 'friend' but here meaning the 'dead founder of the order' or saint) of the Shaikh (the local leader of the order and the bearer of the spiritual power or baraka of the saint). I have an acquaintance whose husband was a Shaikh. The villagers were so fond of him that all the miracles and unusual happenings of the *wali* were connected to the Shaikh. The miracle at his death was that his casket ran towards the mosque, where the members of the order could pray around it. They couldn't hold his casket there either, because it just seemed to run to the grave. So when they praise him, they attach to him miracles he never performed, just because of the miracle of the running casket. His family received lots of gifts from devotees because of this miracle.

The running casket is a well-known motif among the Sufis. It indicates that the Shaikh is being called to heaven to assume a place of honor before God and the angels. It is an indication that great spiritual power is apportioned to the Shaikh by God and therefore he will have favor in interceding for the adherents. In addition, the tomb of the Shaikh becomes a place of special power, and people can come there to present their petitions. Praying in the environment of the Shaikh's tomb is held to be of considerable significance for the devotee, and particularly if the miracle of the running casket is associated with him. Thus the mausoleum of the deceased Shaikh becomes a beneficial place for spiritual exercises and explains why the Shaikh's tomb is placed in the corner of the *zawiya* where the *dhikr* is held. It also demonstrates the sense of continuing presence that the Sufi acknowledges about the deceased leaders.

II. Shaikh Ahmad Jazouli is the founder of his own order. His *zawiya* is set in the old graveyard in Cairo for two reasons: obtaining buildings in overcrowded Cairo is expensive and usually hopeless, and the graveyard is now used by many of the city's poor because the small tombs at least allow them some place out of the cold. While the Shaikh's devotees do not belong to this social group, they nevertheless find the locale congenial to their rituals. Shaikh Jazouli believes that he passes on the blessings of the saint to his adherents; because his followers accept this, they grant him total control over them. They believe that he is the present embodiment of the *baraka* of the saint, and he gives them all the love and concern that is held to reside in the saint. The power he has is reflected in this quote from Jazouli:

> Something from the material world has to be put in the hands of the devotees. They can't see God. So the Shaikh has a chance to help them. He puts his hand in the person's hand to help to do two things: to keep away from everything that makes God angry and get closer to everything that makes God happy. What we care about is the order and the length and quality of the individual's life who belongs to our order. This is an operation of love; it is not a college.[1]
>
> Many people come to celebrate the saints just for fun. They don't know the saint as a saint. Those who come correctly, come with the saint within, so whether he goes to the saint's celebrations or not, the saint still comes to him. It's not a matter of seeing him with your eyes, it's seeing him through learning and *ma^c rifa* (deep spiritual insight). He's with me, regardless of where I am. When love is there, he's present.

III. During the *dhikr* of the great orders, singers attempt to center the thoughts and concerns of the dancers on the saints. Yet these singers have a very special relationship with the saints themselves. Through this relationship, they believe that they are given a crucial task: to make the saint present through the medium of song. Thus Muhammad al-Husaini said:

> I memorize songs from all the great Shaikhs and during the *dhikr*, I bring all the saints together in front of me[2] and then I love one of them and call upon him to save (assist) me. So, when I have them all together in my mind, I call on that one for *madad* ('grace, blessing') to make the *dhikr* longer for me. I am in their hands and I need their help. I am counting on them to assist me.

---

[1] While the Shaikh teaches, he is not passing on information, he is rather 'ministering' to those who need him.

[2] In his mind—editor

IV. A most important dimension of Sufi belief is the perceived relationship between the individual adherent and the local Shaikh. He mediates the *baraka* of the order's founder and provides a personal direction in life. He often counsels the adherent on a wide range of problems and issues. Thus a female Burhani devotee confided:

> The Shaikh is such a beautiful person. He teaches us the right way, he gives us help and assistance, he listens to our problems and gives us good advice. He has such power that he can do extraordinary things, yet he never shows off. It's like heaven just to be around him.

From these selections, it is evident that the line of spiritual masters plays a unique role in the world order of the Sufi devotee. We can see that the line of demarcation between the saint and Shaikh is blurred, so that the human spiritual leader represents and possesses powers associates with the saint's world. It is also possible to see that the role of saints and other spiritual forces (such as God and Muhammad) are seen to be of one piece and even if the latter are above the former, they are on a continuum, not in a separate environment. This environment is not foreign to the adept, because he 'belongs' to the family of the saint, through his adherence to the local Shaikh. In some sense the devotee is also inducted into the realm transcending the human.

Little wonder, then, that the death of the Shaikh shakes the foundations of the adept's world. But, at the same time, it will set in progress a series of adjustments of perspective and spiritual understandings such that the Shaikh rises above his human specificity and becomes part of the saintly world. In effect, deaths as an event will set the stage for a process by which the meaning of the Shaikh's death is transformed from the loss of a significant human to an encounter with the symbolically powerful dimensions of his being. This encounter takes place primarily through the ritual dance, but is also conceived to take place in the life of the individual adept. While this process is underway, the physical death of the Shaikh becomes less important, and the symbolic dimensions of the Shaikh's life are enhanced. In the next section, greater nuance will be given to important aspects of the process sketched here.

THEMES FROM THE PROCESS

On the Meaning of 'Presence'

As can be seen from the discussion above, one of the most important notions is that of 'presence.' The Shaikh becomes allied with the saint, who is perceived to be symbolically present in the lighted candle during the ritual dance. He is also present in the song of the singer, who 'loves' one of the saints held to be seen in his mind's eye. But what appears crucial is that the saint becomes present during the *dhikr*. The Burhani claim that the *Shaikh* becomes present during *dhikr*. The following exchange took place with Tag al-Afsia, a young Burhani singer from the Sudan. It reflects views expressed by a number of members interviewed from among the four hundred adherents at the international meeting held in Cairo by followers of Muhammad al-Burhani. A number of significant themes to be considered later are touched upon in the text:

> Waugh: When you have a good *dhikr*, some people say the Prophet is present. What does that mean?

> Tag: When you call your Shaikh, he comes. So if you call the Prophet, he comes.

> Waugh: How can the Shaikh come if he's dead?

> Tag: If you love somebody, you can see him wherever you go.

> Waugh: But I can make an absent lover present through imagination. How do I make one present as you do?

> Tag: The body is present, along with the spirit.

> Waugh: What does it mean to the people there? How does that happen?

> Tag: The *ruh* 'spirit' is very light, says the teaching. Water (mist) is very light, and fire is lighter than that. Wind is lighter than fire and the Ruh is lighter than them all. We know they all are real. The Prophet is lighter than *ruh*, so he can be present in everything, both body and soul.

The adepts with whom I discussed this issue continued to insists on a body for the saint. The point seems to be that it is not possible to conceive of a personage without a physical form. Thus even the Shaikh is dead, he still inhabits an imaginal world in which he has materiality. The singer, in reality, brings the Shaikh into this world by emotionally involving his inner being with the Shaikh and 'loving' him, so much that his emotional state delivers the impact of his encounter to those who hear him. It would appear that the imaginal world bears the same relationship to this world as the various levels of reality had in Neo-platonic doctrine, where an imaginal world mediated between this world of materiality and the other world of pure spirituality (Waugh, forthcoming). The universe of the Sufi is tripartite, with reality being expressed in three different forms: pure spirituality (God), meditational reality (world of the saints) and pure materiality (our physical world). The meditational world is quite accessible to the Sufi, and appears to operate on the basis of the claims of the pious. The Sufi adept and the singer alike can ask the saint to be present because the adept is part of a heavenly family and thus has a claim. The saint cannot resist the calls of his family.

When asked what kind of materiality this might be, the answer is that it is tangible but not solid; just like Jesus after the resurrection was said to pass through walls, so the imaginal body has the same form without the sense of solidness. But most important is the sense of achievement which delivers the Shaikh's presence in the *dhikr*. The ritual dance can be humdrum or it can be extraordinary. When it is the latter, the adept claim the saint was very powerful that night, meaning that his presence was very strong. On other occasions, he is present but not strong. Thus it is possible for even the most cynical of observers to acknowledge that there is a different 'feel' to a meeting where the saint was said to be very strong. Even I could tell the difference. Thus materiality, at least so far as the *dhikr* is concerned, could be understood as a strong collective sense of being with the saint *ensemble*, and if this feeling is maintained, the *dhikr* is said to be good. The materiality would seem to require collective validation and encounter.

Centering on the Shaikh

The ability to center on the Shaikh is a critical technique for bringing the Shaikh into the *dhikr*, as we have already learned. Centering is the activity that connects the adept with the spiritual resources, something like a spiritual receptor. The process involves rejecting extraneous elements, and 'loving the Shaikh' becomes a phrase meaning a spiritual exercise of great tenderness and sensitivity toward the whole spiritual world. The process brings with it a state of elation as is indicated in this selection: (this segment of the interview was carried on in English).

Waugh: Can you describe how you feel when you sing?

Tag: I am exceedingly happy! I feel light as angels; I concentrate on an image of the Shaikh and other Shaikhs, and then I remember (*dhikr*) and am very happy. I don't know who I am or where I am. I remember the Prophet, he was not a normal man.

Waugh: Why do you sing a particular song?

Tag: Because the song itself has a power to make souls feel uplifted and grateful in the *dhikr*. It has the power in it, just like the Shaikh. Each (song) has the power of the Shaikh in it. When you love the Shaikh, you can feel the power.

Waugh: Do you feel the power of the Shaikh more some nights than others?

Tag: Yes. Angels and Shaikhs can give you power to do things and to sing good songs. We call that *ilham* (inspiration, spiritual expressiveness).

The crucial issue in this selection is that the Shaikh becomes available to the singer through the technique of centering; he appears in the mind's eye, so to speak, where he becomes the focus of the singer's spiritual mediation. The result is an empowerment that delivers the Shaikh to the listener through the vehicle of the song. Thus *ilham* is perceived as the means by which the Shaikh becomes living and real in the ritual dance through the medium of the singer. This technique is of some importance to us, for it aids us in understanding the role that the Shaikh, now dead, could continue to play in the life of the group.

On Word Transference

The following song was sung during the international *dhikr* held in Cairo that brought together the devotees and the Shaikh Muhammad al-Burhani before he died. The selection translated below is filled with Sufi literary conventions, such as the reference to the female beauty, (a metaphor referring either to the pleasurable spiritual path, or God, or Muhammad) to non-existence, (*fana* or passing away into God, the traditional conception of union as the goal of the Sufis), to unrequited love (a reference to the never-ending search for ultimate reality), and to the inauthentic nature of all linguistic formulations of reality.

The Shaikh, the Crown of our Lord

If you are looking to her for the true effect,
Then surely you would be blind to it:
In him is blended spirit, soul and body
He regarded not her features.
Some of my patience, I spent without recompense
And soon it had departed.
The disease of pleasantness for me had vanished.
Instead of Solomon, they gave us Solonuna and Alma,
But the name does not hold the existence nor does it continue to exist
A treasure it is, and the flesh its border only,
The shepherd, if he is ignorant of (that treasure)
Will surely be filled with knowledge.
Anticipating seeing him is like a burning fire.
Ah night! night! You have multiplied the fire's strength
It has imprisoned, like everyone else, all my heart
This rainbow-hued (One) comes to you in the *zawiya* (i.e., during the *dhikr*)
Many tears have I spilled over you!
But compared to others, they were precious few.
Ah, you who drew about me the cloak of non-existence
I will give you the cloak of allegiance
At your door I will beg an answer to my plea,
If you were not generous with kindhearted aid
What a tragedy! What harshness!
If you questioned me of evil
What could I say?
Ah, Please command my heart to resist you!
Beware of bringing your soul (to that door)

Beware also of abandoning the search.
Invite your people in, hear
The call of love by these great ones
Those who have forgotten timidity and speak to her
Commune with her face;
Loving her, you will see the sun
You will walk in the light
From the depths of your awareness
Comes the brightness of the Morning Star.

The elliptical and allusive nature of this language indicates that the hearer must be attuned to special meanings. The adept gradually learns the spiritual impact of each of these phrases as one or another of the conventions ignites the group during the *dhikr*. Thereafter, the phrase connotes not only words but the experiences attending their being heard. Thus, *dhikr* is not merely the transmission of traditional phrases, but moments of encounter. The song is filled with emotive triggers, drawn from Sufi tradition or the Shaikh's teachings, or previous existential occurrences which can explode with psychological power at any time. The words propel the adherent into a certain affective condition. Sufis talk about having an attitude of 'softness' before this can occur, as if they were suspended serenely in the air, regarding expectantly the passing realities. This sensitivity to spiritual forces is said to allow them to jump across the chasm created by words and the logical system that sponsors them. The song is directed to the Shaikh, in this case Ibrahim al-Disuki, the founder of the order, but it could just as easily apply to the Shaikh in their midst, Muhammad al-Burhani. Thus words do not describe things, they intimate psychological directions. Like floating logs, one jumps from one to another on the way to shore. Being mindful that one only reaches stability in God, the adept accepts the words are part of the process, not anything final in themselves.

The themes in the song reflect this ideology to a marked degree. The song begins with the recognition of woman's beauty, but notes it is just a cipher; true beauty is in the Shaikh. It acknowledges that the great wisdom of Solomon, as well as his prowess in love, has been accorded females, but passing away into God is not found in that beauty or that love. The treasure is the Shaikh who fills one with burning desire for God and the urge to perform the ritual of *dhikr*. So attractive is the spiritual ancestor or saint that the devotee begs him to command that the adept's heart resist the saintly attractions. The song ends with a flurry of images . . . sun, insight, brightness, morning star, as an attempt is made to depict the reality which is the goal of love.

It is difficult to capture the depth of devotion one encounters among Sufi members for the Shaikh. In this section, I have indicated that the Shaikh becomes present in a very real sense, when *dhikr* is performed to such a degree that the believer holds him to palpably exist with them. One could say he is just as present as in her real life, only he now cannot be visually apprehended. The most evident example of the new way of perceiving the Shaikh is in the performance of the singer, who utilizes the technique of mental imaging to concretize the Shaikh. Then, in what one might describe as an encounter between them, the spiritual power of the Shaikh is delivered to the group. The words and phrases are well-known in the Sufi *dhikr*, and the notions quite conventional, but they have a double meaning. On the one hand, they represent the phraseology of love as old as the tradition; on the other, they hark back to the occasion when the *dhikr* was powerful, and the adept encountered the spiritual force of the Shaikh in a special manner. Thus the living reality of the Shaikh continues to grace the experience of the adept.

If spiritual states can be sensed as territories, the above points map the terrain. When Muhammad al-Burhani died, the route for coping was available. The Shaikh's influence was retained and comprehended through the ritual system, especially through *dhikr*. What was fascinating was that the chasm between the dead and the living was collapsed even more than the scenario expressed here would have allowed, because of the appearance of songs from the dead Shaikh. This was the most important element in the grieving process.

The Situation in 1985

When I returned to Cairo in 1985, the Shaikh had been dead two years. The loss could be read on everyone's face. The believers were unanimous in reflecting their loss—it was grievous, traumatic and depressing even after this length of time. While the cloak of leadership had fallen to Muhammad's son Ibrahim, it was evident that the transition had not been easy. Devotees still wept at the mention of the Shaikh's name. Nevertheless, the group seemed to have a new lease on life. I expected that normal grief process was responsible, but the real reason was to pose many questions.

One evening at the *dhikr*, I was surprised to hear that a new song had come, presumably from the Sudan. The excitement in the group was tangible for it was a song sent by apparently unknown means directly from the dead Shaikh to the order. The local head spent considerable time trying to explain what the words of the song meant. Finally he gave up, urging his members to find the meaning in the performance of *dhikr*. The statement from the devotee that began this chapter took place at that time. To her, the words from the Shaikh not only guaranteed his continuing presence, but made him more accessible. While he was alive, his humanness had limited him to one locale; with his death, he was able to be present with all the sister orders, wherever they met. Moreover, he bequeathed his power to them through his songs, thus continuing the creative interaction that he so successfully had brought while alive.

While he had lost his fleshly frame, he had lost none of his personality and human grace. He was not just absent in the Sudan or some other place now. He was present to the community of adherents, adding another dimension of reality to their experience. He was transformed into a universal being, beyond flesh and its limitations. But his songs meant he was still directly involved in the growing of their own particular group, for the songs were depicted as being the Shaikh's message for them.

It took quite some ferreting before I could determine how these songs came from the Shaikh to the order. The female devotee refused to say, and the local leader evaded the question. Many of the adepts were vague, saying only that they came from the Sudan. Finally, after some months, an associate in Cairo wrote to me indicating that the new center in Khartoum had a library, and that periodically new songs are found among the existing manuscripts. No one knows how they appear there, since the room was closely watched. The general conclusion was that the Shaikh materialized these songs as messages to his followers.

For the devotee, this was sufficient. The Shaikh was now physically present, through the vehicle of his songs, to continue his influence on their lives. He was still human, in some sense of the word. But his humanity was now supplemented and universalized.

The lengthy two years of intensive grief was now over; the Shaikh's death took on a new dimension. I took the new outlook to be a major shift whose significance stretched far beyond the local Sufi order. It indicated that the death of a critical leader required extraordinary processes to bring closure to grief. In the end, the Shaikh was transformed.

GRIEF AND THE MODELS
OF THE COPING PROCESS

In his study of severe reactions to death loss, Volkan identifies elements of traumatic mourning that were reminiscent of the Burhanis before the songs arrived. Volkan indicates that speaking of the beloved in the present tense, of visiting tombs and mausoleums, of representing the God in the survivor's mind and directly linking unusual occurrences with the dead as pathological (Volkan, 1987:246f). Much research concentrates on loss patterns in terms of control theory, maintaining that the significant dead in childhood must be replaced by some other person or persons if the search for a replacement is not to become a recurring pathological pattern in adulthood. Hales goes so far as to say that "Awareness of the presence of a dead person is both widely experienced and a very unusual symptom" (Hale, 1987:211). Rees regarded such behavior as hallucinatory (Rees, 1971). While all the characteristics described as pathological are found in the behavior of the adepts, neither they nor I would have agreed with that designation. Indeed, we have shown that many of the elements become incorporated into the ritual world of the Sufi and that most are found in everyday *dhikr*. We can conclude then, that, either Volkan's definition is culture specific, or there is a much wider range of behavior possible. Indeed, I would argue that the Sufi adepts were not pathological, but were expressing a different processural system. Such a view is also consonant with Wellenkamp's study (Chapter 8), where the grieving process included retaining the dead in the household until the rituals required could be carried out. It is also present in Badone's study (Chapter 13), where the dead are not truly content until they return to their home area for burial, implying a tension that can only be calmed by an integration into a symbolically significant region. The new, materialized songs from the Shaikh were the instruments that brought about the final integration for the Burhani. For the Sufi, then, we have a case in which the grieving process takes an alternate routing than Volkan's reactions of "predictable sequential phases through which anyone who has lost a loved one can be expected to pass" (Volkan, 1987:246).

In what follows, I shall address three related aspects of the process, hoping to show how the transformation of the Shaikh is a distinctive solution for the Burhani, but also has ramification for our general understanding of the process of grieving. The first aspect is how the Shaikh is part of a special Sufi paradigm for maintaining spiritual authority and group solidarity. The second is the significance of the new songs, and insight into the unique flavor of the Burhani transformation of loss. The third is more theoretical in nature and is directed towards applying models that will help us understand the transformation process as it occurred among Muhammad al-Burhani's followers.

Authority Maintenance and Group Solidarity

The survival of the Shaikh in the religious life of the group is not to be construed according to Western spiritualist's notions of ghosts or manifestations of a persistent personal energy (as one finds expressed in Myers 1961 et al.). The Burhanis do not suggest that the personality of the Shaikh continues to linger around, as if he had unfinished business. They never say they have 'seen' the Shaikh in a ghost form. Nor is the energy that is acknowledged in the *dhikr* and charges the rituals perceived as an individual presence—it is always connected to the great spiritual ancestry that reaches all the way back to Muhammad and his son-in-law Ali. The person of the Shaikh is spiritualized and ritualized, to be encountered solely in the ministrations of spiritual forces within the *dhikr*. This decidedly Sufi understanding of the presence of the Shaikh dates back to the 17th century, when a profound shift occurred in Sufi awareness patterns. Where Sufi groups had originally focussed upon union with God in a spiritual experience, Sufis from that time on began to conceive of the goal of the spiritual life as union with the Spirit of the Prophet (Voll, 1980).

From this came the sense of belonging to the family of the Prophet, of being connected to him through a mystical linkage. The human focus of that lineage was

the Shaikh. In practical terms, Sufism became Shaikh-oriented with direct connections to the power of the Prophet. This connectedness provides one with an entree
into the spiritual forces of the other world, and empowers one's life while in
this one. Hence the song translated earlier can be read as setting forth a Sufi
'philosophy' of the Shaikh, and identifies those spiritual traits associated with
him. After the Shaikh's death, he may be encountered through structures indicated
in that song. Without being exhaustive, some of themes expressed formulate
the Shaikh this way; as a presence (lines, 5, 6, 9); during the *dhikr* (16); as a
provider of life-transforming benefits (22, 23); as an irresistible love (26); as a
treasure with a border of flesh (10); as an inner awareness (35) and as a visualized
fire (13).

Such an interpretation indicates that a distinctive paradigm is at work, a paradigm that differs markedly from traditional Islamic notions. Yet it is a socially
controlled and mediated paradigm that does not require the adept to do any more
than follow the direction of the local Shaikh. The adept is guaranteed participation
in the social group that gives him meaning. He may also strike off on his own,
under the Shaikh's guidance, and tread a more individual path of spiritual enter-
prise. The point is that the Shaikh becomes the means to relate to reality as it is
defined by the group. Hence, at death, he also provides the mechanism to transform the adept's grief into spiritual tranquility.

The New Songs in the Burhani Transformation

As we have indicated, all songs have their central impact during the *dhikr*. Sufi
songs are often signatures of the groups identity and this is especially true of songs
of the Shaikh's composition (Waugh, 1989:163). Muhammad al-Burhani, a singer
himself, was always held to be a most expressive creator of songs. These familiar
songs became a touchstone for connectedness with the spiritual line.

This suggests, then, that *dhikr* is the most logical place for the Shaikh to have an
impact upon the group; it is also the environment in which grief work can be done.
Separating grief work off from the ritual form cannot be done, at least not
according to Burhani codes, because that is the prime vehicle for encountering
reality. Contrarily, trying to handle grief over the Shaikh's death separate from
ritual would be to reduce its importance. Personal loss can be transformed through
the ritual. Grief is incorporated into a new scheme of meaning. (See also Simeone,
Chapter 10, for ritual transformation of grief into joy.)

Then, when the new songs were discovered, the presence of the Shaikh was
renewed at an additional level. General Sufi ideology allowed them to perceive
the Shaikh as present with them in the *dhikr*, as we have seen. The unique aspect
was that the Shaikh was now present in his former role—as a singer
bearing spiritual directions for the group. Moreover, the meaning needed the
decoding of the *dhikr*, as evidenced when Shaikh Gamal gave up explaining the new song and directed them to discover its meaning in the *dhikr*.

The importance of the solution is that every 'good' *dhikr* thereafter at which the song was sung was an occasion for discovering the actual meaning. In that way, the freshness of the Shaikh's presence was experienced anew at each powerful performance.

It is highly significant, then, that the new songs provided the means for completing the grief work. Since *dhikr* does not just provide a religiously acceptable activity, but also delivers reality, the songs activated a new level of engagement with that reality. With the existence of new songs, the adepts were quickly and easily propelled into a scheme of reality where the death of the Shaikh was transformed into a power linking them to the saint and the Prophet. The songs were thus the means of unifying the adept with the Prophet. Grief was overcome by realizing personally the connectedness with the Spirit of Muhammad.

Theoretical Models of the Process

It is evident that group processes of grieving carried the most weight with the Burhanis. For them the pain of loss is transformed into the connectedness with the Prophet. What are the models operative in this process?

Coping Mechanism: The Social-Religious Dimension of the Burhani Sufis — In his important study of health care in Africa, Lambo concludes that "concepts of health within the framework of African culture are more social than biological: (Lambo, 1964:447). Following this line of analysis, I suggest that the Sudanese group has altered the notion of 'real person' to include the dead Shaikh in his modified *dhikr* sense and in the sense of delivery of special 'messages.' In effect, the Sufi social context allows for modification of the strict line of demarcation between the living and the dead with regard to the saintly figures. Hence there is nothing absolute about loss; it is defined in terms of an immediate response to the disappearance of his physical body and his attendant role as guide of the community. Soon, however, contact is re-established through *dhikr*, and more pointedly for the Burhanis, through the specially given songs. Ultimately loss is rationalized and integrated into community ritual. The Burhanis challenge the perception prevalent in the Western culture that loss is singularly a personal experience treatable by a neutral therapist. They also suggest that the loss of a Shaikh can only be handled within a word order/theological schema. Any attempt to see Sufi behavior as pathological would flounder on the fact that a neutral point of view cannot exist in the Sufi ethos. In effect, personal loss is actualized as corporate loss; and corporate loss cannot be pathological.

Some years ago, Kiev, in his introduction to a series of essays on non-Western therapies entitled *Magic, Faith and Healing*, affirmed that the model of grief treatable though interpersonal intervention was undercut by social prerogatives, at least for some cultures:

By shifting the orientation from the interpersonal level of analysis to one that takes into consideration the situation and cultural context, these studies have been most valuable in re-emphasizing the broader fabric in which psychotherapy occurs. The studies are of particular interest because of the attention they have focused on the cultural and social elements of psychotherapy, a particularly difficult step because of the twentieth century emphasis on intra-psychic features of mental illness and the two-person nature of treatment (Kiev, 1964:6).

Du Toit has also argued that many of our therapies over emphasize dichotomies (Du Toit, 1979). As a result, faith is segregated from pharmacopoeia, religious acts from secular rituals, private from public grief. My material suggests that *Dhikr* is far more important for the grieving process among the Sufis than might appear on the surface. In my recent work, I argue that ritual is the central constitutive element of the Sufi world, but that experience is both validated within it, and reality itself discerned through it (Waugh, 1989:36-50). Thus other ways of crisis management can be detected. It may well be that the Burhanis exhibit a larger truth: methods of a corporate sort exist which will allow personal grief to be dispersed and transformed.

Coping Mechanisms: Transforming the Inner Crisis — In his study on the death of Lincoln, Peter Homans proposes that we utilize psycho-biographical models to understand how people handle crisis (Homans, 1987). Drawing on Eric Erikson's analysis of the three crises of Freud's early career, Homans finds a pattern in the way crises proceed. Erikson had held that Freud's three crises involved the rejection of current paradigms of scientific exploration, rejection of work-roles based upon these paradigms and reaction of an intense personal sort to a relationship with Wilhelm Flies (Erikson, 1964). Out of the interlock of these three crises, Freud was able to develop a new sense of meaning, a mission, that was radically different than anyone else had hitherto fashioned. Homans argues that our understanding of the life of great individuals likewise follows similar routes.

Changes wrought by great individuals are understood in terms of a rejection of the established system and an overthrow of accepted methods of working. These lead to new activity structures. Finally, personal relationships are the catalyst for important modification in the great individual's life. By broadening these categories, we can apply them to the loss of the Shaikh among the Burhani. In that way, important aspects of a coping mechanism can be seen.

Rejection of the Current System and Development of the New System

In Islamic tradition, the Angel of Death comes to claim the soul of the individual which in then returned to God for judgment. Once judgment is complete, the individual goes to paradise or to hell, depending upon his confession of faith (or lack thereof). The individual ceases to be available to anyone in the world. Moreover, rituals of separation and disposal emphasize the split between the dead and the living. The individual is washed and wrapped in a shroud, then taken to the mosque for prayers, followed by immediate interment. Often the more pious dead are said to 'run' to the grave, in order to begin their eternal slumber, and thus be "with God." In effect, the participation by the Sufi in the burial rites of the larger Muslim community accentuates the severing nature of death and heightens the crisis.

Then, the very need of carrying on the order requires acts which emphasis the Shaikh's death: a new leader, new directions, new dynamics within the group. The adept's personal involvement with the Shaikh is gone, and the individual must draw on new sources for inspiration and guidance. The Sufi must participate in this severing from the Shaikh because of being first and foremost a Muslim. But he withholds validation of the normative Islamic notions in two key areas— the continuing impact of the Shaikh on the group and the connectedness of the Shaikh with a spiritual lineage. As will be clear from the preceding exposition, a new meaning must be accorded the Shaikh through the *dhikr* form. The adepts re-orient their world to account for the new facts. They do not have to make a radical re-orienting if they belong to the group, because the explanations are present in tradition to account for the new paradigm. But they must relate to a new sense of meaning of the group now that the center of the order is physically unavailable. These usually take the form of "explanations," of ways of perceiving the relatedness of the group to each other and the spiritual world. In effect, the adepts have a significant stake in the spiritual realm beyond, through their connectedness to the Shaikh. This means the group no longer defines itself the same way.

The new songs from the Shaikh provide the principle vehicle for this new sense, but not exclusively; many claim to have had visitation in dreams from the Shaikh. The methodologically significant factor in these developments is the growth of a new body of 'understandings,' including the new songs and their interpretation which push the group onward in coming to term with the situations. Homans, in his analysis of great leaders, suggests that these understandings be viewed as a 'text' and defines it as a new theoretical realm which provides an analytic base. In Burhani terms it is rather an enhanced paradigm, since the new understanding does not require a new world view or revised ideology, but rather the empowerment of certain latent meanings in Sufi ideology. The only really new element is the recently received songs.

The Overthrow and Articulation
of New Work-Techniques

The second crisis relates to work techniques. As Homans remarks, "work-roles are, in effect, the way society makes felt its demands for certain types of performances" (1987:301). But work roles do not define the world of a Burhani quite the way they do for Freud, for secular work is perceived as subservient to the religious world view. The most important work for a Burhani is the discipline of the *dhikr*. It is *jihad* (holy war) of the soul (al-Taftazani, 1985). Yet this jihad is not strictly personal; it sees the individual as part of a corporate whole whose main *raison d'etre* is the building of a true Islamic community. Such an interpretation is linked to a historical development with Sufism itself, when a shift in goals occurred, moving the meaning of the brotherhoods away from a personal union with God to the growth of a comparably spiritually sensitized community. Rahman is regarded as correct by most scholars when he insists that the new Sufism movements, the so-called Neo-Sufism of the nineteenth and twentieth century, have a common characteristic: "They bring into the center of attention the socio-moral reconstruction of Muslim society, as against [the older] Sufism which had stressed primarily the individual and not the society" (Rahman, 1970:638). Defining work as essentially religious activity with community ends means that the Sufis can overcome the crisis proposed by the loss of a personal guide and director by affirming the primacy of the social nexus. Hence, where ordinary Muslim conventions would deny the validity of the Shaikh's presence after death, the "work" of dealing with the Shaikh's death is transformed through ritual acts into encounters with the power and personality of the spiritualized Shaikh as a group endeavour. The empowerment gained leads to affirming Islamic cohesion as well as a brotherhood of discipline.

Where Freud radically altered the direction and technique of dealing with patients when he reacted to his crises, the Burhanis, in effect, came to empower in a new and more meaningful way the latent beliefs of the neo-Sufism to which they belonged. Pain and grief was submerged within the belief of a corporate good now accomplished through *dhikr*, at the center of which was encounter with the spiritualized and universalized Shaikh. Personal loss only heightened group achievement.

The Personal Relationship Redefined

The third crisis deals with the personal domain. Both Erikson and Homans propose the analysis of personal relationships with parents as the model best able to account for the intensity and depth of relatedness.

While the Shaikh was still alive, he embodied in his actions and guidance the role of a parent. Sufi ideology holds that belonging to an order is to have one's identity tied to a spiritual lineage, reaching all the way back to the Prophet. Hence, the Shaikh was the concrete expression of the adept's own great lineage. The adept also takes on roles that psychologists would regard as dependent ones associated with parents. It is clear that the Shaikh becomes a subjective constant, providing assistance, communion, advice, encouragement and discipline. As a kind of substitute parent, he binds the adept to himself. The adept becomes so fulfilled while the Shaikh is alive that the believer becomes identified with him. Many of those elements of parent-child relationships detailed by Volkan apply to the adept-Shaikh connection during the Shaikh's life (Volkan, 1972). Moreover, the Prophet is a powerful model in this, since Muhammad had lost both parents, and found his sustenance in God. Not considering themselves of that spiritual level, Sufis are content to hold the Shaikh as a substitute. The personal crisis also derives from the amount of energy invested in the relationship with the Shaikh. Scarcely any other person can be so significant. The death of the Shaikh raises the question of the validity of this kind of relationship. The individual Sufi may be thrown into severe depression, as, indeed, some appeared to have experienced.

Like Freud, then, a very deep and personal relationship had caused excessive pain for the adepts. Like Freud, the Sufis had to redefine the meaning of that relationship so that it would not be defined, but so that the anguish could be redirected. This they did by centering their spiritual life around the image of the Shaikh as a mediator and (now) saintly-guide. Indeed, by joining the other saints, Shaikh Muhammad now assured their position in the spiritual world. The new relationship supported connectedness to a far more important area of power than had been the case before. Thus the personal pain gave way to a new sense of the depth of personal power.

These three crisis appear to be effectively connected to each other, perhaps in a dynamic manner. Out of this process of coping came the new complex which is the resolution of the grief and the renewing of the group. The process involved an enhanced paradigm of the Shaikh: this is embodied in the new song transcribed above. Among the new markers are the following: the Shaikh brings life—transforming benefits and grace; he is internal yet externally present; he is a medium encountered in the *dhikr*, yet he is loved as he was loved in his 'parental' role. Because of this he becomes the focus for metaphors of praise.

Such a list indicates that a distinctive paradigm is at work, a paradigm that differs significantly from the traditional mediated paradigm that does not require the adept to do any more than follow the direction of the local Shaikh. With the Burhani paradigm, the adept personally senses his stock in the eternal. Muhammad al-Burhani becomes the entree to reality as it is defined by the group. His songs provide the mechanism to transform the adept's grief into tranquility.

CONCLUSION

The coping process sketched here suggests that the traumatic Burhani loss was overcome through activation of certain latent tendencies within Sufi life. The process leads to a revaluation and empowerment of the adepts in several key areas, and ultimately to the transformation of the Shaikh Muhammad al-Burhani from a human spiritual advisor to a universal saint. We may thus conclude that there are other coping mechanisms than those which are sanctioned in our culture. Such mechanisms may likewise provide for a deepening of personal meaning when the process is completed.

Perhaps, even in our culture, there are potentials available for alternate ways of dealing with death's loss. Did not Vachel Lindsay imply this, when, in honor of Abraham Lincoln, he penned: "He cannot sleep upon his hillside now He is among us—as in times before."

Po Starykovsky
(The Old People's Way):
End of Life Attitudes and
Customs in Two Traditional
Russian Communities*

Richard A. Morris

In Chapter 7, Richard Morris compares death, grief, and mourning among two groups of conservative Russian religious isolates now resident in the United States. Different as their practices are from each other, the Old Believers and the Molokans are similar in their strong commitment to community solidarity, especially in the face of death. Death makes manifest their beliefs and their separation from mainstream American society. Morris stresses the important role of universal involvement in ritual as the key to these societies' handling of grief work.

*   *   *

PART 1—OLD BELIEVERS

Ivan was in his berry field, trimming the plants for the next year's growth, when his third son came running to the field to report that Uncle Fyodor had died. Ivan immediately stopped what he was doing, gathered his tools, and accompanied his son back to the house. His wife had already started to pack the car with what was necessary. In minutes, the whole family was in the car and on its way to the home where Fyodor had lived.

When they arrived, his wife and the older girls went into the kitchen to join other women who had collected and already begun cutting vegetables and preparing the meal. Ivan and his older son went to the garage, where several men were measuring boards and making a casket, while a couple of others were making the

*A portion of the research for this report was made possible through a grant from the Oregon Committee for the Humanities, an affiliate of the National Endowment for the Humanities.

eight-ended Orthodox cross. Ivan volunteered to help where there was need. The younger children went out into the yard to join the other children, who were sitting quietly or playing in a subdued manner. More people came. The driveway filled with cars. Each family entered the home and prayed in the direction of the icon in the corner before the family divided into its male and female components, each going separately to help prepare for the funeral activities.

These people are members of the Russian Old Believer community which has settled in Oregon since 1964.[1] They represent, however, an eminently traditional group with ancient Slavic roots. Their way of life is deliberately fashioned after a mid-seventeenth century religious ethic of the Old Orthodox Russian Church. The Old Believers are descendants of what had been the overall population of Orthodox believers in medieval Russia. They acquired their identity as Old Believers, or Old Ritualists, through their refusal to accept the Russian Orthodox Church reforms implemented in the mid-17th century.[2] Hence, this Russian population has steadily preserved many of the traditions and religious practices which were characteristic of the peasants of medieval Russia.

Death is a 'village' affair, and when it occurs, all turn their attention to it and rather rapidly do what they consider necessary to lay the body to rest and to acknowledge the event among all the living present. The process takes very little time: rarely more than 24 hours. The funeral service reflects many aspects of their religious beliefs, rituals, and internalized understandings.

When the casket box was completed, several of the men took it into the room where the body of Fyodor lay. Two men there had just finished cleansing the body: washing it all over and dressing it in a white, loosely based cloth.[3] The men lifted the body into the casket and made the final preparations, crossing Fyodor's arms on his chest and forming the hands into the sign of the cross in the old style, that is, with the first two fingers extended, and the thumb joined with the third and fourth fingers.[4] Under his hands they slipped a prayer sheet, and on his chest they placed a metal icon cross. Lastly, they placed a narrow ribbon with a prayer across his forehead (see Figure 2). By the time they brought the casket into the living room, a large crowd of people had gathered. All had come to pay respects, and were calmly waiting for the *nastavnik*, the 'lay pastor', to arrive to begin the

[1]For a more detailed account of the emergence of Old Belielvers, see (Zenkovsky, 1970). For detailed information on the Oregon descendants, see (Morris, in press). For an account of Russian cultural attitudes on death, see (Kaisers, 1988).

[2]Known as the Great Schism in Russian history, the church reforms of the period 1651-1667 not only made corrections to the written books of the Church, but also modified the ritual used in prayers and services. This latter offended many as being contrary to God's ways, thus justifying their refusal to accept the reforms even in defiance of the patriarch who instituted the reforms and the tsar who later approved them.

[3]Men are assigned to clean the bodies of men, and women to clean the bodies of women.

[4]One of the reforms in the ritual was to discontinue crossing one's self with two fingers, and, instead, join the thumb to the first two fingers to cross one's self with three fingers. For those who refused to accept the reforms, the crossing with two fingers became a symbol of their stand.

Figure 2. Headbands for adult (right) or for child (bottom) and letter
to be placed in the hands of the deceased in the coffin.

funeral service.[5] No one had received an invitation—none was needed. All had come upon merely hearing that Fyodor had passed away. Anyone that knew him, even remotely, would come to pay their respects.

The lay pastor arrived and the ancient prayers were sung using the style of the *znamenny* chant.[6] The casket was placed to face the icons in the eastern corner of the room. All of those present crowded around. They were standing facing the icons and were bowing towards the icon corner as the series of prayers was read and recited.[7] At the end of the service, a procession formed to lead and accompany the departed to the cemetery. Leading the procession, a young man, a direct relative of the deceased, carried the cross which would stand at the foot of the grave. Behind him came the bearer of the lid to the coffin, which would be laid in place only moments before burial. Then came the coffin borne by kinsmen and surrounded by the lay pastor, the widow, the close relatives, and those comforting them. Behind them, in a random, respectful manner, came the friends and acquaintances of the deceased.

SERVICE AT THE CEMETERY

The final service at the grave site once again underlines the Old Orthodox traditions: final prayers; circling the grave three times in a clockwise direction;[8] the final farewell by the immediate kin as they go forward for their last view and, perhaps, kiss of the deceased; affixing of the lid on the coffin just after the lay minister removes the icon from the deceased's chest; lowering the casket into the grave; and filling in the grave, beginning with close kin, followed by distant kin, and then others, all of whom approach to throw three handfuls of dirt onto the casket.

Nearby, a close relative holds a large bowl of *kutya* (a cold, cooked wheat mixed with honey) with several spoons around the edge. As opposed to the symbol of "living bread, the *kutya* represents the cold flatness of death—but with the sweet reminder of life eternal. After each final farewell, each person eats three spoonfuls of sweet *kutya* before leaving the cemetery.

In an Old Believer cemetery, the graves are in a line, oriented in an easterly direction. There is no segregation as to family or kin. As long as a person is "in union," he or she occupies the place next in line. At the foot of each grave stands an eight-ended Orthodox cross (see Figures 3 and 4). Thus, at sunrise, the shadow

---

[5]Circuit priests in old Russia would bless one chosen by the congregation to be the spiritual leader, *Dukhovnyi Nastavnik,* and to conduct partial services and bless marriages, baptisms, etc., in the absence of the priest. On the next circuit, the priest would confirm the actions. Old Believers, however, were left without priests as a result of the severe rules of the government against priests conducting services in the Old Rite. Thus, they have institutionalized the role of the lay pastor for their religious blessings. However, without a priest, they are not able to participate in the fullness of the Rite.

[6]The *znamenny* chant is a medieval form sung in unison.

[7]An eastern corner of a home where the main family icons are displayed on a high corner shelf.

[8]As opposed to the reform-stipulated counter-clockwise direction.

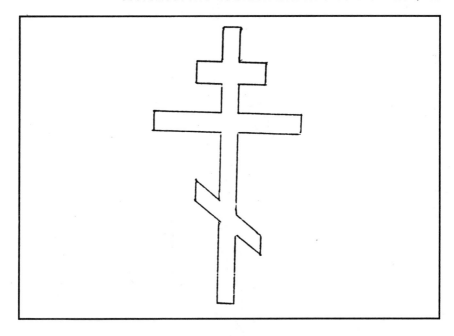

Figure 3. Traditional Russian 8-ended Cross.

of the cross is cast onto the grave, superimposed on the deceased in proper perspective. Additionally, at the Second Coming, when the dead are called from the grave, the deceased will simply rise up to stand next to their crosses and face the East, from whence Christ will come, in accordance with the precepts of the Second Coming.

After the burial, all those in attendance return to the home of the deceased, where a dinner has been set to commemorate the deceased. Depending on the stature of the deceased, comments can be made in tribute to his or her achievements. At the end of the meal, as those present are leaving, the family gives each one a token gift, asking for prayers for the dead. The recipients remember the deceased by name in their evening prayers.

BACKGROUND OF THE OLD BELIEVERS

The rituals of the Old Believers codify their understandings and interpretations and define their behavior in daily life and at major life crisis events. To them, the rituals represent the mysteries and sacraments of life's changes. Their beliefs are not only shaped by this medieval version of the religious aspects of Christianity, but also are influenced by their need to be distinct and clear in their identity, in order to differentiate themselves from those accepting the Reforms. Therefore, the

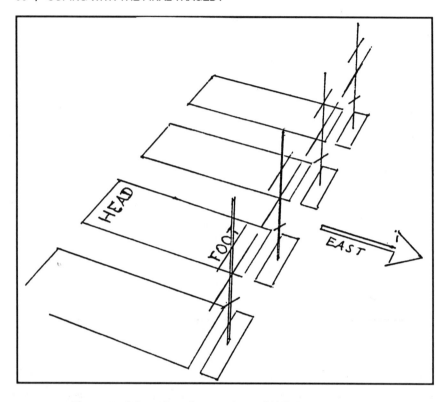

Figure 4. Orientation of graves in an Old Believer cemetery.

proper ways have gradually taken on what could be considered today a monastic form. In turn, they accuse the Orthodox Church of having fallen into the hands of the Anti-Christ for having accepted reforms. Consequently, every change in Orthodox Church ritual since the middle of the 17th century has been rejected by the Old Believers.

Additionally, the Old Believers are motivated in some of their burial rituals by practical considerations. Inasmuch as they have lived in remote areas for a fair portion of their existence over the last 350 years, and have steadfastly remained determined to preserve their traditional ways, they are reluctant to use mortuary services, or any specialized technologies, much less using the services of non-Old Believers. This, in part, accounts for the rapidity with which the memorial and burial services are conducted.[9]

[9]Old Believers are also extremely distressed when required by the State to have an autopsy performed on one of their dead (Kaufert notes this is also true of Canadian native people, see Chapter 14). Therefore, autopsies are not routine, and occur only when required by law.

The forthright quickness with which the funeral takes place does not mean that there is an absence of grief. There is, indeed, real hurt and sadness at the departure of someone close. While an outward show of excess grief is not considered proper, crying certainly does take place, and is a reflection of the genuine feeling of loss. However, one shouldn't cry too much; only the close kin are socially excused for this outward show of emotion. The forthrightness of the funeral service contributes to this containment of immediate grief by having the event quickly handled in a public ritual, and then leaves the family in its own private grief. Moreover, there are periodic rituals to follow which allow for the public to commiserate with the family on behalf of the deceased.

MEMORIAL RITUALS

In addition to the main funeral service, there are four other services which commemorate the deceased. Members of the family, close kin, and any others who are concerned, gather at the prayer hall or church between three and six in the morning to light candles and sing prayers for the deceased. These remembrance services (*Pominky* or *Ponikhidy*) are given at set periods after the burial, and each is usually followed by a remembrance dinner. The first service (*tritina*) is given three days after the death, with the subsequent remembrance services nine days later (*devyatina*), and forty days later (*sorochina*), as well as on the first anniversary, and, if desired, on subsequent anniversaries. In the interpretation of the Old Believers, however, prayers during the first forty days are most important. It is believed that on the fortieth day, if the departed has been forgiven for whatever sins were committed during life, the soul is admitted into heaven. Moreover, a reader is often secretly given money (sometimes as much as $200.00) to read prayers to ask forgiveness for the deceased prior to the fortieth day. This person is referred to as a *sorokovust*. Subsequent prayers and remembrances are considered beneficial to the deceased, especially in the case where the person has not been 'in union' during life, and could be considered as not qualified to be fully forgiven for his or her sins.

The dinner after the service varies with families. Wealthy families can afford to give large and elaborate remembrance dinners during the specified and proper times. Others provide modest dinners after the service. Poor families either serve meager fare, or simply have the service. Still others, who have been buffeted by dislocations, or in the case where a death has occurred outside the community, normally feel obligated to have a remembrance dinner whenever one can be arranged, even years later. By means of the remembrance service and dinner, one pays tribute, reverence, and respect to the deceased, and at the same time re-establishes continuity among the living.

In the cases where the family cannot afford all the remembrance dinners, the emphasis is to have the dinner on the fortieth day and on the first anniversary. The dinner on the fortieth day, normally the period of ritual purification, commemorates the end of the forty-day journey of the soul to the gates of heaven.

The widow will often dress in black, and may do so, if she chooses, for the remainder of her life. Relatives often wear black as well, especially during the first forty days. After the first year, the period of mourning is considered fulfilled for all. On subsequent yearly anniversaries, relatives may continue to remember the deceased by either arranging a remembrance dinner or by giving out *milostinya* 'gifts' to ask for prayers for the departed.

At the church service is a bowl of *kutya* (the cold porridge of wheat mixed with honey) on one table with candles. The table is blessed by incense during the memorial service. All participants at the service take three spoons full of the *kutya* in remembrance of the deceased (*Pomnim kutyei* 'remembering by *kutya*').

PRAYERS FOR THE DECEASED

The importance of prayers for the deceased is paramount. While the order of services is considered important, there are times when services are not possible. They are merely a time-frame by which prayers can be offered on behalf of the deceased, and requested by the kin of others. The request for prayers usually takes the form of *milostinya*, understood as a 'gift of request.' It is used on various occasions. The giver presents his friends with some token to ask for prayers for some purpose which is important to the giver. The gift, therefore, becomes like a payment in advance for prayers to be said on the giver's behalf. In the case of a funeral, of course, the request is for prayers for the deceased.

A *milostinya* is always considered a religious act. The request is always for prayers. The gift is commonly in the form of money, but can also be a small cross that each Old Believer wears around his or her neck, church candles, the long beeswax candles that are hand-made in the community, scarves or fabric for making some sort of clothing, or food—bread or onions or a small box of salt. It is not uncommon to see people after a church service distributing pieces of bread to members of the congregation as a form of *milostinya*.

Secret gifts (*tainaya milostinya*) are left in obvious places for a given person to find: on the car hood, at the doorstep, etc. The receiver is not to attempt to guess who the giver might have been, but is to simply offer prayers ambiguously in behalf of the giver's purposes.[10]

FUNCTIONAL ASPECTS OF THE RITUAL

The ritual provides for several practical features. Normally the Old Believers, as an eminently traditional group, would not think of describing the ritual in practical

---

[10]It is not uncommon that older members of the community who are receiving social security checks, will treat the gifts as a secret *milostinya*, and offer prayers for the government sources of the funds.

terms. However, when confronted with questions as to its practical nature, they would acknowledge that this secular view would have some merit. Not given to analysis of parts, they nonetheless would indirectly agree that the form of the funeral, in terms of its ritual parts, 1) provides a periodic cathartic release of emotion, 2) encourages cohesiveness at the personal and group level, while at the same time underscoring and re-emphasizing the religious concepts involved, and 3) realigns relationships within the family and the group by institutionally acknowledging the departure of one of the constituent members. At the same time, it grants a sense of reassurance of eternal care and of the attention of the supernatural in a manner that re-emphasizes and preserves their religious concepts.

An Old Believer, being steeped in tradition and not accustomed to analyzing ritual in its modular forms, views the listing of practical aspects of rituals—however valid—as a diminishment of events and their significance. There is a larger dimension, and that dimension includes, in a holistic sense, the indistinguishable combination of the comfort of the ritual, the genuine emotion experienced, and the necessity of final disposition. All these elements are simultaneously and indistinguishably taking place within a cohesive religious focus.

RELATIVE FEATURES

The outpourings of feelings focused by the rituals vary according to the age and stature of the deceased. For the young, death is tragic and sad, especially from the point of view that the person has not had a chance to live a full life. On the other hand, the young person is considered relatively free of serious sin, and there is, therefore, little worry as to his acceptability for eternal life. Hence, the services are shorter, and the requests for prayers reduced and more perfunctory.

On the other hand, older members of the community may be taking to their graves unknown sins. Therefore it is important for their kin and others to pray for their forgiveness. If an older person has led a good life within the community, other members are inclined to pray diligently for him or her, in order that forgiveness be offered for whatever unknown sins there may be. Also, many of these people willingly attended the memorial services and dinners that are given. It is common that tributes are given at the dinners: the re-telling of stories of the good deeds and pleasant moments in the deceased's life.

If a person has not maintained his or her stature in the community, and has fallen from grace; that is to say, is not 'in union' (*ymeste*), it is more difficult, regardless of age, to have the proper prayers said in his or her behalf. To be "in union," an Old Ritualist must conform and abide within conventions required by the religious precepts; i.e., attending church, keeping the fasts, and eschewing sinful activity. As long as one obeys these precepts and does not break social cohesion by publicly offending them, he or she is considered to be 'in union.'

However, violations of these precepts, especially in a public and obvious sense, incur various sanctions which determine the relationship of the person to his community. A serious violation results in a person being declared *otluchyonny*, 'excluded' or 'excommunicated.' Examples of such sins are: marrying outside of the religion; closely associating with "unclean" people; shaving for a man, or cutting one's hair for a woman; or using tobacco. A person held in this relationship to the community can return to 'in union' status, provided he or she is seriously willing to repent, request and receive forgiveness of the congregation, do penance, and completely cease the offensive behavior. However, should a person in an excommunicated state die, he or she cannot, in any circumstances, be buried next to those 'in union.' Often they are placed at the margins of the cemetery, or even buried at some other location.

When and if the person's request for forgiveness is accepted by the congregation, the person becomes *oglashyonny* (a word that derives from a root word of 'deaf'), until the period of penance for readmission is over. If death should occur before readmission, they can still, nonetheless, be buried in the central part of the cemetery designated for those 'in union.'

Those who have poor attendance at church, or have participated in activities which make them ritually unclean—such as eating unclean food or eating from the same plate with unclean persons must do penance. By correcting their ways, and asking forgiveness of the congregation, these people can be easily forgiven. Such violations do not involve dire consequences in the case of death.

Drunkenness, an easy sin to slip into, involves severe sanctions by the group, regardless of whether the person is 'in union' or not. A person who dies in a drunken state, usually accidentally, is considered unforgivably unclean. Old Believers liken a drunken person to a dog, and a dog, for Old Believers, is the most unclean of animals. A person who dies while drunk is buried wherever the family can arrange a place, at best along the margin of the cemetery. There is no ceremony, and no prayers are said. The immediate family offer only the simple 'Jesus' prayer at the burial.[11] It is widely believed that God will not forgive someone who dies drunken. The person is laid to rest as a matter of necessity, for "One cannot leave the body lying in the yard."

For those who die in a marginal status, either in the ritually unclean state or excommunicated, the family actively prays and requests prayers of others through *milostinya*, secret or open. On the special church days designated as "parent's days," when ancestors are remembered in prayers, people pass out gifts for prayers to the others in the congregation during the service.[12]

---

[11]"Lord, Jesus Christ, Son of God, have mercy on (X), a sinner."
[12]In Orthodox services, the congregations stand for the most part. Thus, quietly weaving through the congregation to give out gifts is not disruptive.

THE CEMETERY

The Old Believers have established a cemetery for their own use. It is a grassy knoll surrounded by trees, in a remote area which is, nonetheless, fenced. The graves in the center of the cemetery are arranged side by side in straight lines with no family plots or pre-arranged positioning. As long as a persons were 'in union,' they remain with the others of the congregation who are also 'in union.' The graves are oriented to the east: that is, were the person to rise up on his feet, he would be facing east. The cross, as mentioned above, is placed at the foot of the grave so that when all are called from the grave at the Second Coming, they will rise to stand next to their crosses.

Those who are excommunicated are buried on the margins of the cemetery, without the benefit of a cross. Children who died without the benefit of baptism, are also buried on the margins, but not with those who are excommunicated. Unbaptized children, it is believed, will be in the presence of God, but will not be able to see His face. Part of the liability for this restriction lies on those who are responsible for the baptism.[13]

The Orthodox crosses used are the eight-ended type, as opposed to the four-ended Latin crosses. In the past, crosses were made of wood, the main post made of a four-by-four, with the cross sections notched so that they are flush. Little, if anything, is written on the wooden crosses. Occasionally, scratched out by hand, is the statement "slave of God." Most of the wooden crosses are weathering and some of them tipping, with the cross arms falling off.

Recent graves have metal crosses set in cement foundations which are level with the ground. Still, there is little or no identifying information on the several crosses of this type. At recent grave sites, there may be an icon hanging on the cross. This is characteristic during the first forty days as another means of sanctifying the area where the soul may still dwell. After the forty days, the icon is usually removed.

---

[13] The matter of baptism of the young is very important. In one instance, an obviously unhealthy child was born in a hospital. from its appearance, there was a possibility that the child might die. The medical attendants had placed the child in an oxygen tent next to the mother. Soon, a small group of Old Believers came to visit the mother and child. In the group was the lay minister. Apparently, the group had been informed of the frail nature of the child. The nurse left the room so that the group could visit. However, upon re-entering the room, the nurse saw, to her horror, that the child had been removed from the oxygen tent, and was in the hands of one of the men! The lay minister had poured water into a sink and was baptizing the child. The nurse was extremely angry, and shouted at the men to put the baby back under the tent. However, the men could not be hurried. They continued until the baptism was complete. Then, and only then, was the child put back under the oxygen tent. The outcome of this incident is unimportant in terms of the attitudes of the Old Believers. The important issue is that the child, whether it lived or died, was baptized, and it would enjoy all the benefits of baptism in an eternal sense. The urgency was over. The greater danger, that of the child dying before baptism, had been avoided. All those responsible could relax, for they had fulfilled their duties. The immediate family also was contented that the child, should it die, would receive proper care in the next world.

The wooden, decaying, disintegrating crosses with little or no identifying information serve as a powerful reminder that the dead have been consigned to the next world, and that the living must take care of their own. The wooden marker stands, disintegrates, and falls along with the living memory of the deceased in the community.

ATTITUDES TOWARD ELDERLY PEOPLE, AND OF ELDERLY PEOPLE TOWARD DEATH

In the Old Believer community, any older person is referred to as either 'grandfather' or 'grandmother,' again using kinship terms to refer to the sense of union that the Old Believers feel within their group. Old people, especially men, have great stature. One should listen to them. They have survived, and therefore have accumulated great wisdom. They know what is dangerous and where people can make mistakes. They have seen much of this throughout their lives. Therefore, older people have the right to correct anyone, even outside of their particular family. Within their family, they are no longer of functional importance. The immediate parents take charge of the home, and the elderly are simply cared for there. However, in matters of the Church and religion, older people are looked to as a source of wisdom.

The Old Believer attitude toward old age and death seems to be one of frank acceptance. Often in greetings, when one is asked how things are, an older person will sigh and reply "Oh, all is going in an old peoples' way" (*Vsyo po starykovsky*). When questioned further, old people are quick to refer to a number of expressions common among the old. For example, "Old age is not happiness," in which the reference is to the aches and pains and restrictions of old age. Or, "We'll live to the end, but if I die soon, all the better." Frequently, there is an open reference to death: "I'll be dying soon." Or, "I'll soon go into the ground." These statements are made with a matter-of-fact acknowledgment of the physical limitations of age and the obvious approach of death. "Each one has his century." When life is nearly over, these Russian Old Believers do not hang on to it, or avoid mentioning the reality of death.

PART II—MOLOKANS

In the same area of Oregon lives another Russian group, not nearly as large, but equally traditional in their ways. These are Russian Molokans, descendants of those who broke away from the Orthodox Church in the latter half of the 18th century. A large peasant group, dissatisfied with the ceremonialism and obedience required by the Orthodox Church, and inspired by charismatic leanings, they set out on their own religious path, much like the Protestants in western Europe. This movement, unnamed at the time, objected to the ritual ceremonies of the Orthodox Church including the necessity of using the intermediary of a priest; praying towards icons and religious objects which they had begun to consider idolatrous; and other materialistic aspects of Orthodoxy. Instead, they stressed a direct relationship with the Supreme Being through religious inspiration and personal testimonies.

Some became resolutely non-materialistic, even declaring that the Bible was materialistic. This faction later became known as the Doukhobors. However, others in the movement considered this to be extreme, and continued to recognize the Bible as the Word of God. This group later became known as Molokans.[14]

Some of their literate members began reading newly acquired Bibles and discovered issues, especially in the Old Testament, which they considered deserved more emphasis. Consequently, the elders consolidated the beliefs more around the Mosaic law of the Old Testament. Apparently, they not only rejected features of the Orthodox Church—for example the ceremonies, fasting, icons, etc.—but they also reorganized their religious celebrations around the Old Testament Jewish calendar sequence. They are, nonetheless, emphatically Christian.[15]

THE MEETING HALL

Their meeting hall (*sobranye*) reflects much of their philosophy. It is simply a building which becomes a holy place only when prayers are in process and the Holy Spirit is made manifest. Otherwise, the building serves as a hall where administrative meetings of the group can be held, dinners arranged, and a place where all-night vigils can be held before funeral services.

The meeting hall is quite plain. Plain, white shadow curtains hang over the windows. The walls are bare. No crosses, no icons, no pictures. It is an open hall, with portable tables and benches stacked on two of the sides. In one corner, a shelf holds the Bible, the holy writings of key Molokans, and hymnals. During services, benches are set along one side of the hall for the choir. Along an adjacent side, is a bench for the minister (*presvyter*) and the other officials of the church. At a right angle to their bench, are several rows of benches, the front one reserved for the Prophet and the Assistant Prophet. Other men attending the service sit on the other rows. Along the fourth wall are several rows of benches reserved for the women

---

[14]The name 'Molokan' has several legendary sources, all deriving from the Russian word for milk, (*moloko*). One places a prominent group of adherents on the Molochnaya (Milky) River. Another, more popular, relates ethat adherents had ceased fasting and other required outward rituals prescribed by the Orthodox Church. Therefore, during the frequent Orthodox fasts (from animal products, including milk), these people were observed drinking milk. Hence, they were dubbed "milk drinkers."

[15]For their religious stand, Molokans were often persecuted by the tsarist government, and eventually sent into exile along the southern border of Russia, as a buffer against the Moslems. Later, during the Soviet collectivization period in the 1930s, those families who were able escaped over into Iran where they lived for some twenty-five years. In 1949, a sizable group of them, some 150, came to join other Molokans who had come to Los Angeles at the turn of the century. The new group, basically oriented toward agriculture, found it difficult to accommodate to the big-city atmosphere. In 1952, they moved north on the basis of stories and rumors about Oregon.

of the congregation, the more important women sitting on the first bench. In the open space surrounded by this configuration is a table directly in front of the minister, which holds the Bible and other books of the Molokan faith, and a loaf of bread, with salt, brought forward at each service by one of the women. The remaining space beside the table is referred to as 'the circle' (*krug*). It is within the circle that most of the spiritually inspired events take place during the service.

During the worship service, when the congregation stands up to sing and worship, the benches are removed and stacked against the walls. On special days, a dinner (*obyed*) is served after the service. Benches and portable tables are set up in long, neat rows occupying the entire meeting hall.

Thus, the meeting hall takes many forms. Its austere plainness indicates less reliance on a "church" atmosphere, and more on an abstract sense of inner inspiration. Each male member could act in the role of priest for the services, and would be empowered to do so on consent of the congregation.

FUNERAL ARRANGEMENTS AND CUSTOMS

Many of the contrasts to Orthodoxy, enumerated above, are also reflected in the funeral customs. Each member who attends a Molokan funeral plays a personal part in the event, and feels a responsibility and an obligation to attend, even though the travel distance might be quite far.

Funerals are normally held four to five days after the death to allow for relatives and friends to travel the necessary distances to attend. Funerals in Oregon are attended by those from the several locations of Molokans in southern California and Arizona. Likewise the Oregon relatives will travel the same distance for funerals held in those other areas.

The news of a death spreads rapidly through the various communities. Those who can respond—which is most—stop what they are doing and make preparations for the one or two day trip to the funeral. In order to preserve the body for this period of time, the Molokans have no objection to hiring the services of a commercial mortuary for embalming and preparation. The law and practical sense also support this practice since a Molokan funeral lasts almost two days, and usually does not take place until two or three days after the death. It is in this time interval that friends and relatives come as far as 1,000 miles to attend the funeral, console the family, and, as they say, "accompany the deceased to the gates." These visitors are given places to stay with their friends and relatives and receive most of their meals at the prayer hall during the two-day funeral.

THE FUNERAL

The funeral starts just after noon on the first day. The deceased in the casket is dressed in the Russian Molokan clothing, with hands joined at the belt line. In the right hand is placed a folded white handkerchief. (During regular services, which

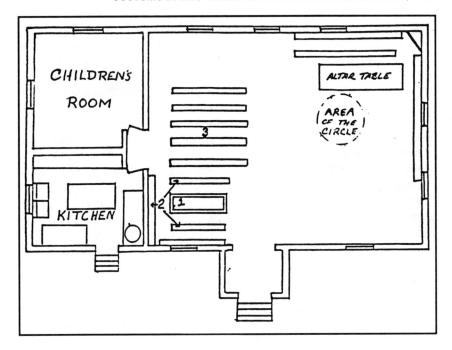

Figure 5. Molokan Sobranye arranged for a wake.
1, deceased in casket; 2, benches for immediate family and kin; 3, other friends.

can become quite emotional, it is common for the worshippers to hold a white handkerchief in hand.) The casket is brought into the meeting hall and is placed on sawhorses in the corner, diagonally across the room from the place where the alter table and 'circle' are located. Benches are placed on three sides of the casket, the end near the door being left open. Members of the immediate family sit in the first rows on the benches around the casket. Other relatives fill up the remaining places, and sit in the back rows (see Figure 5). Each person, upon entering, usually stops at the foot of the casket in order to pay personal, silent respect, then takes a seat on a bench. All afternoon, and on into the evening, the people collect. Some stay only a short time, others stay through the all-night vigil which is followed by the morning service.

During the vigil, the friends who have collected together sing song after song. One person will quietly start a song, and all will join in. At other times, a kinsman or close friend will stand to deliver a tribute to the deceased. In between songs and tributes, people can leave or go into the kitchen where there is a constant supply of hot soup, tea, and food.

According to Molokan belief, the soul of the departed immediately transcends into the other world. For him or here there is peace, there is heaven, there is paradise. One doesn't feel sad for the dead. One of the speakers at a vigil, in honor of the deceased, pointed out with blunt realism, nodding towards the casket, "He doesn't hear us. He doesn't hear or understand anything. What we do here, we do for ourselves. We do this to bring us together and give sympathy to the family." Indeed, the consoling of the family and the unifying of the community is done with elaborate genuineness and touching tenderness.

Occasionally one of the immediate family will be overcome by grief and start crying. Others of the family will normally join in, and often the moment can develop into an intense emotional episode, subsiding only after considerable wailing which can be taken right to the very edge of the casket, and involve touching the deceased.

Molokans also believe that once a person has died, the body loses its spiritual cleanliness. It is, henceforth, treated as unclean. This accounts for the lack of objection to autopsies or mortuary services for preservation, as mentioned above. Those Molokan members who touch the body must wash themselves and their clothing in order to regain their own state of cleanliness so that they can re-join the other members. Members of the family, for instance, who have occasion to touch the body, or touch those who have touched the body, are held apart during the funeral service. After the funeral, they are required to wash themselves and their clothes thoroughly before rejoining the group.[16]

The Molokans do not fear death, nor do they view death as tragic. But they do mourn death, and in their mourning, they strive to comfort those who have lost a relative, a member of the family, or a companion. The funeral becomes a reconciliation.

Grief is open. Upon initially seeing a member of the bereaved family, one usually expresses condolences simply by embracing the person and being embraced, during which time both begin to cry. It is not uncommon, for instance, to see two husky, grown men throw themselves into each others arms and sob openly. After a few minutes, they break apart, one offering the other some halting words of sympathy. They exchange the brotherly kiss characteristic of the Molokans, and part.

Early the next morning, the prayer hall fills to capacity as all members come to pay their last respects. When it is time for the service to begin, the pastor and several elders take their seats at the altar table and arrange the Holy Books on the table. Then, one by one, family by family, people rise from the benches oriented toward the casket, cross the room, with the males giving their entrance prayer oriented on the altar table, and take their seats for the morning service. Gradually

---

[16]Women, during the time of menstruation, are considered unclean, as well. They do not attend services at these times, usually staying home, or, as is said in the old way, "staying in the *banya* 'bathhouse'." However, the matter of the funeral is not concerned with cleanliness, inasmuch as the body is considered unclean. Women can attend the parts of the funeral which do not include the summoning of the spirit.

the room is transformed into the arrangement for the normal service, although the casket remains in the opposite corner surrounded by the immediate family and relatives of the deceased.

The talks at this service are dedicated to the concept of death in the Molokan faith and to consoling the family of the deceased. At one point, one of the chief kin of the deceased is called upon to pay tribute to him or her. The eulogy delivered at the funeral of one of the more respected elders, paraphrased below, contains insights into Molokan values.

> This, our kinsman, is a valuable and respected person, for he is *Rossisky*; that is, he lived in Russia where our ancestors were and where they were sent to exile. He has seen things that we have only heard about. He has heard things we will never think about. He had a chance to hear things from his grandfather and from other elders in those days, and he remembered all those stories. We could ask him, "Dyadya Ivan, tell us about Russia, about Kars, and about how things were," and he would tell us stories of the early days.
>
> He also was a good example of Molokan charity. In Tiblisi (Georgia), we went calling on some friends. They asked us if we knew Dyadya Ivan and we said yes. They told us how he had helped them during a very bad time of repression, a time of terror and famine. He gave them shelter, a hiding place, food, and looked after all their needs. "Thanks to him," they said, "we are now alive."
>
> He did not live in vain; he did many good works; his children and family are here; they are keeping the faith; they are raised in the faith and are strong.

After a song pertaining to funerals from the hymnal, the family moves forward to go into the circle. Male members pick up the casket and bring the deceased into the circle for the last time. The family and kin, on their knees, ask forgiveness and make a request for blessings for the deceased and for all his departed relatives and ancestors as far back as can be remembered, as recited by name by the head of the family. As the family bows forward to pray, the choir and others join in song and await the presence of the Spirit to bless the request. After the blessing is received and confirmed, the family take the casket from the circle, carry it out of the Meeting Hall and on to the cemetery. The lid of the casket is held high above the casket and is not affixed until the very last moment.

In earlier days, the congregation would form a column behind the casket and would walk the entire distance to the cemetery, singing as they went. However, with the present day distances, the custom has been extended to allow the mortuary service to carry the casket in a hearse, accompanied by the family.

THE CEMETERY

At the grave site, the casket is placed over the grave, with the foot of the casket pointing east. After the final prayer by the pastor, amidst the sobbing and wailing of the relatives and the fierce passion of the Molokan songs, the casket is covered and lowered into the grave. Four or five relatives step forward with shovels and offer shovelfuls of dirt around for the other kin members and friends to take and throw token handfuls of dirt into the grave. Then the shovel men begin to shovel dirt vigorously onto the grave. Periodically, other kin and friends step forward to spell them in the shoveling. Once the grave is covered the people slowly depart to their cars. Later, a solid stone marker will be placed at the head of the grave with the name and commemoration in English on one side, and in Russian on the other.

The family members, and any others who have touched them or the deceased, return to their homes to wash and change into clean clothes. Then all assemble back at the Meeting Hall to take part in a memorial dinner (*obyed*). During the dinner, elders of the church and close friends stand to give testimonials and exhortations and to reminisce about the deceased. At the end of the dinner, during the benediction, special prayers are made for the safe return of those guests who have come from afar to attend the funeral.

MEMORIAL CUSTOMS

Ideally, there are three memorial services (*pominky*) with dinners given three days in a row. On the fortieth day, those who wish to, will have another memorial service and another on the yearly anniversary, if the family desires. On these occasions, the elder of the family, during his prayer, will repeat all the names that he can remember of the immediate and extended kin of the family. Also, on Judgment Day (*Sudnyi Dyen*), those offering prayers bring to mind the names of kin who have passed on. However, the full schedule of memorial services is rarely practiced. There also appears to be no designated period of mourning for the Molokans. More consistent with Molokan precepts is to do what one feels is right according to the Spirit. For instance, one widow, approximately six months after the death of her husband, announced and arranged a thanksgiving service (blagodarnost) which was held at the meeting hall. A thanksgiving service normally signifies an expression of joy and happiness, and a time for counting blessings. In this case the woman and her husband, while he lived—albeit terminally ill—had planned to arrange a thanksgiving so that they could publicly express the blessings that they had enjoyed throughout their life together. The thanksgiving she arranged after his death was, then, actually the fulfillment of their mutual wish. There was no seeming contradiction in holding a thanksgiving after the death of a family member. According to Molokan belief there is no need to mourn the death of a righteous person, for the righteous enjoy the reward of paradise.

ACTIVITIES OF ELDERLY PEOPLE

"Honor the hoary head" is an expression that is often used to refer to the elderly. It indicates the honor and respect which is accorded them. They represent accumulated wisdom. When men and women grow older, and their direct responsibilities for raising a family and maintaining a household are considerably lessened, they tend to spend more time doing handicrafts themselves, and teaching handicrafts to the young. Also, the men of the community are looked upon as elders in a religious sense. They usually spend more time in discussing scriptures and writings that have been passed down, and they spend more time in church work and church activities. As elders, they are looked to with respect, and their words have authority.

ELDER ATTITUDES TOWARDS OLD AGE

The attitudes towards old age of the elders among the Molokans vary according to how one's life has gone. Those who have been active in the church feel more comfortable, more assured by the respect given to them by the other members, and deserving the promise of eternal rest when the time should come. They decrease their activities in the overall community, and seem to prefer either to stay at home or to attend church. Movies, television, and frivolous types of entertainment are not common in the Molokan community. There is, therefore, plenty of time to attend the activities of one's church and the activities of other neighboring church areas as well. A respected elder is usually known in all the parishes.

An elderly man who has held a position of high status in his home church will usually be accorded the respect of occupying the place on the bench that he had earned when he was active, even though he may be too old to perform the duties of that status. For instance, a first singer who had been absent from church for some time due to old age or illness would be accorded the place on the bench as the first singer should he return to visit the church. He may, and frequently does, defer to the current first singer with the proper gestures of gratitude for the respect.[17]

SUMMARY AND CONCLUSION

These two Russian communities living outside the Soviet Union and away from their cultural roots in Russia have managed quite successfully to preserve their traditional attitudes toward old age and customs for death and grieving. A good case can be made to show the similarities between the attitudes and customs of the two communities, and their common, ancient Christian roots. Obviously, while having common roots, the Old Believers, who precede the Molokans in history by

---

[17]Singing is an honored activity among the Molokans. They consider it an obligation to sing, for through singing, one renders service to God. It is usually during periods of intense singing that the Spirit descends and is manifested by members of the congregation. Songs of blessing and of prayer are sung by men only. Also, a song is begun by a man, either by invitation or on his own initiative. Rarely are women asked by the men to start a song. This usually occurs after the main service, during the rejoicing. At these times, the entire congregation sings with full, spirited voices.

some 150-plus years, serve as a base culture from which the Molokans have borrowed extensively. Nonetheless, there are distinct differences. These differences reflect the variations in the religious interpretations affecting the rituals which follow in reaction to death in each community (see Figure 6). Central in the rituals is the presumed location of the newly deceased spirit. Molokans assume that the spirit of the deceased has immediately transferred to the domain of God. Old believers anxiously conduct forty days of prayer on behalf of the deceased, at which time, according to their teachings, the spirit may be accepted into heaven.

Differences between the communities are also seen in the historical and social experiences, and the subsequent development, of each community. The Old Believers, on one hand, have insisted on preserving over the years an unchanging ritual, yet have faced limitations in their ability to do so. The Molokans, on the other hand, have interpreted their rituals in ways that would fit with their new insights and understandings.

The Old Believer rituals reflect the medieval ethic of the Orthodox Russian peasant. Prior to the church reforms which gave rise to the Old Believers, the overall Orthodox peasantry was nominally loyal to the church and tsar. With the reforms, large numbers of the population, unwilling to accept the changes, sought safety by exodus. Separate Old Believer groups, remote and isolated, gathered

Reaction at Death	Among Old Believers	Among Molokans
Disposition of the Dead	Rapid	Prolonged
Ritual Period of Liminality	Periodic memorial services over the first year. First forty days of greatest importance.	Generally confined to the funeral period. If desired memorial services any time afterwards.
Extent of Grief	Restrained. Restricted to periodic memorial services over the first year.	Unrestrained at time of funeral, when the spirit of deceased leaves. Of little note afterward.
Assurance of Acceptance by God	Tenuous. People pray for mercy on behalf of the deceased over forty days. Priest also intercedes with prayer.	Members responsible to gather for blessing. Visible sign manifested at the funeral.

Figure 6. Reactions at death among Old Believers and Molokans.

their immediate kin under the guidance of their spiritual leader: either a priest or a 'lay pastor.' They were independent and self-sufficient. Old Believer communities, widespread and often out of contact, felt no compulsion to notify others at a distance in order to assist in the blessing, as do the Molokans. The crucial blessing was performed locally by a priest or 'lay pastor.'

Moreover, in their Orthodox understandings, Old Believers continue to hold that the soul of the departed is still somehow associated with the body for the first forty days. The body should not be disturbed by embalming or any other artificial means to preserve it. The funeral is accomplished quickly. Their ritual is fashioned to support this. Consolidation of the family is incorporated according to these precepts.

On the other hand, the Molokan community, starting with a few and adding adherents over time, was never large. The separate groups were—and are—relatively small, cohesive, and interrelated. Kinfolk and friends are supportive by their presence. Moreover, having gathered together, they contribute in the request for blessings of the Spirit. Hence, Molokans come from afar to be present at these and other crucial events. The funerals are delayed in order to allow the kin and friends to attend. The interpretation that the soul has left the body of the deceased at death allows not only for the delay but also for the necessary artificial preservation of the body during the delay.

Additionally, Molokan customs reflect the individual responsibility each member has assumed in matters of the Spirit. Hence, the Molokans take a far more active participation in the mourning, the wake, and the funeral service than do the Old Believer individual members. Having denied themselves the services of a priest who bears the bulk of the responsibility for intercession and conduct of prayers, the Molokan members must assume joint responsibility for requesting blessings and preserving the cohesion of the group. This is mirrored, as well, in their open grieving, both individually with members of the family, and collectively at the vigil.

With the Old Believers, dependence on the priest and the institution of the Church brings comfort and reassurance. The request for blessings resides with the priest or the lay substitute for the priest. Sanctions are administered by him, as well. Various categories of burial placement serve to underscore and emphasize social norms. These understandings preserve group solidarity and encourage desired social behavior. Furthermore, there is a concerted effort on the part of the Old Believer parishioners, as urged by the kin, to pray for the forgiveness of the deceased, especially during the first forty days after death. Although these prayers are performed alone on an individual basis, there is a group acknowledgment that this happens. Moreover, there is confidence that others will pray for them at their death. These are assurances and rewards of keeping one's self 'in union.'

The attitudes toward old age in both communities are generally similar. Those in elderly status are respected for their wisdom and years. The elderly in both communities face the realities of age and death with frank openness. Their stark references to their own approaching death are compensated by their confidence in the promises of the next world.

In both communities the death and departure of a member, especially a righteous member and one who has taken active part in the maintenance and furtherance of the group, creates a disruption in social continuity, a disruption that is mended only with the active participation of all in attendance. It is a reconciliation for the people suffering the loss of the newly deceased, and in a wider sense, a reaffirmation of traditional religio-cultural values. The continuity of those values undergoes subtle stresses and strains in daily life within a larger host society, and now, a more direct threat by the loss of a member of the group, especially an elder who represents the virtues of traditional culture. Yet the reconciliation is complete with the proper blessings and assurances, and the immediate kin are comforted and eased back into activity. The group continues to function. Life goes on.

ACKNOWLEDGMENTS

A portion of the research for this report was made through a grant from the Oregon Committee for the Humanities, an affiliate of the National Endowment for the Humanities.

CHAPTER
8

Fallen Leaves:
Death and Grieving in Toraja*

Jane C. Wellenkamp

*In the four chapters that follow, we are asked to consider societies that urge on
their members restraint in the face of death. The presence of death is accepted
and inevitable, and society expects composure when it comes. The first of these
chapters, by Jane Wellenkamp, draws on her work among the Toraja of Indonesia, whose exotic death rituals have long been of note to anthropologists.
Wellenkamp focuses her analysis on the Toraja handling of grief, rather than on
the exotica of the funeral and burial ritual. The question she raises is how people
handle the emotional storm of grief when they regard death as fated and are
granted only limited opportunities to express their feeling of personal loss.*

*   *   *

Although death only recently has become a topic of interest in anthropology, a
longstanding concern with religion and ritual has indirectly provided us with
several accounts of cultural practices and beliefs concerning death and the afterlife
(see Palgi and Abramovitch's 1984 review). Commenting on the variation in
cultural responses to death, one set of observers remarks:

> What could be more universal than death? Yet what an incredible variety of
> responses it evokes. Corpses are burned or buried, with or without animal or human
> sacrifice; they are preserved by smoking, embalming, or pickling; they are eaten—
> raw, cooked, or rotten; they are ritually exposed as carrion or simply abandoned; or
> they are dismembered and treated in a variety of these ways (Huntington and
> Metcalf, 1979:1).

Some anthropological accounts of death describe public mourning behavior and
ritual which, along with death practices and eschatological beliefs, vary considerably from culture to culture (Rosenblatt et al., 1976; Huntington and Metcalf,
1979; Eisenbruch, 1984b). Benedict (1934), writing about the cultural differences

*The author conducted fieldwork in Indonesia together with Douglas Hollan in 1981-1983 with the
permission of the Indonesian Institute of Sciences (L.I.P.I.) and the sponsorship of the Universitas
Hasanuddin. Funding for the research was provided by a National Institute of Mental Health
traineeship and by the Wenner-Gren Foundation for Anthropological Research.

113

between Pueblo and Plains Indians, highlights the contrasting ways in which the two groups approach mourning: Pueblo Indians "do not deny sorrow at death. . . . They treat it as loss, and as important loss. But they provide detailed techniques for getting past it quickly and with as little violence as possible" (1934:109). In one Pueblo area, on the evening of the fourth day after the death (following various ritual actions expressing a formal breach with the deceased),

> . . . the chief speaks to the people telling them that they shall not remember any more. 'It is now four years he is dead.' In ceremonial and in folklore they use often the idea that the day has become the year or the year the day. Time has elapsed to free them of grief. The people are dismissed, and the mourning is over (Benedict, 1934:110).

In contrast, Plains Indian cultures emphasized the indulgence of violent, uninhibited grief: "All their behavior stressed rather than avoided the despair and upheaval that is involved in death" (Benedict, 1934:111).

The cultural response to death—the way in which the body is handled, beliefs about the afterlife, cultural expectations regarding proper mourning behavior, and so forth—would seem to have an important effect on individuals' experiences of grief. To date, however, there have been few studies of the personal experience of grief in other cultures (Rosenblatt et al., 1976:14) and thus it is not clear to what extent the grieving process varies culturally (in intensity, duration, etc.), either as a consequence of the cultural response to death or because of other factors (for example, the nature of interpersonal attachments in a particular society).

In part, the lack of information on individuals' experiences of grief may derive from an assumption on the part of some anthropologists that there is a close correspondence between public mourning behavior and individuals' emotional responses to death. Rosaldo (1984:189) notes that many anthropological treatments of death center around symbolic analyses of formal ritual behavior and tend to conflate ritual processes with individuals' grieving processes (cf. Lofland 1985:173). The problem with this is that death rituals "do not contain the entire process of mourning. It is a mistake to collapse the two because neither ritual nor mourning fully encapsulates or fully explains the other" (Rosaldo 1984:192). Thus, anthropologists interested in grief and mourning need to supplement their studies of cultural practices and rituals with information on mourners' personal experiences in both ritual and non-ritual contexts, and in private as well as public settings.

When in 1981 I left to conduct research among the Toraja in the mountains of South Sulawesi (Celebes), Indonesia, I went with the specific intent of investigating personal experiences of grief among a people with elaborate and in some respects highly unusual death practices, including keeping the body of the deceased in the house for weeks or months prior to the funeral. This chapter reports some of the results of my research, beginning with a brief description of Toraja death rituals followed by a discussion of beliefs about death and the fate of the soul, the treatment of the dying person, and aspects of grief and mourning. My central concerns in this chapter are: 1) to discuss aspects of the cultural response to death in Toraja and provide mourners' reactions to, and evaluations of, their culture's death practices and beliefs; and 2) to examine similarities in, and differences between, Toraja grief reactions and those reported in the Western psychological literature and by the other authors in this volume. I argue that some Toraja practices and beliefs facilitate mourners' adjustment to loss, while others typically are experienced as onerous or anxiety-provoking. I also suggest that there are both major similarities and differences between Toraja grief reactions and those reported elsewhere, and I explore some of the factors responsible for these. In conformity with the conventions established by the editors, I define mourning as "the overt, public expression of grief" and grief as "the experience of distress following a loss." By grieving process I mean "the conscious and unconscious psychological processes set in motion by loss."

Much of the material I present derives from loosely structured interviews conducted with Toraja villagers regarding their bereavement experiences (and other aspects of their lives). The following provides a brief introduction to some of the individuals whose statements are quoted in subsequent pages.[1]

> **Ambe'na** ('Father of') **Doko** is a poor, middle-aged Christian man. His wife and one of his children died suddenly about a year before my fieldwork.

> **Indo'na** ('Mother of') **Lu'pang** is a young, recently married Christian woman and the mother of an infant. One of her older sisters drowned during my fieldwork and her father died some months earlier.

> **Indo'na Rante** is a middle-aged Alukta woman of elite status and moderate wealth. Several of her children have died and she herself nearly died in childbirth.

> **Indo'na Tiku** is a divorced, middle-aged Christian woman with five children of her own and two foster children. She is a teacher at the village elementary school and is well-liked by many in the community. She was raised by her maternal grandparents and two sets of foster parents.

> **Nene'na** ('Grandparent of') **Limbong** is an elderly Alukta man possessing much wealth and high status. He is a prominent political and ritual leader in the community. He remarried after his first wife died and has thirteen children.

> **Nene'na Tampang** is an elderly Christian man of moderate means and status. His wife died of typhus during my fieldwork.

---

[1] All of the names are pseudonyms. Only direct quotes taken from tape-recorded interviews are placed within quotation marks. In extended quotes, my remarks are placed within parentheses. Some of Nene'na Limbong's statements are from interviews conducted by Douglas Hollan.

Tasik is a young, unmarried man who attends school in Rantepao (one of two Toraja towns). His foster mother, Indo'na Sampe, died after a period of illness during my fieldwork.

To Minaa Sattu is an Alukta ritual specialist (a *to minaa*) in his late forties. He is married and has six children and one stepchild.

ETHNOGRAPHIC BACKGROUND: THE TORAJA AND THEIR DEATH RITUALS

The Toraja (or precisely, the Sa'dan Toraja) are wet rice agriculturalists, numbering around 350,000. They speak an Austronesian language and traditionally had a stratified social system consisting of three major classes: nobles, commoners, and dependents or slaves. Prior to the early 20th century, the Toraja were politically decentralized and relatively isolated from outside groups. Today, a majority of the population is Christian (primarily Protestant) but many in the rural areas continue to adhere to the traditional religion, Alukta.[2]

Alukta centers around the worship of ancestors and gods (*nene' sola deata*) through the performance of various rituals and the observance of numerous prohibitions. Many of the prohibitions serve to separate two opposing, but complementary ritual spheres: the east or 'smoke-ascending' (*rambu tuka'*) sphere, concerned with the promotion of prosperity and fertility, and the west or 'smoke-descending' (*rambu solo'*) sphere, which includes death rituals (for a fuller discussion of the nature of this division see Wellenkamp, 1988a). Although smoke-ascending rituals are also dramatic and rich in symbolism, the Toraja are best known for their elaborate death practices. One of the more striking sights one encounters when entering the Toraja area is the massive limestone cliffs, dotted with burial vaults and (in some locales) wooden balconies on which nearly life-sized statues of the dead stand. (See Figure 7.)

The Toraja have two main death rituals: funerals and a form of "secondary burial" (Hertz, 1960; Huntington and Metcalf, 1980) called *ma'nene.'*[3] I provide a brief description of these as a background to the discussion. Considerable regional variation in terminology and beliefs and practices exists in Toraja; my material is largely based on fieldwork conducted in the village of "Paku Asu" (a pseudonym) located in the northwest region.

In many areas of Indonesia, death is treated as a gradual process rather than an abrupt event (Hertz, 1960; c.f. Ramsden, this vol.). Among the Toraja, there is often a lengthy interval between a person's physical demise and the performance of his or her funeral, especially in the case of wealthy, high status individuals. The

[2] See Hollan (1988a) for a discussion of religious change in Toraja.

[3] There is some disagreement about whether the ma'nene' should be classified smoke-descending, smoke-ascending, or is intermediary between the two. See Wellenkamp (1984:48-49).

delay is caused by several factors including the need to make preparations for the funeral and the desire to await an auspicious date. During this period—which may last several weeks or months, and in rare instances, years—the body of the deceased is kept in the house, either wrapped in several layers of cloth or injected with formalin and placed under reed mats or in a wooden coffin.

Alukta adherents do not formally acknowledge the death and refer to the deceased as *to makula'*, 'person with a fever,' or *to mamma'*, 'sleeping person.' The deceased is offered food and drink, informed of the departures and arrivals of household members, and in general treated as if he or she were still alive (cf. Hertz, 1960:36, 48; Metcalf, 1982:45). Throughout this period, someone must remain at the house to guard and watch over the body.

Although the death is not formally acknowledged, the village nevertheless is considered polluted by the presence of the deceased and the staging of any smoke-ascending ritual is, in principle, prohibited. One way of alluding to the death is to say, "A leaf has fallen in the village" (*Den daun kayu rondon*

Figure 7. Toraja cliffside burial vaults and balconies containing statues of the dead (*tatau*).

laku tondok), a statement that refers to the littering of the houseyard with leaves which are swept away each morning in an effort to keep the village clean and tidy.[4]

Not until the funeral begins is the deceased referred to as *to mate*, literally, 'dead person.' The funeral itself may take several days or weeks to conclude as the body of the deceased is gradually moved from inside the house to the houseyard, to the funeral ground, and finally to the burial site. All Alukta ritual is structured around food offerings and animal sacrifices. For funerals, pigs and water buffalo are the main sacrificial animals; in former times, human sacrifice (in the form of headhunting) was also an integral element of the funerals of wealthy nobles.

In conjunction with the offerings and sacrifices, funeral songs, flute music, and wailing may be performed, and various effigies and memorials may be constructed, depending upon the age, status, and wealth of the deceased. There are several levels of funeral ritual. Children and poor, low status adults are given the most simple funerals, while older, wealthy nobles are accorded the most elaborate, "highest" ones. Christian funerals retain many traditional elements including funeral songs and wailing, and the slaughter of pigs and water buffalo. Many funerals are held in the dry season, following the rice harvest.

The *ma'nene'* ritual involves bringing offerings to the burial tombs, cleaning and repairing the gravesites, and attending to the remains of the dead (for example, repairing damaged coffins, rewrapping the remains). The continued attention paid to the body of the deceased, even after burial, is explained in terms of the survivors' feelings of love and respect and their expectation that in return for safeguarding the remains, they will receive blessings from the deceased. As one man said, the Toraja care very much about the bodily remains, even though they appear worthless, because it is believed that the souls of the deceased, seeing that they have not been forgotten, will bring assistance to the living. (Cf. Badone's and Weigand and Weigand's discussions in this volume of the value placed on the bodily remains.)

Although there is some wailing at the *ma'nene'*, it is intended to be a happy occasion on which the community meets again with the ancestors. The *ma'nene'* is held annually in some areas of Toraja, while in others (including Paku Asu) it occurs at seven to ten year intervals. It is performed after the rice harvest and before the funeral "season" begins. Christians are officially prohibited from taking part, and yet Christian participation continues to various degrees in a number of places. (For further information on Toraja death rituals, see Wellenkamp, 1984; Volkman, 1979, 1985; Nooy-Palm, 1986.)

---

[4] The use of botanical metaphors to refer to the person, and to interpersonal relationships, is common.

ATTITUDES AND BELIEFS ABOUT DEATH AND
THE FATE OF THE SOUL

The Toroja believe that each person has a predetermined life-span, or *sunga'*, the thread of life' (Nooy-Palm, 1979:129). Many deaths are considered natural deaths in the sense that the deceased are thought to have reached the end of their *sunga'* (*nalambimo sunga'na*). Some say that because the time of death is predetermined, one should not worry about one's own death and that one should be accepting of the deaths of others. When Nene'na Tampang's wife died, To Minaa Sattu said (in a somewhat self-congratulatory way) that while others in the community were upset over her death, he was not, because he felt she had just reached the end of her life. Similarly, Nene'na Limbong said that while many people are fearful of dying, he is not, even when he goes on long journeys outside of the village, because he believes we die when our time has arrived. The notion of a fateful death is often expressed in terms of having been 'called' (*natambamo*) or 'taken' (*diala*) by the ancestors or, for Christians, by God.

Although there is an emphasis on viewing death as a matter of fate (in part, it seems to me, as a means of coping with death), some deaths are viewed as premature in the sense that those who die are thought to have not yet reached the end of their *sunga'*. Deaths caused by suicide, homicide and, according to some people, accidents and (reportedly) poisoning and magic fall into this category (see the chapters by Lieber and by Preston and Preston in this volume for discussions of similar beliefs). Also, the Toraja believe that death can be hastened by the performance of activities normally associated with death (e.g., wearing black; sleeping with one's head facing south, the direction of Puya, the afterworld), and by one's own misdeeds as well as those of family members and forebears. When several of Indo'na Rante's children died, for example, she suspected that her husband had been conducting illicit love affairs with other women which had resulted in the deaths. When a specialist was consulted, however, he concluded that the deaths were a matter of fate and had not been caused by any transgressions.[5]

Death is also said to be hastened by imprudent living (e.g., continually becoming angry and upset (Wellenkamp, 1984:94; Hollan, 1988b:10)). Conversely, people claim that one will be assured a long life if one lives properly and responsibly (cf. Simmons, 1945:221). The deaths of children and young and middle-aged adults are more likely to be viewed as premature than are the deaths of the elderly.[6]

---

[5]There are three culturally recognized categories of illness: saki biasa, 'common' illness, saki to lino, illness caused by humans (through the use of poisoning and magic), and saki deata, illness caused by transgressions.

[6]People do not necessarily agree on which deaths are fateful and which are premature.

Past events are commonly viewed as harbingers of a death. For example, Nene'na Limbong interprets several dreams he had before his first wife died as foretelling her death. In one, he was sleeping alone in the forest; this, he now believes, represented the period when he would guard his wife's body during her funeral (a period when the surviving spouse is identified with the deceased and is symbolically separated from the rest of the community). When Tasik's foster mother died, more than one person said that before her death, they had seen her soul (*bombo*) and thus knew she would die in the near future. The souls of those about to die are believed to temporarily leave the body to wander around, especially at night. Only a small minority are thought to be capable of seeing such souls (*pakita bombo*), and it is said that if they report to others what they have seen (and attempt to warn others of their impending deaths), then they themselves will be the first to die.

Puya, the traditional land of the dead, is said to be located to the southwest of Toraja between Kalosi and Enrekang (cf. Metcalf, 1982).[7] Traditionally it was believed that in order for the souls of men to gain entrance to Puya, they were required to have scars produced by burns on their forearms. Up until about twenty years ago when the practice was discontinued, scarification was performed by groups of boys roughly between the ages of five and ten years, with each boy responsible for producing his own scars.[8] Paku Asu men, who were around the age of thirty and older in 1983, have these scars. Many say that the scarification process was very painful but that they were afraid that if they did not participate, after death their arms would be cut off before they would be allowed entrance to Puya. Entrance is believed to be denied altogether to certain people, including the souls of those who commit suicide (*mentuyo*) and the souls of very young children who are buried not in the limestone cliffs but in a tree or kettle.

Life in Puya is thought to closely resemble the present life (cf. Rivers, 1926 and Ramsden's chapter in this volume). The souls of the dead are said to have bodies and to live as humans do in this world. If one is poor in this life, then one will be poor in the next; if one is wealthy, then one will be wealthy in Puya. Beyond this rudimentary description, villagers do not usually elaborate or speculate and they prefer not to consider at length their own deaths.[9] As Nooy-Palm notes, the Toraja "are more interested in what after death the souls are going to do to the living than in questions of what their private fate will be" (1979:124). In general, people avoid thinking about death and other undesirable and unfortunate events. To dwell on such things, people say, will only endanger one's mental and physical health

---

[7]Heaven is thought to be a separate place from Puya, a belief that deters some Alukta Toraja from becoming Christians because they do not wish to be separated in the afterlife from their Alukta relatives.

[8]According to some informants, ear piercing served the same function for girls.

[9]Ritual specialists have more detailed knowledge about the afterlife. Also, some people claim to have visited Puya in their dreams. See Wellenkamp (1984:42).

(Wellenkamp, 1988b), and will increase the likelihood that something bad will happen.

Although people are reluctant to think too much about their own deaths, some people do make advance preparations, including, for example, leaving instructions regarding details of their funerals and burials. The survivors are said to be obligated to carry out any such instructions, and if they fail to do so, people claim that the soul of the deceased will somehow make his or her displeasure known. An illustration of what can happen if such instructions are ignored is provided by Indo'na Tiku. She related that her foster mother had requested that she not be buried in her family's *liang batu* 'cliffside vault' but rather be placed in a *patane* (a separate burial structure built on the ground). The reason for her request was that she did not want the decay from the other bodies in the vault seeping down on top of her body. At the time of her burial, Indo'na Tiku had not yet been able to have a *patane* built; furthermore, she did not think it was possible that a dead body could feel anything or have any preferences. Thus, she did not tell anyone about her mother's request. Later, however, when there was a great deal of difficulty getting the body into the vault, Indo'na Tiku was asked if her mother had made any special requests about her burial. Indo'na Tiku then "remembered" her mother's instructions and repeated them to the others. Even though her mother had been a Christian for several years, an offering was made to her soul, which was told, "Be patient. Later when there's an opportunity . . . a gravesite will be made for you." After three hours of unsuccessful attempts to maneuver the body into the vault, it finally went in. Later, at the *ma'nene'* ritual, Indo'na Tiku kept her promise and moved her foster mother's body to a separate burial tomb.

THE DYING PROCESS

When someone is injured or ill and near death, his or her close relatives are called to attend to the dying person. Culturally recognized signs of impending death include delirious speech, often interpreted as conversation with the souls of the dead, an inability to recognize those present, and requests for what are considered luxury food items, such as poultry, water buffalo milk, palm wine, and various kinds of fruit. Indo'na Rante said, "if our parent sends [us] to buy fruit, we understand that this [person] must die. Thus, we're happy if we give them all [he/she desires] and he/she eats until satisfied." If one is remiss in fulfilling a dying person's request—for example, if one decides to wait for the local market instead of going to a distant market, and the person happens to die in the meantime—then, according to Indo'na Rante, one will "certainly be upset" and one will "always remember it."

Some die suddenly (*mate poso*) without any forewarnings, but even in the case of illness, people say that there may be no outward indications that death is imminent. Indo'na Tiku said that she was not called to her grandmother's house before she died, even though she had been ill for two weeks, because there had been no signs that she was dying. Sometimes self-diagnoses are made. To Minaa Sattu reported that on the day of his father's death, his father sent him to attend a ritual, but after he left, his father called him back to the house because he thought he was dying. He waited for To Minaa Sattu, his youngest child, to arrive and then he died.

I was never present when someone was dying, but people say that the atmosphere in the house of someone near death is subdued. One woman described how one feels when in the room with a dying relative:

> [We are] just quiet. Because we are sad to see someone suffering. Thus, we want to speak [but the words] won't come out, we want to walk [but] it is as if someone were holding onto us. Thus, our body is [too] heavy—[too] heavy to stand, to converse—because our attention is just focused on the person who is suffering.

At the time of death, recognized as the cessation of breathing (and the separation of 'breath' (*penaa*) from the body), the dying person should not be left lying down but rather should be cradled in a relative's arms, "just like when a child is given the breast."[10]

Once a death occurs, close relatives who are not present are informed of the death. As Geertz (1973) reports for another Indonesian group, the Javanese, the death is not usually mentioned directly; instead people are often told, at least initially, that their relative is very ill. It is considered too emotionally shocking to bluntly convey news of a death to close family members. When Tasik's foster mother died, for example, a messenger was sent to Rantepao to inform him and to accompany him back to the village the following day. Tasik was initially told that his foster mother was gravely ill. At first, he said, he did not suspect that she had died, but that night, "[I] felt it in my heart, you know, that probably my mother had died." The next day, when they set out for the village, his companion informed him of her death.

GRIEF AND MOURNING

The Expression of Grief

In many Indonesian and Malaysian cultures, emotional restraint and equanimity are highly valued. This is also true for the Toraja, who in their daily lives attempt to avoid the experience and expression of intense emotions, particularly negative or unpleasant emotions such as anger, fear, and sorrow. The emphasis on emotional equanimity is not linked to self-reliance and autonomy as in the Cree case

---

[10]Similarly, among the Alorese of eastern Indonesia, "when a person is dying, it is customary for one of his grown children, or failing this, some near kinsman like a sibling, to hold the sick person on his lap much as parents hold children" (DuBois, 1944:152).

(see Preston and Preston, this volume), but rather stems from: beliefs about the potentially detrimental effects of intense emotions on one's mental and physical health; an abiding concern with maintaining smooth interpersonal relationships; and a sense that it is unseemly and disgraceful to appear visibly upset (cf. Lieber, this volume) especially in the case of anger (see Hollan, 1988b).

Although emotional upset is avoided, at the same time the Toraja believe that in certain special contexts, including a death, it is appropriate and even salubrious to express intense emotions (Wellenkamp, 1988b). Thus, while in everyday life, separations (from both people and things) should be met with emotional calm, even casualness; following a death the expression of grief through (limited) periods of crying and wailing is both expected and encouraged. (See Figure 8.) The Toraja thus differ from the Javanese and Balinese, among whom there is reportedly very little crying, at least public crying, following a death (Geertz, 1973; Rosenblatt et al., 1976; Siegel, 1986). Siegel reports that among the Javanese, "one seldom sees expressions of grief or mourning" (1986:257) and that

Figure 8. A Toraja woman, with her head covered, wailing during a
pause in a burial procession.

even the family members closest to the deceased "often, perhaps usually, are *iklas*, 'detached,' within minutes after a death" (1986:258).[11]

Crying on the part of Toraja adults is usually subdued, while wailing (a combination of crying and calling out to the dead, interspersed with sobbing) can be loud and dramatic. Wailing, however, is limited to certain times and places; for example, it should occur near the deceased's body or some representation of the deceased (such as an effigy), and while people may wail immediately after death and during the funeral, wailing should not occur during the time the body is kept in the house (the one exception being when a close relative of the deceased returns home for the first time following the death). Unlike in Kapinga as reported by Lieber (this volume), in Toraja anyone who desires to wail is free to do so. It is recognized that not all those who wail are expressing sadness over the loss of the deceased. Some may wail out of sympathy for the bereaved, or because they are reminded of the previous deaths of those close to them.

Viewing the Remains

Viewing the deceased's body before it is wrapped is very important to many Toraja. I was often told that children of the deceased have a strong desire to view the body, and my observations and interviews support this claim. Indo'na Rante, for instance, said that she is glad she did not settle permanently in the city because then she probably would not have been able to see her mother's body after her death. I also found that the photographs taken of Indo'na Sampe's body before it was wrapped were requested more than any others. These photographs were sent to Indo'na Sampe's son in the coastal city of Ujung Pandang and to other relatives who had not been able to view the body. Siegel (1986) maintains that among the Javanese, photographs of the corpse and coffin are also very popular and play an important role in the grieving process. I return to Siegel's discussion later in the chapter.

The importance attached to viewing the body is further illustrated by Nene'na Limbong's response to his first wife's death. Nene'na Limbong was in Ujung Pandang when he received word that if he did not return to the village soon, he would not see his wife again (that is, she was dead and would soon be wrapped). At the time there was considerable political unrest in the rural areas and it was considered risky to travel outside of the city. Despite the dangers, however, Nene'na Limbong petitioned for permission from government officials to return to Paku Asu and after several days, his request was granted. He felt, "better that I am killed than I don't see my wife." By the time he reached the village, several days

---

[11]However, Javanese fictional characters often cry privately in connection with loss (see, for example, Pramoedya, 1975). Also, Wikan's (1987) work among the Balinese suggests that crying in private may be more common than previous reports have indicated.

after her death, her body had already been wrapped; seeing her face was so important to him, however, that he ripped open her wrappings.[12]

Even after the burial, many people look forward to occasions (such as the *ma'nene'*) when they can view the remains again. When I told one older man that in America the body of the deceased is buried in the ground, his response was: If ground burials are used, how can the body be seen later? If, instead the body is put in a rock tomb, two, three, or five years later, one can open the graves and see the body. Even grandchildren can see their grandparents, he added.[13] It is not clear to me precisely why, from a Toraja perspective, viewing the deceased's body is important. My guess is that for the survivors, viewing the body shortly after death helps to confirm the reality of the death; later viewing of the remains seems to offer a tangible link with the deceased (cf. Siegel, 1986; Volkan, 1981).

If, following death, the body cannot be recovered (e.g., in cases of drowning), then for Alukta Toraja, a substitute body is constructed.[14] On the one occasion on which I observed this process, the body was made from burlap sacks and dried bark; a photograph of the deceased was attached to the head which was then wrapped with red cloth. The substitute body is treated as the actual remains—it is wrapped, wailed over, and entombed.

Bowlby (1981), citing studies conducted on grief in Western societies, maintains that a period of yearning and searching for the deceased is a common aspect of the grieving process. One would expect that searching would be prolonged or intensified if the body is not recovered. Although my material is limited on this subject, the practice of constructing a substitute body would seem to be of great psychological value to the bereaved, especially for the Toraja, given the importance attached to the remains of the deceased.

Guarding the Body

The period during which the body is kept in the house is a very trying one for the survivors. With the exception of Indo'na Tiku who said that some people do not mind having the dead body stored in the house because they feel "at least we are still together," family members consistently reported that they and others they know find it burdensome. One source of stress is the smell of the decaying body. Although it is hoped that the preparation of the body (by wrapping or injecting it with formalin) will eliminate or at least reduce the odor, it is not always effective

---

[12]Her body by that time had become swollen and "very rotten." Nene'na Limbong was apparently surprised and probably distressed to find her body in this condition. He only briefly discussed the incident and then abruptly changed the subject. Although people tend to emphasize the survivors' desires to view the deceased, many are also concerned that their own bodies be viewed at death (see Wellenkamp, 1984:193-194).

[13]However, at least one person (Indo'na Rante) is frightened by the sight of the remains. See Wellenkamp (1984:240).

[14]The substitute body is not constructed until the onset of the funeral.

and I was told that some bodies smell intensely.[15] In addition to the odor, the family must contend with the *bombo* 'souls' which are thought to be present throughout the time the body is in the house. According to some people, the survivors should endure their discomfort and refrain from complaining about their situation as a sign of respect and affection for (and to avoid offending) the soul of the deceased.

The presence of the deceased is also burdensome because it serves to constantly remind people of their loss. One woman said that prior to her mother's funeral, she would sit and look at her mother's body and think, "Oh what a pity, when my mother was alive [she would say] . . . 'Here's some hot water. Drink some.'" Many said that once the body is buried and thus no longer in constant view, one's grief is considerably lessened. One person, for instance, said, when the body is in the house, "we look at [the dead body]. Our sadness comes again. . . . But when [the body has been moved to] another place, even if we remember [the deceased], if we don't see him/her with our eyes, we don't remember as much."

The practice of keeping the body in the house interferes with the way in which many Toraja would prefer to deal with death and other distressing events, which is to try to avoid dwelling on, or even thinking about, the matter. Keeping the body in the house, while very distressing, has the consequence, it seems to me, of forcing people to deal with their loss. When the body is later removed during the funeral, people seem both relieved and saddened by the final departure of the deceased.

Mourning Regulations

With the onset of the funeral, the death is formally recognized, and the period of mourning begins. Among the more salient mourning requirements still observed by Alukta adherents are the wearing of black clothing and abstinence from certain foods. The type and length of abstinence are set by tradition (thus the responsibility for ending the taboos does not lie with the mourners themselves (see Counts and Counts, this volume)) and vary depending upon the level of the funeral and the specific role played by the person observing the taboo. The primary taboos concern eating rice and, during shorter periods, any cooked or heated foods or beverages.

Most villagers view these taboos as very demanding and some decline to 'fast' (*merok*) for fear they would not be able to tolerate the restrictive diet. Serious consequences, such as blindness, insanity, or a swollen stomach, are said to result from breaking these taboos. Indo'na Rante reported that during her mother's funeral, when after two or three days of abstaining from rice she could no longer tolerate it, she resumed her normal diet. Her father has since told her several times that the reason she has lost many of her teeth is because she broke this taboo.

[15] I personally did not encounter any intense odors when visiting houses in which bodies were stored.

In addition to clothing and food restrictions, one person is designated to remain in the close vicinity of the deceased (sleeping next to the body at night) and to participate in various offerings to the soul of the deceased. This role is performed by the spouse (if he or she is still alive) or by a close relative of the deceased, often a grandchild.[16]

With the end of the funeral rites (which for high level Alukta funerals does not occur until a few days after the burial), the official mourning period comes to an end and any taboos still in effect are lifted for all those except the spouse of the deceased. In the Paku Asu area, the spouse of an Alukta adherent continues to observe certain mourning regulations until a ceremony called *pakendek* (literally, 'to raise' or 'elevate') is held, after which he or she is considered 'pure' (*malino*) again. The *pakendek* is a simple marriage ceremony performed between the surviving spouse and another person who is also widowed. The timing of the ceremony is left up to the participants, although a common time for holding pakendek is after the rice harvest.

Following the ceremony, the couple stay together for a few nights, during which time they are permitted, but not required, to have sexual relations. After this, if the couple so desires, they may continue to live together as husband and wife. Otherwise, a simple divorce ceremony is performed and then each is free to marry whomever he or she pleases.

Responses to Loss

Some of the physical and psychological responses to loss are similar to those described in the literature on grief in Western societies. Decreased appetite, a sense of confusion, and a lack of interest in one's work are culturally expected and commonly reported. Ambe'na Doko described how he felt after the deaths of his wife and child: ". . . my feelings were like a crazy person. My head wasn't thinking in a fixed way. What it was that I was thinking in the house, I don't know. I never thought about the work in the fields. . . . My heart was very full."

Suicidal thoughts on the part of the bereaved are recognized as a possibility and occur occasionally, but they do not seem to be especially frequent (in contrast to the Huichol case described by Weigand and Weigand, this volume). Although a very popular traditional story recounts the suicide of a young man following the death of his sweetheart (Wellenkamp, 1984:122-123, 263), I know of no actual cases of suicide following a death (although suicide does occur in other contexts (see Hollan, 1990)).

Although their sources and targets vary, feelings of anger or hostility in connection with loss have been reported in several studies (Counts and Counts, this volume; Weigand and Weigand, this volume; Rosenblatt et al., 1976; Bowlby,

---

[16]Christians do not observe specific mourning practices. However, black clothing is customarily worn and the body of the deceased is watched over by close relatives.

1981; Rosaldo, 1984), and such feelings are given ritualized expression in many cultures (Rosenblatt et al., 1976). Among the Toraja, however, anger and hostility are not culturally highlighted and do not seem to be consciously experienced by many bereaved people. I did not observe any overtly angry or aggressive behavior following a death (although such behavior is uncommon in other situations as well), and people did not spontaneously report feeling angry. When asked about such feelings, many denied having them. For instance, when I asked Indo'na Rante if those who have experienced a death sometimes feel angry, she replied, "Oh, no! (Oh, they don't feel angry?) The only thing is that we don't know anything. Our thinking is confused/dizzy." One of Nene'na Tampang's daughters, when asked the same question, responded, "No, not in my opinion. How could one be angry?! (In America, sometimes people feel angry because they think, Why am I the one who has been left behind?) No, no. As for here, no." Her neighbor added, "Here, there isn't any of that. It [the death] is not intentional."

For Ambe'na Doko, angry feelings are incompatible with the sadness of grief. When asked, for instance, if he had ever felt angry in connection with his wife's death, he replied, "I'm never angry now. Because I feel the loss. . . . People here, if their wife is dead, or their mother or father, or anyone in the family, they don't have any anger because they think of the death." The only instance I recorded in which someone expressed some anger following a death involved a man who told me that even though the local doctor had said that his wife had died of typhus, he was certain that she in fact had been poisoned.[17]

The survivors' distress following a death is said to be greatly exacerbated by the hardship involved in financing and preparing for the funeral. At the same time, however, many aspects of the funeral, such as providing tributes and memorials to the deceased, are viewed as a source of consolation and satisfaction (see Wellenkamp, 1988b:489-490). People also report that it helps to be reminded that others are also struck with misfortune and loss. Indo'na Lupang said that when the family members of the deceased hear other people wail (those who perhaps were not particularly close to the deceased, but join in the wailing because they are reminded of their own losses), "[We think], 'I am not the only one who has suffered a loss. This person has also suffered a loss.' Then we feel a little bit better. We think, 'I have a friend. Someone who has suffered a loss. [Someone who] has experienced hardship/grief.'" Another person who has lost six of his thirteen children said,

> Often it happens that I feel sad/upset. I usually say, "I'm not alone. Lots of other people are like that [have had children die]." That's medicine [for me]. If . . . I were

---

[17]It is possible that angry feelings are experienced but are not easily expressed or disclosed given the strong cultural disvaluation of anger (see Hollan, 1988b). Also, it may be that angry or hostile feelings are symbolically expressed during the funeral through the slaughter of animals, especially water buffalo (which are identified with the deceased). In former times, headhunting may have involved the expression of anger over a loss.

to think about it [the deaths], probably I would be dead [by now]. [I would be] thin if I were to think of that, but—but, lots of people, lots of people throughout the world [have suffered losses].

Funeral songs also remind the bereaved of the inevitability and non-discriminatory nature of death. (Cf. Obeyesekere's (1985:144) discussion of the Buddhist parable of the mustard seed.)

The Toraja recognize that there is variation in the duration and intensity of people's responses to loss. In some cases, particularly those in which repeated losses have occurred, feelings of sadness and distress are recognized as potentially intense and persistent, leading possibly to illness, insanity, and even premature death (for similar views regarding the dangers of intense or prolonged grief, see the chapters by Lieber, Preston and Preston, and Weigand and Weigand). In others, it is said that feelings of grief may be relatively mild and brief. People say, for example, that there are those who do not particularly love their spouse and when the spouse dies, they quickly remarry.

A complete lack of distress following the death of a close family member, however, is considered either not possible or somewhat contemptible. Tasik, for example, when asked if there are people who are struck by a loss at death but do not feel anything, responded, "No. They must feel something. Everyone, when there's a dead person, must feel something. [They] feel upset/grieved." Indo'na Tiku said that those who are arrogant and those who have not experienced much hardship or suffering in their lives may not grieve at death. But, according to Indo'na Tiku, "Those who do not know sadness and difficulty are despised."

Although several researchers have emphasized the cultural downplaying of grief in Indonesia, I suspect that in many groups, some distress is expected, and a complete absence of grief is viewed negatively. Geertz (1976:97) reports, for example, that a Javanese man attributed an illness he suffered to suppressed anger felt over the fact that his son's mother-in-law did not seem at all grieved over her daughter's death. Similarly, Acciaioli (n.d.) reports that a Bugis woman (from the Lindu area of Central Sulawesi) "was incensed with the rapidity with which her son's wife remarried after her son's death, calling Hasu [the wife's new husband] a 'man of ten hands'—always ready to grab at what lies around unused, even if he has no right to it."

Among the Toraja, there are two general, culturally encouraged ways of dealing with loss. First, although some expression of grief through crying and wailing is expected and encouraged, the bereaved are often counseled to not allow themselves to be preoccupied with the loss or dwell on past memories of the deceased, especially once the body has been entombed and the funeral has been completed (cf. Preston and Preston, this volume). One man said that he tries not to think about his dead parents and grandparents or to visualize their faces for if he did, "I might get tuberculosis. Or go crazy. That is how illnesses of the mind arise. Don't think [of them]. Don't visualize [them]." He added, "If [our dead relatives] are visualized, how can we make a living?" (that is, he would be too sad and depressed to work).[18]

Second, the survivors are encouraged to focus on the ways in which their relationship with the soul of the deceased continues, but on a new, transformed basis. That is, the bereaved are reminded, through funeral songs and other means that while the deceased is now separated from the living, his or her soul continues to exist and can provide the survivors with spiritual protection and blessings (cf. chapters by Waugh and by Weigand and Weigand).

Siegel (1986) and Hoskins (1987) report similar cultural themes among the Javanese and among the Kodi of West Sumba (Indonesia), respectively. Siegel, for example, maintains that the Javanese response to death entails a focus on the soul of the deceased as a source of blessings, and an avoidance of specific memories of the deceased. "When death arrives," according to Siegel, "it brings with it a view of the person that is intended to replace thoughts of him or her alive" (1986:260). Photographs of the corpse and coffin (and other aspects of the funeral) serve to create a fixed, unchanging image of the deceased which, Siegel argues, obviates the need for active grieving as we think of it. According to Siegel, "it is a mistake to speak of mourning in a Javanese funeral if this means working through memories of the deceased in order to put them to rest" (1986:259).

An avoidance of specific memories of the deceased, and a focus on the continuity of the relationship between the living and the dead are also noted by Hoskins (1987). She maintains that Kodi funeral songs, sung not by the official mourner who remains silent but by another woman (often a complete outsider), replace "personal memories with evocations of socially appropriate emotions—how a mother feels at losing her child, how a wife feels in grieving for her husband. Sorrow is 'generalized' in terms of categories rather than worked through in terms of personal experience" (1987:181). This cultural process, according to Hoskins,

> . . . goes very much counter to Western expectations; we tend to see mourning as the gradual exteriorisation of grief, as the living come to accept the fact that the deceased is no longer among them. Freud has referred to this as the 'work of mourning,' and he describes grief as a process whereby memories are re-lived over a certain period of time until the ego is able to accept the separation. . . . Kodi death songs, in contrast, do not focus on the content of individual hopes and memories but rather on their links to enduring social roles . . . and the culturally specified emotions and attitudes which go with these roles. Moreover Kodi do not lose all of their dead as thoroughly as we do. Certain named ancestors continue to hover as invisible presences in the village. . . . Others . . . recycle their essences to their descendants. . . . Living and dead are members of the same enduring social community (1987:181-182).

---

[18]However, visualizing one's deceased relatives in dreams is a very positive experience (see discussion on page 131).

Siegel's and Hoskin's accounts both emphasize contrasts between Western and Indonesian cultural responses to loss; furthermore, Siegel maintains that the grieving process itself is absent or at least attenuated for individuals in Javanese society. In Toraja, many aspects of the cultural response to death seem to assist the bereaved in adjusting to loss, and in particular, the belief that one's relationship with the soul of the deceased continues and that the deceased is a potential source of blessings and protection does seem to make the experience of grieving very different.

The cognitive and emotional "saliency" (Spiro, 1984:325-330) of this belief for Toraja is evidenced by the fact that many people have had dreams of their deceased relatives aiding them in some way.[19] Such dreams are interpreted as actual communication with the soul of the deceased and are believed to foretell future prosperity.[20] Indo'na Lu'pang had had three dreams of her sister in the months following her death: "The first time when I dreamed [of her, she] came bringing clothes. The second time, [she] brought letters. Lots of them. The third time, she came bringing clothes. Pretty clothes." Indo'na Tiku dreamed that her foster mother brought her vegetables to feed her pigs. She said, "Elders say that's good. . . . They say [it means they] will always respond to/ supply their children. . . . if someone who is dead comes and helps us" (that is, the dream indicates that the soul of the deceased is still concerned with the well-being of the dreamer and sometime in the future will send blessings in one form or another). Another woman dreamed of her aunt who "came bringing a basket full of vegetables. [She] brought them for me. Yes! Because she loved me that mother. . . . She was walking that way. I called out, 'Oh, my mother has come bringing vegetables.' She gave [them to me]! . . . I was very happy."

In contrast to Siegel's findings regarding the absence of active grieving in Java, however, I found that in Toraja, while the bereaved were expected and encouraged to respond to loss by avoiding specific memories of the deceased, their personal experiences did not always match cultural expectations. Many villagers, including Indo'na Lu'pang's mother and Tasik's foster father, continued to recall memories of the deceased and to be preoccupied with their loss even after the conclusion of the funeral. Indeed, one woman claimed that

> it's not possible that our grief will disappear, disappear completely, once we have experienced a death. When there are a lot of people around, yes, usually it disappears. But when there's another dead person, and we go there [to the house of someone who has died], grief arises in the heart again. Thus, we always remember.

Also, during the course of my fieldwork, I encountered one case of severe and prolonged grief. Over two years after the deaths of his wife and child, Ambe'na

[19]The psychological importance of cultural beliefs needs to be established by anthropologists and not just assumed.
[20]See Hollan (1989) for a discussion of Toraja dream beliefs.

Doko was still very much upset by and preoccupied with his loss. Sighing repeatedly, he told me that since the death of his wife "[when] people come bringing women here, I don't accept them. I refuse them! Because . . . I think within my heart, I imagine in my eyes or in my heart, that my wife is probably within the house. I am thinking short-term. I—because of all of these children, I [should] think long-term. [There are] eight of them." Ambe'na Doko's lengthy grieving is probably related to the sudden nature of the deaths; both his wife and child died suddenly in the same month (see Bowlby, 1981:180). Also, since Ambe'na Doko is Christian, he has not taken part in a *pakendek* ceremony, which might have helped him adjust to the loss.

CONCLUSION

Toraja death practices and beliefs are elaborate; I have discussed only some of the many elements of the Toraja response to death, focusing on those of most importance to mourners. What is it like to experience bereavement in a culture with such elaborate and unusual death practices? My material indicates that some aspects of Toraja practices and beliefs, such as mourning regulations, the costly nature of the funeral, and the practice of keeping the body in the house, are experienced by mourners as very burdensome. In one area of Toraja where the survivors' responsibilities to the corpse are especially demanding (Wellenkamp, 1984:206), nearly all of the residents have converted to Christianity as a means of escaping from the "heaviness" of the traditional regulations. However, many other aspects of the funeral and burial, and of cultural beliefs about death and the soul—including, for instance, the belief that many deaths are a matter of fate; the reminders that the survivors are not alone in their suffering; and the practices of viewing the remains and providing tributes and memorials to the deceased—seem to provide much consolation to the survivors and to facilitate their adjustment to loss.

How much do Toraja grief responses vary from those reported elsewhere? What accounts for similarities and differences between the Toraja and other cultural groups?

(1) One of the most central aspects of the cultural response to death in Toraja is the emphasis placed on maintaining the tie between the living and the dead. This is connected to what is probably the most dramatic difference between grieving in Toraja and grieving in many Western cultures. Although an emphasis on maintaining some tie between the living and the dead is present in many places (Lifton, 1979:98-99; Malinowski, 1954:49), in Toraja this tie is culturally reinforced in several ways, including through periodic interaction with the remains of the deceased during the *ma'nene'* ritual, and through dreams of the dead which are interpreted as direct communication with the souls of the deceased.

The possibility of continued contact with the soul of the deceased, along with the belief that the soul is a potential source of protection and material blessings means that important aspects of one's previous relationship with the deceased theoretically can be continued (see Wellenkamp, 1984 for a discussion of interpersonal relationships in Toraja). On the basis of interviews and other sources of information, I believe that for many Toraja, this is not just a theoretical possibility but an experiential reality. That is, although Toraja recognize and outwardly state that when someone dies he or she is irretrievably gone, their sense of loss is lessened by the fact that some important aspects of their relationship with the deceased are maintained. As Indo'na Tiku said when discussing her dream of her deceased foster mother bringing her vegetables, "thus, indeed, it's like . . . . . . like when they were still alive."

Waugh (this volume) reports similar experiences among his Burhani informants who also believe that continued contact with the soul of the deceased—in this case, the soul of their shaikh—is possible. Waugh notes that Burhani continue to speak of the shaikh in the present tense and maintain that since his death his accessibility to others has actually increased. It is important to note, however, that for both Burhani and Toraja the experience of grief is still a difficult and painful one.

(2) Although the existence of feelings of anger has been reported in several studies of grief, angry feelings do not seem to be commonly experienced following a death in Toraja. The apparent absence of anger is probably due in part to the belief that many deaths are predestined. Bowlby (1981) suggests that anger is more common following a death judged untimely, and is directed toward those held responsible for the death. This interpretation is consistent with the presence of anger in Kaliai (Counts and Counts, this volume) where many deaths are believed to result from the malevolent actions of spirits or other human beings. Similarly, Weigand and Weigand (this volume) report that anger is common among the Huichol when witchcraft is the suspected cause of death.

The absence of anger in Toraja is also consistent with the general cultural attitude toward misfortune. From a Toraja perspective, the ideal way to respond to misfortune of various kinds is a combination of resignation, attempting not to think about one's misery, and adherence to the traditional belief that by continuing to carry out one's spiritual obligations, one will eventually recoup one's losses (see Hollan, 1988b:60-62; Wellenkamp, 1984:105-115).

(3) Finally, in their view of the dangers of intense grieving and in their attempt to limit the expression of grief, the Toraja are similar to the Cree, the Huichol, and the Kapinga (see chapters by Preston and Preston, Weigand and Weigand, and Lieber) but very different from the Kaliai (Counts and Counts, this volume). Some differences exist between the Toraja and the three former groups. For instance, among the Toraja, expressions of grief are not as formalized as among the Huichol and Kapinga, and are allowed for a much longer period of time than among any of the other groups. Furthermore, unlike in Kapinga, Toraja mourners need not fear

that their grieving will attract the dead and thus endanger people's lives, and in fact, Toraja mourners are encouraged to engage in some crying and wailing as a means to prevent later illness.

However, when the Toraja are compared to the Kaliai, among whom dramatic expressions of sadness and anger are commonplace following a death, the similarities between the Toraja and the Huichol, Cree, and Kapinga seem striking. Among the Toraja and perhaps among all four other groups as well, the attitude taken toward the expression of grief is consistent with, and perhaps derives from, cultural attitudes toward emotions in general. The extent to which the open and dramatic expression of grief at death is viewed negatively or positively in many cases seems to be related to the way in which emotional expression in general is evaluated and managed in a particular culture.

ACKNOWLEDGMENTS

I thank Larry Mai for putting me in contact with the editors of this volume. I also thank Michael Lieber, Peter Ramsden, Dorothy and David Counts, and the other participants of the conference for their valuable criticisms and suggestions, and for their friendship. I am also very grateful to Douglas Hollan for helpful comments on several drafts of the paper.

CHAPTER 9

Death and Grieving among Northern Forest Hunters: An East Cree Example

Richard J. Preston
and
Sarah C. Preston

The chapter by Richard and Sarah Preston focusses on the Cree people living east of James Bay in the Province of Quebec in Canada. The chapter is an example of collaboration by researchers coming from different perspectives after more than a quarter century of research and residence among the Cree. Their perspectives differ because Richard began his sojourn among the Cree as a trained anthropologist whose primary interest was in mental culture, values and symbolism. Sarah first accompanied Richard in her role as wife, and came to know the Cree as neighbors and friends. She has since taken an undergraduate and graduate degree in anthropology and followed her own independent work among Cree with a special interest in women's work and life histories. The Cree place great value on personal autonomy and competence and do not intervene in each other's lives. Their restraint, even in the face of death, is a hallmark of their culture. The Prestons, after so many years of residence among the Cree, also speak of their own grief at the death of their friends.

*   *   *

INTRODUCING THE CREE

The patterns of death and grieving we represent here are, we believe, characteristic of the native people living on the Quebec side of the coast of James Bay, Canada. Our interpretations are derived from experiences shared during sojourns between 1963 and 1984, and from narratives of events which we take to be true to life and of value as they provide a guide for living. It is a simple but difficult fact of human mortality that some of our friends would meet their deaths over this twenty-year-period. These deaths would have been difficult for us to discuss a few years ago. We are comfortable now presenting these events with some objectivity derived from some years' passage of time, and with the social distance of this volume's comparative research.

The cultural events we discuss in this chapter were considered to be traditional by Cree adults in the 1960s. By traditional we mean a recognition of continuity with the past which gives people a feeling of authenticity. Eastern Cree traditional culture is characterized by an ideal of personal autonomy, with pervasive attitudes, themes, and values of interpersonal composure and reticence. They attend to subtle cues in interpersonal relations, but have a remarkable capacity for non-interference in the personal autonomy of others (R. Preston, 1976, n.d.; S. Preston, 1986). The Cree cultural focus or premise is an ideology of egalitarian personal autonomy. The authority of the individual person is primary; giving orders to another is insulting, for all are responsible for their own actions. Most perceptive sojourners in this area are impressed, first with the superficial similarities to, and later with the fundamental differences from, our own ideology of individualism.

For many Cree people, the 1970s and 1980s have seen a turning away from traditional attitudes and sensitivities, a diffidence towards listening to narratives for guidance, and the adoption of more cosmopolitan values (J. Blythe, P. Brizinski and S. Preston, 1985). We doubt our ability to make a precise assessment of the effect of these changes on the topic of dying and grief, so we focus on the not too distant 'traditional.' On the other hand, the last grieving we were a part of occurred in 1984, on the death of Malcolm Diamond, an exemplar of tradition and the old chief at Waskaganish. We were aware at that time that grief was powerfully felt and expressed in traditional mourning, while concern for the behavior of the departing spirit seemed to be much less evident. The death of the old chief may have signalled the end of an era, but some of the events and feelings we shared at that time were certainly traditional.

We wish to emphasize three main themes from Cree Culture:

1. People can and should control themselves in sustained synchrony, or cultural coordination, both with human others in personal community, and with non-human others in an inclusive community of human, spiritual, and animal persons;
2. Living and dying are full of contingencies that are only partly predictable and to which human beings must adapt by trying to meet them competently.
3. Life is viewed metaphorically as a journey. All who make this journey in its various aspects—from the daily following of trails, to longer hunting trips, to seasonal periods of camp movement through a hunting range, to movement through the life course—are guided by paths. The narrative is such a path.

Our presentation centers on several narrative texts which provide primary evidence for our discussion of cultural aspects of Cree dying and grieving. By providing examples of what others have done and the consequences of their actions, Cree narratives traditionally offered guidance for living one's life competently and wisely. Stories are intended to draw the listener into vicarious participation with the narrator and with the persons involved in the events recited, so that one can learn not only to tell the story but also to guide one's life accordingly.

CREE BASIC ATTITUDES, NOTIONS, AND CONCEPTIONS

Death is at once a commonplace event and one with much significance. Hunters chronically pursue, cause, and perceive death of the animals that are their food as part of the ordinary process of living. Cree believe that animals give themselves to humans gladly (or they would never let their whereabouts be known) and yet, somehow, not willingly (because they try to escape). That is, it is the purpose of animals to give themselves, so that humans can obtain their food and live. The human who is capable, once given a clue to the location of the animal, of playing out the strategy and action of the hunt, and who then is competent in the respectful use and disposition of the remains, is destined to continue to be the recipient of these covert gifts of love (R. Preston, 1975:198-234). The consequences of incompetent hunting or disrespectful acts toward the animals through the casual disposal of their remains are expected to be failure and hardship.

Human death, in contrast to the death of an animal, is an intensely emotional event, and dangerous in its potential for difficult consequences. It is not necessarily a crisis, but it *may* become one. Like birth (S. Preston, 1982), a person's death is an occasion for unusual effort at self-control. As with the person in the act of giving birth, self-control is expected of the person who is dying, and it is hoped that others present will not give way to fear. If you are dying, a controlled death is the ideal for your own composure and for the composure of those around you. If others are dying, you hope that they will not only die well, but will continue to manifest composure in their activities after death, and that they will soon depart.

Death is normally regarded as a letting go of the body, and a subsequent departure of the spirit. In some narratives, this is given the explicit metaphor of a voyage or journey, when the person goes out to meet his or her death, perhaps not much interrupted from life's voyage. There is an ideal of a good death, one that maintains human and other-than-human relationships much as they were before death. This emphasis on continuity constitutes a moral pattern for the subsequent behavior of spirits of the deceased, both human and other-than-human. The behavior of the spirit is the final test of that person's true character and attitudes towards the living. On the occasion of a human's death, people watch for signs of the person's final intentions. At the same time, people watch to see the animals' intentions towards the human survivors. The animals may leave the region that was used by the deceased, requiring the survivors to move elsewhere or starve, or they may choose to make themselves available for hunting and eating to the surviving humans. Cree say that the deceased human may influence these animals' decisions to make themselves available. Belief in the ability of the spirit of the deceased to influence animal behavior is dramatically illustrated in the following recollection by an Anglican priest:

> An old Indian woman . . . died about the middle of April, when the snow was beginning to melt. . . . This was my first funeral and it had a somewhat surprising climax. After the service I walked at the head of the funeral procession with her husband, the chief mourner, who had his capote over his head. It was very solemn. As he and I walked together in front of the coffin towards the graveyard, a flock of Canada geese returning from the south suddenly appeared over the trees. A person who has never lived in the north could not realize the thrill of the first wild goose call in the Spring. Often it means the end of hunger. It always means fresh meat.
>
> The whole procession dropped on its knees. The pallbearers crouched and the bereaved husband dashed back to his tent for his gun. Meantime the whole congregation were answering the call of the geese. As they came overhead, Manitoshans raised his gun and brought down two geese with a shot from each barrel. One dropped on the coffin. A smile came over his face as he handed the geese to his daughter. "I knew she'd bring me luck," he said (Renison, 1957:31-32).

The man's words speak for themselves, with the same kind of mystical certainty that the arrival of the geese expresses. If it seems odd to us that only the widower ran for his shotgun, we may wonder what restrained the others. Were they simply afraid of scaring the geese by their movement, or did they recognize who sent the geese, and to whom?

SOCIAL DEATH CONTRASTS WITH DYING IN COMMUNITY

"Social death" is an awkward concept in the Cree case, because ostracism is such an extreme measure, and because it is normally an individual's autonomous action that brings it about. The most extreme form is the mythic windigo condition, a person's transformation into a monstrous, damaging state of being. Windigo is thought to be the dying of a person's humanity through a loss of self-control, a giving up of community, and becoming a hunter and eater of humans (R. Preston, 1980).

The Cree consider death to be natural more than social or symbolic. It may be rendered premature by sickness, by accidents, by errors in judgement or actions, or by hardship or sorcery. Nonetheless we suspect that the Cree think that even a death by sorcery is primarily a natural death with social and symbolic causes, as Evans-Pritchard explains for Zande witchcraft (Evans-Pritchard, 1937). There is a notion of fate, at least to the extent that no one, not even a powerful conjuror can give himself more days than he was allotted (perhaps at birth). While anyone may be caught earlier by one of life's many hazards, we are not aware that the Cree think of this as unfair. They do understand, certainly, that premature death is an unfortunate event that requires some effort to accept; it is not considered an imposition of fate. This understanding seems to us to emphasize the essential contingency of the Cree world.

People differentiate between good and bad deaths largely on the basis of what we currently call 'cognitive control.' For the traditional Cree the good death is a well composed act of 'going out to meet one's death.' We are not certain whether we can say confidently that people—like the animals they hunt—seek the ideal of dying a good death, not willingly, but gladly, but the idea has an intuitive fitness to it. That is, a person ideally goes to meet his or her death with composure and an acceptance that he or she may engage with, but not delay, this event, since this mysterious meeting implies a human destiny that will lead to some further experience.

The following narrative is an example of meeting one's death with composure. The understanding that death is a continuation of life's journey is implicit in the behavior described. Also implicit in the narrative is fore-knowledge and acceptance of an event which could not be delayed. The preparation for further experience on the part of the man making the transition from life into death is explicit in the way he chose to dress. Dressing in one's best clothes for this journey is the means through which one shows respect for the relationships one may be about to enter into, and one hopes that this respect will be reciprocated.

THE DEATH OF PHILIP DIAMOND
(REMEMBERED BY MALCOLM DIAMOND)

I'm going to tell you the story about when my brother died. That morning we were supposed to go out to cut some wood. We had some snares over there and we were going to check those snares. That morning he got up very early. I wasn't even out of bed yet and he was all dressed, all ready to go. He came and stood by the doorway of the bedroom and he asked me when we were leaving. My wife had made a new pair of moccasins and new mittens for him and he'd never worn them before. That morning he dressed up, he wore those moccasins and the new mitts she had made for him. He was all ready to go by the time I got up. Then the old lady got up too, to make some breakfast for us. My brother never used to do that. This was the first time I knew that he was up so early and so anxious to go.

While I was eating my breakfast, the telephone rang. It was the chief, asking me if I could be here that day. He told me he wanted me to be here because they were bringing two men in from the trapline. Their mother had just recently died and he wanted me to meet the plane to tell them about the death of their mother.

When we left here on the skidoo my brother was sitting on the sled, behind. He seemed OK. He didn't look like he had any problem at all. He used to carry this stick that he used as a cane, and as we drove along over there where those small islands are, up the river, not too far from here, he threw his stick ahead of the skidoo to alert me. When I stopped and looked back he said, "I see some white birds on the island." When we stopped near the island the white birds flew off to the other side where there were small willows and bush. So he told me to go and get our snowshoes. We usually leave our snowshoes when we come down the river, and hang them up in a tree. I told him, "We can't waste time too long here because we have to get back soon." My brother said, "You shouldn't say that. If we get those white birds, then the old lady will have something to eat. We catch rabbit and she doesn't eat rabbit. She doesn't have any other kind of meat except what you can buy that she can eat." I guess he was thinking of my wife, that she won't have anything to eat even if we catch some rabbit in our snares, because she didn't eat rabbit. That's the last time he talked to me. Those were his last words.

I decided to leave him there and go with the skidoo to get our snowshoes. I'm sure it was only about a 15 minute ride and then I would be back again. I told my brother to wait there and look for the white birds in case they fly somewhere else. I left the gun and said, "If you see them out in the open away from the willows maybe you can go and shoot them." That's when I left him there, and he was OK. He didn't say he was feeling sick or anything like that.

When I was on my way back from the bush, I saw another man on his skidoo. He didn't have anything else with him. He waved and I stopped and he stopped too. I asked if he saw my brother over there where I had left him. He said, "I saw him and I gave him a ride a little ways. He said he wasn't feeling very well." So we both started back. We didn't drive very long and we could see where my brother was. He wasn't sitting up anymore. He was lying on the small sled and he had his face down. He didn't even look up and show he could hear the skidoos coming. I was thinking to myself, "He doesn't even move. He must be in great pain, why he doesn't move when he hears the skidoos coming." Then we stopped and still he didn't move. The other man didn't get off his skidoo. He waited for me to go and see what was happening. He said, "I don't think he's breathing anymore." I guess he could tell because he wasn't moving at all. When I got closer I pulled the hood (of his parka) up because it covered his face, and right away I knew he wasn't breathing anymore, he was gone. I said, "He's gone. He's not breathing anymore." And the other man said, "What are we going to do?" I said, "We have to go back. You drive the skidoo and I can sit at the back." So we came back to the village on one skidoo.

When Sarah asked Malcolm if he thought Philip knew this was to be his last day, Malcolm answered, "I'm sure there was a way that he knew this was going to be his last day, because when he got dressed, he dressed just like he was going somewhere." Although Philip Diamond met death deliberately, with self-knowledge and composure, it is possible that his departure from this world took place more quickly than he had anticipated; an event which he was prepared to meet, but could not postpone. It would seem that he had hoped to speak to his brother one last time, but the expected journey began before he could say his farewells to his relatives. When he was buried, his family left him dressed as he was, assuming that he had prepared himself for this journey by wearing the new moccasins and mitts.

Because they cannot know the future, either in this life or the next, Cree do not know when or if departing loved ones may be seen again. Unforeseen death may intervene. It is, therefore, important to say farewell before leaving on a journey of lengthy duration or distress. Saying farewell affirms relationships and is a recognition of friendship. It is important for those who are dying as well as those who are living to be able to make this statement. Even though people may be afraid, it is considered strange and unfriendly to fail to make their goodbyes when there is the chance to visit the dangerously weak or dying person. Dying persons share the attitude that it is important to say farewell. Ideally, even in the extremity of dying, Crees will make their goodbyes in a way that comforts the survivors.

Accidental or conjured death may pre-empt composure, but we do not know whether the Cree think that the manner of death influences or determines experiences in the afterlife. It is our impression that the afterlife, being unseen, is necessarily left vague in Cree beliefs. If the character of spirits is known at all, it is known only vaguely. Spirits speak only rarely or indirectly (as in the gift of the geese noted in Renison above) before they depart for good. Most people would be skeptical of claims of knowledge based on mere surmise. Following the example of the Cree, we prefer to leave our consideration of the spiritual realm indefinite.

Successful hunters have to be practical, to see tangible signs in order to know the character of a person, animal, or spirit. In the contingent universe of the Cree there are no guarantees. A person does not know what might be found at the end of a track. There may be caribou there, but one may never catch up with them. It is up to the hunter and to the animals who are unseen.

In the same way, one may not know what is on the other side of death, but the following near-death experience of a nine-year-old girl provides some indication of what Cree might expect. The narration suggests that the dying may enter into relations with spirits whom they encounter on their journey. These may be spirits with whom one already has a reciprocal relationship or they may be spirits with whom one hopes to establish new relationships.

A CHILDHOOD VISION
(REMEMBERED BY ALICE JACOB)

I was so sick, it seems like a dream, but at the same time, I thought I went away. I thought I was walking in the clouds. I came to a large house with a door in the middle. When I came to the door it opened and I went inside. Straight ahead of me I didn't see anyone, but on either side I saw a fence and a stairs. And I saw children, just children, very happy children.

During this vision Alice thought she was met by a tall man dressed in white. She laughed as he came toward her and she felt happy. But the man told her she was going to go back to her mother. When she was told this, instead of turning to go, she waited. She was given a small dish which she thought contained food which she was told to take home to her parents. Then she turned to go. She turned again to see the man hold his hands up to her. . . . When she woke she was told she had not been sleeping, her eyes had been open and she had been gazing upward. She had tears in her eyes and she felt as if she had just returned from being away. "I just went out and came back again." She tried to give to her mother the food she thought she had brought with her, but her mother had only been aware of her illness, not of her 'journey,' and did not understand what she was talking about.

In Alice's near-death narration, she meets a spirit person who is generous to her, but does not let her stay in this happy place. She had no foreknowledge of this meeting, or indeed of her travel to another realm and return to this world. She follows a new path, discovers what is there, and then returns with this new knowledge. There is no certainty that she or anyone else will again take this path, or encounter the man dressed in white. But it might happen, or another path might be taken, and other spirits might be met. As with their hunting, the Cree cannot know the outcome in advance, but only have some idea of what has happened in previous hunts, and a sense of how to conduct oneself along the path to discovery.

The following narrative provides an illustration of foreknowledge and preparation for death. The events exemplify a good death. Although these events may have been experienced by relatives as sudden and unexpected, they were experienced by the dying man with composure, self-control, and understated competence.

I'M ALMOST FALLING OFF MY CHAIR
THE DEATH OF JIMMY MOAR
(REMEMBERED BY ALICE JACOB)

Near the time when my foster father would die, I knew about that. I really loved him, like a father. . . .

Late one evening, I went to see him. He knew I came into the house because he heard me talking. He was sitting in a chair and he said to me, "What are you doing?" And I said, "Nothing, I just came by, dropped in for awhile." He said, "How is my grandchild?" I told him, "I already put her to bed." The he said, "Take care of my granddaughter all the time. Take good care of her. I'm almost falling off from my chair. That's all I can sit here. I'm very tired. It's quite awhile since I was blind. I really love you because we brought you up. I always stopped Maggie from beating you or spanking you. I am very happy we never hurt you."

Then I said to him, "Why are you talking like this to me?" I felt in my heart there was something I didn't like, the way he was talking to me. I felt like crying when he said all this to me. His wife said to him, "Don't talk that way." Then he said, "I wanted to tell you so you would be ready." I never even sat down. I was standing when he was talking to me. So I decided to go outside because I was wondering about what he said to me. I told him, "I'm leaving now." I said, "Good night" to him, and he said, "I love you, my child." Then I went home.

As soon as I went out from their house, he started to sing a hymn from the hymn book. He sang in English and he stood up while he was singing. Then he felt for the string, (which was about the house for him to get around on his own) and started walking while he was singing. After he finished singing, he asked for his suit-coat. Then his wife asked him, "Why do you carry on like this?" He acted very different, and he didn't tell her why. Then he went to bed; he lay down on the bed with his suit on. My foster mother thought he had gone to sleep.

My foster mother went to bed too, and when she touched him on the bed, she thought she couldn't hear him breathing. There was another old woman there with them, my foster mother's sister. Then she made sure, she looked at him and watched him to see if he was already gone. He wasn't breathing any more. And my foster mother told her sister, "Go and get Alice;" When I got there I checked and he had no pulse. So I believed what he told me (S. Preston, 1986:71-72).

When Jimmy Moar told Alice he was almost falling off his chair, his meaning went beyond the literal statement that he was so tired that he felt as if he might fall out of the chair. He was also stating, indirectly, that his death was near, and he was preparing himself and his family for his leave-taking. He made every effort to create a disciplined experience; expressing his respect and concern for those persons closest to him, saying his goodbyes, and reaffirming his relationship to his daughter and her child. He also expressed his respect for those persons he might be expected to meet on his journey from this life into the next through singing and dressing in his best clothes.

It is the rare individual who can both create and sustain the balance between the ideal and action achieved by Jimmy Moar. Others strive to achieve this ideal through their efforts to meet death as one should meet life: with equanimity and conscious deliberateness imbedded in reticence, friendship, and as much self-reliance as possible. The response of the old man's wife to his words and actions is a reminder that subtle cues are not always readily understood, or accepted, even among Crees. She seemed to avoid sharing his foreknowledge, refusing his cues or teasing about them instead of taking them into composed acceptance and acknowledging his indirect message that he was about to leave them. Although Alice was reluctant to act on the basis of what she knew in her heart, she did not avoid the foreknowledge, but went outside to keep her composure. Both women were in some sense avoiding a recognition of loss and a premature expression of grief. Although this may not be the ideal response, the measure of disengagement allows the women to maintain emotional control.

BEHAVIOR FOLLOWING A DEATH

The body of the deceased is carefully washed, usually by older relatives. New moccasins and sometimes new or fancy clothing is put on. In cases like that of Philip Diamond, however, where it was thought that the person had dressed himself for his journey, people would not interfere, assuming that the person had chosen those things to be buried in.

The place at home, where the deceased spent his/her final days, is scrubbed down, and some personal things of little value to others may be burned by spouse, parent, child, or other close relative. In one instance even a small house was demolished. Useful personal property of the deceased is stored away by immediate family for a year, then distributed to relatives. The family puts possessions away partly to keep from being reminded of the death, and partly as a sign of respect for the deceased. This is also a demonstration that family members are not anxious to claim these possessions. One man who did not wait a full year to claim the rifle that a brother might have claimed was the focus of gossip censuring his possessiveness.

Delaying a burial is not good for the dying person or for those who grieve. Delay may interfere with the forthcoming journey and result in unusual activity by the departing spirit. Delay may also result in over-long and intense expression of grief and a loss of emotional control on the part of the bereaved. The death of a person whose body is lost or a death which occurs while a person is 'outside' (and so may be casually disposed of), is a cause for real concern. Whenever possible, a person who dies 'outside' (for example, in hospital) is brought home for burial.

In this century a funeral service conducted by an Anglican priest in the church building and burial in a marked and decorated grave in the churchyard are considered to be appropriate, but burial in the bush is also acceptable and sometimes necessary. Graves in the graveyard are visited, tidied and decorated, especially on an annual day set aside by the Anglican Church for that purpose. Graves in the bush may be visited, especially when they are located within a family hunting territory. After some years, however, feelings of grief are let go in favor of acceptance and remembrance; prolonging grief or brooding is unhealthy for the mental well-being of the living. The following narrative provides an example of the continued love and respect which is expressed to the deceased through the care of the gravesite.

A STORY OF A MAN FROM EASTMAIN (RECOUNTED BY MALCOLM DIAMOND)

The man and his family were out on their trapline and they were very short of food. The man's older brother went hunting and was gone for two days. When he didn't return, the man told his mother, "I think we should follow his tracks and check on him, to see what happened." They walked all along the lake shore. The wind had shifted from the north and there had been quite a snow storm. Finally they came to a hump, partly buried in the snow. They discovered this was the man's brother and they gave him a burial.

What they used to do to identify where the burial site was, they just removed the bark (from a tree). The only thing is, every year you do that. Every time you pass the grave, you peel it or cut it more, so it's bare on that side.

Every time he went to the bush, if he was near the grave, he always removed the bark. He said, "That's just to show respect for my brother, that I loved him. But now that site is where they were going to put the Eastmain River Dam, so it's under water. Of all the things that happened as far as all that damming around here, that's what hurt me the most. Seeing that grave under the water like that. Even though my whole trapline is under the water, I think that showing that respect for my brother, marking that tree like that, is what I really feel bad about. I feel bad about losing my land to trap on, but I feel worse about losing the site of my brother's burial."

Death, being so much a part of the hunter's world, is also associated symbolically with some categories of animals. For example, the stuffed and decorated head of the first goose that a boy killed, was kept as a tangible sign of the continuing relationship of a hunter to geese, and finally was hung on the hunter's grave pole. This may be symbolic of a transformation of the relationship of the man with the geese into an unknown but hoped for continuity.

To our knowledge, people do not make any associations between death and particular categories of person. Old women, usually family members, prepare the body for burial and an older man, either family member or respected elder of the community, will probably coordinate the burial activities, but this is not necessary. After a lifetime of experience older people are willing to assume a leadership role, making decisions about what is to be done in a variety of situations, including preparations for burial. They have acquired both the knowledge of what needs to be done and the ability to handle the stress which accompanies death and grief.

Cree characteristically accept death rather than deny it. We are aware of no mandatory or ritual behaviors to ensure acceptance of death, but the attitude seems to be strongly and generally held. We think that it is accurate to say that people may be able to bring their attitudes and actions into accord with the process of their dying, as indicated by the narratives we have cited above. The dying person knows that death is close at hand and makes an effort consciously to act in a manner reflecting the deeply held, unconsciously patterned, beliefs about appropriate social behavior.

Hardship and death may be brought about through the incompetent actions or the poor judgment of a person within the group. Two narratives of the same events illustrate death as a consequence of misjudgment. In the first an old woman recalled her daughter's death in the bush.

REMEMBERED BY MARY DIAMOND

I want to tell you about when we were in the bush when my daughter had a baby who was just about two months old when the mother got sick. It was too late to come (to Waskaganish) to get the airplane. My daughter got sick very suddenly and she was nursing the baby, and then, she died. I didn't have any milk and there were two women in the same tent that were still nursing their year-old children, so they had to breast feed the baby. And I had to boil some oatmeal and take the juice out of the porridge, that's what I used to feed the baby before I put him to bed. I think it was about two weeks those women had to breast feed the baby. Then at last there were people coming down the river and they had a little bit of powdered milk with them. One of the women had a nursing bottle which she gave me, so I boiled the milk and that's the way I fed baby. Then we came down to the village and I raised the baby. Now he's grown and I am staying with him.

Another woman's account of these same events suggests that the loss of the daughter was so great that Mary was able (or willing) to recall and retell only the story of the infant's survival and not the story of her daughter's death. Her omission may be the result of her grieving over this death and her regret at having misjudged the situation. Silda's account tells us, among other things, why one should listen carefully to what others have to tell, as well as why one should always say goodbye when leaving.

REMEMBERED BY SILDA DIAMOND

The next fall, in September, we went out on the trapline by canoe and we stopped at Middleton Island. Walter Diamond and his son and son-in-law and all their families were camped there, but when we left to go up the river, they stayed. Walter Diamond's youngest daughter, apparently liked my little boy, Joey, very much. When we left we didn't go to see them (to say goodbye). She didn't even see the baby, my little boy, before we left their camp. After we were gone, she said she didn't know (we were leaving) and she was sorry she didn't get to see my little boy. She told her mother, "I guess they are so sure that we're going to live until we see them again, is the reason why they don't even come to shake hands and say good-bye to us when they leave." She wasn't very old, this woman, she'd just been married two years at that time. She acted as if she really wanted to be friends and she really loved us, because she used to come to see us all the time, before she was married, and after too. Then, they came up the river after us (to go to their camp). We had to go farther up than they did.

Everything went fine at the camp for us, nobody was sick out there, and we were there all winter. The men did very well with trapping and hunting. We had meat all the time, all through that winter. Later on, some of the families that were with us went down to Waskaganish for the spring and some stayed behind with us. We spent spring out there and came down the river after breakup. Sometimes Walter Diamond and his family would come to our camp and we were surprised when he didn't come that spring, because we could hear their shots. We could hear them shooting at something and Malcolm wondered what happened, why they didn't come to see us. So we decided we should go and check on them, to see what happened. Before we reached their camp—they were already quite a ways down river—we found a letter they had written telling us their daughter had passed away. And then Malcolm told everybody we should go and camp where they were camping.

Walter Diamond's daughter had a baby boy, born on March 6, and she died on April 19. She had been breast-feeding this baby, and after her death they didn't have a bottle to use to feed the baby. One of the women told us that after the baby was born, the young mother got worse. She got very sick and then she started to lose weight very fast. She got worse and worse. She used to complain to her mother that she was losing weight very fast, and her mother would just say to her, "That's because you're nursing the baby, you're going to lose weight." Louisa Diamond (the young mother's sister-in-law) told her husband, "I think your sister is very sick. I think you should go to Waskaganish and try to find a way for her to be taken back to the settlement."

Louisa told us the parents didn't seem to notice or pay any attention to the fact that their daughter was sick. They weren't worried at all, because they thought it was the effect of the birth that was why she's losing weight. Then, she really was sick, and they didn't seem to notice that she was that sick. They weren't really worried about her. Louisa was very surprised, because Mary really worries about what happens when somebody is sick. But, that's the way, I guess. They didn't worry about their daughter, but that's the way things went.

About a month after the baby was born they were moving to another place, and Mary told her daughter, "Get your baby on the toboggan and pull the baby on the toboggan while we're traveling." Not too long after they left the camp, they were behind all the others, she told her husband she wanted to stop and rest because she felt very tired. It hurt her chest when she walked and she told her husband, "Let's sit down and rest for a while." So that man told his wife, "Never mind, don't pull the baby, just take some of our stuff off my toboggan and I'll pull you on with the baby. I'll pull you on the toboggan."

When they got to the camp they were already putting up the tent. When Mary saw her daughter bundled up on the toboggan with her husband pulling her she asked why did she have to ride on the toboggan. Her daughter said, "I didn't feel well at all, I couldn't walk." Then Mary told her, "You would feel better if you had walked for quite a while, but it was just the beginning when you're trying to walk that you felt like that." All of a sudden the daughter was unconscious, and that's when they started to wake up and begin to worry about her. Then it was hard to come down to Waskaganish because it was thawing already, it was spring. She was unconscious for three days before she died. So it was very hard on them, what happened, and Mary tried to look after the baby herself. After we moved to the camp with them, we tried to help her with the baby and we came down the river all together.

The baby didn't have very much milk when we saw them and we were able to give them nipples and bottles and milk, too. Everybody would give them some. Mary wasn't well after that, that spring, after we came back. She went to see the doctor here when he came, but he said she wasn't sick. It was because she was taking her daughter's death so hard, that's why she thought she was sick. They took her to the hospital in Moose Factory, but apparently after they did all the tests that they did on her, the doctor told her the same thing again, that it was because she was taking her daughter's death very hard, that's why she though she was sick.

Mary had only two children, one girl and one boy. Apparently that girl was always well, before she was married, she was never sick. This was an arranged marriage and then she got sick after she was married.

Silda's narrative presents the events in their full complexity, with a sense of the tragic fate of a young woman to whom people did not pay enough attention. Silda is a very competent, wise and graceful person, and we can see from her story that she recognizes the mistake, accepts the tragic consequences, and forgives Mary's uncharacteristic lapse of competence. Silda's group, after all, also made a serious mistake. They did not say their goodbyes, and the young woman's comments carry a foreboding of what is to happen. Mary's error of judgement is twofold: she is too ready to interfere and direct the actions of her daughter, and she does not perceive her daughter's fatal illness until it is too late. She is not the cause of her daughter's death, but she did not respond to the illness quickly enough.

COMMUNICATION WITH THE DYING
AND THE BEREAVED

The first person to realize that death is approaching may be the dying person, or an astute observer, or someone who has received the knowledge in a dream. Cree do not normally tell a person directly that he or she is likely to die, for such a statement probably would be taken as a personal insult or as a threat instead of as a diagnosis. A person may, however, make such a statement if care is taken to avoid implications of threat or sorcery. Alternatively, the person who discerns that another is dying might show concern by some caring inquiry or action. In contrast, if a white man with authority, such as a trader, missionary, or medical practitioner informs a person of oncoming death, the diagnosis usually does not imply ill intent.

The news that someone has died should be told simply, directly, and promptly so that grief may be expressed quickly and fully. The consequences of delaying the report of a death may be difficult and unpredictable. Part of the reason for this has to do with the pattern of quick, full venting of grief. Adult women do not cry often, though they may do so when hunters return, long overdue, with needed food, or when sharing a sad story, or in remembrance, while in the security of a church service. The event of the death of a relative is perhaps the only time that an adult man will cry openly. This brief expression of grief is followed by the appearance of fully regained composure, even when the inner feelings are still troubled. Part of the reason is that the strong emotions may lead to a misconstruing and misreporting of events, if they are not already known clearly and quickly. But mistaken understanding is not so risky as unpredictable actions.

If the death is accidental, badly managed, or complicated in some other way, the details may be discussed as gossip by those only distantly related, and cause implied. For instance, a reputed sorcerer had a severe stroke and survived for many months in a distressed and disorganized way, shouting profanities and in other ways being out of control. This was widely regarded as an awful way to die.

In the 1960s we observed several times that no one went out the night after a death. A candle or lamp was set into the window of a house or kept in a tent to discourage the spirit from entering. It is possible for a spirit to remain for up to seven days, before continuing on his or her way. In a few troublesome cases, this departure may take even longer. There is an assumption that the spirit of a dying person will visit those persons for whom he or she had strong feelings, whether positive or negative. Those who are visited may be at risk of being taken by the dying one. On the other hand the visitor may be mischievous, or may simply wish to say farewell, as a good person should.

The death of a woman who had been involved in an affair with a philandering widower was preceded by a premonitory dream in which the man's deceased wife was seen to call to the indistinct image of another woman, "Come on, _____." The situation was regarded as one of considerable risk for the philanderer who was advised to keep his food covered up against poisoning. In another case, which was regarded as less ominous and more mischievous, and old man finally shot his rifle at an old woman's spirit to hurry her away. This unusual step was taken only after she repeatedly disturbed her belongings, which first had been put away at home, then later in the Hudson Bay Company warehouse. In a much less troublesome case of simple farewell, another departing spirit was unexpectedly heard by a man to say to him, "Boy! I didn't come to tease you."

EXPRESSIONS OF GRIEF

What expression of grief is appropriate? The immediate, open expression of personal, spontaneous grief by relatives and friends is expected, accepted, and normally is expressed by both publicly and privately. People cry freely and are quickly supported, comforted, and encouraged to carry on with their lives by those less affected. This support is part of the lifelong process of renewing and strengthening the bonds of friendship and kinship. The outpouring of grief will be repeated in spells until the burial. Cree hope that the mourners soon will be able to let go of their grief, for to hold it and brood for a long time is unhealthy, and may lead to madness.

The following vignette demonstrates that the appearance of equanimity after the burial can be disconcerting to an outsider and can contribute to the outsider's brooding and social isolation. (See Figure 9.)

Figure 9. Death and grieving among northern forest hunters:
an East Cree example.

THE DEATH OF WILLY WEISTCHEE
(REMEMBERED BY DICK PRESTON)

I was present at the death of a good friend in 1964. The events are still vivid. Willy was my first good Cree friend, my advisor ("Never get excited; never lose your nerve."), practical helper, interpreter, and teacher about life in this Cree settlement. We were the same age. He had been out to the Hamilton Sanatorium for five years as a teenager in the 1940s, with tuberculosis of the spine. Consequently, he was fluent in English as well as Cree, and could swear in Hungarian and Chinese. He had few relatives in the settlement where I knew him. His parents were dead, and some brothers lived in mining towns to the south. He was aware that, as a cripple, he could probably never marry; however, he held the hope that with his intelligence and fluency, he might be chief someday.

At the time of his final sickness, his old Aunt Maria and a girl who lived in their tent were gone to a fishing camp, so he was alone. I knew that he had a persistent feeling of something stuck in his throat, and we had delayed a trip inland until it would clear up. I also knew that he had been concerned about telling me some things about an old man whom he believed to be dangerous. The throat did not clear up. A traditional healer made an herbal concoction for him, but it didn't help. I asked if he wanted to go to the nursing station, but he declined. Then, one night, I had a premonitory dream in which my friend died.

The next morning I went next door to his tent, and he said, "Boy, I almost died last night." He showed me a teaspoon that was strangely blackened, and told me he had got up in the dark and used the spoon to take some Emo laxative salts, and then felt much worse. He looked quite ill, and I urged him to go to the nursing station, only a few hundred yards away. He balked again, this time saying that he was not sure he could walk that far. I interfered a little, saying that if he could not make it, I could carry him.

He made it, and the nurse put him in bed and seemed reassuring. Next morning I went there and she said he was doing well, and had eaten a little porridge. I went in his room and was shocked at how wasted he looked. When I told the nurse that I thought he looked much worse, she became concerned and radioed for a plane to take him to hospital. Willy gave me the key to his tent, and asked me to get him a few personal items, and to "tell someone that I am leaving, Lawrence maybe."

I told Lawrence, brought the things, and sat with him. He was sweating and wanted fresh air, but I was afraid he would chill. Time seemed to go too slowly for him. Then he wanted a bedpan, so I went for the nurse. She put it under him, and came out into the hall, where we talked for a minute. I thought I heard him call, but could not be sure. Then he rang the hand-bell. The nurse went in, and when she came out she was crying. She said she just picked him up from the bedpan, and he died in her arms.

Willy had a married sister, Emily, living with Rosie and Anderson, her in-laws. I went straight to their house and in the door, holding my grief. Emily was pregnant and in a bed in the corner. I walked halfway to her, and she pulled the blanket up closer to her. I stopped and said, "I am sorry to tell you this, but Willy is dead." She and others started to cry right away, and I stood there, choked up. Then Rosie came and put her arms around me to help me to cry. I can't recall for sure, but I think I did. Then I sat down with Anderson, and he started to tell me about Charlton Island, the land where he trapped, how good the water was to drink there, and how many kinds of berries grew there in the fall. I was confused by this. It seemed to make no sense to try to listen to these things in such a situation. After a while, I went to my cabin.

The plane came, with a young doctor. I went to speak to him at the Nursing Station. He wanted to do an autopsy right there. I sensed his inexperience and arrogance, and spoke strongly against this, saying that if an autopsy was to be done, it must be done fully and properly, at the hospital. He resented my skepticism of his ability, but I saw that the nurse also did not respect him, and insisted. He said that if he agreed to that, then the Indians would expect the Northern Health Service to pay to return the body for burial. I told him that I would pay the charter. He was unhappy with this, but accepted it. The nurses' aide told me she wanted to help pay, but had a debt still from her father's funeral. I went back to get Emily's permission for the autopsy, and then he was taken out.

That afternoon, or perhaps it was the next day, the chief came to tell me that some of the men were saying they would put some money to pay for the charter, and he heard that I said that I would do that, too. He said that he just wanted to know how much money I wanted to put in. I told him whatever was needed. My vague answer was not helpful, he wanted to know an amount. I did not know what to estimate for an amount, and repeated my first answer. They went away.

Northern Health Service paid the charter. I went to the funeral, and one of Willy's friends made room for me and showed the places in the hymnal. We went outside and the casket was put in the grave. I did not know, or try to find out, how to be a part of any of the work of preparation or burial.

Following the funeral, I withdrew to my cabin. The night after the burial, it was extremely quiet; even the dogs were silent. The next morning, a neighboring boy opened my door to ask if I had been in my cabin that night. "Yes, it was pretty quiet."

The board walls and floor of Willy's aunt's tent were scrubbed twice. Some small things were burned, and others gathered and put away. Willy's missing pliers were, for some reason, a problem, and I was asked for them three times although I explained that I did not have them. It is unusual to persist in requests for something; the death may have made their location more urgent for someone, or perhaps they thought I was lying.

I remained withdrawn and brooding. I thought that Willy had been ensorceled by the old man. I then thought that the old man would wish me the same ill condition, since I had learned about him from Willy, and he might somehow know about this. I wondered if my questions about sorcery had been a cause of Willy's dying. I wanted to pack up and run away from the situation and from anthropology. I was afraid to eat. I felt terribly alone. Then I determined that I would pit my will power against the old man's, so that he would not beat me.

Old John Blackned took a unique initiative and came to see me. He came with an interpreter, to tell me "The Beaver Wife," a particularly entertaining story. I wrote it down carefully, but it was difficult to get it straight because the interpreter was not competent. Some days later, with a good interpreter, I checked it with John.

The first day or two after the burial, when I went out to the store, I looked depressed, and people seemed to avoid eye contact. When, in a few days, I shook off my depression and began speaking in a normal, casually friendly fashion, the avoidance disappeared, and with it my sense of isolation. After a few days, someone told me, "We feel badly, too, even if we don't show it." I asked if anyone had been visited by his spirit on the night after the funeral. Maybe one or two people; it wasn't certain. There was no trouble, I didn't ask anyone else. He was a good man.

At the burial, grief is openly shown in crying, but, so far as we know, is not expressed in more violent actions. Indeed, while the relation of hunters to animals routinely includes bloody injury, human interaction emphatically should not be violent and rarely is this stricture broken. Similarly, one should not inflict violence on oneself. It would, for example, be wrong to gash oneself in grief. After the burial, close relatives go into formal mourning, with an arm band of black or some other visible sign, for a year. Gaiety, flirting, or remarriage are inappropriate during this period. These outward expressions of mourning may have been introduced by Anglican missionaries in the 19th century. In a culture where emotional reticence is a distinctive characteristic, the brief period of open grief is particularly striking, and perhaps particularly effective as a catharsis. It may be that a mourner's expression of deep feelings of grief is directed not to those around him, but directly to the person of the deceased, now only present as spirit.

Relatives and friends of the deceased will differ in the strength of their feelings of grief, according to the strength of the love they feel for him or her. We would not be confident, however, in differentiating the kinds of feelings experienced or shown to others, and we intuitively resist the notion of categories of loss value. Social categories are resisted by the Crees, even when they manifestly exist. In our experience, people may help the bereaved by simply being present, by talking about the deceased, or by talking of other, seemingly irrelevant and distracting things, according to their leading.

A RECENT DEATH

In 1984, when we received the phone call that the old chief, Malcolm Diamond, had died, Dick was away giving a lecture at a university in New England. Sarah, responding to many years' close friendship with the old man's wife and daughters, as well as her great respect for him, felt the need to return to Waskaganish for the funeral. Sarah made hurried and complicated travel arrangements which she thought she had fully organized. On our arrival at Timmins, however, we met Diamond family members who were being brought in from the bush by charter, as well as those who were arriving from Manitoba. These relatives had been told that we would be arriving in Timmins also and they expected us to join them for the last portion of the journey.

It was a solemn meeting and trip, but open expression of grief did not take place. We flew into Waskaganish late in the evening and were met by the deceased man's sons who took us immediately to their parent's home. One of the daughters, with whom we normally would have stayed, arranged for us to stay at the Anglican mission, because her house was filled with family. When we entered the Diamonds' house, we came into the front room filled with relatives, friends and neighbors, sitting together, weeping. (See Figure 10.)

Figure 10. Death and grieving among northern forest hunters:
an East Cree example.

THE FUNERAL OF MALCOLM DIAMOND
(REMEMBERED BY SARAH PRESTON)

I went immediately to Silda to hug her and join the weeping—then I remember shaking hands and greeting all those in the room, hugging and weeping with all the women I knew. Then I sat beside Silda's daughter Annie, who has been like a sister to me. I continued to weep and to hold Annie's hand—or perhaps Annie was holding my hand. I remember experiencing intense sorrow, not only because I considered many of those around me, who were weeping, to be close friends and I shared their grief—but also, over the years in and out of the household, the old man had begun to treat me as another daughter. I felt the loss as I might have felt the loss of the father I never knew.

I was able eventually to control my weeping as those around me were doing, but at the funeral service the following day I clung to Annie's hand and continued to weep. Finally, because I was aware that Annie was beginning to control her tears, I tried to also. After the burial service I visited with sisters exchanging family news and cheerful small talk. One of the sisters told stories about her adventures with their father when she was young. We shared in the cooking and child care and household duties which continue even in the face of grief.

I greeted Alice Jacob with Annie, and the weeping was part of the greeting, then there was effort to encourage each other and to cheer each other up. I visited in Silda's house also, where all the relatives gathered and exchanged family gossip, cheerful memories and encouragements. Silda remained in her room most of the time, but I had the opportunity to visit with her there and tell her of my respect for the old man, and that my feelings were those of a daughter for a father. She acknowledged my expression of care and I joined the relatives in the front room.

The second day, signalling the ending of open grieving, Silda, with sons and son-in-law, was in the basement putting away Malcolm's tools. Finally, when we came to say our goodbyes before returning home, Silda and I hugged and wept together for a moment, no doubt both of us wondering if we would ever see each other again.

Dick recalls the evening that we arrived: "Malcolm's oldest son, with whom I had travelled and camped, held onto my hand for what seemed to me a very long time, and Malcolm's closest brother came and spoke at length, firmly and gently, to Silda, offering her encouragement and guidance rather than tears."

CONCLUSIONS

In this chapter we have sought to craft a balance of text and discussion, and have ordered these nine texts with our audience in mind. We began with a text that would have a familiar cultural style, that of an early sojourner with the Crees, an Anglican priest (and later bishop) of the James Bay region. The core of the chapter is six Cree texts, which we hope conveyed something of their cultural style. The final texts are ours, recent sojourners who brought to their experience of dying and grieving an earned measure of bicultural empathy. We found this chapter a chance to objectify our experience, and offer these for the reflexive goals they may serve.

The 1980s are a point in history when we can expect to find that we share some bicultural empathy with most contemporary young Crees, with one critical difference. They have experienced and internalized substantial parts of Western civilization's youth culture and protest politics, while we have experienced and internalized substantial parts of Cree "old ways" and reticence. In some of this we are facing in opposite directions.

Some of the young Crees are impatient with the Cree past and with its value of patient quiet composure that is maintained by traditionalists despite chronic failures of fairness by white men. For our part, we tend to be impatient with the Euro-Canadian present and with the barrage of words used for advantage rather than for community; whether it is the strategic use of ordinary language for persuasive marketing, the strategic use of technical vocabulary by social methodologists, or the strategic rhetoric of competition between ethnic group identities. We could use a bit more reticence in our lives, and solitude (not loneliness, which is endemic, but solitude, which is rare), and patience. And we could use friends. As one Cree lady told a departing anthropologist guest who had not stopped to say goodbye, "Don't you realize that the only thing we have in front of death is friends?"

And so to summarize. The ideal for Cree dying combines 1) harmony with others and with the process of dying, 2) maintaining competence in the face of this, the greatest of life's contingencies, and 3) setting out on a journey to a little known domain of the after-life. These three themes emphasize the importance of self-reliance, preparing one's self and one's friends, and going out, solitary and with composure, to meet death. This ideal is close to our somewhat narrower, technical concept of cognitive control. If it is the ideal way to set off on a next voyage, it is also only realistically a very solitary trip.

The ideal for Cree grieving is an immediate, shared, emotional release, with mutual support for those most at loss and perhaps at risk. But the release of crying and support is soon followed by a return to outward self-reliance and composure, though the inward, private feelings may still be strong. Realistically, much of Cree life, too, may be a solitary journey.

The Crees are not primitive existentialists, but this abstract comparison is not a trivial one. Their emphasis on an egalitarian, individual autonomy was nurtured not by a European-style interior struggle with the question of faith and hierarchies of sacred and secular power, but by unknown centuries of hunting for a living in the great Circumpolar Boreal Forest. They had few other humans for company, and periodic starvation as certain, though as contingent on the whims of nature as anything else in life.

Depending upon our culture and particular circumstances, we may meet death with equanimity or with anger, rage, and fear. Through the process of grieving we are brought face to face with our own mortality. These culturally defined attitudes toward death may reflect our attitudes toward the value of life. For the Cree, grieving is an intense expression of bonding between those with whom one shares a community. It is reestablishing community with those still living and at the same time reaffirming a relationship with the deceased, now transformed into spirit. Anger is out of place here.

We find that the Cree deal with death as well as anyone we know.

The Northern Athabaskan Potlatch: The Objectification of Grief

William E. Simeone

In Chapter 10, William Simeone presents an analysis of death and grief among the Tanacross Athabaskans of Alaska. As with the Prestons' Cree, Wellenkamp's Toraja, and the Kapinga material that follows in Chapter 11 by Lieber, Tanacross culture permits very limited expression of the emotions of grief and loss that follow death. Fearing for the health of the bereaved, Tanacross people enact rituals whose goal is to transform grief into joy and reknit the bonds of community. In its transformative practice, Tanacross society recalls the material presented by Waugh in Chapter 6 on the Burhani Sufi, but here it is the community that works to transform grief on the occasion of every death. It does so because, while loss is inevitable, grief is dangerous.

*   *   *

This chapter describes how Northern Athabaskan people objectify and ameliorate their grief in the ceremony of the potlatch. Frequently associated with Northwestern Coast cultures, the potlatch is practiced among the Athabaskan speaking peoples of east central Alaska and the western Yukon Territory. The research for this chapter was conducted in the Athabaskan village of Tanacross, Alaska, located just off the Alaska Highway, 100 miles from the Canadian border. First established as a mission in 1912 by the Episcopal Church, Tanacross became a village during the 1930s after native people took up residence so their children could attend school.

My acquaintance with the Tanacross people began in August of 1971 when I went to the village to serve as a lay worker for the Episcopal Church. Since then I have lived in the village intermittently, both as a resident and to do research. Most recently my research has focused on history and cultural identity as it appears in the contemporary potlatch. While I have not studied death, it has become a part of my research because the potlatch is, among other things, a mortuary ritual.

Among Athabaskan people death and the potlatch are considered personal affairs. Some people feel I have transgressed their boundaries by simply conducting research on any aspects of the potlatch. During the year I conducted research for my Ph.D. dissertation, one man refused to talk to me at all. However, not everyone in the village feels so strongly. There are those who think research is important because it may help in their struggle to maintain a distinct cultural identity. Yet most people believe their personal feelings are not a legitimate area of enquiry. This view stems, in part, from a distrust of anthropology and anthropologists, and partially from the cultural perspective that personal feelings are private and should not be discussed openly. In this respect long-term research has both advantages and disadvantages. Throughout the eighteen years I have known Tanacross people, I have experienced a number of deaths, attended many potlatches and come to know some people very well. In establishing mutual trust we have talked about very personal feelings. Most recently, for instance, my friends in the village helped me through my divorce, which took place while I was doing research. However, knowing how people feel about certain topics makes it more difficult to ask questions. In fact, asking questions is a sign of bad manners. One either waits for a person to talk, or watches to see how things are done and learns from experience. Under these circumstances the potlatch is a particularly important and revealing event. It is the major vehicle for the public display of emotion.

Consisting of a sequence of activities repeated over a three-day period, the ritual of the potlatch provides a "dramatic frame" (Scheff, 1977) for the expression and discharge of grief. The sequence includes feasting, dancing, singing, and oratory, climaxed by the distribution of gifts on the last might. Through this last act the grieving relative, or potlatch host, symbolically dissolves the corpse, thus "letting go" of the deceased and ending the period of public mourning.

Death produces bereavement affecting all members of the community and creates a particularly dangerous and contradictory emotional situation. This situation is mediated by the potlatch. In a culture that values emotional reserve, any emotion as strong as grief is dangerous because it can produce unpredictable behavior. Consequently, it is important that a grieving individual be supported and attended so that she or he is not overcome by sorrow. At the same time, emotions are private and no one would presume to interfere. By intensifying and objectifying grief through singing, dancing, oratory, and distributing gifts, the mourners and their guests become capable of managing and then eliminating emotion through public and autonomous actions.

Contemporary Athabaskan society in east central Alaska is divided into two matrilineal exogamous moieties. These are further divided into matrilineal sibs or descent groups. According to the anthropologist Frederica de Laguna, the moieties "function primarily in dividing individuals into 'opposites' who intermarry, help each other at life crises, particularly death, and who entertain each other at potlatches" (de Laguna 1975: 89-90).

Although a funeral is always followed by a memorial potlatch, and the two events are intertwined, they are distinct in purpose. Funerals are concerned with the physical treatment of the body and entail the preparation of the corpse, the building of a coffin and grave fence, and a Christian religious service. The burden, or obligation, of preparing the body and building the funeral structures falls to the guests, who are members of the moiety opposite to that of the deceased. Whether the corpse is considered polluted, as in the case of the Tlingit (Kan, 1986), is uncertain. Certainly, the spirit of the dead person is thought to be dangerous to the relatives, which is why non-relatives handle the body. In return the deceased's own maternal moiety, the hosts, prepare a feast and accumulate gifts which are then distributed to those who have fulfilled their obligation. This is the memorial potlatch. It marks the separation of the deceased from society and is the last public expression of grief. In the presence of the guests, who provide a safe, supporting environment, the grieving relatives are allowed to experience the unbearable pain of loss and to grieve freely. By extending the event over a three- or four-day period, the potlatch hosts are permitted to fully experience and come to terms with their loss. As this process unfolds, the mourners are expected to relinquish their grief. For, like the Cree mentioned in the Prestons' chapter (Chapter 9), Athabaskans think that to prolong grief, or brood, is unhealthy for the mental well-being of the living.

GRIEF

As suggested above, grief is considered to be a powerful emotion. For example, in the past people say that when someone brought news of a death the messenger was supposed to stand close to the person while giving the message. In this way the messenger could, if the need arose, throw his arms around the person and prevent him from injuring himself. While the deceased's relatives were expected to show some signs of grief by singeing or cutting their hair or acting despondent, there was the possibility that grief stricken persons would lose control and severely harm themselves, either by throwing themselves into fires or slashing their arms with knives.

Today even these expressions of grief are regarded as extreme and unacceptable. Crying by both women and men is accepted, although women seem more free to express their grief by crying uncontrollably or wailing. I never saw a man do this. Powerful expressions of grief almost always take place during the funeral, as the congregation pays its last respects and walks by the open coffin. It is also acceptable for mourners to cry while they sing 'sorry songs' which occur after the funeral service. During the singing of these songs everyone should be very quiet and serious. People are not to talk or laugh and children are supposed to remain with their parents.

DANCING AND SINGING

People use two kinds of music in the potlatch: 'sorry songs' and 'dance songs.' Each is integral to the mourning process as a medium for expressing emotion and changing the mood of the mourners. Both are accompanied by dancing and drumming. Dancing and singing are, like caring for the corpse, part of the reciprocal obligation the guests are expected to fulfill. That is, in exchange for food and gifts, the guests are expected to sing for the hosts both to entertain them and to support them in the mourning process. In fact, dancing is so important that particularly good dancers are singled out and given especially large potlatch gifts. Dancing and singing are also competitive; guests from different villages compete with each other and with their hosts to see who are the best dancers.

Dancing is important because it stabilized life in a very crucial period. The following vignette illustrates this point. Several years ago there was a funeral and potlatch in one Upper Tanana village where the people danced but they were unable to "break out the good time," as they say. Suddenly someone rushed into the hall and exclaimed there was some trouble outside. Everyone went out to find one whole family had been asphyxiated in its car right in front of the hall. After the dead were taken care of, all the people went back into the hall and danced hard until they were finally able to break the spell of bad luck. After this everything was all right.

Before the songs begin, the older men gather and sit in one corner of the community hall quietly talking and occasionally spitting tobacco juice into a coke can or styrofoam cup. The lead drummers slowly warm up, initially tapping the drum heads lightly, feeling the tension of the skin surface. At the same time they warm their voices. Then, as they find a common tune, the men burst into song and are immediately joined by groups of elders situated in different locations around the hall. This signals the beginning of the mourning.

The only instrument used is a tambourine-like drum made of moose hide stretched over a birch frame. Usually men are the drummers, although on some occasions I have seen young women pick up the drum and use it. Not everyone has the ability or predilection to be a good drummer, and the importance attached to a man's ability to drum and lead songs is reflected in what people say about the drum. The drum is an essential part of potlatch because, as one man told me, "it leads the potlatch." He said it is like an important person and, like a person, "makes noise . . . and good news in the dance." He compared it to a speech for "good favor and good feeling." Furthermore, its reverberations make people "feel friendly" and enable them to have a "good time." Without the drum ". . . it does not look [or feel] like a good time." In essence, the drum reminds people of the importance of the potlatch. When people hear the drum they know something important is going on.

I think the drumming, accompanied by the presence of so many friends and relatives, produces a safe environment. The reverberations of the drum produce the same soothing feeling as a heart beat. It also produces a sound on which the dancers can focus so they can concentrate on their feelings. During the 'sorry songs' the beat is slow and comforting, allowing the mourners to feel secure while dwelling on their grief. By contrast, during the 'dance songs' the beat is fast and vibrant, lifting the spirits.

To expel their grief, mourners used to dance for days on end, but nowadays dancing is limited to the three days of the potlatch. The mourning begins with a 'sorry song' made expressly for the deceased. During this first song only the hosts and relatives of the deceased dance. Following this all the guests join in and a succession of 'sorry songs,' interspersed with dance songs, are sung. By singing a number of such songs the guests are reminded of their own loss and can more easily empathize with their hosts.

Though sung almost in a monotone, 'sorry songs' fill the hall with excruciating emotion, bringing people to tears. As the immediate family of the deceased rises to dance, others rise with them and, gathering tightly around, they offer both physical and emotional support. Heads bowed, hair falling over the faces of the women, the dancers sway their upper bodies to the beat of the song, shuffling their feet in short abbreviated steps. Their hands are held flat, palms up in a supplicating manner, moving up and down to the beat expanding away from the head of the skin drum. As the mourners sing they pull their arms away from the body to the rhythm of the drum in an attempt to pull the grief out. At times this action is reduced to an up and down motion dramatizing a sense of fretting. In circumstances when the pain is particularly intense supporting dancers gather close by the mourners in physical support.

The intensity of 'sorry songs' varies, depending on the circumstances of death and the feelings of the composer. Because grief is considered to be a particularly powerful emotion, it has to be physically expelled from a person's mind and body before he or she is taken over by it. The structure of the songs provides the needed release. Each 'sorry song' is made up of a lament which draws on the emotions by creating an image of the dead person and expressing the feelings of loneliness and loss. Repeated over and over, the lament is interspersed with a chant.[1] One 'sorry song,' for example, was made to the sound of a river boat whistle which conjures up loneliness. Another song, made for a young man shot by the Anchorage police, was made to the sound of a church bell with the refrain, "the church bell calls for you, where are you?" These chants and accompanying dance movements help the mourners physically expel their grief.

'Sorry songs' are sung one after another as the dancers dip farther and farther into their grief. The first song is about the deceased, but subsequent ones may be sung about people who died from ten to fifty years before. Songs about more recent deaths produce floods of tears as family and friends recognize it to be about their son, mother, father, daughter or cousin. When the drummers judge that the

---

[1] Kan has noted similar expressions of grief among the Tlingit. He writes that four special "crying songs" were sung followed by four prolonged oo sounds which are said to "expel sadness" (Kan, 1986:200).

mourning has gone on long enough, they begin to intersperse 'sorry songs' with an occasional 'dance song,' gradually altering the mood. Finally, dance songs predominate and come one after another, transforming the sober scene of moments ago into a joyous occasion.

By manipulating the songs the lead singers are able to control the grieving process and keep it within socially acceptable bounds. As one person put it, the mourners ". . . sing WU WU back and forth, singing the sadness away and then out comes the calico!" In other words, after they have expelled their grief, the mourners' mood is expected to change and they can then dance joyfully with the long strips of calico that are a sign of a good time. 'Dance songs' encompass a variety of topics including songs about the dangerous business of fighting forest fires, the beautiful woman of Northway, a village near Tanacross, or driving to Fairbanks. This last is based on the sound of a running automobile (Guedon, 1974:222).[2] These songs are accompanied by quick, loud beats which excite people and get them moving. Dancing rapidly the participants forget themselves and loosen up. No one is "supposed to hang back," as one person said. Guests are expected to dance hard because the movement of the dance helps to "break out the good time." The dance should loosen up the bad luck and push it away. Otherwise, the people say it will remain with them. That is why they say that to dance at someone's potlatch is to do "a favor for the hosts."[3] Through intense dancing the visitors accomplish something and satisfy both themselves and their hosts.

Bodily movements accompanying these songs are flamboyant, particularly for the men, who dance with their feet planted wide apart, their arms jabbing the air in time with the drum beat. Women form a circle around the men and either stand still while moving their arms or dance in a shuffling movement carrying the circle counter-clockwise. Everyone is supposed to dance, and women often playfully pull men on to the dance floor. To keep the dancing going, the drummers and lead singers sing one song after another until they are exhausted. The point is to dance until everyone is satisfied and happy.

ORATORY

Public speeches are an important aspect of modern potlatches and continue to be part of the reciprocal obligation each moiety, guest and host, owes the other. Guests always offer public condolences that are aimed at transforming the experience of the mourners and removing their grief.[4] For their part, the hosts are

[2] Guedon (1974) records that these same songs were sung at a potlatch she attended in Tetlin in 1969.

[3] Both McKennan (1959: 134) and Guedon (1974: 212) record that a guest's participation in the potlatch is done as a favor to the hosts because they care.

[4] cf. Kan 1983: 48 for a discussion of Tlingit potlatch oratory which serves much the same purpose.

expected to explain their reasons for giving the potlatch and to express their gratitude for the guests' participation. Often these speeches are traded back and forth, each side using expressions of love and respect which, like the drum, strengthen harmony and cooperation, or "good favor and good feeling" among the participants. Traditional condolence speeches are offered by older men who understand how to use the metaphors which can assuage the grief of the mourners and establish a tone of harmony and cooperation. At one potlatch held after the funeral of a very old woman, one of the leading old men walked to the middle of the floor and stood directly in front of the hostess to offer his condolences. He said in the Upper Tanana language (I paraphrase):

> Don't make yourself too cheap by grieving deeply for your beloved sister. You come from *Diichaagh*, "people who are really great." I know who these people are.

As he spoke he pointed to Mt. Sanford, the 14,000 foot volcano that symbolized the ranking men of the deceased's sib. He continued by saying:

> Your people were so great that you do not have to feel bad and you should remember not to let your grief get you down. You should be happy because all of these people came to see you and make you happy during your bereavement.

It was later said that the speaker had ". . . hung *Diichaagh* around her [the hostess's] neck." This condolence speech fulfilled the guest's obligation to the hostess and her *sib*. His speech also reiterated important features of the potlatch: exchange, love, and respect. With his words he wrapped the hostess in love and respect which, like the special potlatch blankets given to the close friends of the deceased, were supposed to warm her and assuage her grief. By telling her not to cheapen herself her meant she should not grieve too deeply and lose control of herself. Rather she should emulate her ancestors who, in effect, were standing right there in front of her in the guise of Mt Sanford. By acknowledging the status of her ancestors, he also acknowledged her status. His recognition was supposed to make her feel better and emphasize the harmony and cooperation between moieties. Thus everyone was supposed to be comforted by the speech. As it turned out, not everyone was.

While people today stoutly maintain that potlatches are not political events, the harmony of the occasion can be disrupted by sharp arguments over particular aspects of etiquette. These disputes, although sometimes phrased in ambiguous terms, illustrate the rivalry between sibs and moieties over power and prestige. For example, on the day after the foregoing condolence speech was delivered, a man got up to speak. He was dressed in a bright red beaded coat given to him by the deceased's husband. This coat represented the intimate connection between the deceased and the speaker. He spoke in both the Ahtna language and English. Apparently annoyed, he criticized as disrespectful the absence of the extended family from the village after the body had been returned. They should have been in the village to greet the deceased and to accept the condolences offered by attending members of the opposite moiety. He went on to say that members of the opposite moiety from other villages should have been there as well. At that juncture, he pointedly excused several of the guests, because they had had to travel long distances, but he ignored others who were in the same circumstances. The speaker then said he was always the first to go to the village when someone died. Thus he admonished those who had not been in the village even as he built himself up.

This speech caused no little tension and was immediately followed by another in which the speaker excused himself for being late because of family problems and transportation difficulties. Then another man made some remarks trying to smooth over the increasing tension. Next a man from Tanacross responded to the first speaker's criticism. He prefaced his talk by saying he was, at seventy-five, a little young to understand all this, a remark both self effacing and designed to put the younger speaker in his place. While the man said he bore no malice against the first speaker he did feel slighted because he had not been excused while others had. He went on to point out that no one had telephoned him, or they had called the wrong person. For this reason he had not known exactly when the body was to be returned to the village or the exact time of the funeral. After he sat down the tension relaxed. By excusing some people and ignoring others the first speaker had made a serious breach of etiquette. Because of his status the Tanacross man should not have been ignored. He had the right to be angry because he was not properly informed of the date or time of the funeral.[5] Furthermore, he had met his reciprocal obligation by assisting in the grave digging. As well, he had both danced and sung, and donated money to the potlatch. Finally, his wife, who was a sibmate of the deceased, had also made a substantial donation of blankets and cash to the potlatch. This conflict was not immediately forgotten but discussed for several weeks afterward.

Condolence speeches are only one form of oratory associated with grief. Often there are also very emotional gratitude speeches, given by the host in return for the guests' participation and assistance in the potlatch. In the following speech a woman explains that she put on a potlatch to memorialize her son, who had died of cancer some years before. Just before the distribution of the gifts she stood in the center of the community hall and said 'it was for him,' pointing to the picture of her son which was fastened to a Hudson's Bay blanket hung on the wall. Then she said (I paraphrase):

> In giving this potlatch I am doing the best for my son whom I love very much. I have done all I can now it is time to let him go. From this point I cannot think about or worry about him anymore.

[5] Guedon (1974: 211) writes the ideal way in which to invite important people to a potlatch is to send one or two messengers to the 'chiefs' and older people.

She said this several times, She also expressed her gratitude to both natives and non-natives who attended the potlatch and helped her, and she spoke for her granddaughter and her granddaughter's husband who had lost their own small daughter. Eloquent and emotional, the woman was able to express her grief publicly and to share it with the guests.

THE DISTRIBUTION OF GIFTS

The major gifts distributed at a potlatch are guns, beads, and blankets. As potlatch gifts these items become more than mere objects. They are objectifications of the host's most deeply felt emotions. By giving away guns, blankets, and beads infused with feeling the host can express and discharge his or her grief. To understand how this happens we have to know something of Athabaskan concepts of property.

In Athabaskan culture objects have an essence I would compare to the Maori concept of *hau* which is a ".. vital essence of life found in human beings, in land, and in things. Because the *hau* is connected through people to land and things, things take on the power of personification" (Weiner, 1985: 212). Objects such as knives, arrows, and guns have an essence received in manufacturing which enables them to "do their job," that is, to kill or sustain life. When a person obtains an object it is personalized by being infused with the power of the owner. For example, I was told that a beaded knife case, once owned by a knowledgeable and powerful man, had retained some of his power even though he had died. In fact some believed that the sheath retained enough power that it could guard a sick person against further illness. Through its association with this powerful person the sheath had become 'personalized' or 'spiritualized.' Similarly when a person works to purchase or to make potlatch gifts he or she personalizes the objects by infusing them with emotion. Then, by distributing the emotionally charged gifts, the host can purge himself or herself of grief. Thus the host and guests become bound in a reciprocal relationship based on shared emotional pain and goods.

Not just any object will do, for not all goods can be personalized. Objects purchased for a potlatch can only be personalized through money earned by the host's "own hand." Acceptable money includes wages, but excludes cash won through gambling. The sanction against using gambling profits to purchase potlatch gifts may reflect a Christian attitude, but is also suggests that such objects cannot become potlatch gifts because no labor has gone into them. Without labor, such things remain alien objects; that is, they are objects that are not connected to a person. Guns are the most important potlatch gifts. They are equated with food and individual autonomy. It is said that without a gun a person cannot make a living. Guns are, therefore, objects of great power, both in the material and symbolic sense. The ideal is that a host collect at least seven guns: one for the chest or torso, one for the head, one for each arm and leg and a seventh to stand for the whole body of the deceased. Further, the number of guns collected is always supposed to be increased in increments of seven.[6] I believe this reflects the larger concern of the host to express his\her love and respect for the deceased by symbolically covering the body with love. Each gun metaphorically represents, or 'covers' a part of the body with an object of great value, thus objectifying what the host feels for the deceased. By giving a gun representing a part of the deceased's body, the host shares the love felt for the deceased and shows respect for the guest. At the same time the distribution of the guns metaphorically "destroys the body" so "people won't miss that person" and "have to worry about it [the body anymore." In other words, as each weapon is given away the host nullifies his grief which is concentrated in the body.

The potlatch host also shared his\her feelings for the deceased by distributing blankets. Because of their tactile qualities blankets symbolize a feeling of comfort and warmth which soothes distraught feelings. As one person said (I paraphrase):

> . . . giving a person a blanket is just like you put your arm around, or wrap somebody up with your love and warmth.[7]

Fancy blankets, particularly the Hudson's Bay style, are always in and on top of the coffin, wrapping the body in warmth and love. Identical blankets are given away to those especially close to the deceased. By giving an identical blanket the host shares a part of the love that is buried with the deceased. The emotional content associated with Hudson's Bay blankets was expressed to me after I had given some as Christmas presents to my close friends. One man said that "it was a great Indian potlatch" and that it made him feel good, almost beyond words. His wife told me that when she died she would like to be buried in hers.

CONCLUSIONS

In this chapter I have discussed the northern Athabaskan potlatch, focusing on how the hosts and their guests manage and transform emotion by objectifying it. The potlatch is central to modern Athabaskan life. Death creates a rent in the social fabric, a tear which is mended through the ritual reaffirmation of society in the potlatch. Beginning with the funeral, the "phase of disaggregation" (Bloch and Perry, 1982: 4), the corpse is prepared and then disposed of by members of the opposite moiety. The potlatch is the "phase of reinstallation" (Bloth and Perry, 1982: 4) in which both hosts and guests reaffirm their relationship through shared

---

[6] In have never heard anyone express the reason for this symbolism and I suspect that the reasons are known only to a few people.

[7] Kan (1986: 206) notes a similar significance for blankets in the Tlingit potlatch. The physical feeling of the soft, warm blanket conveyed warmth to the guests who thanked their hosts for "warming them."

sorrow and joy. This reaffirmation occurs as each group responds to the other in a culturally appropriate manner. At the beginning of the ceremony the feelings of the mourners are demonstrated through the medium of music. In the performances of 'sorry songs' and 'dance songs' the mourners are helped to confront and manage their grief. They are led by the guests from sorrow to joy and from grief to celebration. Additionally, the guests comfort the mourners and rebuild their confidence with condolence speeches praising the hosts' ancestors. In response the mourners answer with their own oratory and the distribution of food and gifts. By distributing gifts which are symbolic of the dead and filled with emotion the hosts begin to purge themselves of grief. At the same time they reaffirm their relationship to the guests by giving them powerful objects, guns and blankets, which are also symbols of love and respect. While mutual reaffirmation is the ideal, we have seen that the harmony of the ceremony can be disrupted by conflicts over power and prestige. It is this underlying tension that provides the dynamic in which society as a whole is reaffirmed. This competition is implicit in every aspect of the ceremony and is used to assert and reaffirm the hosts' and guests' social positions. For just as the gifts are symbols of grief, they are also symbolic of the host's ability to accumulate and distribute goods. By distributing objects of value the host asserts his prestige and reaffirms his ability as a provider. At the same time, the guests assert their superiority by accepting the gifts and acknowledging the host's abilities. Such mutual affirmations provide the ongoing context for the continuation of society in the face of death.

Cutting Your Losses: Death and Grieving in a Polynesian Community

Michael D. Lieber

In his chapter Michael Lieber draws on his lengthy acquaintance with the people of Kapingamarangi in the Federated States of Micronesia. He explores the ways that a people whose culture bids them beware of any intense public display of emotion handle the trauma of death and its attendant grief. In this society of people from a tiny atoll in the Pacific it is not death that poses a problem, but the danger that comes with loss of control by grieving survivors. Kapinga attitudes and practices surrounding death and grief described in this chapter stand in sharp counterpoint to those of the Lusi-Kaliai in the chapter that follows.

*   *   *

I had been in the village for about six weeks before I first heard that piercing, ululating wail. It came from a house very close to mine, and I followed a crowd of people into the yard to see a young woman keening inside the house beside her mother's body. Outside the house was a buzz and bustle of activity, all very confusing to me in the fading light of evening.

This was 1965, and I'd come to this Polynesian village on Pohnpei Island in Micronesia to compare this resettled community with its home island, Kapingamarangi Atoll 485 miles south, as part of a larger project on resettled communities. Twenty-five years old, naive, eager, and determined to record everything around me, to miss nothing, I stood in that yard watching and writing furiously in my small notebook. I felt a hand on my shoulder, and one of my friends (interpreters) told me that the headman of the village was waiting to see me at my house. "Why now?" I muttered under my breath as I dutifully followed. I had to obey, since this man was responsible for me as long as I lived in the village—gaffes and all. The wiry, wrinkled old man sat imperiously on one of the two chairs I'd managed to scrounge and ordered me to light the lantern and get ready to write. We had never before talked for any longer than a few minutes. Careful not to convey my frustration over missing the action, I obliged. He began as follows:

> A Kapinga funeral is very complicated because so many different things are going on at the same time. You haven't been here long enough and you don't know the language well enough to understand what you're looking at. So I am going to tell you step-by-step what has already happened, what you've already seen, and what you are about to see.

He followed this brief introduction with a two hour, beautifully organized account of a typical Kapinga funeral including comparative commentary on the difference between present day Christian funerals and those of pre-Christian days. Then he answered my questions. He concluded with this:

> I know you're in a hurry to get back to the funeral, but I want you to take a little time, go over your notes, make sure you understand the order of events, and then go out and visit each place where things are being done. Make sure you write down who is there and what they're doing. Then compare what you see with what I've told you and see if I've told you the truth.

I did, and he had. What I describe to you now is pretty much what the headman described to me with some detail added and with one major difference. This bright, wily old man is a keen observer whose generalizations about Kapinga practice are precise and thorough—and I have since observed enough instances of death and grieving to know this. What he did not tell me is *why* things are done as they are. The WHY of it took another eighteen years and four stints in the field—and a bit of luck—to figure out.

If there is a single message in all this, it is the same one you will encounter elsewhere in this volume (e.g., the Weigands' Chapter 5 on the Huichol): *ritual saves lives*, both literally and figuratively. You will find much that is familiar in my description, not very different from our Western ideas and practices dealing with death. But you will also miss some things that you would expect to find in any account of death and grieving. You would expect to find some account of people's inner, emotional and psychological experiences with death—that of others (in Wellencamp's account, Chapter 8) or, with their own impending deaths (as in Badone's Chapter 13). These things are missing from my account because Kapinga do not talk about these matters, not with me and not with one another. Kapinga will, in conversation, reveal very intimate details about their lives that make them appear to be very open people. Their openness is about what they have done, however (much of which is known about or gossiped about anyway), not how they feel about any of it. It is this reticence to express or talk about spontaneous emotion that is most different from Westerners. This is the most exotic aspect of my presentation—a *non-event*, and one whose very absence *is* the why of the funeral ritual the old headman described to the young neophyte.

A whole chapter of a book dedicated to the proposition that a non-event is the cause of events? Yes indeed—it happens all the time. In mathematics, a zero is nothing, like 3 - 3. But zero in the world of human communication is not nothing, and it can be a cause of other things. Think about the letter you did not write, the phone call you did not make, the bill you did not pay. All zeros, and all can bring on angry responses. Think about the lengths to which we all go to bring about non-events, like not having an auto accident, not getting wet in the rain, not getting ill, not allowing our kids to be junkies. Non-events can be causes of events, and events can cause non-events (see Bateson, 1972; Carroll, 1977). Kapinga people go to great lengths to make the spontaneous expression of emotion a non-event. The way they respond to death is but one example of many possible examples of the lengths to which they go. To explain what ties together a Kapinga funeral ritual with the absence of spontaneous expression of strong emotion is to understand a single Kapinga idea: *what it means to be a person.*

I begin with a description of the setting—the island and its people. Then I explore the idea of personhood and how it explains much of what Kapinga do and think. This exploration of Kapinga culture—their universe of meaning—sets up the description of the meaning of death and what makes it a crisis for the living. Once it is clear why death is a crisis and what kind of crisis it is, then the funeral makes sense as a strategy for crisis management. My explanatory procedure is to use the cultural construct of personhood to show how people's behavior in particular contexts such as death and grieving makes sense. This procedure is similar to the Prestons' use of the Cree concept of *autonomy* in understanding how they prepare for and respond to death (in Chapter 9).

KAPINGA COMMUNITIES

Being on Pohnpei and being on Kapingamarangi are two very different sorts of experiences. Pohnpei is a high, volcanic island like Hawaii with a rugged, mountainous interior surrounded by a narrow strip of low land that most of its 30,000 residents inhabit. The Kapinga village is on the outskirts of Kolonia town, the administrative center for what is now Pohnpei State in the Federated States of Micronesia. There is the state hospital, government buildings, stores, warehouses, movie theaters, bars, and dwellings of cement and of native wood construction. The town, even with its many cement block houses, some of which approach suburban elegance, still looks like the old Wild West town I first saw in 1965, just a bit tidier and less interesting. The roads are all paved in town now, and there are fewer bars and more restaurants. The movie theaters have been replaced by Video stores.

More than 500 miles north of the equator, Pohnpei is hot and wet. Its growth is luxuriant with all the tropical fruits and flowers you could want, including wild orchids. But there are no beaches, just brown volcanic soils mixed with reddish clay. The Kapinga village, called Porakied, used to be the showpiece of Pohnpei when I first lived there, the Polynesian village that every visiting big shot and tourist was taken to see. That was when there were less than 300 people living there and the village seemed spacious, the native style thatch houses interspersed with coconut, breadfruit, papaya, soursop, and other trees. Though people had lots to do, the pace seemed very relaxed to a wide-eyed, East coast boy.

By 1982, the population had more than doubled, and houses had crowded out many of the trees. The Kapinga had converted from a mixed cash and subsistence economy to a full time cash economy. They had abandoned their homesteads in the southern part of Pohnpei and the large taro field that a Pohnpeian high chief had given them in the 1950s. They had cut off most of their trade relationships (vegetable food for fish) with local Micronesian farmers in favor of commercial fishing, wage work (mostly for the government), and handicrafts for the tourist market (Lieber, 1984). The village is crowded, noisy, and not very healthy. The diet these days is mostly white rice, canned mackerel, and popsicles with occasional purchases of local taro, coconuts and bananas. In some respects, the running water and electricity have made people's lives easier.

Dinner is a lot quicker to prepare. But the life style, in my view, has deteriorated. People are hungrier than they used to be, especially the kids, thirteen of whom died of protein malnutrition and its attendant dehydration while I was there in 1978 and 1979. A lot of money was being spent on alcohol.

Kapingamarangi is another kind of experience. It is tiny and flat. Approaching this atoll on the government ship, it looks like a bunch of reeds growing up out of the ocean. As the ship clears the channel into the lagoon, you can see the wide arc of green that are the thirty-three islets bordering the lagoon waters. As the ship gets close to the two central islets that hold the bulk of the atoll's 450 inhabitants, you see the white sand beaches and the row of thatched canoe houses. The first time I saw it, I had butterflies in my stomach. I still get the same sensation every time I go back.

Going inland on the central islet, Souhou, reminds me of Porakied village. Lots of houses close together, but it is tidier, since each plot of land has its own boundaries. A white sand path circles the islet, lined by a low rock wall on one side. Houses sit on the ground here, their yards covered with white limestone pebbles. There are coconut and breadfruit trees everywhere and hibiscus lining the lagoon sides of many of the house compounds. The next islet north, Welua, is different. On Welua, house compounds make a half circle around the channel between islets and curve round the lagoon beach up to the north end of the islet. Inland from the houses is a huge taro patch that fills the center of the islet. Then on the ocean side of the islet, there is thick growth of coconut, pandanus, and hardwood trees. The school is located here. You get the impression of luxuriant vegetation here. But a close look tells you that Kapingamarangi is really an atoll and Pohnpei is really a high island. The quantity of greenery is not matched by much variety. Pohnpei will grow all sorts of plants, fruits, hardwoods (like mahogany), and flowers. Kapingamarangi has only ninety-three different species of plant, and many of these are weeds. There are only four food plants here—coconuts, pandanus, breadfruit, and taro. There are a few papaya trees and a few banana trees (most of which bear no fruit). Of these, coconut and taro can be harvested year-round, while breadfruit and pandanus are seasonal. As you can guess, there is not much variety in the diet. You quickly understand that an extended drought in a place like this means famine. The atoll has had these disasters in the past, the last one resulting in ninety deaths between 1916 and 1918. This is what led to the founding of the Porakied village on Pohnpei.

But on Kapingamarangi we eat fresh fish. Kapinga men define masculinity in terms of fishing. Their sturdy, single-outrigger canoes are built for speed and stability in the deep sea, which is how they established themselves on Pohnpei in the first place. They had a virtual monopoly over yellow-fin tuna until the 1960s.

Kapinga daily life revolves around food—producing it, producing the gear to produce it, controlling the land that produces it and the gear, consuming it, and, above all, sharing it. Food is a metaphor for love and well being; it is the medium for expressing the important things in a human relationship, the other thing that Kapinga produce most consistently. Not surprisingly in a place this small (less than a half a square mile of total land area), control of land is a pivotal issue in people's lives. Land is owned, shared, and used mainly by family groups (Lieber, 1974). To share rights in land is to share a kin relationship regardless of genealogical connection (if any). So to share land and kinship is to share food. It is simple, logical, and true.

Unlike the Pohnpei community, life styles have not changed much here. Western goods, like cloth, steel tools, coffee, tea, sugar, white rice, and such have been around since the 1870s. Outboard motors mounted on outrigger booms, waterproof flashlights, electric generators, snorkeling gear, and (ugh!) chainsaws are recent innovations. They are time savers, but they seem not to have made all that much difference in the scheme of things. Christianity has been the most important organizational change, followed by the abandonment of the traditional chieftainship in favor of an Americanized tri-partite democratic polity—chief magistrate, municipal council, and local court judges constituting a municipality of Pohnpei State. This includes Western schooling, a local co-operative store (money coming through copra sales and government jobs), and a medical dispensary with a trained nurse. The difference these institutions have made is the introduction of context specific roles by which Kapinga interact with other Kapinga, wherein one's family and one's biography make no difference whatever in the interaction. Nothing could be further removed from traditional Kapinga thinking about personal interaction and what it means to be a person. To understand how profoundly different, say, a customer-clerk or a doctor-patient relationship is from what Kapinga normally think of as human interaction, I must now introduce you to the cultural universe of the Kapinga person.

KAPINGA PERSONHOOD

Like most other westerners, I had always assumed that people everywhere were *individuals*. I had thought and acted in terms of that assumption during my first field stay, and it proved to be the cause of many mistakes, both in the ways that I communicated with people and in how I interpreted what I saw and heard. Let me give what seemed at first to be a trivial example of what I mean. I had determined to be polite to everyone, so the first Kapinga phrase I learned was "Thank you," and I used it liberally for anything that faintly resembled aid and comfort. One day, I borrowed a screw driver from a man and thanked him. He replied, "No! Bring it back!" Puzzled I recounted the incident to an older man, who explained that Kapinga never thank one another for loans. Moreover, there is no Kapinga word for 'gift.' The verb, to give, cannot be turned into a noun. It took me five years to figure out this puzzle.

To us, being (or identity) can be distinguished from behaving. Kapinga make no such distinction. The reason they do not is because they assume, unconsciously, that identity and behavior are components of a higher order entity: a relationship. *It is social relationships that define the person.*

Put in more formal terms, the person, in Kapinga conception, is a node of intersection of social relationships. The boundary of an individual is his or her skin. The boundary of the Kapinga person is much wider—the particular network of kin, friends, enemies, and colleagues in which the particular person is embedded. The reason that Kapinga do not thank each other for loans is that loaning and borrowing are not what people *do*, but what people *are*. The relationship defines the person. So, for example, what we would call a 'comedian' Kapinga would refer to as 'a person who causes other people to laugh.' We locate humor in the person, as a property of a person. Kapinga locate humor in the relationship between people.

But language is only part of the story. Kapinga, for example, explain the difference between people and animals by citing examples, such as the fact that dogs will mate with siblings and parents, and that two dogs that have been amiable will suddenly turn on each other in a vicious fight. The points of these examples—'Dogs don't know who their relatives are; people do.' 'Dogs don't know who their friends are; people do.'—illustrate a single principle. It is the ability to establish and maintain social relationships that distinguishes people from animals. It is, moreover, consciously knowing about these relations that makes one human. Thus, Kapinga refer to incest and promiscuity as 'acting like animals.' Another term for incest is a word that also means 'delirium.' It turns out that 'knowing' in Kapinga terms means 'to be aware of differences,' and difference is a *relationship*.

The history of a person's relationships with other people and with his or her environment constitutes the person's biography. What distinguishes one person from others besides such formal criteria as birth order, age, and sex, is the *style* with which he or she conducts those relationships, the emphases on particular relations, and their management. The style that one develops is what gives shape to one's biography and makes one predictable to others. It is not your status that other people use to predict what you are likely to do, as in the West. It is knowledge of one's biography that makes that person predictable. This being the case, consistency, of style and responses is a minimal demand made on everyone. For example, Kapinga tolerate a wide range of social conduct, including insanity, with gentle good humor. They will not tolerate inconsistency. One man who was alternately quite mad and quite lucid was taunted unmercifully throughout his lifetime, while a patently mad woman was kindly cared for by everyone.

The term I employ to label personhood as defined by relationships is Alfred Schutz's "consociate" (Geertz, 1973: 364-367). Kapinga personhood is just one instance of consocial personhood, a concept that we find throughout Oceania. The consocial person contrasts with the individual in the West in that almost every consocial relationship involves the whole person, while the individual participates mainly in status relations involving parts of, properties of the person. Individuals live in a world of statuses and roles; consociates live in a world of biographies. The way we describe individuals is by listing their properties. The way Kapinga describe others is by listing the kinds of relationships they emphasize and the style by which they conduct them.

An important implication of Kapinga personhood is the way the self is defined. Although Kapinga do not have a term that can be translated as 'self,' they do distinguish between the public person and the inner, private person by the term 'my inside' or 'inside me.' The Western self is characterized ideally as being a set of physical and psychological properties which are 1) complete and 2) integrated. Completeness and integration are the goals of the maturation process. They enable the individual to be competent and self-reliant enough to handle any situation he or she confronts. The stress on completeness and integration is reflected in popular idioms as "not playing with all his marbles" and having "a screw loose." Incompleteness and lack of integration are looked at intellectually and legally as pathologies that may make people not responsible for their actions (or not mature enough to be responsible). Some pathologies make a person *incompetent* to stand trial, for example. The Kapinga self is nearly the opposite of the individual self.

The Kapinga self is composed of physical characteristics and four other things—desire, emotion, will and thought in order of their first appearance in the infant. Each of these develops separately and each is thought to operate totally independently of the others. Rather than being integrated, the Kapinga self is the domain of true chaos. Self-control is possible among individuals because of their integrated selves. Self-control in the Kapinga case is a contradiction in terms.

Control of the self is an absolute necessity because uncontrolled expression of each of the components of self is potentially disastrous to oneself and to others. Uncontrolled desire leads to acts that disrupt social relations, such as theft, assault, gluttony, and incest. Uncontrolled emotion is dangerous, especially in infants, where it can lead to soul loss and death. Unconstrained will is the most dangerous since it often leads to acts that, in the past, offended the gods, who retaliated with famines, epidemics, and by bringing castaways who slaughtered over half the atoll's population (Emory 1965: 53-56). Uncontrolled thought is the cause of all insanity.

Control of the self must come from outside the self. It is, thus, located at some higher order of the person. An obvious source of control is the social relationships in which everyone is enmeshed. Indeed much of the constraint on self is nested in the watchful eyes, mouths, and hands (depending on one's age) of others. Lack of thoughtfulness, diplomacy, and common courtesy are taken very seriously by Kapinga. There is no such thing as an unintentional slip of the tongue.

It makes systemic sense to infer that people internalize social contraints on the self, permitting people to operate habitually without conscious effort. As Gregory Bateson points out, "No organism can afford to be conscious of matters with which it could deal at unconscious levels" (Bateson 1972: 143).

Kapinga appear to do precisely this by internalizing not so much abstract moral principles as a model of the community, i.e., one's significant categories of relationships. When contemplating an immoral action that might be or has been taken, a Kapinga would not say, "I am doing something wrong, therefore I am a bad person," but rather "If other people (or if X) know about this they (or X) would say that I am a bad person." It is shame, not guilt that gets internalized. Thus, even internally, morality and surveillance are delegated to others.[1]

The development of personal style in one's social interactions is part of the internalization process. One's decisions about what one can and cannot do are filtered not only through the likely opinions of others, but also through the likely mismatch between the act and the hard won consistency of personal style in one's personal style in one's public persona. The complexity of levels of constraint on the self helps to insure their effectiveness. Children, for example, learn very early that their reputations depend at least as much on what others think as on what they say and do, and that they should not expect others to be fair in their judgements. The pejorative nicknames that every child receives from his or her peers is but one example of how children learn about the surveillance of others in the formation of their personal reputations.

If this analysis is correct or nearly so, then another critical difference between the individual and the consociate becomes clear. One of the minimal social demands on individuals is that their public personalities and assertions be an

---

[1] While it should be obvious, let me say explicitly that I have moved from one inference about the constitution of the person to another inference about internalizing social relationships, couching the this second inference in terms that appear descriptive. For the sake of brevity I have condensed a long and detailed argument to be published elsewhere comparing the Kapinga social-conceptual hierarchy with a cybernetic system hierarchy. The comparison teases out the differences between the minimal assumptions that must be true in order for each system, given its structure, to work. I present here only the results of that analysis. The idea of internalizing shame comes from a conversation with Vern Carroll and is not original with me. I should also point out that I have tested this analysis in several different ways, the most interesting of which was a series of conversations with Kapinga in the U.S. getting advanced degrees in educational psychology.

accurate reflection of their inner beliefs, feelings, intentions, and thoughts. They must, in other words, be *sincere*. We insist on a nearly one-to-one correspondence between self and public image, modulated by constraints of etiquette, consideration of others' feelings, and diplomacy. Kapinga also value honesty but not sincerity in our sense. No one wants to know what is really inside anyone else's self. Kapinga are constrained to mask the self in public personas. To fail to do so is to expose oneself and others to danger. This is the origin of an unresolvable dilemma inherent in Kapinga personhood. Kapinga are well aware that one's public image is a carefully constructed artifice, and no one trusts anyone else's stated intentions, motives, or excuses on their face. But they are comfortable with these artifices, which mask the underlying selves that everyone trusts as being real but of which everyone is utterly terrified.[2]

Given this dilemma, it follows that not only does one's own death present potential danger, but also that other people's responses to death are just as fraught with danger. The death of a loved one (or for that matter a hated one) occasions natural emotional responses from the self—grief, rumination, and anger to name a few—whose expressions, as we have seen, are hazardous to one's own welfare and that of others. Death, therefore, occasions extraordinary demands of constraint on those most intimately affected by it. The rest of the chapter describes these dangers and how people manage them.

DEATH

Kapinga, like Westerners, see death as part of a cyclical process common to all living things. People, like trees, get old and die. Sometimes people become ill and die—and older people are more prone to lethal illness. This is to be expected and not particularly feared, though not always particularly welcomed either. The Kapinga view of death as a natural cycle is in stark contrast to many of the Kapinga's Melanesian neighbors to the south, who see every death as murder (e.g., the Kaliai, Chapter 12). Kapinga distinguish between natural death and untimely death, and they do whatever is necessary to avoid the latter. Between these two poles is a kind of social death.

Social death for Kapinga is not the kind of formalized procedure that the Counts describe in Chapter 12. As a person grows old, the number of people who have the right to constrain him or her, older relatives and friends, become fewer. Men in particular are cut out of the gossip networks that carry information about one's foibles, so that they get very little information about themselves or anyone else.

---

[2] I am indebted to Don Handelman for this way of viewing the problem of self, gotten in a personal conversation. For an interesting and insightful comparison of the same problem in the context of assumptions about the individual, see Handelman (1983).

They become socially isolated, and that is social death for a Kapinga, personhood being what it is. The response of the aged to this situation is to show symptoms of senility. In the twelve cases of senility I witnessed, all men but one, only three were physiologically senile. The other nine, when it came time to make a will, were as lucid and querulous as college professors. Women tend to be active in their household's affairs until they are physically unable to respond to anything. They are, thus, privy to all the current gossip, including third party comments about themselves. when a woman shows symptoms of senility, she is usually senile.

Untimely death through injury, drowning, soul loss, starvation, sudden illness, attack by a spirit, and more recently, sorcery are all very much feared. To the extent that they can, people try to anticipate and either avoid or take precautions in dangerous situations. I should mention here that death attributed to spirit attacks was more frequent before Christianity than since conversion. Death from sorcery is an import from Micronesian castaways (about 1780), supplemented by contact with Micronesians on Pohnpei. The more lethal bronchial ailments, such as tuberculosis, are also post-contact phenomena.

The most serious injuries appear to have always been those sustained by males through falls from coconut or breadfruit trees and by women burned while cooking. Injuries sustained from beatings were more common but less lethal than murder, which was very rare. Drowning has always been a major cause of death of children past infancy (while infant mortality appears to have been much higher before than since World War II). Finally, starvation and illness related to it have always been a threat on the atoll, which has suffered protracted droughts in the last two centuries.

People could anticipate and deal with many of these misfortunes. Boys were taught how to climb, move about, and position themselves in trees. Children, who were usually supervised by elder siblings, were taught where and when to swim in the lagoon. Pregnant women were taught how to sit and what to eat during pregnancy, and midwives learned how to manipulate a fetus during birth to reposition it for a normal or near normal birth. Special foods were used for people with one or another form of illness. Gods were prayed to and pampered in hopes of gifts of abundance. Attacks from spirits could also be prepared for, but they were less predictable and required constant attention.

There were three classes of spirits in the aboriginal Kapinga universe, two of which remain as more or less of a threat to some people today. There were the high gods, the 'line of ghosts,' and two lagoon spirits. The high gods were the subject of all major and many minor rituals. Incurring their wrath or having direct contact with them could be lethal, but they have little to do with people otherwise. The 'line of ghosts' inhabit the outer reef near the large channel at the southeastern quadrant of the atoll. They are mainly the spirits of deceased people, active only at night. They come in a line to the inhabited islets at night, searching for some person who has gone to sleep outside his house, taking his or her soul with them either out of malevolence or, in the case of spirits of the recently deceased, out of loneliness for loved ones. These spirits are much more predictable than the gods, though not as powerful. They avoid light so as not to be seen. They are also unable to crawl under the low roof of the house. These spirits would sometimes protect a potential victim from harm when they knew the person was a kinsman, driving off another spirit who intended to take the person's soul. This was the case when the protecting spirit was that of someone long deceased.

Finally, there were two spirits in the lagoon, a male in the southern lagoon and a woman in the northern lagoon. Each would approach a member of the opposite sex at night when the unfortunate person was unaccompanied. Contact with the spirit was followed almost immediately by insanity.

Forfending an attack from the line of ghosts and from the near-lagoon spirits was a matter of exercising reasonable caution, like staying indoors to sleep and not attracting the attention of the ghosts, such as by loud singing or crying at night. The most immediate danger with the recently deceased is that (a) he or she is lonely, and (b) he or she feels pity for the grieving relative left behind. The wish to have company and to comfort the pain of one's loved ones are strong incentives for the recently deceased to seek out a living relative. The longer and more overt the grieving, the more likely it is that a deceased kinsman will notice it and come for the griever (or take another unwary kinsman instead). Mortuary ritual is designed to deal with this contingency.

The Funeral

Funeral preparations are much the same for all ages and both sexes, differing (by age) mainly in their elaboration. I will describe the precolonial form of the funeral, which has undergone only minor changes since Christian conversion. I will also describe the post-colonial changes and explain why they are so minor.

A person's death initiates a flurry of activity that proceeds in stages. These stages, in outline, are as follows:

1. Organizational: The female head of the deceased's descent group assigns initial tasks. She appoints women to organize cooking and recruiting of workers and men to organize fishing to provision workers and guests. Other tasks include preparing the body for viewing—washing, dressing, closing orifices—and preparing the house for the wake. Children are recruited as messengers. Organization is worked out rapidly, and as soon as the body is placed in state, the next phase begins. No weeping or other emotional expression is permitted during this first phase.
2. The Wake: Chanting and Work: This stage begins with women inside and outside the house performing a high-pitched wail, or keening. This is the first public sign that a death has occurred, and it is the official notification that guests and other kin may assemble to view the body and join the family.

Keening ceases when mourners and guests assemble (both inside and outside the house). Only now is weeping permitted, and then only soft intermittent sobbing. Chanting begins at this time and continues until this stage is complete.

Chants are about fishing expeditions, beached whales, and memorial chants composed by and about the deceased and/or his or her relatives (Emory, 1965: 186-192). People move into and out of the house to sit near the body, chant, and help with food preparation that proceeds during the chanting. Guests are fed during the night.

3. The Wailing: This stage begins very late at night and is called *hangihangi* 'wailing.' Wailing is performed as a low, throaty, rhythmic cry, distinct from weeping and keening and similar to a chant. It is performed only by intimates of the deceased, and the subject of wailing, lyrics composed on the spot, concerns wrongs done to the deceased by relatives, family disputes involving the deceased, admissions of wrongs done, and exhortations to the family to settle their arguments and act as kin should. Names are named and admission of culpability is expected to be forthcoming from those named. Wailing is expected to do in an hour or so what sitting *shivah* is expected to do among Jews in eight days. It appears that 'wailing' accomplishes these goals effectively, at least in the short run.

4. Chanting: Chanting begins again after the wailing is complete and continues until mid or late morning, depending how long it takes before food for the feast is ready. Food preparations are stepped up at this time, and fishing expeditions are already out either in the deep sea or the lagoon, depending on the season and weather conditions. Chanting bridges the period between wailing and disposal of the body.

5. Disposal of the body: Bodies of older people, particularly male and female heads of descent groups, were buried under the floors of the ancestral houses, called 'grave houses' of the group's compound. Kapinga say that others were weighted with stones and buried in the lagoon. At the time of disposal, close relatives bring packages of their most valuable goods, jewelry, clothing, or fish hooks, to be buried with the body. This is called *heihei* 'caring.'

6. The Feast and next stage of chanting: Food is served to all guests and mourners after disposal of the body, the eldest and most prestigious being served first, and younger people thereafter. The most prestigious people, mainly men, receive the highest quality foods, such as taro puddings and deep sea fish, and others get whatever else has been prepared, particularly if there is a shortage of higher quality foods. Chanting begins again after people have eaten and continues until the next morning. But the nature of chanting at this point is more animated and competitive, the mood is more festive and the chanting is more entertaining. New compositions are sung, and people, particularly younger men, compete not only to show off their

songs, but their talents as good singers, i.e., being able to chant in good voice continuously without getting hoarse.

7. Renaming: All of the closest kin of the deceased are given new names by one or more elder relatives when chanting is finished. All personal names are derived from chant lyrics and are usually names that ancestors used. A child receives several names at birth, and the elder may select one of these or give a new name. Like goods given at burial, old names are said to be 'thrown away.' They are abandoned to symbolize the rupture of a relationship, rather than simply as a sign of loss. As several informants put it, "I abandoned that name because that is the one X called me by." To continue to use the name would be a painful reminder of one's personal loss of an important relationship. The new name simultaneously connects the person with family history by connecting him or her with ancestors.

For the next eight days following the funeral, life returns to normal, but those close to the deceased are watched very carefully by other relatives and friends. There is a good deal more visiting of the bereaved than is normally the case. The evenings are taken up with chanting, conversation, and storytelling. At the end of the eight-day period, a small feast for close family signals the end of the mourning period. The occasional tears and understandable moroseness that were permitted (if not protracted) are no longer permitted. Grieving after this period encourages the deceased's spirit to remain near the compound at night at worst and is considered to be 'thinking too much' at best. People literally demand that grieving end.

Modern Christian ritual differs very little from the traditional model. Western clothing and a wooden casket have replaced the native kilt and the sleeping mat. Hymns have replaced chanting. Each compound on the atoll has its own cemetery, and the Porakied community has a village cemetery. The memorial chants that formerly punctuated chanting have been replaced by prayers recited by the pastor or by church elders. The funeral now ends after the post-burial feast, which is initiated by prayer by the pastor. The eight-day mourning period is still observed but is less formal, as people, particularly on Pohnpei, no longer fear the 'line of ghosts' as they once did. The threat of insanity through 'thinking too much' still remains. A cement gravestone is set on the first anniversary of one's death, accompanied by a feast for those who contributed money and labor for the stone setting.

Having outlined the format of funerals, we now turn to the more detailed analysis of key elements of the format to show how the palpable dangers of unbridled expressions of self are constrained and managed.

Funerals as Crisis Management Strategies

Whatever else a death may provoke in particular cases, it always triggers organizational activity as the first social response. Expressions of emotion must be deferred until the work of planning and delegating responsibilities is complete. Initial organizing is done by the oldest capable woman in the deceased's descent group. She assigns tasks and positions of responsibility for directing them. If there is competition among relatives for these positions or over where to bury the body, she has to manage it with firm diplomacy to ensure that work gets done efficiently and to prevent alienation of family members with conflicting interests. The attention of those most closely involved is, thus, focused on work and potential crises of family politics that will affect the family's social and economic integrity later on.

It is only after organizational matters are settled and the first project, preparation of the body and the house, are complete that any expression of grief is permitted. But even here, grieving is constrained to a very narrow range of expression—keening, a highly stylized communication device, and soft, periodic weeping. Uncontrollable sobbing is heavily sanctioned on the spot, either by remonstration of an elder, or subsequent ridicule and gossip. Moreover, some people are considered to have the right to be grief-stricken while others have not. In one case, a man's sister-in-law was overly sincere in her sobbing, occasioning the anger of both her own and the deceased's relatives. Her uncontrolled sobbing was embarrassing enough, but even worse was the fact that her relation as in-law to the deceased did not warrant that sort of emotion.

Mourners around the body are expected to join the chanting that initiates the wake. But this obligatory social activity has its own pitfalls. Mortuary chants are inserted into the wake at various points by family members who have the right to sing them. These chants are family property, and only family members can sing them. But this can be tricky, because someone who considers himself family may not be thought of as a family member by others. On the other hand, signaling alienation by not singing may expose one to accusations of callousness toward the deceased. Obviously, when a mortuary chants begins, everyone, mourners and guests, sees who sings and who does not.

Family members who are not keeping vigil by the body and chanting are hard at work preparing food and coordinating the cooking of various dishes. Women in particular are doing both, moving into and out of the house to take their turns at both cooking and vigil.

Up to this point, we see that personal emotion is subservient to social obligations of various sorts—organization, funeral preparations, and communal expression of grief through song. Each of these involves personal decision making with social implications that are immediate and public. Grief is constrained to expression through these channels and always in concert with and under surveillance of others. Communal chanting becomes particularly important at night, when the 'line of ghosts' are likely to be about. The crowd of people, the noise, and the lights of cooking fires and whale oil lamps inside the house prevents the approach of ghosts. Thus, ghosts are prevented from claiming victims during that period of greatest emotional stress when people are most vulnerable.

The first and only time that crying is permitted is during the part of the vigil called 'the wailing.' But even this expression of personal emotion is channeled through an intensely social form with a publicly social function. Crying is structured by the chant format. Rather than being expressed, it is *composed and performed* in proper rhythmic structure. Non-rhythmic crying is punctuated with the lyric, rhythmic stanzas. Only here are men allowed real tears. In wailing, personal emotion is transformed into social performance. The contents of wailing, moreover, represent yet another sort of transformation of personal emotion.

The content of 'wailing' is of intense interest to mourners and guests. This is the only context in which open airing of family animosities and disputes is permissible and expected. What had been gossip and speculation now becomes history and fact. Grief is transformed into righteous indignation, demands for amends, admissions of culpability, and, above all, embarrassment. The wailing continues until culpability for wrongs done to the deceased is admitted and admonitions to heal old wounds are acknowledged by promises to do so. Embarrassment drives the reintegration of those formerly alienated. The work of exposing and healing wounds is public to a fault. The chanted format constrains the anger, hurt, and embarrassment to highly conscious expression that demands careful thought not only about what one is to communicate, but also about the proper aesthetics of communication. Hurt is felt, but its expression is composed. The drama of wailing is intensely absorbing, and its stylistic rules help to ensure that the deep emotions being expressed are constrained within manageable limits. Stylistic rules are not the only constraints on emotional expression, however.

Those kin most closely involved with the deceased must be present at the 'wailing.' Their participation is not simply a matter of how they feel or how to express their feelings. Given that relationships in any family have their conflicts and antagonisms, each person must consider what accusations might be made against him or her (and how to respond) and whether or not to bring up an issue in wailing or remain silent. A person's relative age and family position are important determinants of what he or she can say. Some family issues, like a land dispute, can be resolved during wailing and some cannot. One has to judge the situation and the possible consequences carefully before deciding to chant or to be silent. Failure to help the deceased when help was most needed is the most common sort of accusation, and it often is used to indicate a pattern of neglect of one's relatives. It is less common for a mourner to bring up a land dispute but it sometimes serves to reintegrate squabbling family members. If it fails to do so, it can make matters worse. When resumption of chanting marks the end of the wailing, it is a relief from the intensity of the drama it concludes.

At the time of burial, mourners are faced with yet another set of decisions that transform personal emotion into social performance. Their selection of grave goods to be buried with the deceased requires the same sorts of considerations involved in memorial chants and wailing. These goods are not given to the deceased but are said to be 'thrown away' to signal the enormity of one's loss. The value and amount of the goods signal the value of the relationship ruptured by death. Stinginess invites gossip and invidous comparisons. Overgenerosity raises suspicions of 'showing off' or of having some secret that has been previously hidden.

The feast following burial is socially, economically, and politically demanding on the family of the deceased. The quality and quantity of food to be served require planning, collecting, and preparation that begins during the first phase of the funeral. The family's prestige demands that it put on a good show. How difficult this is depends on the social position of the family, its land holdings and relations with other families from which use rights to land are available, the season, and the weather. If death occurs during windy season, when the lagoon is choppy, lagoon fish are unavailable. Fish may only be gotten from the outer reef and deep sea areas that are shielded from the wind by the islets. In pre-Christian times, this meant that either the family had to commission a number of canoes to go out for deep sea fish or to get a group of men to go out to the reef flat for a netting surround. Given that canoes were owned mainly by the privileged sacred class (those eligible to be priests) or favored men of the secular class, the family's ritual position determined whether canoes were immediately available, If they were not, then one or several canoe owners had to be convinced to help. This meant exploiting kin connections and engaging in delicate negotiations that meant incurring new debts or calling in old ones. This in turn meant selecting a responsible elder whose directing of fish collection depended on his connections with other fishermen. Once canoes and crews were gotten, then the problem became one of the catch. Few categories of bait are available during windy season, so the fishermen were often restricted to those fish that would take crabs as bait—mainly triggerfish. Triggerfish might be better than reef fish, but they certainly did not have the prestige of, say, blue jack. Anglers would take whatever they could get, given the time constraints. If deep sea fishing was impossible, the elder directing fishing might send out one or two crews to net goatfish on the outer reef, assuring at least reasonable quantity.

Once the fish were brought in and cooked, the old woman directing preparations would have to decide how to distribute them.

Given the amounts and kinds of deep sea fish available, this woman would have to gauge how many people had to be fed and how many prestigious people— priests, descent group headmen, men's house headmen, and, possibly, sacred class women—would have to be given the best quality fish. The remainder would get reef fish. If there were not enough deep sea fish for the prestigious people in attendance, then the family might have to supplement fresh fish with dried tuna. This posed yet another problem. If the family had its own store of dried tuna, then the problem was simply one of how much to deplete its resources. If the family had little or no dried tuna, then negotiations would have to be opened with kin who did. Dried tuna was a resource used to get through the windy season when there were fewer fish available and few techniques to get them. Negotiations for this resource were, therefore, delicate indeed.

Calm season was a time of plenty, since almost every technique in fishermen's repertoires could be used. But if death occurred during tuna season, when no other canoes than tuna canoes were allowed on either lagoon or reef, getting fish could be complicated. The high priest might be importuned to delay the tuna fishing canoes for a day, so other canoes could go out for other deep sea fish. But this depended on the family position and the closeness of its members to the high priest. Alternatively, importuning a men's house headman might get one a large crew to go out for a surround on the reef under the pretense of providing bait for the tuna fishermen. Some fish would be given to them and the rest to the family for their feast. This surreptitious arrangement depended on the family's relations with the leader of the men's house, of course. Still, it wasn't the same as having deep sea fish. Even the privileged families with their own canoes would be in a position of expending resources and incurring debts, since they would have to form crews for either or both deep sea and reef fishing.

Modern practice, aside from the changes already noted, has ameliorated some of the economic pressures on the family of the deceased. Canoes are far more plentiful and far more evenly distributed through the population than they were in pre-Christian days. The use of lures and outboard engines mounted on the outrigger booms makes for a wider range of deep sea fish available even in windy season. The need for cash, however, has become the analogue for access to canoes. Rice and flour are now mandatory for a good show. In the Pohnpei community, where fresh fish means money and where subsistence fishing is all but nil, the expenditures of money for a funeral absorbs ready capital and creates debts in the same manner as the need for fish and taro did on the atoll in the past.

The chanting that ended the funeral, while being more entertainment than anything else, had an intensity all its own. The competition among singers was an obvious one. A much more subtle one was that among composers. Chanting up to this point included only well-known chants, memorial chants, and occasional chants of praise to the gods. This phase of chanting, however, included both old standards and more recent compositions. This was the pre-colonial community's version of the hit parade, when composers learned just how popular their songs were. The introduction of a recent composition had to be carefully gauged according to how enthusiastic the audience was in general, how they had responded to previously introduced compositions, what chants had just been sung, and whether the rhythm of the recent composition to be introduced was too similar or too discordant with the mood of the audience. Composers deploy all the considerations of timing that any entertainer uses. Given that the family's attention was being directed away from the deceased, that they and many of the guests were physically and emotionally exhausted, and that no one was in the mood for mediocrity, this was no time for a singer to introduce a dud.

The return to normal life over the next eight days carries not only the dangers of spirit attack and insanity, but also the danger of permanent family splits and animosities. If an oral will had been made, this was (and still is) the time that it will be enacted. Descent group succession and the distribution of rights over land and taro plots is finalized during this period. This can be more or less complicated according to the number of extant versions of the deceased's will. Parents sometimes manipulate their children by giving each a different version of the will favorable to that child. Adopted children, who are supposed to have full rights of inheritance with natural children, are either included or excluded from the will. There is likely to be much manipulation of an adoptee's rights at this time (Lieber, 1970). If the deceased died intestate, then descent group elders may have to negotiate the distribution of rights, and their own personal interests may be reflected in the negotiations.

There is practically no aspect of Kapinga life and Kapinga social organization—from cult house organization to household organization, men's work and women's work, kinship, marriage ties, and friendship, economics, politics, and aesthetics—that is not somehow vitally involved in the Kapinga response to death. The problem of controlling the self is met at every level of constraint in the Kapinga social and conceptual order. This has the effect of transforming personal crisis into a sequence of social crises that must be dealt with quickly and correctly. It is the shape of these social crises that manage the personal crises of the potential dangers of self-expression.

BUT DOES IT WORK?

But does it really work? Jane Wellenkamp, Ellen Badone and Richard Preston (personal communications) have been particularly (and rightly) insistent about this question. Even if the kind of control that Kapinga (and most other Polynesians, by the way) demand of each other is routinely possible, does everyone always live up to the cultural expectation? Are there no deviants? Of course there are people who lose control. What is so striking is how very few people do, at least in the grieving context.

I have managed to find two instances of people who were taken by spirits following intense grief, both women before the turn of the century. There was another instance of a woman who, according to Kapinga people, went crazy after prolonged grieving following her father's death. I met this woman, and her behavior was bizarre by my standards as well as theirs. There were two other instances of women who were hysterical during funeral preparations both involving very sudden deaths. I witnessed one of these. People's reactions to both were very negative—disgust and ridicule. That's it. Those are all the cases I have, and believe me, I asked.

Keep in mind, however, that grieving is not the only context involving control. Uncontrolled desire is common, particularly among babies and dirty old men. Desire is the earliest component of the self to develop, and infants are nursed and pacified whenever they look like they might be getting frustrated. This is because unfulfilled desire can cause hysteria, which leads to soul loss and possible death. Death through soul loss is said to have been the most common cause of infant mortality, and it is still blamed for much infant illness. Uncontrolled desire among adults is usually sexual in nature, but it does not take the form of rape, lewd exposure, or the other usual kinds of perversions we find in the West. With Kapinga, uncontrolled desire usually takes the form of incestuous liaisons (sexual relations with any relative up to third cousins) or what could be called blundering. Certain men are known to be constantly, shall we say, fraught with horn. They fall easy prey to young men who promise them a willing woman or to young women who lead them on, usually for a fee. They are then taken to some house in the dead of night by boys or told by a girl to meet her at a certain spot. The assignation turns out to be a hoax, yielding new grist for the gossip mill within minutes. There are many stories about these buffoons, as good as any you will read in the *Decameron*, but I will resist the temptation to tell them, since this chapter is already too long.

Uncontrolled will was, in pre-Christian times, the most dangerous way of losing control because, as I said before, the results could affect the entire community. Yet, of all ways of losing control, this appears to be the most common, particularly after colonial contact in the late 19th century. The history of Kapinga political leadership since 1870 is littered with shattered careers of the once powerful who became victims of their own willfulness. My data show no less than twenty-three such people since 1900, all but one of them men, and the pattern for each of them is identical. It is as follows:

> The would-be leaders begin their careers in their late twenties or early thirties as hard working, generous people who accumulate wealth or skills or connections with powerful outsiders, all which they use to help their families, friends, and community. They gradually build up a clientele of those in their debt, people who become dependable supporters. Over a period of years they build up reputations as shrewd, knowledgeable, generous, and trustworthy people. Eventually the reputation is converted to political position and/or religious office, such as chief, chief magistrate (or some other executive office), headman, deacon, and the like. Then a transformation takes place. The humble, generous facade disappears, and in its place is an imperious, self-indulgent presence, a power broker who gives orders to minions, takes what he wants, and listens to no one not in his 'league.' At this point, the fall is very rapid, always precipitated by some over-indulgence or political ploy that no one will accept. Within a few months, the person's capital is used up, and he has been voted (or hounded) out of office. In most cases, ignominy follows the fallen one to the grave.

This is a fascinating pattern of self-destruction that only four men have managed to avoid in the last 100 years, and three of these men were pastors with the fourth in the process of becoming one.

Now compare the percentages. There were only twenty-two political-ritual positions in pre-Christian times, only eight during the Japanese period, and up to about twenty-two political and ritual positions since World War II. On the other hand, everyone in the society becomes a mourner a number of times during his or her lifetime. So the rate is about twenty-three blowouts for maybe several hundred chances for uncontrolled will while it is only five for several thousand chances for grieving. In other words, compared to other crises of control, the Kapinga mourning practices work very well indeed. There are three reasons why this is the case.

First, the dangers inherent in grief are obvious and immediate. The dangers of passion and power are more insidious. They appear only gradually, so it is harder to take steps to avoid them. Besides that, it is not at all obvious what steps need to be taken to control passion and willfulness. There are no *ceremonies* for them. This leads us to the second reason for the success of funerals—the ritualizing of grief.

No matter what the circumstances of death are or what sort of relation a survivor had with the deceased—and these are every bit as variable with the Kapinga as they are with us—the first responses to death are entirely predictable. Everyone involved knows exactly what has to happen and in what order. Yet within that ritualized, predictable framework of response, there are details of making the ritual happen that are unpredictable and require conscious attention, labor, negotiation, and performance while being aware of others' responses. The demands of the funeral ritual provide comfort in their predictability, yet present participants with a series of social crises to which everyone's personal crisis must be subordinated. This leads us to the third reason why the funeral ritual works so well.

The funeral makes grieving intensely social. The grieving person is locked in to a continuous barrage of social demands requiring immediate and correct responses. One is also surrounded by those who simultaneously demand from and support one another. They demand work, goods, and quick decisions, but they also demand expressions of emotion, appropriately couched at appropriate moments. Grief is (literally) worked out, choreographed, staged, and judged in a public arena. It is, thereby, *regulated*. By contrast, the person in power is alone, without the social network that provides control for the mourner. This is the young politician's analogue of social death.

The genius of Kapinga funeral ritual, if I can call it that, is its message about life rather than about death. The intensity of social demands has to do with getting things from people and converting them to other things, like food, to give to people. Giving and taking, loaning and borrowing, remember, are not what people do, but what people *are*! The funeral embodies the meaning of personhood. It is about living.

ACKNOWLEDGMENTS

Research for this chapter was conducted between June, 1965 through September, 1966, funded by the National Science Foundation. Subsequent research was conducted in the summer of 1977 with help from the Office of Social Science Research at the University of Illinois at Chicago, who also helped with research from June, 1978 to January, 1980. Further research was conducted on Pohnpei and Kapingamarangi in the summers of 1980 and 1982. I am grateful to Jane Wellenkamp, Ellen Badone, Richard Preston, Esther Lieber, Dorothy Counts, and Eve Pinsker for their kindness and comments on this manuscript.

CHAPTER
12

Loss and Anger:
Death and the Expression
of Grief in Kaliai

Dorothy A. Counts
and
David R. Counts

The following chapter by the Counts stands in sharp contrast to the preceding one by Lieber. Kapinga society stresses control because powerful emotional aspects of the self, once released, are dangerous to others and to society in general. The Lusi-Kaliai treated in this chapter, see death itself as the problem, for it comes to most as the result of human malevolence. Death, hence, becomes a marker of the danger already present in Kaliai society, and a bereaved person's grief is compounded with anger and the desire for revenge.

*   *   *

When Abner and Lola left for their distant garden at dawn they had no way of knowing that they would never see Agnes, their sixteen-year-old daughter, alive again. It was mid-morning when a villager found her still-warm body hanging from a tree near one of the major paths leading from the village to nearby gardens. Alerted by the man's shouts, the men of the village brought her to the house of a kinsman. A young man was sent to take the news to Abner and Lola. When they returned to the village in mid-afternoon, Lola went directly to the house and began to weep and caress the body of her daughter. Abner staggered into the village plaza where he fell writhing in the dirt and crying, "Why did you kill my child? Why did you not kill me instead? Why did you kill my child?"

Months later, when the village moot had named those responsible for the girl's death and had required the guilty to make compensation payments to her kin, Abner refused to accept either the pigs or the shell money. Tears running down his cheeks, Abner insisted that the wealth should be given instead to Agnes' maternal relatives. As for him, he said, the gifts would neither cool his anger nor end his sorrow. They could not return his daughter to him, and he wanted nothing to do with them. The wrong done his child could not be so easily settled or forgotten.

191

Abner's cry, "Why did you kill my child?," and his refusal to accept the compensation payments offered for his daughter's suicide, are expressions of angry grief; grief that is based on assumptions about the cause and meaning of death (a more detailed discussion of this case is found in Counts, 1980b).

People everywhere lose friends and family to death. The shock and grief that people experience when they first learn of a death—especially an unexpected or premature one—seem to be similar across cultures. Indeed, grief may be experienced in similar ways by all primates and throughout the animal kingdom (see Averill, 1968 and Zeller in this volume [Chapter 2]). However, the way in which people experience and express their grief is culturally patterned and constructed. This construction begins only moments after they learn of the death. After the initial shock has subsided, people of different cultures react in a number of different ways. They may, for instance, seem to lose all inhibition as they erupt in a frenzy of wailing and self-mutilation, or they may behave in a circumscribed and restrained manner as they emphasize one or more of the components of grief: sorrow and depression, denial and disbelief, fear, despair, anger, guilt, and perhaps relief (Jackson, 1963; Kalish, 1985). Thus, in this volume we learn that the Toraja (Chapter 8), the Cree (Chapter 9), the Tanacross (Chapter 10), and the people of Kapingamarangi (Chapter 11) tightly control grieving behavior; that the Sufi (Chapter 6) and English Canadians (Chapter 3) deny the expression of grief; and that for the Huichole (Chapter 5), the Maori (Chapter 4) and the Kaliai—like the Ilingot (Rosaldo, 1984)—anger and guilt are major components in grief.

In this chapter we argue that Lusi-Kaliai assume that most death is premature and has been caused by a human agent. This assumption colors the way in which the Lusi-Kaliai respond to death and the way that they experience grief. We explain what constitutes good and bad death in Kaliai, and we argue that the form grief takes is defined by the mourner's evaluation of whether the death was good or bad. We also distinguish between immediate grief and the long-term grieving process, and we explore the extent to which grieving is a publicly monitored process that expresses the relationship between the bereaved and the deceased.

The Lusi-Kaliai are Austronesian-speaking people who live in five villages along the coast in the Kaliai area of West New Britain Province, Papua New Guinea. The people of Kaliai remain isolated, even though the town of Kimbe, which is the capital of the province and the site of a hospital, is only about 160 kilometers to the east. Because there are no roads linking Kaliai villages to one another or to the rest of the province, most travel is by sea. The significance of this is that the only locally available health care is at the Kaliai health center, located at the nearby Catholic mission. The health center is staffed only by nurses and provides basic care: first aid, medication for minor infections and illness, obstetrics, and a well-baby clinic. People with severe or chronic illness must travel to Kimbe. This is an uncomfortable trip. It takes up to twelve hours on a canoe fitted with an outboard engine to reach the road connecting the western part of the province with the town. Even severely ill people are frequently unwilling to make this journey. As a result illness and death and the grief that follow them are unfailing presences in Kaliai life.

Most death in Kaliai is premature, and the people do not usually consider it to be a naturally occurring event in the life cycle. They almost always attribute death to an external agent, a spirit or (more frequently) a hostile human being. The assumption that ill health and death are the result of human malevolence, is not uncommon around the world. It is also discussed in this volume by the Weigands for the Huichol and by Mead for the Maori of New Zealand. The Kaliai believe that a human agent may cause death by an act of violence; by shaming or slandering other persons, thereby causing them to commit suicide (they call this "killing with talk") or—most commonly among Lusi-Kaliai—by the practice of malevolent magic: by sorcery. As one of our consultants declared, "If we had no sorcerers, we'd have no death."

A good death occurs naturally in old age after a person has settled unfinished business and concluded the cycle of sharing and exchange that dominates adult social life. It is rare. Instead, death is usually untimely and strikes children, teenagers, and adults in the prime of life. People feel anger and the desire for revenge at a premature death because they believe it to have been the result of someone's action.

THE MEANING OF LIFE AND DEATH

The Lusi-Kaliai do not define life and death in the same way that English speakers do. They have no generic term for 'life.' They oppose existence (*imoro* 'it is') and a condition they call *mate*, a word that may be translated 'dead,' 'unconscious,' 'ruined,' 'fatally injured,' or 'terminally ill.' Persons who are *mate* may return to life at any time after they begin the process, including after they are 'really' and 'completely' dead.[1]

People know that dying is almost complete if the breath smells of death, if the person stares without blinking or shame at another person's face, is restless and must be moved frequently, or loses bladder or bowel control.

Dying is complete when breathing stops, when the heart ceases to beat, and when the eyes and mouth hang open. The spirit usually leaves through the eyes or mouth or, if both are closed, by the anus. Adults are buried twenty-four to thirty-six hours after death is complete. Infants and uninitiated children are often interred more quickly, for there are fewer people in a young child's social network

---

[1] A more complete discussion of this phenomenon and near-death experiences in Kaliai as well is found in Counts, 1983.

to come to the funeral. People are permitted to view the corpse until it begins to bloat. Then it is wrapped in pandanus mats and hidden from view.

Even though Lusi-Kaliai recognize complete death by the various physical signs, the emphasis in any discussion of *mate* is on the process rather than on the event. This process may begin with the social disaffiliation of an aged and decrepit person, or with the perception on the part of an ill younger person that he or she is dying. The death process continues after the body is buried, though it is usually irreversible after burial. Death for Lusi-Kaliai, then, is processual, reversible, and has boundaries other than the ones Westerners recognize. The separation of spirit from body is not necessarily permanent or instantaneous. The spirit leaves the body during dreams and visions, during serious illness, and in death, and it may return in all these cases. We know of a number of people of all ages who have been defined as 'completely dead' only to return to life. Three of these were men for whom mourning ceremonies had begun (Counts, 1983).

For the Lusi-Kaliai, death is not an end to life but a transition from one type of life state to another. As is true for the other peoples in this volume who believe in ghosts and the reality of the spirit world (see the chapters by Lieber, Waugh, Wellenkamp, the Weigands, and Mead), people who are physically dead are not necessarily socially defunct. Those who experience bodily death are in transition from human to non-human or spirit life. Lusi-Kaliai think that the newly dead remain aware of events in their community. This assumption has implications for people who commit suicide, for they expect to know how their death affects their survivors and to take grim satisfaction from revenge by their kinsmen on those who drove them to the act. The newly dead also are able to contact the living. They show themselves to kin who fail to avenge their death and may be called to appear at rituals held to identify those responsible for their deaths. The long dead normally have little interest in human affairs, but even after people forget their names, they are not completely separated from human society. Their voices are heard keening in the bullroarer's cry when someone dies, and they may steal children who are neglected or who wander away from the village.

Lusi-Kaliai separate a human village from the forest by scraping the ground free of all grass and weeds and by marking the perimeters with a fence or a hedge of crotons, plants that signify the borders between the human and spirit worlds (Counts, 1980a). They use similar markers to confine the dead within the boundary of human society and culture. People were once buried under the men's house or the woman's house. Today they are buried in a graveyard that is scraped clean and bordered by crotons. The graves of the newly dead are sheltered by small houses, and are often lined with shells or beer bottles.[2] Relatives tend the graves of the recently dead by maintaining the gravehouses, planting crotons, and

---

[2] The customs of scraping the grave and building a house over it are also found in Africa and in North America among native peoples and in the traditional American South (Jordan, 1982).

scraping them clean. A neglected grave signifies that no one remembers with affection the person buried there and is evidence of social death (see chapters by Badone and Ramsden for a similar point).

Lusi-Kaliai notions of the fate of the spirit after death have been influenced by the teachings of the Roman Catholic mission, established in Kaliai in 1949. Nevertheless, much of the old belief system remains intact. According to tradition, human spirits have two aspects: the *-tautau* 'spiritual essence' and the *-anunu* 'shadow' or 'image.'[3] The *-tautau* is the essence of self, the essential part of one's being, while *-anunu* means 'dream' or 'reflection.' Either may leave the body during illness and maya be seen by persons miles away from a dying person. When death occurs both aspects permanently leave the corpse; one remains near the body until it decomposes (decay and the spirit's departure are signalled by the collapse of the structure built over the grave). The other aspect goes to the land of the dead.[4] The departure should occur immediately, but if unavenged the spirit appears to its relatives—usually at dusk—to remind them of their duty. Nowadays people say that a unitary soul goes to Purgatory or Heaven, but it may remain near the grave or appear to its kin until a Mass has been said to send it on its way.

Catholic theology holds that the fate of the soul depends on how a person lives; traditional belief held that the spirit's fate was determined by how the individual *died*. Ordinarily, the spirit goes to one of several spirit villages located at specific sites in the New Britain interior. Although we know of no Lusi term for the concept, it is as though the spirit villages are located in another dimension. Humans who come upon one of the sites can smell the smoke of cooking fires and hear distant village sounds, but they can see nothing. The living cannot enter these villages unless they are accompanied in a dream by a resident. Then, like Persephone, if they accept the food or drink that is offered to them they may be unable to return home. As Ramsden observes in Chapter 3, "societies construct a notion of what comes after death as a mirror image of what precedes it." Life in Kaliai spirit villages mirrors life in human villages. People garden, hunt and fish, celebrate marriages and the affiliation of children to their kin group, and are otherwise occupied with human-like endeavors. Some people are, however, permanently excluded from this village life. The spirits of suicides and of women who died in childbirth exist on the outskirts of the spirit village, unable to enter and partake of spirit society. Instead they are outcasts and, like the Huron warriors discussed by Ramsden, they may be angry and dangerous to the living. Theirs are

---

[3] The notion of a unitary spiritual aspect or soul (Tokpisin *sol*) was introduced by the Catholic church. The notion that there are at least two nonmaterial aspects of life is not unusual among Pacific people. Mead (Chapter 4) discusses a similar concept among the Maori.

[4] Although our informants disagreed as to which aspect remained near the corpse while the other departed, most opined that it was the *-tautau*, the essence and perhaps the core of individuality, that went on to the spirit village while the person's *-anunu* or shadow lingered around its body.

the spirits captured as familiars by powerful sorcerers. One duty of these familiars is to seize the spirits of the sorcerer's victims and cause their death.

The transition from human to spirit person is a process, not an instantaneous event. Death requires the severing of human social relationships and the separation of the spirit of the dead person from his or her body. This takes time, especially for those who have become fully social beings. The corollary of this is that the spirits of the very young and the very old, being less tightly tied to their bodies and to their societies, are easier to separate. They are, therefore, more vulnerable to death. Young children who have not yet been fully integrated into society are not fully human (cf. Ramsden, Chapter 3). Consequently, they do not require public ceremonies of transformation. In some ways, young children are similar to the very old. Both lack the ability to reason and to make critical judgments. The boundary between infancy (which does not require a death ritual) and full human status (which does) is marked by the child's ability to discuss its dreams. The death of a young child, even one who has not yet become fully human, may be intensely tragic for the parents. In the terms used in this volume, they will grieve. However, the death tears no web of social relationships, for they have not yet been constructed. The death is not, therefore, a public matter and there is little or no mourning.

GOOD DEATH

Although it is relatively rare, a Lusi-Kaliai may die a good death in old age as a natural conclusion to the life cycle (Counts, 1976-77). No one is culpable in a good death. It does not suggest a breakdown in social ties, and it does not disrupt community life. It neither expresses or represents the destruction of relationships. A good death is usually the quiet death of an elderly person that takes place with his or her acquiescence. It is appropriate, it is under the dying person's control, and it permits time for the social connections that have bound the person to the community to be brought to satisfactory closure. These relationships are usually expressed through a reciprocal flow of wealth items. Everyone in Lusi-Kaliai society who enjoys fully human status is entangled in a web of exchange, sharing, and obligation that holds the society together. The persons with the greatest prestige and influence in the community are those who have most successfully manipulated their relatives, friends, and affines in order to direct the flow of great amounts of wealth. The ties of prominent persons are intricately entangled and extensive. It is, therefore, essential that an influential person, especially a bigman, sort out these complex relationships, settle debts and fulfill obligations, and bring both his social and economic affairs to a steady state before death. Until this occurs, until social and economic ties are balanced and severed, a person retains his interest in the affairs of the living; his death and transformation to the spirit world remains incomplete.

Most people prefer to settle their own affairs. This is why Lusi-Kaliai political leaders (*maroni* or 'bigmen') usually begin to withdraw from exchange activities and enter semi-retirement when they approach old age. Retirement permits a person to start the lengthy process of settling obligations and concluding business. Because death much more commonly strikes when people are young and vigorous than when they are old and feeble, only rarely do individuals complete the process of severing social relationships. When it does happen, the death is seen as being a natural occurrence and there is no suspicion of evil intent. Then survivors express their grief as private sorrow rather than public shock, or anger. Consider, for example, the good death of Koroi. Koroi was an elderly, senile *maroni* whose social death occurred two years before his physical death.

The Death of Koroi

In 1981, at the age of eighty to eighty-five years, Koroi was one of the oldest living Lusi-Kaliai. He had clear memories of the coming of the German colonial rule to western New Britain shortly after the turn of the century. He had become very feeble, could walk only with a stick, and spent most of his time asleep or reminiscing with others in the shade in front of his men's house. As a young man and as an elder, Koroi had been the village's most prestigious leader. Now, on those occasions when he attempted to reactivate his former status of *maroni* by directing the rituals sponsored by his sons, he was gently pushed aside and ignored.

In 1981, Koroi's sons began to acknowledge by public ritual his retirement from active life and the closure of his affairs. They held the first stage of Koroi's *ololo*. This mortuary cycle culminates in the distribution of the heritable property to the heirs and the termination of all obligations. An *ololo* is usually held several years after a death, when the heirs no longer feel angry. It is not an occasion for mourning; rather it celebrates the deceased's life. Koroi's *ololo* preceded his *physical* death by two years. It is most unusual for an *ololo* to be held for a still living person, but Koroi's sons explained that they were doing it "so that he can see, before he dies, how much we honor him."

The completion of Koroi's mortuary ceremony also enabled his sons to become leaders in their own right. They had increased their reputations and validated their claims to leadership by sponsoring the ceremony for Koroi. This accomplishment is normally denied to men until well after the death of their fathers.

Koroi's *ololo* was completed during the summer of 1982 with a distribution of hundreds of fathoms of shell money, cash, pandanus mats, clay pots, wooden bowls, and forty pigs. When his *ololo* was finished Koroi was socially dead. His sons had severed the network of debts, credits, and social ties begun for Koroi by his father and grandfather and upon which he built his reputation as a leader and bigman. He no longer had any business. It was done. The final ceremony marked the end of Koroi's life. His physical death in 1984 was of no consequence. He was buried where his men's house had formerly stood in the center of the village, in a quiet ceremony marked by only token funerary rites. With one exception there was no public mourning, only the private grief of his family. His widow, Gaia, began her public display of grief by wearing black and rubbing pig fat in her uncut hair after Koroi died and was still in mourning in 1985.

It is rare in Kaliai for social death to be so formally signalled before physical death. As Leenhart (1979) suggests, a person who is socially dead is not only excluded from social life, but is physically irrelevant. No apparent significance is attached to the condition of such a person's body. Some villagers say that Koroi died because his physical condition was neglected following his *ololo*. They claim he was not taken to the clinic for medication for a series of problems that eventually caused his death. If Koroi was neglected, it should not be attributed to callous indifference. His family believed that his body was only a husk from which Koroi's vitality as a social person had gone.

Less formal social death in Kaliai has been experienced by both women and men. It is preceded by the classification of the person as *taurai* 'decrepit and dependent.' It is, therefore, appropriate only to elderly people. It does not apply even to severely handicapped young people.[5] Dependence, which precedes social death, is a negotiable state that a mentally aware individual enters only with his or her acquiescence. It is a condition that may be refused, as is illustrated by the case of Sally who declined to be defined as a *taurai*, a 'decrepit old person' and set on the road to social death.

Sally's Refusal of Social Death

Sally, in her late sixties in 1991, is the only child of one village leader and the wife of another. She earned a reputation as a strong-minded and independent woman, active in political and economic affairs in her own right and in support of her husband. She suffered for years from blinding headaches and continuous eye infections and was totally blind by 1981. Nevertheless, she continued to weave fine baskets and participate in ceremonial exchanges. She also had a number of people—including a powerful sorcerer from a neighboring village—in her debt. In 1981 Sally attended a ceremony that culminated in releasing dangerous ancestor spirits. Ordinarily, women must flee the village when the spirits are fed. In this case, however, the men—including the sorcerer—announced that, because of her age and infirmity, they would consider Sally to be a *taurai* and invite her to remain in the village. Sally contemptuously refused the offer and fled with the other women to a secluded spot where they feasted and mocked the men. If Sally had

---

[5] Formerly children who were obviously severely handicapped at birth were exposed; today they are cared for by their parents and may live to adulthood.

accepted the appellation *taurai* she would have ceased to be an effective social being who could participate in a meaningful way in ceremonial exchanges. As well, her rightful claims for reciprocity would likely have been rejected by her debtors. She would have lost her status as a socially significant woman and a person to be reckoned with. Therefore she refused to present herself, or to allow others to classify her, as a decrepit and dependent old person in the first stages of social death.[6]

BAD DEATH

A bad death is premature and inappropriate. Even when the dying person seems to acquiesce in his or her death and tries to exert control over it—as in the case of suicide—it is a death out of time. It is always seen by survivors as being caused by a human agent. Suicide is always a bad death, for it represents the ultimate expression of the breakdown of social relationships. This breakdown continues into the afterlife where the suicide is excluded from the community of the dead. Inevitably, the suicide's survivors argue that the person was driven or forced to this extreme action.[7] Similarly, the victim of unrelenting sorcery may beg for death in order to escape constant pain (Scaletta, 1985).

The agent who causes a bad death is usually human and, nowadays, usually a sorcerer. There are two kinds of responsibility in cases of sorcery death: 1) the responsibility of the sorcerer who cast spell on the victim; and 2) the responsibility of the person(s) who hired or cooperated with him. The sorcerer's aide may have gathered the victim's hair clippings, fingernail filings, or sweat encrusted clothing. Or he may have slipped ensorceled material into the victim's food or drink. A sorcerer's collaborators are usually the victim's kin or affines. Therefore, a serious illness or death attributed to sorcery is especially traumatic for the victim. Not only do victims suffer pain and face death, but they are convinced that someone they know well—neighbor, brother, spouse—hates them enough to conspire in their deaths.

Bad deaths may either be sudden and unexpected—in which case the victims have no opportunity to settle their affairs—or lingering. In either case, the mourners assume culpable human agents and, like the Huichol who respond to deadly witchcraft with vengeful anger (García de Weigand & Weigand, Chapter 5), the grief of the Lusi-Kaliai is mixed with rage and the desire for revenge. Such feelings are amply exemplified in the aftermath of the death of Bruno.

[6] Also see Counts, 1985a; Counts, 1985b; Counts and Counts, 1985b.

[7] For additional discussion of suicide in Kaliai see Counts, 1988; Counts, 1987; Counts, 1984; Counts, 1980b; Counts and Counts, 1983-1984.

Premature Sudden Death: The Death of Bruno

In 1967, while returning from a long trading voyage with his father, twelve-year-old Bruno became lethargic and complained of a sore throat. By the time they arrived home the next day, the boy was seriously ill. When we saw him Bruno was lying on a mat, the inside of his mouth and throat covered with running ulcerated sores. His back was arched, his head thrown back, and he had a very high fever and was in great pain. Kevin, Bruno's father, took the child to the mission clinic in mid-afternoon. He was dead by dawn the next morning.

The news of his death reached our village in early morning. Bruno's body soon arrived home, and canoes filled with grieving relatives from nearby villages began to arrive. His mother's kin did not immediately come ashore after they dropped anchor, but sat in their canoes rubbing their hair and faces with powdered lime to indicate their grief. When they landed, they gathered at one end of the village and then strode together through the village carrying their spears in attack position. Kevin's kin, carrying shields and spears, met the visitors who drove their spears into the waiting shields. When their expression of rage at Bruno's father's kin for failing to care for their child was finished, his mother's relatives dropped their spears. Then the two groups of keening men embraced and went together to view the body of the boy.

People arrived all day and sat together by the body which had been dressed by his mother's female kin and placed under a lean-to in front of Kevin's brother's house. As the day faded, the crying and keening became more intense. With darkness, the bullroarer—the voice of long dead ancestors—was heard from the forest crying in sorrow and anger at Bruno's untimely death. As the bullroarer's crying died, Bruno's mother and other women began quietly to keen "Aeee, Aooo" as accompaniment to Kevin's song of lament:

> My own, my own. Why did you die so young? You have died without issue. Why did you leave me? Why did you die without bearing children? My own, my own.

All night the voices of Bruno's grieving relatives alternated with the cry of the bullroarer. The following morning the body, in a simple wooden coffin, was carried to the village cemetery a couple of miles to the east and buried there.

After the burial, Bruno's parents moved to a spot near the grave where their kinsmen had built a small shelter for them. They moved to be near their son because they were concerned that he would be lonely. As we noted above, the spirit of a newly dead person is thought to remain nearby as the corpse decays. So the villagers believed that Bruno's spirit lingered at the grave, near his body. He was so young, and he had died so suddenly, people explained, his ghost would not understand what had happened and would be frightened and lonely. In earlier days they would have buried him under the floor of the men's house where he could be near his kin. Australian law forbade such burial and the cemetery was far from the boy's home. If his parents were nearby, Bruno's ghost would be aware of their presence and comforted while he became accustomed to his new condition.

The family remained there for the next month. During that time they took care of few of their physical needs. They did not garden, collect firewood, draw water, or cook food. All their chores were done for them by relatives. Their only task was to stay near their dead child and think of him. After a month had passed, their kinsmen came to the cemetery bringing food and began preparations for a ceremony they called a *kap ti* ('cup of tea'). They quickly constructed long tables and benches and served a meal which included cups of hot tea liberally laced with sugar and (for the men) rum. When they had finished eating, the villagers dismantled the lean-to where Bruno's parents and siblings had been living, and the family returned to the village to resume normal life.

The sudden death of Bruno, an apparently healthy child, left no one in doubt that he had been a victim of sorcery. For the two weeks following Bruno's death, the identity of the sorcerer was a primary topic of conversation. People reasoned that, because a child "has no mouth"—that is, a child's words or actions would not cause an adult to kill him—Bruno was not killed because of anything *he* had said or done. His death was a result of his father's deeds. Because he was an only son, his death would be excruciatingly painful for his father. Not only is there affection between a man and his only son, but the child is his father's replacement in his kin group. Bruno's death would also, in a sense, be the death of his father because he would, as the Kaliai say, "have no one to take his bed." Kevin's rage was almost palpable during the early weeks following Bruno's death. He accused several prominent men of sorcery and tearfully threatened to get revenge. People dismissed Kevin's accusations and threats. He was, they said 'crazy with grief,' and they carefully monitored his behavior, concerned that in his anger he might attack an innocent person.

People also gossiped about Kevin's relationships with his fellow villagers in an effort to discover who hated him enough to kill his only son. The concern over finding the killer culminated in a divination rite. During the ritual one of Bruno's relatives asked his ghost to identify the person who had poisoned him. Because the spirit belonged to a weak child, the specialist asked other ghosts residing in the cemetery to add their strength to the boy's and help him identify his killer.

During the divination, Bruno's ghost suggested that his father had ensorcelled him. Villagers rejected this suggestion, so the ritual did not fully resolve the question of the sorcerer's identity. Nevertheless, the prime suspect feared for his life and left the village for good. Had he remained, our informants agreed, someone would have killed him either by violence or sorcery.[8] By 1981, the attitude of the villagers toward Bruno's father had changed because he had

---

[8] We also give details of Bruno's case in a more general discussion of Kaliai dispute settlement in Counts and Counts, 1974.

become a sorcerer. People explained that in 1967 Bruno's ghost had correctly identified his father as his killer. People had come to believe that the child had touched or eaten some ensorcelled item of his father's. Then, though the poison was not intended for him, he had succumbed to the power of his father's magic. Villagers have never considered the possibility that Bruno died from a natural illness. Bruno, most now believe, was his father's first victim.

All the elements of the Lusi-Kaliai reaction to a sudden death are present in the responses to Bruno's death. First, shock and anger are dramatically illustrated in the attack by Bruno's mother's relatives on the kin of the boy's father. Although they did not hold Kevin or his relatives culpable for Bruno's death, the mother's relatives felt their in-laws were guilty of negligence. If they had been alert, if they had diligently guarded against sorcery, if Kevin had not made enemies who hated him enough to kill his innocent son, then the child would not have died. The immediate response of Bruno's relatives was to assign blame for his death. A malevolent human agent could not have been successful if the adults responsible for the child's well-being had performed their duty.

A second element was community grief. By the first evening, people had arrived from neighboring villages to participate with the boy's immediate family in their mourning. The grieving kin were also joined by the dead, the ancestors whose cries of anger and sorrow were heard in the voice of the bullroarer.

Third, the conviction that the child's death was caused by a human agent is emphasized by the determination to identify the person who was responsible for it. To this end, the kin engaged a divination specialist whose ritual included an interview with Bruno's ghost and solicited the cooperation of other spirits. In their grief, both the living and the dead collaborated to assign guilt so that the killing could be avenged.

Finally, although the immediate pain of bereavement fades with time, the angry suspicion sparked by the death remains. More than twenty years later, villagers continue to attempt to identify the culpable party. Because there was no solution to the mystery in 1967, they now suspect that Kevin was indeed responsible. The persistent anger, determination to assign guilt, and desire to exact retribution is a characteristic response to a bad death. Among the Kaulong, another people of West New Britain, desire for revenge resulted in a sorcery war that killed many people before the exhausted remnants of the population declared a truce (Goodale, personal communication; see also Lindenbaum, 1979). We see another example of the Kaliai determination to assign responsibility for premature death in the case study of the death of Tim.

Premature Lingering Death: The Death of Tim

Tim was only seventeen in December of 1979 when he became ill with a persistent high fever that his relatives could not bring down by sponging him with cool water. The symptoms were consistent with those resulting from a common type of Kaliai sorcery. Although his kin took him to the clinic to be treated for malaria, they did not expect it to help. When he failed to respond, they brought him back home and engaged a local healer to try to stop the spell. Tim seemed to rally, but his recovery was temporary. After about two weeks of high fever, delirium, and great thirst, Tim died. Shortly before his death, Tim begged his father to protect him from two visitors who ostensibly had come to offer curing spells. In fact, Tim said, they had reinforced the original poison and had whispered to him that he would certainly die. During his illness, Tim's relatives tried several healer/sorcerers in a frantic attempt to avert death. Believing that the cause of his illness was sorcery, they tried to find someone who could reverse its course and restore him to health. Such attempts are always chancy because most Kaliai assume that *only* the person whose sorcery is causing an illness is able to reverse its course. Therefore, a curing implicates the healer as the cause of the victim's illness. Another widely held assumption is that most sorcerers have no malice toward the victim. They cast their spells as agents of a third party. Often the employer is a relative or affine of the ensorcelled person. Once found, the sorcerer is urged to identify his employer. If he does people can learn the reason for the ensorcelment, a reason usually found in the social relationships between the victim and the sorcerer's employer.

Tim's relatives' efforts to find the cause of his death were confused by his allegation that two men who had claimed to be healers were the real sorcerers. The confusion had several roots, all explored in the months following Tim's death. One confusing aspect was that one of the accused was Tim's brother-in-law, Bob. Almost no one believed that Bob knew sorcery or had any enmity toward Tim. The other man charged, Sammy, was widely believed to be a sorcerer. Although he had no known grievance against Tim, Sammy had a long history of conflict with Tim's father. As in the case of Bruno, this conflict could provide the motive for Sammy to kill Tim.

Despite this possible motive, Tim's relatives had no firm evidence of Sammy's guilt. So Tim's death remained unsolved and unavenged. From time to time the festering grief and anger would boil to the surface and involve the community in an anguished attempt to get positive identification of the killer.

Two years after Tim's death, Simon tried a divining ceremony somewhat similar to the one in Bruno's case. He hoped to establish the guilt or innocence of the two who were under suspicion. For a number of reasons the results of the divination were not accepted by the community. Kolonga, Tim's father, still visibly in mourning, was angered by what he regarded as the stupidity and danger of allowing an illegitimate divination ritual to slander innocent persons. He called a public meeting to make clear to everyone that he wanted such antics to stop.

During the meeting Kolonga faced Sammy, whom he believed to have killed Tim. He systematically ticked off the evidence that led him to his conclusion and cited the evidence that eliminated everyone else from culpability. Kolonga's anger and disgust were palpable, as was his frustration at being unable to do anything to rid his community of this killer. Kolonga's inability to do more than accuse stemmed from his commitment to living by the rule of the nation's law. Although he *knew* who had killed his son, his own values precluded his avenging his son's death, and his anger and grief continued unabated.

Because Tim's bad death could be neither resolved nor avenged, his family's grief stretched over years and resulted in his father's publicly accusing a fellow villager of murder by sorcery. His accusation, in turn, is almost certainly regarded by his surviving kin as a factor in Kolonga's own death in 1987.

GRIEF AND MOURNING

It is useful to distinguish between grief and mourning and to differentiate between the short-term and long-term expressions of grief. The Lusi-Kaliai term that best translates as 'grief' is *lolo-sasi*, literally 'bad guts,' also 'sad,' 'unhappy,' 'sorry,' 'upset.' This is the emotion people say they feel at the death of a beloved friend or relative, but it is also the term that is used to describe the emotion that can precipitate suicide (Counts, 1980b). An important component of this emotion is *lolo- ipaipai*, literally 'burning guts,' the term for anger. The term for 'mourn' is *oaso*, used for a person in mourning, a period of mourning, or the black paint used by people who are in mourning. The phrase *ikaro oaso* means he/she is mourning, while the term *mok* refers to the taboo that a bereaved person places on himself. Though closely related, grief and mourning are not inseparable. It is possible to engage in mourning behavior without feeling grief. Kaliai assume that this happens because a person's failure to mourn may cause others to suspect him of culpability in the death. So, as in the case of Akono below, villagers cynically observe that form may be empty of content and that intense mourning may demonstrate fear for oneself rather than grief for the dead.

Short-term Grief and Mourning

Short-term grief is the feeling of loss immediately after death occurs. It is usually a compound of sorrow and anger, but may be complicated by 'shame' *mamaea*- if the bereaved person has accepted responsibility for the death. Shame is felt if, for instance, a husband who has battered his wife accepts culpability for having driven her to commit suicide.[9]

Radcliffe-Brown suggested the utility of distinguishing between public reciprocal mourning which affirms social bonds and private weeping of the bereaved (1944:239-240). Reciprocal mourning is expected of everyone related to or

---

[9] We know of no Lusi word for the English word 'guilt,' and suspect that guilt is not an indigenous concept. Shame is, however, a powerful and driving emotion in Melanesian society and is "closely allied to the affect of grief" (Epstein, 1984:21).

friendly with the deceased. Failure to mourn suggests that one is not sorry about the death and may be responsible for it. Kaliai public mourning expected immediately after death includes singing mourning songs and keening—a high pitched combination of weeping, moaning, sobbing, calling to the dead, and song. Keening is self-consciously learned. Our young neighbor—a ten-year-old girl—practiced keening while looking in a mirror to observe the effect. She had watched her parents and other relatives keening after her younger brother's death and was concerned because she did not know how to do it correctly. She determined that the next time a relative died she would mourn properly, like an adult.

Because anger is so large a part of grief in Kaliai, people commonly offer expressions of regret and sorrow to deflect suspicion that they are somehow responsible for a death. For instance, if a person dies away from home, the residents of the village where he dies send the body back home with a small amount of wealth—usually several fathoms of shell money—as a sign of their sorrow and of their innocence in the death. If relatives accept these symbols of grief and innocence, they double the gifts and return them within a few hours.

One expression of grief that immediately follows a death, especially the unexpected death of a young or an important person, is the cry of the bullroarer representing the angry keening of the ancestors. The task of sounding the instrument is performed by a kinsman or fellow villager who was not intimately associated with the deceased.

After people die, their relatives immediately demonstrate their sorrow and anger by destroying property that was closely associated with them. Coconut palms that were planted in a child's name shortly after its birth are cut down if the child dies. Relatives also isolate themselves. Bereaved persons, especially members of the immediate family, withdraw almost entirely from normal social activity, as Bruno's parents did. They do not provide their own food, take part in ceremonial affairs, or even use the house they shared with the deceased. Instead they move to a vacant house, a cooking shed, or a lean-to near the grave.

The mourning state of recently bereaved persons is obvious from their physical appearance. Mourners rub their faces and hair with lime powder because white color symbolizes death. They rub charcoal on their bodies and clothing. They do not cut their hair. For Lusi-Kaliai men, a beard is a sure sign of recent bereavement. Mourning women rub their untrimmed locks with grease and soot. The bereaved continue to wear the same clothing worn when the loved one died, do not bathe, and often wear relics—a bit of the deceased's clothing or a wrapped lock of hair—around the neck.

These conspicuous expressions of grief last about six months. Each is brought to an end with the performance of a small ritual. A man's hair and beard are publicly shaved and he makes a small payment to the barber. Mourners discard their soiled and ragged clothing only when someone presents them with new ones. The filthy rags are burned and the mourner pays the person who caused him or her to resume a normal life.

In Kaliai the short-term grieving process of the living mirrors the process that the dead undergo in joining the society of the spirits. The relationship between grief and the condition of the dead is an extension of the connection that exists between the corpse and the soul of the dead. This relationship was first noted for southern Borneo by Robert Hertz who commented on "a kind of symmetry or parallelism between the condition of the body . . . and the condition of the soul" (1960:45). Metcalf observes that the Berawan of Borneo understand the character of the soul of a newly dead person by metaphorically linking it with the corpse (1982). This link also exists in Kaliai where there is a bond between the dead and the living who cared for them during their lifetime. As we discussed in reference to the death of Bruno, so long as the physical body of the dead person exists the spirit remains bound to it. As the body decays and the spirit is freed, it takes up residence in the land of the dead and participates in society there. He or she becomes an *antu*, a 'spirit person.' For the living who were closely tied to the dead person there is a similar transition. Grief requires that while they retain their bonds with the dead, the living cannot participate fully in normal social life. Indeed, immediately after a death the bereaved are removed from society. As the body decays and the ties between living and dead loosen, the living are gradually reintegrated into social life in the same way and at about the same time that the dead person becomes incorporated into the spirit community.

LONG-TERM GRIEF AND MOURNING

Long-term mourning does two things. It keeps alive the memory of the deceased, and it may signal that the death is unresolved. One function of long-term mourning, vivifying the memory of the dead person, applies to nearly all adult deaths in Kaliai. The existence of persons in a non-literate society continues past their death only so long as they are remembered by the living. The Lusi-Kaliai have a number of mnemonics that serve, by rekindling grief, to keep alive the memory of those who are dead. One of these ways is by song. Consider the following song memorializing Mary.

> Oh, who comes to break my walls? Ohhh!
> Children of Kandoka, you are naughty. Ohhh!
> Oh children, you don't listen to your grandmother.
> She calls in the daytime, in the afternoon, in the middle of the night.
> Night is falling and she calls, "Some firewood, some water, some food.
> "Bring it for me to eat.
> Ohhh! Hunger is cutting me deeply."
>
> Oh, who is that disturbing my fire?
> Oh, who comes to break my walls? Ohhh!
> Children of Kandoka, you are naughty. Ohhh!
> Oh children, you don't listen to your grandmother.
> She calls in the daytime, in the afternoon, in the middle of the night.

Night is falling and she calls, "Some water, some food, some firewood.
"Bring it so I can warm myself.
"Cold is cutting me deeply."

Composed by Clement Maro Laupu
Kandoka Village, 1985

Mary died in 1975, the victim of neglect. As she was decrepit and blind, responsibility for her care rested with two of her foster children, each of whom had a large family. Mary dwelt with neither, but passed her time in a small lean-to near the house of her foster son. There she was easy prey for the thoughtless—and to her cruel—teasing of the children. There, too, left alone during the day, she stumbled into her fire and died later of her injuries. The whole village shared the shame of her foster children at the neglect of a dependent and needy person. This shame is kept alive by Clement Laupu's plaintive and poignant song which captures her endless calls for help and her chiding of the teasing children. When it is performed, it rekindles the grief and shame of Mary's neighbors, and they often weep for her death and for themselves.

Other Lusi-Kaliai death mnemonics include the following: bestowing death nicknames on the closest survivors; wearing death relics long after short-term mourning has ended; and self-imposed tabus. These tabus include prohibition of bright colors, of items of food and drink that were favorites of the deceased, and of going to places with which the dead person was associated—such as a swimming hole or shade tree.

Death nicknames are given only to the closest survivors and often refer to some circumstance of the death itself. For example, one man was nicknamed *Balus* 'Airplane' after a relative who was flown out for medical care in hospital, while widows are called *Rais* 'Rice,' *Biskit* 'Cookie,' and *Tapioc* 'Cassava' in memory of dying husbands who craved these foods. Another person is nicknamed *Sosonga* 'Sweat' for a kinsman who perspired profusely during his last illness.

Death relics, usually a lock of hair or a scrap of clothing, are also used by close survivors to keep the dead person constantly in their memories. Two things about the use of such mnemonics should be noted. First, both the nicknames and the relics memorialize the *death* of the person, not his or her life. Second, the mnemonics differ from each other in the way that they are acquired and in the way that they are terminated. Nicknames, for example, are bestowed on the bearer by others and may last for decades, even when the bearer no longer finds the name appropriate. Second, the mourner who chooses to avoid a place, to forego bright colors, or to wear a memento of the dead also decides when to discard that memento.

In contrast, although bereaved persons establish tabus on food and drink for themselves, they cannot bring the tabu to an end. A mourner may do this to demonstrate that he or she cannot accept the death and is still grieving. Parents who have lost a first-born or an only child often tabu food or even water for this reason. Or a bereaved person may self-impose a tabu to acknowledge that there were unresolved bad feelings between him or her and the deceased. The tabu is usually on a staple food item such as sweet potato or taro, or on something that is highly desirable such as tea or sugar. It may even be on a necessity such as water. Mourning tabus are considered to be a severe hardship and may lead to real deprivation, especially in time of drought or famine. They are, therefore, a powerful public claim that grief continues unabated. It is only when others judge that the mourner's expression of grief and his or her separation from full social life through self-denial has gone on long enough, that the tabu is brought to an end. This decision is usually made by the mourner's relatives. They signal the end of the tabu by giving the bereaved some of the prohibited food or drink with a small portion of shell money. The mourner accepts the judgment by eating or drinking and then returning a gift of shell money. The grief of three of Kolonga's children—Mary, Paul and Bob—provides an example of mourning customs and the circumstances under which tabus are established.

The Grief of Kolonga's Children

Mary and Paul and their families shared a compound where their houses, a garden patch, and a copra dryer were located. All the adults of the compound were in mourning. Each week Mary went to clean the grave of her brother Tim, dead over a year, and she observed a tabu on sweet potatoes in his memory. She cleaned Tim's grave because she continued to grieve his death. She observed the food tabu to attest her anger that his death was unresolved. No culpability had been established and no one had paid compensation for Tim's death.

Mary's husband, Lou, was observing a tabu on taro in memory of his mother. She died estranged from him, still disapproving of his marriage to Mary. Earlier Mary had been married in a church wedding. Although wife beating is common in Kaliai, Mary's relatives considered her to be excessively abused. After a particularly brutal beating, Kolonga gave her refuge in his house and helped her to marry Lou, a widower with young children. They were wed in a customary marriage in which a small amount of shell money was distributed. The marriage was condemned by the local priest who suspended Lou and Mary from the sacraments as long as they continued to live together. Lou's mother, a devout Catholic, was shamed by their relationship and pointed to Mary's barrenness as proof that it was sinful. When she was unable to persuade Lou to leave Mary, she declared that he was no longer her son and refused to speak to or acknowledge him. Even as she lay dying she turned her face from him. Lou's tabu on taro was not undertaken to appease her ghost or to prevent her from harming him. It was an expression of his sorrow that she had died without their reconciliation.

Mary's brother Paul and his wife Tina were mourning the death of their only son Charles, who had died seven months before. When Charles died, Paul severed two joints from one of his fingers, a custom learned from his mother, a migrant from the New Guinea Highlands. Tina placed a tabu on tea, a drink that Charles had especially liked. Unable to endure the house where their son had played, Paul and Tina left their home and moved under Mary and Lou's house, which was on six foot pilings. When Bob, Mary and Paul's brother, and his wife, Rose, lost their infant son Hubert, they joined the other two grieving couples. All six adults lived on the ground beneath the house. When monsoon storms caused the ground to flood, they built slat beds so they would not have to sleep in the water, and put up blinds to protect themselves from the driving rain. Otherwise they continued to live in wet, cold, uncomfortable conditions, without cooking or gardening or otherwise attending to their needs. As Mary expressed it, "We just sat under the house and wept." After three months the local priest visited them. He advised them that their self-denial had gone on long enough and urged them to resume their normal lives. Bob and Rose returned to their home, Lou and Mary moved back into their house, and Paul and Tina built a new house in the compound with Mary and Lou.

The custom of imposing on oneself tabus that must be lifted by others illustrates the second aspect of long-term mourning. Lengthy mourning may signal that the death remains unresolved and unavenged. As such it is a source of anger both for the spirit of the deceased and for its living kin. Or long-term mourning may indicate that conflict existing between the deceased and the mourner was unresolved before death. The relationship between the two remains, therefore, marred by continuing regret and self-reproach or by anger.

We return here to the point made earlier. Just as the state of the soul reflects the state of the corpse, the condition of the mourner mirrors the condition of the deceased. We observed that if there are no extenuating circumstances, the decay of the corpse frees the spirit to join the community of the dead, and that the integration of the spirit in the society of the dead is reflected by the reintegration of the mourners into human social life. If, however, broken relationships between kin were not mended before death, or if a person's kin have not avenged his death or demanded compensation for it, then the spirit of that person does not sever its ties with the living. It cannot, therefore, participate fully in the world of the dead. In its loneliness it may lure away the souls of small children or enchant persons walking alone in the forest and entice them to their deaths. Such a spirit is potentially dangerous to the living because it cannot sever its ties to them. Its continuing interest is a result of lonely desolation, resentment, anger, and a desire for revenge—the same emotions felt by its living, grieving relatives. It continues to be a social person who cannot resolve its grief and, as such, poses a threat to the living.

The ability of the living to ease an unhappy spirit's grief and anger is limited. They can avenge the death or demand compensation for it and hope that the spirit can go to the land of the dead. If, however, the spirit lingers near the village because of unresolved conflict with the *relatives*, there seems to be little that they can do. They cannot change the fate of the spirits of people who commit suicide and are condemned to a liminal existence exiled from community with either the living or the dead. These spirits cannot re-enter the world of the living, but neither can they leave it. The cannot enter the spirit village where they belong but must hover on its outskirts, observers of but never participants in spirit society. The mourning customs that the living practice are not thought to assist spirits to move into the spirit world. Instead they allow the living to express intense grief. Such customs are a catharsis that permits the living to suffer self-imposed denial as an expression of sorrow over a ruptured relationship that can never be healed.

There is no mystical tie between the grieving relatives and the recently dead, but there is an important similarity between them. A spirit whose death is unavenged depends on someone else to take this responsibility and release it to enter the land of the dead. Similarly, mourners depend on others for their food, and those who have imposed on themselves tabus requiring self-denial can only be released by others who judge that it is time for this expression of intense grief to end.

We have described the grief and anger of a person whose loved one was killed by sorcery. We have also noted that the Kaliai assume that often a kinsmen of a victim engages the sorcerer who killed him. What of the grief of a person who is accused of culpability in the death of a relative? The following is a composite of several cases that have in common the widespread belief that the bereaved person was, in fact, responsible for the death for which he or she grieved.

Culpable Grief

Akono sat disconsolately on a stump by his house, his hair and beard untrimmed and dirty, his filthy clothing in rags. Six weeks earlier his wife, Galiki, had died. Some said she died as a result of drinking poison. Most believed that she had died by Akono's hand, either as a result of injuries she suffered from being beaten or because he had held her head and forced poison down her throat. During the twenty-four hours that her body had lain on a mat under the canvas lean-to in front of their house he had been inconsolable. He had insisted that she be dressed in all her finery, her shell bracelets on her arms and many strands of fine shell money around her neck and spread over her chest. As she lay in state he had refused to leave her side and had sat for hours holding her body, cradling her head against his chest while he keened and sang the songs of grief. Now he remained in deep mourning. In addition to his filthy condition, his only nourishment was coconut liquid and rice—all other foods were tabued—and he had restricted his activities to the area immediately adjacent to his house. His gardens were neglected, his children were in the care of relatives, and the shelves of his trade store were empty. In his grief he had invited the villagers to take everything. The door hung open, a reminder to everyone that he was now 'rubbish.' He was ruined. Despite Akono's display of the physical manifestations of profound grief, many of his fellow villagers were unimpressed. They believed him directly culpable in his wife's death. "When I was a boy," one villager commented, "my father told me that you could always tell a killer by looking at his eyes. 'Don't listen to his words.' he told me, 'look at his eyes for they will be sunken and hollow.' Look at Akono's eyes. They are the eyes of a killer."

A woman related that when she and the other women had gone to cry over Galiki they had been disgusted by Akono's display of grief and had stayed only a few minutes. "Why are you carrying on so?" she had asked Akono under her breath. "Why are you crying? Have you no shame? You killed her."

Still another villager observed ruefully that Akono should be grieving for himself. Even though he might make a large compensation payment to Galiki's relatives, it was unlikely that shell money and pigs would soothe their anger. Akono should be weeping with fear for his own life, for Galiki's family was known to hold onto their anger and several of them *were* sorcerers or had close ties with known sorcerers.

We do not know if Akono's grief was mixed with shame for his wife's death and fear for his own future. We are uncertain whether his mourning was a desperate attempt to convince his neighbors that he was not culpable for her death. We do know, however, that Akono did die a few years later, while he was in his prime. Following his death, Akono's relatives called a village moot to determine who was responsible for it. As the third villager had predicted, one of the area's most notorious sorcerers admitted that Galiki's father had employed him to cause Akono's fatal illness in retaliation for his daughter's death.

Unlike other Lusi-Kaliai who are bereaved, those who are held culpable for the death of a spouse or close relative find that neighbors doubt the sincerity of their expressions of grief. Villagers suspect that excessive display is motivated by fear for their own future rather than by sorrow and anger at the death of loved ones. Furthermore, they cannot express any anger that may be an aspect of their grief. Instead they must expect the anger of others to be directed at them.

DISCUSSION

We began this chapter with the observation that for the Lusi-Kaliai there is both a good death and a bad death. In the final analysis, of course, no death is ever really *good,* for all death is followed by sorrow and grief for at least some of the living left behind. The quality of the grief felt by the survivors, though, gives a clue to how bad or how nearly 'good' that death was, and so constitutes a commentary on it.

The Kaliai custom of expressing grief by a self-imposed tabu enables the mourner to express shock and profound sorrow at the loss of a loved one, and it is an observable link between the living person who cannot fully engage in human life and the dead one who cannot participate fully in spirit society so long as there is unfinished business. It also allows bereaved persons to acknowledge unresolved bad feelings between themselves and the dead and to expiate their responsibility for the rift. And it allows them to bring their grief to closure.

Lusi-Kaliai expressions of grief are shaped by their assumption that premature death is bad death. They consider it an unnatural occurrence resulting from 1) social relationships gone bad and 2) the malevolent actions of a (usually) human agent. As a result, Lusi-Kaliai grief is almost always a mixture of sorrow, anger, and desire for revenge. The mixture of grief and anger is nearly universal. As Rosaldo observes in his moving essay on understanding the cultural force of emotions, this combination of feelings—rage, born of grief resulting in the desire to kill—has an overwhelming power that communicates cross-culturally. It is experienced by North Americans as well as by headhunters and/or people who believe that death almost always has a human agent.

For some peoples (see chapters by Lieber, Simeone, Wellenkamp and the Prestons), death is a part of life and the emotions of grief that follow from it are a problem that must be solved, a danger that must be controlled. For Kaliai, *death* itself is the problem. The Kapinga, Cree, and Toraja fear that uncontrolled grief will destroy society. The Kaliai consider a premature death to be evidence that the dissolution of social life is already underway. For them, then, the emotions of grief are natural, expected, and may be given full rein. Calculated vengeance, born of angry grief, against persons that the community agrees are responsible for the death of a loved one is legitimate, expected, and reasonable. Grief is dangerous only if it leads the bereaved persons into irrational action or if it results in further killings that tear apart a community or result in a state of war between communities. Instead it is dangerous to fail to express grief and avenge death, for such failure results in a restless ghost who may lure away children and cause illness and further death.

Does the way the Kaliai express grief help to reintegrate bereaved people into the community and aid society to adjust to the loss of one of its members? Yes and no. Society supports bereaved individuals, considers their rage to be legitimate, and also tells them when they have mourned long enough. This works very well for people who grieve the death of the very old or the very young, but not for those who have lost people in their prime. A premature death is evidence of poisoned social relationships and puts the very existence of the community at risk. Because people assume that premature deaths are *caused*, almost the only way for the grief to be resolved is by another death. When one grief is brought to closure another is begun. Consequently, almost any dispute in a Lusi-Kaliai village occurs against a background of unresolved anger and suspicion and the fear of death. The potential always exists, in these cases, for the destruction of community.

Finally, grief springing from an unresolved death is dangerous because it involves *both* the still living and the newly dead in anger and loneliness. For Lusi-Kaliai, physical death is not coterminus with social death. In life as in myth (Counts, 1980a) the dead must break all their bonds with the living before grief can be stilled and its potential for social chaos averted.

CHAPTER
13

Memories of Marie-Thérèse

Ellen Badone

In Chapter 13 our attention is drawn away from the exotica of the isolated or encapsulated societies that provide the bulk of anthropology's material. Ellen Badone's research on death and grief took place in the (almost) familiar culture of rural Brittany in France. Her chapter brings us to the realization that the exotic may be found in the familiar, that the death of memory may be more final than the death of the body, and that it is not only persons who die. Societies also die and their deaths may be yet another source of grief for human beings.

*   *   *

The experience of confronting death is one of the few human universals. To study death as an ethnographer is to come face to face with one's own mortality. Death, grief and loss are the points in common which bridge the distance separating Self and Other, Subject and Object (Danforth, 1982:5-7). Too often, anthropological writing on mortuary customs in "exotic" cultures maintains a detached stance which drains death of both its emotional intensity and its power to threaten the ethnographer along with those whom he or she studies (Fabian, 1973; Rosaldo, 1984). In this chapter, I have specifically sought to avoid the pitfalls of this approach. Elsewhere, I have published more "objective" accounts of death in Brittany, although I have always made room for local Breton voices alongside my own (Badone, 1987a; 1989). Here, however, I have tried to go further, by experimenting with a literary stylistic framework. It is my hope that this has enabled me to evoke in a humanistic way some of the emotions which I shared with my companions during fieldwork.

During 1983-1984, I lived for thirteen months in La Feuillée, a small impoverished and depopulated rural parish in the Monts d'Arrée region of interior Brittany. I set out to study the impact of rapid social change on Breton responses to death. Much of my time in La Feuillée was spent thinking and talking with people about bereavement, solitude and, in the words of the La Feuillée priest, the "great mystery" of death which awaits us all. In the pages which follow, I have tried to set down on paper some of the conversations I had with people in La Feuillée, and in so doing, to translate the worldview that their words convey.

Known locally as *"la montagne"*, the Monts d'Arrée are a chain of hills which bisect the *département* of Finistère, rising nearly 400 m. above the Breton coastal plain which borders on the Atlantic and the English Channel. Although the Monts d'Arrée are in no sense "mountainous," the rocky outcrops at their summits and the contrast they provide with the surrounding countryside give these hills the impression of height and ruggedness. It is a harsh landscape, but not without beauty. Clumps of gorse and heather nestle against the rocks. The land is not fertile: "This is a poor country," as local people say. Market gardening and dairy-ing provide lucrative incomes for the people of the coastal plain, but here in the mountain, the soils are too heavy, rock-laden and acidic, the rainfall too high, and the temperatures too cool for successful crop production. During the 19th century, large herds of sheep roamed the Monts d'Arrée, but few people keep sheep today. Most of the active farmers in the area raise dairy cattle on a small scale.

According to local legend, the Monts d'Arrée have always been haunted by death. Here, one risks encountering the *Ankou*, death personified as a skeletal figure who comes with his cart to carry away the souls of the dying. To hear the sound of the *Ankou's* cartwheels creaking past one's house at night is a sure omen that someone from one's family is about to die (Le Braz, 1928:I:111-163).[1] To the south of La Feuillée, there is a marshy area, ringed by barren, windswept hills. Here, it is said, is located the Youdik, a turbulent pool which marks the entrance to Hell. In generations gone by, spirits of the malevolent dead, exorcized by priests and transformed into goats or large black dogs, were led by their keepers across the Monts d'Arrée to the Youdik. Hurled into the chasm, they disappeared never to return (Le Braz, 1928:II:251, 281-293).

Ironically, since the 1960s, the "entrance to Hell" has been the site of a nuclear power station. Built under de Gaulle, the nuclear plant was touted as the panacea for the economic ills of a troubled region. However, the secondary industry it was supposed to attract never developed. Since 1984, its technology obsolete, the nuclear station's operations have ceased. There is no other industry in the area, and with the financial instability of small-scale agriculture, most of the young people of the Monts d'Arrée move elsewhere, leaving their parents and grandparents behind to complain that "This is a dying region."

This pattern of rural exodus, the *exode rural*, has a long history in the Monts d'Arrée. As early as the 18th century, men from the area were travelling to other parts of Brittany, selling and trading livestock, wooden clogs, charcoal, chestnuts and grain (Cambry, 1979:130). By the 19th century, they were working as *pilhaouerien*, rag-and-bone men, collecting rags throughout Finistère to sell to paper manufacturers in the large Breton cities. More recently, Monts d'Arrée men travelled to England as "Johnnies," itinerant onion-sellers, or migrated seasonally to work as agricultural laborers on the rich farms of the Beauce. Some tempted

---

[1] For more discussion of omens in Breton folk narrative, see Badone (1978b) and (1989).

their fortunes in the New World, working in the lumber industry of northern Ontario, the textile mills of New Jersey, or the hotels and restaurants of New York city. In La Feuillée, where a special program offering the secondary school diploma was established by an enterprising teacher during the inter-war years, many men and women received training for careers in the French civil service, armed forces, police force and state school system. Their work took them far from the Monts de'Arrée—to Paris, Brest, Marseille, Toulon and North Africa. Many, however, conserved a strong sense of nostalgia for their home region. On retirement, many of these emigrés have returned to re-settle in the Monts d'Arrée (Chaussy, Emeillat and Messager, 1976:18-22).

In 1911, the population of La Feuillée was 1889 (Chaussy, Emeillat and Messager, 1976:Annexe 1:1). By 1984, there remained only 627 inhabitants, of whom 36 percent were over sixty-five years of age. Approximately half of these retired persons have lived their entire lives as agriculturalists in the Monts d'Arrée. The others are "returned emigrés." Most of the elderly grew up speaking Breton as their first language, although most now are also fluent in French, which they learned through school and used while working outside of Brittany.

Living in a community populated largely by the old, I was naturally drawn into conversations about death. Much of what I learned about death in La Feuillée came through my friendship with Marie-Thérèse, my eighty-four-year-old neighbor. Marie-Thérèse and I both rented rooms in one-half of a large house in the *bourg*, or town center of La Feuillée. Our landlord and his wife, *Monsieur* and *Madame* Postic, occupied the other half of the house, which had a separate entranceway. Marie-Thérèse and I shared a front door, hallway, washroom and staircase to the second floor. The Postics had refurbished the rooms I was renting, installing a modern stove, refrigerator and hot water heater to attract tourists during the summer season. They had done little to Marie-Thérèse's side of the hallway, however. Her sink ran cold water only, and her sole source of heat was a wood-burning stove, although she cooked on a gas hot plate. (See Figure 11.)

Marie-Thérèse's main floor room served as kitchen, bedroom and sitting room. Arthritis made it necessary for her to walk with a cane, and she negotiated stairs with difficulty, so her upstairs bedroom was reserved for use during visits from her son, Paul, who lived in a Paris suburb. I can never recall seeing Marie-Thérèse's room when it was not scrupulously tidy. The bed with its orange coverlet was pushed against the back wall, next to a solid oak *armoire*. A grandfather clock, whose chimes woke me at night, stood by the doors. In the center of the room was a wooden kitchen table, covered with an oilcloth and flanked by two low wooden benches. The stove and sink in one corner, a wooden chair with crocheted cushions next to the window, and a cupboard for dishes and linens completed Marie-Thérèse's furnishings. The wall opposite the door was occupied by a vast fireplace, with an embroidered linen valance suspended from the mantelpiece.

Figure 11. The author with Marie-Thérèse in her kitchen, 1984.

I spent a lot of time talking to Marie-Thérèse, sitting at her kitchen table in the evenings, chatting by the front door, or sitting on the bench—made from a converted Breton box-bed or *lit clos*—in the hallway that we shared. One conversation, in particular, stands out in my memory. It was close to the start of my fieldwork, in the summer of 1983, shortly after my husband and I had moved into the rooms on our side of the hallway. Marie-Thérèse invited us into her kitchen for coffee, and as we sat around her table, she recounted the story of her life.

Like many elderly persons in the Monts d'Arrée, Marie-Thérèse chose first to talk about the dead. The first time the *Ankou* passed by her household, he came for her infant sister, who was buried in her christening dress. Before Marie-Thérèse was ten, her mother, too, had died. Later, during World War I, two of her brothers were killed, while disembarking during a military landing in Turkey. A third brother survived to return to the Monts d'Arrée at the end of the war.

The two World Wars stand as major landmarks in Marie-Thérèse's personal history. During the German Occupation of the Second World War, she walked miles across the Monts d'Arrée visiting mills to buy flour in order to feed her son, her nephew and her ailing father. Marie-Thérèse's husband, Yves, spent the war as a P.O.W. in Germany, and she managed regularly to send him packages of home-made *crêpes*. At that time, Marie-Thérèse was living with three members of her family in the same downstairs room she now occupies in the Postic's house in La Feuillée. She could not then afford to rent the upstairs bedroom. On one occasion, German soldiers came to the house to requisition supplies. However, she recalls, "They just took one look and turned away, saying, 'Great misery.' They knew it wasn't worth the bother of trying to find anything to take here."

The next landmark event for Marie-Thérèse was the death of Yves, in 1975. After the war, he had found work on a road construction and maintenance crew. Retiring in his sixties, he had devoted himself to cultivating the large garden behind the house. At seventy-one, he seemed to be in good health. Both Marie-Thérèse and Yves regularly visited the doctor in a neighboring parish, and looked after themselves. One day in late February, Yves went as usual to buy his newspaper in the *bourg*. On his return, he purchased a piece of fish for their mid-day meal from the fish-merchant who visited La Feuillée each week. Then Yves decided to fill in the hour before lunch by digging up a patch of the garden, where he planned to plant shallots. Marie-Thérèse told him it was too cold for outdoor work, but he insisted. She followed him out to the garden, since she wanted to pick some leeks to make soup. As Marie-Thérèse recalls, she was about five yards away from where Yves was digging. When she started to pull up the leeks, he was working. When she raised her head again to look at him less than two minutes later, he had fallen over, with his face down in the earth. Marie-Thérèse screamed for *Monsieur* Postic to come with help, and ran to Yves' side. But it was too late, for he had stopped breathing. She knew as soon as she saw him fallen to the ground that he was dead.

Marie-Thérèse remembers every detail of the day Yves died. The landlord's wife *Madame* Postic was the first to get to the garden, because *Monsieur* Postic was slightly deaf, and had not heard Marie-Thérèse's call. She gave the fish Yves had bought to her sister and brother-in-law to cook because she could not think of eating that day. At first, Marie-Thérèse recalls that she cried uncontrollably. Then, her son Paul, with his wife and family, came from Paris for the funeral, and afterwards, Marie-Thérèse returned for a month to their home. During that time, strangely, she could not cry. "My nose was dry. I didn't need a handkerchief to dry the tears from my eyes." For Marie-Thérèse, this inability to express her grief was somehow unnatural. Since Yves' death, she has been very weak, and she sees her bottled-up grief as the source of her physical decline. Her arthritis has worsened and she tires easily. The doctor has recommended a salt-reduced diet, and she has little desire to eat: "Food doesn't taste the same without salt, and besides, when you can't eat salt, how can you have any strength?" Marie-Thérèse feels that knitting or reading makes her head ache, and talking too much with people makes her weary. "That really shook me," she says of her husband's death. "Before, I had much more strength. I used to walk without a cane."

I asked Marie-Thérèse if she thought about her husband often. "Yes," she replied. "Every day, every day. One doesn't forget. And every night, I say a prayer before going to bed." At the time, I wanted to ask her whether her prayer was directed to God, to her husband or to some saint. However, I could not bring myself to pose the question. Marie-Thérèse was not an overtly religious person, and I strongly suspect now, as I did then, that her prayer is addressed directly to Yves; that it is a way of continuing to talk with him.

It was the suddenness of her husband's death that was shocking to Marie-Thérèse. He died too quickly, and she did not have time to prepare herself as one does when a spouse declines slowly, or suffers a lingering illness. For Marie-Thérèse, as for many others in her generation, the "good death" is one which comes forewarned.

At the end of the first summer I spent in La Feuillée, my husband left to take up a teaching position in Canada. When I drove him to the Brittany Ferries terminal, we knew that we would be apart for four months, until he could return for Christmas vacation. My kitchen seemed very empty and quiet when I returned to La Feuillée alone. Within a few minutes, however, Marie-Thérèse found a pretext to pass by my open door. "That's it, you've said goodbye?" she asked. I nodded, and managed a smile, although I felt miserable inside. "At least you'll see one another again before too long," she encouraged me. "Think what it is like to say goodbye forever."

During the year I lived in La Feuillée, Marie-Thérèse walked only once into the main part of the *bourg*, a distance of about two city blocks. Usually, she would take a short walk daily along the laneway beside the garden. On the sole occasion that she did venture into the *bourg*, the goals of her trip were the town hall and the cemetery. A Breton proverb, told to me by Jannick, another La Feuillée widow, aptly expresses Marie-Thérèse's self-perception:

Pa vez dirodet ar c'harr
When the cart loses a wheel
Ne ya ket pell.
It will not go far.

As Jannick explained, a marriage is like one of the two-wheeled carts used on farms in the past for hauling hay. When one spouse dies, the survivor, like the cart with a missing wheel, cannot continue. For Jannick, the proverb metaphorically describes her emotional state. However she also interprets it in a more concrete sense. Like Marie-Thérèse, Jannick has literally "not gone far" from home since her husband's death. She prefers to stay near her hearth, knitting: "I don't enjoy being with other people. I've lost everything." This tendency among widows to renounce active social life stems in part from fear that conversations will evoke memories of the past, making it difficult publicly to control expressions of grief. Another widow in her seventies confided to me that she prefers to stay at home where she can "keep my sorrow to myself."

Anniversaries constitute especially difficult moments for widows in La Feuillée. Many families mark the first anniversary of a death with a religious service, the *messe d'anniversaire*, followed by a family meal. In the past, when formal mourning was observed, the first anniversary mass marked the end of the period of full mourning, when black clothes were obligatory.[2] Some widows explained to me that their inner grief began to diminish once the first anniversary of a husband's death had passed: "After the *messe d'anniversaire*, things get better." Even if the daily experience of grief wanes, however, grieving is renewed annually as the anniversary of the death approaches. During the month of February, 1984, Marie-Thérèse was extremely irritable. She complained daily about her health, which as far as I could see, was no worse than usual. Sometimes, I found myself close to losing patience with her gloominess, but I reasoned that it must be the product of the cold, grey weather and the interminable winter rain. Then, one evening while writing notes on my day's activities, it came to me that February was the month in which her husband had died. I was able to see beyond the complaints I had thought were trivial to the underlying cause of her depression, and I was ashamed of my earlier lack of perception. In some ways, the nine years since Yves' death had passed slowly for Marie-Thérèse, but her sense of loss had remained acute.

---

[2] However, the length of the mourning period was variable and many widows continued to wear black for the rest of their lives. I do not recall seeing Marie-Thérèse in clothes of any color except black, dark green, grey, or navy blue.

Despite her desire to withdraw from social contacts, I noticed that Marie-Thérèse's spirits actually seemed to improve when she had visitors. This was especially true when her son Paul came with his wife and family to spend two weeks of their vacation in La Feuillée. At fifty-five, Paul had just taken early retirement from the Paris police force. His wife, Denise, continued to work in an office job. Their son, a truck driver, was married with two young children. Paul's fifteen-year-old daughter, Michelle, was in love with Michael Jackson, and during these visits, the house echoed with his music, played on Michelle's portable turntable, to Marie-Thérèse's chagrin. Neighbors hinted to me that after Yves' death, Marie-Thérèse could have stayed on in Paris with her son, but she chose instead to return, finding it hard to adjust to the "modern" lifestyle of the younger generation.

Unlike some of his contemporaries, Paul has not chosen to return to La Feuillée on retirement. For some people from La Feuillée, the forty odd years spent working outside the Monts d'Arrée seem to be an insignificant interval, joining the truly meaningful periods of life—childhood and old age—which are spent in La Feuillée. Seventy-one year old *Madame* Tanguy who lived in the next house down the road from Marie-Thérèse and I, was one of these "returned emigrés". Born in the hamlet of Kerberou, one kilometer outside the *bourg* of La Feuillée, she left to attend boarding school in Brest at age eleven. At nineteen, she moved to Paris, where she married and stayed, working as a nurse, until age sixty. On their retirement, she and her husband returned to La Feuillée and moved into the house she had inherited from her parents. Each year, *Madame* Tanguy and her sister, who also lives in La Feuillée, have a special meal with the Kervellas, who live in Kerberou. *Monsieur* Kervella, who is three years older than *Madame* Tanguy, also grew up in Kerberou. He, too, left at age nine or ten, with his parents who went to work in northeastern France. As *Madame* Tanguy explains, "We know each other well. We were children together and now we are old together." At the opposite pole of life, one rediscovers companions from childhood. Through return migration, life comes full circle, and one rediscovers one's origins.

This construction of the life cycle is not uniquely a women's perspective. *Monsieur* Mahé, in his early seventies, retired to La Feuillée after making a career in the Navy, during which he was stationed in Paris, Toulon and Brest. When I asked him if he had found it difficult to readjust to the pace of rural life, he exclaimed, "On the contrary! It's an imperative to return *au pays*. You find the friends of your childhood again. Their characters have not changed and we talk about the old days, about our youth. We get along very well."

To some extent, return migration, or the *retour au pays,* is motivated by a desire to trade the noise and congestion of the city for an attractive rural retirement setting. Beyond this, however, the *retour au pays* forms part of a worldview within which it is perceived to be important to die and to be buried in the place where one was born. Such a perspective is voiced by a forty-seven-year-old La Feuillée man who currently lives near his workplace in Brest. As he explains, he intends to be buried in La Feuillée: "I was born here, and one must end up in a *la terre natale* for eternity." Others express the desire to be buried in La Feuillée "because all the family is there." Here, the connection between genealogical and geographical origins is clear. Even people in their thirties voice their unwillingness to be buried in cities such as Paris, "where we have no roots." Such comments suggest that from the perspective of La Feuillée emigrés, the term "life cycle" is indeed appropriate, for birth and death are symbolically linked in a circular fashion through return migration.

For demographers and sociologists, population statistics confirm that in upland regions of interior Brittany such as the Monts d'Arrée, there is typically

> . . . an emigration of the young, who start their families in urban zones, while the elderly return in more or less large numbers to finish their days in their natal region (Beuchet, 1982:6 my translation).

Among those from the Monts d'Arrée, it is not difficult to explain this demographic trend. As La Feuillée people say,

> Piv 'zo ganet e gwall vro
> He who is born in a miserable country
> War zu henni a zistro
> Always returns.

Regardless of the economic conditions which forced them to leave the Monts d'Arrée, it is believed that the emigrés are impelled to return, especially as death approaches. "Once they reach a certain age," comments a local woman, "they all return."

This permanent return is prefigured annually by a temporary return migration to La Feuillée at *Toussaint—la Fête des Morts* (All Saints' Day and All Souls' Day), the Catholic festival of the dead on November 1 and 2. At *Toussaint*, the number of people in the community increases by two or three times. Nearly every household entertains children, grandchildren or other kin visiting from the urban centers of metropolitan France. More people return to La Feuillée for *Toussaint* than for Christmas or any other calendrical festival. The parish *curé* ministers to his largest annual congregation at the *Toussaint* mass. As La Feuillée people explain, *Toussaint* is the most important religious occasion of the year "because it is for the dead, and as you know, everyone from the parish has some people buried here."

As many people from La Feuillée observe, *Toussaint* is a day of remembering. The dead achieve a kind of immortality in the thoughts of the living. Flowers are offered as a token of remembrance, in a symbolic transaction between the living and the dead. The day before *Toussaint* is the occasion for a pilgrimage to the cemetery, as people bring pots of chrysanthemums, heather or azalea to place upon their family graves. Previously, the tomb monuments have been scrupulously cleaned and weeds have been uprooted from the surrounding gravel.[3] To clean and decorate a tomb is perceived as a message to the dead "that we haven't forgotten them." People remark that "If there are no flowers on a tomb, people think 'Their relatives could have spared a thought for them, after all.'" Those graves which are left undecorated are regarded as *triste*, or sad. An abandoned grave signifies that those buried within have passed out of living memory. They have suffered a second death through being forgotten.

In the past, the souls of the dead were believed to return to their former homes on the night of *Toussaint*. A special meal of cider, buttermilk, and *crêpes* was left on the kitchen table and a large fire was kept burning in the grate throughout this night for the benefit of the returning dead (Cambry, 1979:173; Le Braz, 1928:II:75, 79-82). Now, it is not the dead kin but the living—emigrés dispersed by the *exode rural*—who return at *Toussaint* to families in their natal communities. Symbolically, this temporary reversal of the migratory trend is itself a type of return from the dead. Like the dead whose graves lie untended at *Toussaint*, those living members of the community who do not return are gradually forgotten. To return to La Feuillée for *Toussaint* enables one to re-establish contact with relatives in the community and to renew ties with childhood friends living elsewhere who have also returned for the festival. To return for *Toussaint* is to be remembered and to be talked of by one's kin and former neighbors. In returning, one reaffirms one's commitment to family and community, through fulfillment of obligations to their dead. Not to return forfeits one's identity as *Feuillantin*, someone from La Feuillée. As Marie-Thérèse told me, those emigrés who, in leaving the region, have lost touch with family are said to be "aet 'maezh ar kar," or "gone outside of the kin." Socially, they are equivalent to the forgotten dead.

Return migration to La Feuillée is closely linked to a desire for reunion of family members in death. The elderly hope to be buried in the same tomb where other relatives have already been laid to rest. Frequently, older people voice the hope that their children and grandchildren will be buried with them in a common grave. Expensive arrangements, sometimes involving exhumation, are made to transport the bodies of relatives who die elsewhere back to the Monts d'Arrée for burial in a family tomb. When she was no longer capable of travelling to Lorient, a city on the south Breton coast where her daughter and son-in-law were buried, *Madame* Ploneis, a La Feuillée woman in her eighties, had their bodies exhumed and brought to La Feuillée to be reinterred in her own tomb. Like many others of her generation, *Madame* Ploneis thinks of these family members as "waiting" for her to join them in the grave.

---

[3]See Brandes (1981) for description of similar celebrations on All Saints' Day in Andalusia.

Not all of the emigrés who leave La Feuillée seek to return, however, in life or in death. One of those who is not drawn back to the parish is Marie-Thérèse's son, Paul. At *Toussaint* in 1983, I asked him whether he hoped to be buried in his parents' tomb in the La Feuillée cemetery. His negative reply was distressing for Marie-Thérèse. "I have only one son," she told me later, "and I find it hard to accept that he will not return here." Paul's principal ties are in the Paris suburb where his son and family are now established. The parents of Denise, Paul's wife, are buried there, and she will most likely choose to be interred with them. If Paul decided to return to La Feuillée, it would mean that he would be separated in death from his wife. Marie-Thérèse understands his reasoning, but she is nonetheless saddened. Not only will she be interred separately from her son, but in addition, since Paul does not intend to be buried in La Feuillée, he is unlikely to return after her own death to tend the family tomb. At *Toussaint*, there will be no one to make sure that her grave is cleaned and decorated. She and Yves will enter the ranks of the forgotten dead.

It is painful for Marie-Thérèse to think that she will be forgotten after she dies. Beyond this, however, she fears that her undecorated tomb will be an annual source of shame at *Toussaint* for herself and her family. Marie-Thérèse talks of her situation after death in the tomb as if she will be conscious of the events which take place in the world of the living above her. It is as though she feels she will be able to hear in embarrassment the comments of her former neighbors, as they look with pitying and critical eyes at her neglected grave.

Once, while reading the obituary notices in the local newspaper, *Le Télégramme*, Marie-Thérèse remarked to me that often nowadays the notice specifies that no flowers or wreaths are to be offered at the funeral. She suspects that these cases are funerals of people whose children live far away—in Paris, for example—and cannot return to remove the flowers from the tomb during the days following the funeral. Rather than leave wilting flowers to decay on the grave, Marie-Thérèse thinks that these families request that no flowers be offered at all. I could tell she was thinking of her own situation when she ventured this explanation to me. I am certain that Marie-Thérèse has many times visualized her own funeral in her imagination, as she sits in her chair by the window, on rainy winter afternoons. In her mind's eye, I am sure she sees exactly who will be present, how full the church will be, and who will offer Masses for the repose of her soul. I think too, that she supposes, or fears, that the obituary notice which Paul will place for her in the *Télégramme* will state "No flowers, no wreaths." Lacking flowers, her funeral will be *triste*, sad and lacking in sacred dignity. Again, as she imagines herself lying in the coffin yet still fully aware of her surroundings, she sees the *triste* funeral as a source of public shame.

For Marie-Thérèse, death itself, or the state of being dead, is not a source of fear. "We have to die," she states simply. "It's the most natural thing there is." Along with many others of her generation in La Feuillée, Marie-Thérèse sees death as a deliverance from health problems and loneliness. "All the old are glad to die," remarked another eighty-three-year-old La Feuillée woman to me once, in a conversation about old age. Death puts an end to human suffering, and holds out the possibility of eternal reunion with those who have gone before.

It is not death which is frightening for Marie-Thérèse, but rather the process of dying. "We all have to have something to take us away from here," she would tell me. Likewise, a neighbor in her eighties explained. "The worst misery we will go through is in leaving from here." One cannot tell in advance what illness is going to carry one off, nor how one will suffer. Many elderly La Feuillée widows, including Marie-Thérèse, have difficulty sleeping, and as they often told me, it is when lying awake at night alone that they start "To reflect on things one shouldn't think about." I am sure that the nature of one's own dying belongs in this category of "black thoughts." Sometimes, now, if I am alone at night and cannot sleep, I too listen to my heart beat and think of Marie-Thérèse. Like her, I wonder what it is that will "take me away from here," and when the *Ankou* will come for me.

Despite their fears of dying, however, the elderly in La Feuillée face their illnesses with equanimity. Frequently, they suspect that health care professionals try to "keep the truth" from those who are about to die. Most La Feuillée people claim that they would want to be informed if they were suffering from a fatal disease. "I would prefer to know," Joséphine, a spinster in her seventies, told me. "I said to the doctor, 'If it's cancer, I would rather know.' You have to face up to it." For Joséphine, each individual must endure whatever illness it is that is going to put an end to his or her existence on earth. It is better to know if one is going to die, because foreknowledge allows for preparation.

Many La Feuillée women have organized in advance the details of the rituals that will take place after their own death. Fine linen sheets and crocheted white bedspreads are kept in readiness in the *armoire*, sometimes wrapped in plastic film or paper and marked "In case of death." Some women have knitted the white sweaters or bedjackets which they hope to wear when they are laid out for the wake. It is rare to find an elderly person who has not planned where he or she will be buried, either through the construction of a family tomb, or by renting a tomb emplacement in the cemetery.

Since the state of death is not dreaded but the pain of dying generates anxiety, attitudes towards euthanasia in La Feuillée are generally positive. Several people told me they would rather die quickly from "a good injection" than suffer lengthy months of pain. After the death of a local woman who had been receiving dialysis treatment for over a year, her neighbor speculated that the doctors at the hospital had administered "*la piqûre du trépas*," or the "death injection" to free her from her misery.[4]

---

[4]The conception of the *piqûre du trépas* presents an interesting comparison with that of the in the *remédios da desempata* or "medicine of the deciding game" recorded by Pina-Cabral for northwestern Portugal. In this region, local people believe that doctors administer a certain type of medicine (*remédios da desempata*) to those who are extremely ill at the point when they are hovering between life and death. Pina-Cabral (1980:3) writes:

If the person has life in him or her, he or she will survive; if on the other hand, the person is fated to die, death will immediately ensue.

Although the Portuguese and Breton beliefs appear to differ, they may be related and further investigation on this point would be valuable.

While the idea of euthanasia is not difficult for La Feuillée people to accept, cremation represents a far more problematic issue. Whenever we discussed the topic, Marie-Thérèse would pronounce the French word, "in-cin-é-ra-tion," very carefully and deliberately. It was obviously a troubling concept about which she had little occasion to speak. Once she told me about a certain person in the bourg who had requested to be cremated. However, this was considered sufficiently bizarre that she added, "You don't need to tell anybody in the neighborhood about that." Cremation is difficult to accept in La Feuillée because it abruptly destroys the body and ruptures the possibility of lasting ties between the living and the dead. Although especially important at Toussaint, visiting the cemetery is a central part of the grieving process throughout the year in La Feuillée. By visiting the graves of relatives, one can in some sense continue to communicate with them. As widows explained, by visiting their husbands' tombs each day, they were able to overcome the feeling of having abandoned their spouses in the cemetery. The visit to the tomb enables one to carry on an internal dialogue with a deceased husband, telling him one's problems or sharing events that he would have enjoyed during life. This kind of on-going relationship with the dead is, however, linked to their physical presence in the grave.

At one level, the grave is conceived to be the place where, in a very material sense, the dead continue to "live." People rarely speculate about a spiritual afterlife, despite their education in a traditional Catholic milieu which emphasized the reality of a tripartite otherworld in which one was relegated to Heaven, Purgatory or Hell (Croix and Roudaut, 1984; Badone, 1989). In contrast, the most commonly expressed contemporary vision of post-mortem existence is extremely materialistic. Asked about death, people say, simply, "We go into our tombs." The tomb is sometimes jokingly referred to as the "*maison secondaire*," or vacation home for the future. I have also heard people from the Monts d'Arrée jest about how they will play cards after death with neighbors buried in adjacent tombs. By reducing the body to ashes, cremation precludes the possibility of this kind of physical existence after death. Moreover, it prevents the living from recovering a kind of communion with the dead at the grave.[5]

Many of the attitudes toward aging and death shared by the elderly in La Feuillée are revealed in the following conversation, which I had on the doorstep of our house with Marie-Thérèse and her eighty-three-year-old friend, Madeleine Bleunven. Madeleine had come to the *bourg* to do her shopping, and she stopped with us to talk and rest on her way home.

Madeleine: All the old people have something wrong with them, everyone, everyone does. Me, sometimes I have a bit of arthritis there (pointing to the back of her neck).

[5]Contemporary attitudes toward cremation in La Feuillée have also been shaped in part by Catholic teachings prior to the 1960s, which emphasized the incompatibility of cremation with the doctrine of physical resurrection.

Marie-Thérèse: You too? So do I!

Madeleine: And after that, it's in my arms, or my legs. I get cramps.

Marie-Thérèse: Oh, cramps!

Madeleine: Well, well, we have been young and we won't be young again.

Marie-Thérèse: No, at least not unless we return again for another life on earth.

Madeleine: (giving Marie-Thérèse a skeptical look) We don't return. We go into our coffin and we decompose. Eaten by the worms. (As she spoke, she looked hard at me to reinforce the awful finality of this statement). And to think that everyone will end up the same way . . . But what does it matter—eaten by the worms? After one is dead, one has no more pain.

Marie-Thérèse: No, it's before that one suffers.

Madeleine: As long as we are spared our sight, so that we can wash ourselves and stay in our own homes. As long as we aren't reduced to a state worse than infancy.

Madeleine's final comments underscore the importance attached by the elderly to independence. Although geriatric facilities have expanded rapidly in rural Brittany since the 1960s, the elderly resist what they perceive as the impersonal character of these institutions. To die in the publicly-funded retirement home, located in Huelgoat, 13 kilometers south of La Feuillée, is also interpreted as a source of shame, for it means that one has been abandoned to the care of strangers by one's family. Family care is, however, no longer practical in many instances, especially when children and other relatives live far from La Feuillée. Throughout rural Brittany, a home-helper service which fills part of the gap left by the absence of family care is maintained by the organization *Aide à Domicile en Milieu Rural* (ADMR). The ADMR is partly staffed by volunteers, although the home-helpers are paid at the minimum wage and some public funding is provided to the organization. Daily visits from a home-helper who did laundry, shopping and heavy cleaning, enabled Marie-Thérèse to remain independent in her own home during the time I lived in La Feuillée.[6]

At New Year's in rural Brittany, neighbors keep up the tradition of visiting to wish one another well for the coming year. It is the duty of younger people to call on the elderly, who have difficulty moving about in the winter weather. On the second day of January in 1984, our neighbor from the house across the road came to wish Marie-Thérèse happy New Year. She served him the traditional *apéritif*, and they chatted about local news. As he left, he promised that he would be back

---

[6]For more detailed information on the ADMR home-helper service and Breton geriatric institutions, see Badone (1989).

again to see her next year. "If I am here," she called after him as he walked away. Turning to me at the door, she reflected, "It's sad to get old. Things are not always gay." Then, with an expression of resignation she sighed, "But, life is like that." I remember commenting, tritely perhaps, that it is unfortunate that we cannot all stay young forever. Marie-Thérèse looked at me and replied, "Yes, but the wheel turns for everyone. And one stays young for a good length of time. For me, it's finished now." She looked slightly bitter, but less so, I thought, at the prospect of death than about being left to face it alone. Death, after all, as she said, is something "we will all pass through. The old must give way to the young."

The elderly in La Feuillée accept their deaths as part of a natural order in which death and regeneration are closely linked. Autumn is seen as the season of death in La Feuillée. It is said that "Here, more people die when the leaves fall. The elderly who are not well, many die at the same times the leaves fall."[7] However, in the same way as spring follows autumn in the seasonal cycle, those who die will be replaced by the young. Like Marie-Thérèse, many elderly persons who have passed their entire lives in the Monts d'Arrée express the view that their deaths will provide opportunities for a new generation. "We are not here to stay," it is said. "It is necessary to make room for the others." Such a perspective is finely tuned to an earlier period, when more young people remained in the Monts d'Arrée and those who wanted to work the land depended on access to family property for their livelihood. Death marked the transfer of land through inheritance from parents to their children.[8] In such a setting, the older generation could meaningfully interpret their passing as a process of "making room" for the young. In contemporary La Feuillée, however, the *exode rural* has threatened the certainty of this cyclical continuity. It becomes more difficult to give credence to the natural justice of death when few children remain to take over the farms where the elderly have labored for a lifetime. Even the continued existence of the community seems in jeopardy. The comment of a farm woman in her seventies poignantly expresses the challenge which social change has posed to the traditional interpretation of death: "It is necessary to make room for the others, but there are not many who will come after us."

For the emigrés, death is given meaning through the metaphor of return rather than by reference to the natural replacement of one generation by another. The symbolic linkage of death, family and return is an important *leitmotif* of worldview for the returned emigrés. The dead compel the living to return to La Feuillée for *Toussaint* and also for funerals. It is often observed that "There are certain relatives we only see on sad occasions." At funerals, as at *Toussaint*, the dead provide a reason to reassemble the extended kinship group which has been dispersed outside the Monts d'Arrée.

---

[7]In fact, although autumn is *perceived* to be the time when many people die, statistics for Brittany indicate that seasonal differences in mortality are minimal (INSEE 1980:64).

[8]For a sensitive discussion of aging, death and inheritance in Spanish context, see Behar (1986).

Ties to the dead, to the family and to the land—*la terre natale*—draw Breton emigrés back to their communities of origin. For emigrés, the death of the self is also envisaged as a return. Return migration at *Toussaint* prefigures the more important *retour au pays* of the elderly. Retirement and resettlement in La Feuillée is a rite of passage which marks the beginning of socially recognized old age. More than a physical event, death is a long-term social process which begins for emigrés with the *retour au pays*. This permanent return is foreshadowed annually by the temporary return migration to La Feuillée at *Toussaint*. For the emigrés, as for life-long La Feuillée residents, time moves in a circular fashion. The circle begins and ends in La Feuillée, although the greater part of its circumference may pass through Paris, Toulon or Brest. Ultimately, one returns to one's origins, to join one's dead in *la terre natale*.

Epilogue

I have not made my own return pilgrimage to La Feuillée since I left the field in August 1984. Every year, I send New Year's greetings to fifty or more households in the community. Every year, one or two letters are returned unopened, with the word *"Décédé"*, deceased, written across the envelope by the postal clerk. In January 1985, I received a two-page letter from Marie-Thérèse, written in her own hand. She was well, although, as she wrote: "I have trouble walking. I go slowly, very slowly." In 1986, I learned from neighbors that she had spent part of the winter in a convalescent hospital following an illness, but in January 1987, she was in La Feuillé again, aided by the home-helper. This year, 1988, I have had no news, but my letter was not returned. I hope for Marie-Thérèse's sake that this does not mean she is now living in the retirement home in Huelgoat, which, as *Monsieur* Postic once told me, is "the antechamber of death." To leave one's home community for the retirement home is tantamount to social death, for one is no longer part of the daily networks of gossip and reciprocity. Few people from La Feuillée visit friends or neighbors in the retirement home, partly because there is no public transportation to Huelgoat for those who do not drive, and partly, I think, because it is seen as a depressing institution.

When I lived in La Feuillée, Marie-Thérèse would meet me with a *"Bonjour"* each morning as I came downstairs to my kitchen. On my final morning in La Feuillée, she looked as distressed as I felt, and I think she had passed a wakeful night. *"Bonjour,"* she greeted me, *"Bonjour,* for the last time." I would like to think that there will be another time, but I am afraid that as each year passes, this becomes less and less likely. I cannot return to Brittany this summer, and if I go back next year . . . ?

Looking back over what I have written, I am not sure whether Marie-Thérèse would approve. I do not think that she would feel I have misconstrued her words or misinterpreted their significance. It is rather a case of modesty. She would probably protest that she had told me nothing of great interest, and that it is somehow inappropriate to make public her thoughts and feelings. After all, she always sought to avoid other people, and here, in effect, she is being pushed into the limelight. I hope, however, that she would understand why I have chosen to write about her, that she would feel I have told her story as it should be told, and that she would find pleasure in whatever immortality these remembrances can bring.

ACKNOWLEDGMENTS

I would like to extend my gratitude to Marie-Thérèse and her family, as well as to the people of La Feuillée for their friendship and warm encouragement of my research. Financial support for the fieldwork on which this paper is based was generously provided by the Social Sciences and Humanities Research Council of Canada, the Wenner-Gren Foundation for Anthropological Research, and by a Lowie Scholarship and Humanities Graduate Research grant from the University of California, Berkeley.

CHAPTER 14

Cultural Mediation of Dying and Grieving among Native Canadian Patients in Urban Hospitals

Joseph M. Kaufert
and
John D. O'Neil

Joe Kaufert and John O'Neil are medical anthropologists working in the Faculty of Medicine at the University of Manitoba in Winnipeg. For several years they have been conducting research on the problems Canadian Native people face when they interact with the mainstream medical system, and especially when illness forces them into hospital. They have also focussed on the role conflicts experienced by Native Canadian medical interpreters—Native Canadians who serve as brokers between indigenous people and the medical establishment—as they attempt to translate the medical culture of one society to the members of the other. This becomes a particularly critical task when there is conflict between Native Canadians and hospital personnel over the nature of death, the appropriate expression of grief, and the proper treatment of dying and dead persons. This conflict, and the ways in which interpreters attempt to cope with it, is the topic they address in the chapter to follow.

*   *   *

This chapter focuses on the process of interpreting culturally based understandings of dying, grieving and post-mortem care for Native patients in urban hospitals. Case examples will be used to illustrate conflicts between Native patients' and Euro-Canadian health professionals' interpretations of appropriate care for the dying and grieving processes. We emphasize the role of Native interpreter/advocates who mediate between conflicting interpretations of dying and grieving among patients, family members and clinical staff in urban hospitals.

We draw our case studies describing the work of medical interpreters in terminal care settings from a continuing program of research on interpreter roles in health communication in Winnipeg hospitals and Inuit communities in the

Northwest Territories. The case studies are used to illustrate the following: 1) contrasts between biomedical and Native cultural understandings of viability, death, and grieving behavior; 2) problems of interpreting the organizational structure of the hospital for Native patients receiving palliative care; 3) impact of conflicting cultural values related to autopsies and post-mortem disposition of the body; 4) conflicts between biomedical beliefs emphasizing rational causation and technological intervention, and Native beliefs emphasizing spiritual causation and non-interference; and 5) problems of integrating traditional healing practices into terminal care in urban hospitals.

Palgi and Abramovitch (1984) have suggested that experience with death in Western societies is characterized by extreme mortality anxiety reflected in the definition of death and dying as a 'private affair.' The dying person is likely to be referred to a hospital when the family and wider support group can no longer cope with the range and intensity of caring functions. For Native Canadians this recourse to care of elderly, chronically ill and dying patients in institutional settings evokes fundamental conflicts with cultural values emphasizing the kin group and communities' obligation to take care of its own. Cultural ideologies emphasizing family care contrast with the reality of managing long-term care of chronically ill and terminally ill patients in northern communities with minimal home care resources or in urban migrant households without community support. Although Native people recognize the need for the technical and personal care services provided by the hospital, the problems of maintaining communal support in the hospital environment are profound.

In urban hospitals, the organizational structure of the ward and professional control of terminal care further isolates the patient from family and community support networks. It also interferes with rituals that integrate the family's experience of dying and grieving into community life. Sociological studies of terminal care management by Glaser and Strauss (1965) emphasize that hospital-based management of terminal care shifts the responsibility for support of the dying person from the kin group and community-based support networks to specialized care provided by professional staff.

In both Euro-Canadian and Native Canadian cultures, dying and grieving are defined as pivotal events of transition and passage within the life of the community. However, when terminal illness occurs in the specialized and technologically oriented environment of hospital wards, the work of caring and providing psychosocial support is performed by health professionals who may not share the patients' framework for interpreting their experience (Glaser and Strauss, 1968). The fundamental differences between the interpretive perspective of patients and the outlook of health professionals may be amplified by differences in the culturally based explanatory models used to interpret illness and healing. In addition to the overlay of biomedical cultural values, health professionals also come from a wide range of ethnic backgrounds. This diversity introduces another dimension of variation. Although health professionals generally subscribe to biomedical and dominant Euro-Canadian values, their own ethnic identities may introduce a second set of cultural values that influence their response to dying patients and grieving families.

CONTEMPORARY NATIVE EXPERIENCE OF DEATH AND DYING

Technological and organizational approaches to caring adopted by health professionals may conflict with traditional cultural ideologies emphasizing kin support and spiritual intervention. Among Indian and Inuit patients treated in urban centers, cultural and linguistic barriers compound the feeling of alienation and depersonalization experienced by all hospitalized patients. Native Canadians are unfamiliar with the institutional and professional culture of the hospital. They are also geographically and culturally isolated from their families and community support systems.

In most parts of Canada, the federally supported medical services program and provincial health insurance plans provide tertiary care for Indian and Inuit clients through a highly centralized system of treatment and referral. Health services on reserves and in other Native communities are generally provided by nurse practitioners in local primary care clinics or nursing stations. This care has usually been oriented towards management of minor health problems and disease prevention. The capability of northern community-based health facilities to treat and provide personal care services for a growing proportion of the Native population who require care for chronic conditions is limited. Native people with chronic illnesses and acute life threatening health problems are, therefore, referred for specialized diagnostic studies, surgery, and long-term care to urban tertiary care hospitals. The current system of triage and referral means that Native people with acute illnesses and long-term chronic conditions are increasingly likely to die in hospitals distant from their home communities. Physical relocation of the patient, often without accompanying members of the family, means that death occurs in the alien cultural environment of the urban hospital.

Within this organizational and institutional context it is not surprising that Native perceptions are dominated by images of hospitalization as an experience isolating the person from the cultural context of kin group and community support. Perceptions of hospital-based management of terminal care is also influenced by Inuit and Indian historical experience in which acutely ill patients were evacuated from northern communities to southern hospitals for treatment for infectious diseases. Polio, tuberculosis, and measles epidemics devastated Inuit and boreal Indian communities during the lifetimes of older members of some communities. Many people were evacuated without systematic records of their family and community of origin. Few interpretive services were available, and systematic information about the patient's death or recovery were seldom returned to home communities. Present day evacuation of acutely or terminally ill patients to southern hospitals is frequently interpreted in the context of older peoples' experiences as long-term inpatients in isolated sanitorium and city hospitals during the tuberculosis epidemics of the 1940s, 1950s and 1960s. Evacuation to a sanitorium was described by older patients as "being taken out of the community to die in southern hospitals."

In response to the problems of alienation associated with urban hospitalization, many Native communities are trying to develop community-based services for managing chronic care and terminally ill patients. For example, the Baker Lake Health Committee recently expressed interest in converting their old nursing station into a hospice facility. The hospitals in which our own research was conducted also had an informal policy of working with the Native Services Program and reserve nursing stations to discharge terminally ill patients to enable them to return to their home communities. Unfortunately, northern community-based health services cannot provide the supportive pain management and palliative services which are available to terminally ill patients receiving home care in urban centers. Despite these initiatives, most Native Canadians with acute and degenerative conditions will die in urban hospitals.

THE ROLE OF HOSPITAL-BASED INTERPRETER/ADVOCATES IN CARE OF DYING PATIENTS

In this chapter our primary objective is to examine the process of mediation between Cree, Ojibway, and Inuit patients' views of death, grief, and post-mortem care, and the views held by health professionals. The basis of our study of mediation processes was observation of the work of medical interpreters who act as culture brokers and patient advocates in urban hospitals (Kaufert and Koolage, 1984). Our study of Native interpreters working in Winnipeg hospitals found that they performed a primary role in mediating between the cultural models of death, dying and grieving of Native clients and those held by health professionals. Opportunities for cultural mediation of terminal care experience were also expanded as work by language interpreters in patient advocacy, counselling, and health education became recognized and legitimated (Kaufert and Koolage, 1984). We found that Native interpreters played multiple roles as 1) language translators; 2) cultural informants describing Native health practices and community health issues; 3) interpreters of biomedical concepts; and 4) patient and community advocates (Kaufert, O'Neil and Koolage, 1985). In each of these roles interpreter advocates mediated between biomedical and Native approaches to care of dying persons.

The narrowest definition of the medical interpreter role emphasizes technical translation of biomedical concepts into linguistically appropriate terms in Cree, Ojibway, or Inuktitut. The policy of involving interpreters in clinical interaction with Native patients who had little or no English gave dying patients access to a person with both language competence and a knowledge of their culture and community. In the confusing surroundings of the hospital ward, the interpreter was able to clarify complicated and impersonal procedures. They explained biomedical intervention in aid of life support and pain control using parallel terminology from the Native language where possible. In many cases, however, interpreters had to develop appropriate metaphors or examples which had personal meaning for the client. Interpreters also played a pivotal role in communicating the dying person's choices about alternative treatment, intervention, and palliative care proposed by clinicians. In several cases, interpreters played a critical role in informing patients that they had rights and could choose between, or reject, proposed treatment plans.

In caring for dying patients, interpreters also preformed a pivotal brokerage function by explaining Cree, Ojibway and Inuit cultural perspectives on terminal illness and post-mortem rituals to clinical staff. Interpreters were also able to act as "informants" for clinicians by explaining environmental factors in Native communities and the constraints of local and regional medical services which limited treatment options for palliative care on reserves. Interpreters worked with patients to develop culturally meaningful translations of terminal prognosis, relative risk associated with alternative treatment measures, and options for palliative care.

The expanded role of the Native language interpreters in patient advocacy and counselling involves mediation between strategies of patient management based on biomedical approaches to causation and treatment and traditional beliefs maintained by the client and family. Until recently, interpreters had no systematic training for involvement in advocacy and counselling for terminal care patients. However, in 1985-86, four of the hospital-based interpreters in Winnipeg graduated from a two-year para-professional training program which included instructional modules on counselling, care of dying patients and integration of traditional healing practices. Several parts of the curriculum emphasized client-centered counselling skills based on standard social work and family therapy interventions.

However, training modules also included an emphasis on utilizing Native elders and traditional healers as resource teachers. In contrasting biomedical and traditional knowledge components of their training, several interpreters felt the overall training had enabled them to more effectively deal with death and other family crises. Some of the graduates also reported feelings of dissonance related to their experience in attempting to combine more directive social work counselling strategies with "traditional" approaches to supporting dying patients and their families. Other informants described their personal problems in reconciling traditional beliefs emphasizing family and community responsibility for care of the dying, with the increasing inability and unwillingness of relatives to provide terminal care on reserve communities. A third interpreter described her difficulties in reconciling the models of patient's acceptance of dying (emphasizing the framework developed by Elizabeth Kubler-Ross) with the framework of traditional Ojibway beliefs about the process of dying (Kubler-Ross, 1969). She emphasized that themes of denial, anger and reconciliation in the palliative care literature could not be reconciled with the themes of self-control and non-interference idealized in Cree and Ojibway beliefs.

In response to the general aversion of Native People to hospital-based care, interpreters often played pivotal roles in making arrangements for Native patients to return to spend their final days with their families. Over the past seven years we observed that the role of interpreters in Winnipeg hospitals evolved to include a wider range of caring and mediation activities. These activities have particular significance for dying patients and grieving family members. The expanded role played by medical interpreters in cultural mediation and advocacy for Native patients contained the potential for conflicts of loyalty. Although interpreters were hospital employees and thus indirectly controlled by administrative and clinical managers, most maintained their primary loyalty to the client and the family. Consequently, they had to represent the dying patients individual interests, and in some cases the perspective of family and community groups, in situations in which clinicians and administrators favored alternative courses of action.

Although the role of medical interpreters was legitimated and professionalized through training establishing their credentials, their main source of power in clinical communication continued to be based upon linguistic and cultural access to the patient and family. While co-workers value the interpreters' capacity to interpret the patient's concept of illness, these same co-workers sometimes resent advocacy activities which counter organization rules or standards of clinical practice. For example, the involvement of interpreters in integrating traditional healers and healing practices into the care of dying patients is met with resistance from some clinicians and pastoral care workers. Several interpreters emphasized that this sort of situation involved loyalty conflicts and personal dissonance resulting in stress and "job burnout" (Kaufert and Koolage, 1984). Divided loyalties were also present in situations in which the interpreters' identity as a kin group or community member conflicted with their role as professionals, and hospital employees. In these situations, cross-pressures were reduced by referral to other interpreters and through intervention by supportive clinical supervisors and administrators who defended the interpreter's role as advocate for kin or members of the home community.

METHODS

Data on interpreter work in interpretation, mediation and advocacy were collected using a variety of methods. We conducted sequential, career-focused interviews with nine Cree, Ojibway and Island Lake language-speaking interpreters working in two Winnipeg hospitals. We supplemented interview data from interpreters by field observations carried out over a three-year period in two urban hospitals. Clinician/patient encounters and family participation in terminal care and grieving were observed by the investigators and two research assistants with fluency in Cree and Ojibway. We followed up field observations with focused interviews with patients, family members, physicians and hospital administrators. We video-taped a small number of clinical encounters to facilitate more detailed analysis of the impact of interpretation on the linguistic and social aspects of clinician/patient interaction. Audio and video-taped encounters were followed up in separate interviews documenting varied perceptions of terminal care encounters from the standpoint of the interpreter, the client, the kin group and the clinician. The impact of the hospital organization and professional ideology among clinicians and medical administrators was documented through observing clinical staff meetings, case conferences, and medical rounds.

The primary device for illustrating conflicts between the cultural interpretations of concepts of death, dying and grieving of Native patients and clinicians was the in-depth case study. Case examples provided a mechanism for describing situations in which the explanatory models of Native patients conflicted with those of the clinicians and administrators. In previous publications we have referred to case examples involving conflicts in culturally-based definitions of illness-related interaction as trouble cases (Kaufert et al., 1984). The "trouble case" approach was developed by legal anthropologists and focuses on situations in which the participants disagree over definitions of legitimate behavior (Hoebel, 1964). In hospitals, conflict situations arose when clinicians, clients and cultural intermediaries disagreed over what constituted appropriate response to impending death and suitable means for accommodating family grief. As initially developed in legal anthropology, analysis of trouble cases included documentation of the impact of organizational or socio-political factors upon the specific conflict situation. By dealing with case studies of conflict in terminal care situations, it is possible to examine the impact of organizational factors and professional ideologies upon cultural mediation of dying and grieving. Unfortunately, case examples do not provide a detailed ethnographic profile of the specific content of Native beliefs about death and dying. Rather they take the explanations from the biomedical or client perspective as they are elicited in the actual situation.

The study did not support a coherent political analysis of the role of racism in cross-cultural medical interactions. Although we recorded many statements from informants which suggest that racism plays an important role in structuring the response of care providers to Native patients, we were unable to obtain detailed case study information to support a systematic analysis of structural barriers in health organizations or bias among clinicians. In focusing upon 'cultural mediation' and 'brokerage,' we recognize that these concepts are most often applied in arguing for systems maintenance and as half-way mechanisms for moderating the impact of institutions. We also recognize that cultural mediation of terminal care occurs in highly political contexts structured by the relations between the powerful and the powerless.

MEDIATING THE ORGANIZATIONAL STRUCTURE
OF THE HOSPITAL

A critical function of interpreter/advocates in their work with Native patients in terminal care was to explain and mediate the effects of the organizational structure of the hospital. The social science literature on institutionalization (Goffman, 1961) and medicalization (Zola, 1973) emphasized that the organizational structure of hospitals reinforces institutional and professional control over all clinical situations, including terminal care (Strauss et al., 1986). For all patients, the organizational structure and function of large hospitals is difficult to understand. Like inmates in archetypical "total institutions," patients must be socialized to fit into the hospital's basic organizational structure. From the provider's perspective, organizational rules and care regimens are justified on the basis of rationales emphasizing the "good of the institution" or the need to "consider the rights of all patients and staff." For Indian and Inuit people, the problems of understanding how specialized diagnostic and treatment wards function and how they effect the person's own care are compounded by cultural and linguistic barriers.

Our wider research program examining the expansion of interpreter roles suggested that Native patients felt "powerless" because of their lack of familiarity with the organizational structure of the hospital. Hospital rules and sanctions imposed by clinicians were therefore often perceived by Native patients and their families as oppressive as well as confusing.

Our observation of medical interpreters' work provided several examples of situations in which the organizational rules of the hospital conflicted with Native concepts about family involvement in terminal care. In one case, an elderly Cree woman with terminal gastric cancer was assigned to a double room on the post-surgical ward. Her extended family assembled at the hospital to attend the patient. The kin group included recent urban migrants and other family members who had travelled two hundred miles from the women's home community. As the patient lapsed into unconsciousness, eight members of the family arrived at the ward to attend the patient. The hospital-based interpreter who was translating for the family described the initial encounter between the family and the nursing staff:

> The head nurse called the assistant head nurse for an emergency meeting, and asked why there were so many people there. The head nurse then said there was no need for all these people to be here, so the assistant was to remove all these people from the hallway. The charge nurse went over to the patient and adjusted her I.V. She looked at the people there and said "I'm sorry, but you'll have to leave! At least some of you, anyway. She is only allowed two visitors at a time!" Everyone just got up immediately and started leaving.

The interpreter later commented that her presence may have influenced the nurse's response. As the interpreter became involved in translating, the nurse emphasized that the restriction of the number of visitors was necessary to protect the patient from unnecessary disturbances. The interpreter described her interaction with the nurse.

> The nurse commented to the patient's daughter, "The thing is, she was doing so well yesterday when she was not being bothered by anyone. She was so active in the morning, and after she had so many visitors all day, she's not doing so well today." I, [the interpreter], just stood and looked at her after everyone had left the room, appalled at the tone of voice and the implications of her words, as if reproaching the family for visiting their mother.

Despite this encounter, the support group of family members on the ward continued to grow as more members in the group learned of the patient's condition. Family members slept in the lounge and hallways and rotated to maintain a twenty-four hour vigil in the patient's room. Until the interpreters intervened, no attempt was made to accommodate the needs of the patient and/or the family by providing either a single room or placing the patient in a ward with other Cree-speaking patients.

The head nurse had asked the interpreter to explain the rules governing visiting hours and limitations on the number of visitors. The head of the interpreter program talked to the family and explained that hospitals had their own rules which sometimes were hard to understand and respect. The nurses explained that rules limiting visiting privileges were enforced to prevent infringement on the rights of other patients and to avoid tiring the patient. The head nurse later complained to the interpreter that she had observed that Native visitors did not seem to "do" anything for the patients during visits. She commented that Native visitors "just sat in their chairs and knitted." When the Director of Native Services was asked about this perception, she explained that Native people feel it is important just to "be with" someone who is acutely or terminally ill and that it was not necessary for visitors to interact. She emphasized that Native people found it inappropriate when clinicians and non-Native visitors expected patients to converse throughout a visit because this seemed very tiring for the patient. As the Prestons' contribution to this volume indicates, East Cree people emphasize the importance of visiting terminally ill friends and allowing kin to "say good-bye." In urban hospitals, paradoxically, both clinicians and the family members perceived each other's approach to attending terminal care patients as culturally inappropriate and "tiring" for the patient. Other values defining appropriate dying and grieving behavior (as the Prestons describe for the East Cree) also were difficult to realize in setting of the medical ward. Traditional emphasis upon the need for the dying person to maintain autonomy and personal control were overridden by organizational rules and ward schedules that minimized the ability of the dying patient and his/her family to control time or personal space. The related values of self knowledge and personal competence were also difficult to achieve in the unfamiliar institutional setting of the ward. The notion of a "good death" in which continuity and balance is maintained in human and environmental relationships, contrasts sharply with "decontextualized death" of persons on the ward (see the Prestons' chapter).

Faced with a situation of conflict between two value systems, the Director for Native Services also asked the head nurse whether it was necessary to be inflexible in applying rules limiting the number of visitors in terminal care situations. The Director explained that rules defining the level and duration of family visits resulted from the belief that several family members should be present continuously to protect the patient from spiritual malevolence. The Director asked whether the regulations governing the life of the ward should be applied inflexibly in the care of dying patients. She pointed out that limitations in visiting hours and number of visitors meant that the patient could not go through the process of "leave taking" with members of her community who had travelled from the home community. The nursing supervisor incorporated a more transcultural perspective into the patients care plan and allowed the extended family group to attend the patient on a twenty-four hour basis. The interpreter organized a schedule in which several members of the family could visit the patient on a rotating basis.

The case was one of several examples of terminal care situations involving Native clients characterized by conflict between the formal organizational rules of the hospital and patient and family assertions or their right to follow traditional practices for attending the dying. Although such incidents were discussed widely by the clinical staff, few Native patients were referred to specialized hospice units.

Hospice units are designed and staffed to provide for flexible involvement of the family and more psychosocial support of the patient than could otherwise be provided. When a physician working with the hospice program was asked about the under utilization of the program by Native clients, he responded that the system of referral seldom transferred Native clients to the unit. One barrier to native participation in the hospice program was felt by interpreters to be the cultural model of terminal care emphasized by the unit. This is because the psychosocial orientation to patient management in the hospice was partially based upon the model of staged acceptance of dying developed by Elizabeth Kubler-Ross (Kubler-Ross, 1969), a framework incompatible with Cree and Ojibway values defining a "good death" (see the chapter by Preston and Preston). While problems of reconciling the values of Native clients and hospice staff are significant, members of the unit are currently examining ways to accommodate Native beliefs in their care programs. In the future, hospice units may adopt pluralistic models for terminal care, thereby accommodating the culturally based interpretive frameworks of Native people. Interpreters also are currently working with clinicians and administrators to develop more flexible policy guidelines to govern ward organization and nursing practice.

INTEGRATION OF TRADITIONAL HEALING PRACTICES

The broader context of health care for Native Canadians is increasingly recognized as a 'pluralistic' system in which patients may consult both biomedical practitioners and practitioners of traditional Cree and Ojibway medicine. One critical role of Native interpreter/advocates working with terminal care patients and family groups involves ensuring that hospital patients have access to traditional healers (O'Neil, 1988).

Native Services workers estimate that one-third of the Cree and Ojibway patients entering Winnipeg tertiary hospitals continue to value traditional ideas about illness and medicine. The general perception among physicians and nurses was that adherence to traditional belief systems was more prevalent among older Native patients. However, the interpreter/advocates observed that a significant proportion of middle-aged and young adult patients also believed in traditional medicine. They further observed that a growing number of patients of all ages wanted to participate in traditional healing rituals while in hospital. This growing interest was particularly apparent in terminal care situations.

Although some hospitals adjoining Native communities have developed policies which incorporate healers as members of the consultant staffs, the two teaching hospitals in Winnipeg had no formal provision for involving traditional healers. Despite this lack of official legitimacy, Native language interpreters frequently became involved in helping hospital patients to contact elders and healers. They also assisted terminal care patients and members of their families to contact traditional practitioners, and participated in rituals surrounding death and the post-mortem care of the body.

The integration of healers and traditional care practices into palliative care was observed in the cases of several older patients in oncology wards. For example, a seventy-year old Ojibway patient was referred for palliative care on a specialized medical ward of a teaching hospital. Although the man was diagnosed as having advanced gastric cancer, the attending physicians initially prescribed a chemotherapy regimen to sustain minimal digestive function. During his initial interview with the interpreter the man indicated that he knew he was dying, and the interpreter asked whether he would like to involve an elder or traditional healer in his care. At the patient's request, the interpreter consulted with several healers living in the city. None were willing to perform rituals on the ward because they felt that the hospital environment was alien to their approach to healing. Several days later the interpreter was able to contact an elder in a neighboring reserve community who was willing to perform a healing ceremony in the hospital.

Once the informal arrangement was made, the interpreters had to get official permission and financial support to facilitate the healer's travel and his access to the hospital ward. The oncologist initially rejected the interpreter's proposal to involve the healer, because he was concerned that traditional interventions might conflict with the prescribed biomedical regimen. The physician emphasized that the patient was still actively receiving treatment and he was afraid that the healer's botanical medication might interact with chemotherapy. Transportation expenses for the healer were available from the federal government through the Medical Services Branch, but the attending physician was asked to approve the request for consultation with the healer. After extensive negotiation with the interpreters, assurances were given that no plant medication would be administered. The oncologist finally consented to the involvement of the healer. The healer ultimately agreed to perform a healing ceremony within the cancer center, but requested that some of the more invasive monitoring equipment be turned off while he worked with the patient.

In a similar case, a female patient with advanced renal cancer was being treated by an oncologist who was also initially reluctant to involve a healer in the patient's care. In this case the interpreters' roles as patient advocates involved them in circumventing hospital rules. The interpreters brought the elder to visit the patient during a slack period on a Sunday. The healer performed a healing ritual which required burning ceremonial offerings of sweet grass and tobacco. The interpreters recognized that burning sweet grass might set off the ward smoke detector system so they helped the family cover the smoke detector with plastic and participated in the ceremony themselves. These cases illustrate the expansion of unofficial interpreter roles to include brokering relationships between traditional healers and clinicians.

In both teaching hospitals, health professionals and administrators were sometimes reluctant to accommodate or recognize the role of Native elders and healers in terminal care. This is true even though interpreters from one hospital were themselves active in traditional cultural activities and used community elders and medicine people as their spiritual advisors and as a personal support group. Nevertheless, their efforts to facilitate consultation with spiritual advisors and healers were often limited to unofficial interventions or subterfuge.

BIOMEDICAL AND SPIRITUAL UNDERSTANDINGS OF CAUSALITY: THE TRAGEDY OF CO-TERMINUS SYMBOLS

Several incidents illustrate the potential for culture conflict that can arise when biomedical and traditional interpretations of terminal prognosis and cause of mortality do not coincide. One case involved a female infant born to an Ojibway family living on a reserve 100 kilometers from an urban tertiary care hospital. The child was diagnosed as suffering from a genetically-based degenerative condition with a survival prognosis of a few weeks.

Biomedical explanations of the child's illness emphasized the genetic origins of the problem. The pediatrician and a genetic counselor attempted to explain to the parents that positive and negative traits are passed from one generation to another. When the genetic explanation was translated for the parents, the mother became distraught. Her interpretation of the genetic cause was that the medical diagnosis confirmed her responsibility for the child's condition. In talking with the interpreter the mother stressed that the child's problems were the result of a personal transgression of traditional rules. The Native interpreter explained to the attending physician that the mother understood the child's condition in terms of the concept of *ondjine*. The Ojibway belief system explaining courses of illness or misfortune is based on the belief that individuals may receive retribution for previous transgressions (Hallowell, 1955). Transgressions may include harming animals, ridiculing the physical characteristics of another person, or desecrating grave sites or the physical remains of the deceased (Hallowell, 1936). Retribution may miss the guilty person and strike his or her family members. The root meaning of the word *ondjine* implies "earning" or "receiving in return." In traditional interpretations, the concept had both positive and negative connotations, stressing that individuals might be positively rewarded for acts of kindness or respect to elders or kind acts to animals. However, in contemporary usage the concept of *ondjine* is primarily related to behavior which has resulted in illness or misfortune befalling a family member. Although the genetic explanation was congruent with the mother's belief that she was responsible for her child's condition, she refused to accept the idea that the condition was degenerative and irreversible. She requested assistance from the Department of Native Services to bring a traditional healer into the hospital to see the baby. The Director contacted an elder who was recognized for her success in working with Native children suffering from convulsions. The elder, who lived on a reserve in a neighboring province approximately 400 miles from the hospital, talked on the telephone with the mother and indicated that, while she could not travel to treat the child directly, she would pray for spiritual intervention.

The interpreter's explanation of the mother's spiritual beliefs and request for a healer were recorded in the case notes by the medical staff. However, no formal accommodation was made to involve healers or work with the parents to reconcile discrepancies and conflicts in their interpretation of the child's illness. In the days that followed, the mother became increasingly depressed and began to distance herself from her child. The mother's withdrawal was particularly distressing to the nursing staff because of their own cultural expectations regarding parental involvement in the care of terminally ill children. Pediatric intensive care nursing staff placed great value on the self-sacrificing parent who spends twenty-four hours a day at the child's bedside. Nurses evaluated the level of the parent's concern in terms of their commitment to be with the child on a round-the-clock basis. As the mother began to withdraw from interaction with the infant, her behavior was described as 'uncaring' by the ward staff.

The woman's behavior did not fit the staff's previous experience with other Native families who attended patients day and night. Constant attendance is based on the belief that a dying person must have family present in order to ensure the spirit or ghost of the deceased is not angered. The mother's belief in her own responsibility for the child's illness meant that she had to withdraw from the child in order to protect it from further spiritual malevolence associated with her presence. Her behavior was considered callous by the attending clinicians, and the nursing staff committed extra time to the child's care.

The attempt by the nursing staff to compensate for the mother's withdrawal was perceived by the family as a further assertion of the hospital's control of the process of dying. One of the interpreters compared the terminal care experience on the ward with the alternate scenario of the child dying at home:

> Now if the child had died at birth the parents would have just gone ahead and buried the child and accepted it as something that just had happened. However, when the medical profession became involved they took the child away from the parents and maintained the child in hospital to try and find out what was wrong. From the parents' perspective it looks like experimentation. They felt disconnected from the child . . . as though it wasn't their child anymore. From the parents' perspective they were prohibited from taking their child out of hospital and from their own cultural standpoint were seen to be deficient parents.

The intensive medical and social management of the child extended to the ward staff's management of the parents' involvement with the child. One of the interpreters described the feeling of alienation that the parents experienced as they were forced to take part in token caring activities for the child.

> When the parents came to Winnipeg the nurses would get the mother to bathe the baby, to hold the baby and nurture the baby. I'm not sure how she felt, but she must have felt anguish in looking after a little child with all those machines around her. I asked the parents how they felt about it at first and they didn't respond. I asked them whether they felt their baby was continuing to grow and thrive, they hesitated and then he [the father] said, "Yes, she's growing," but there was no facial expression. He said in Ojibway "she is not part of us anymore." This is very difficult to translate into English without sounding callous, it doesn't mean she's dead or gone, but more like there's no hope or what's the point? We're here you've got our child—its yours—you took our child away from us.

As the interpreters sensed the growing level of alienation in the parents, they enlisted the aid of a consultant pediatrician with extensive experience in Native health, asking him to assume the role of advocate for the family. In conveying the family's wish for withdrawal of life support equipment one interpreter described the mother's perspective on the child's impending death:

> If the child had died in her arms shortly after birth that would have been more acceptable than the way the child is today with all those machines. That is what we believe in—that part of us—we have to accept it. We've lost other children and that was the way it was meant to be. They feel badly because they've lost other children and the chances are that this child will die as well. For me its the medical staff who can't accept this approach to dying and they see the parents as being fatalistic.

The interpreter also attempted to convey the perspective of the medical profession to the parents. She described physicians' and nurses' commitment to sustain life.

> From the perspective of the medical profession the loss of three other children is enough to go to extraordinary lengths to try to save this baby. Medical ethics demand that they always try to preserve life. They live by that, they eat it, they administer drugs that way, its their primary goal to save life.

As the child's condition worsened, the clinical staff continued to provide intensive care, and openly expressed their frustration with the parents' apparent callousness. During an informal clinical consultation, the interpreter overheard one of the residents describing the child's case history. The physician commented on the apparent lack of parental concern over the child's terminal condition. Speaking with a colleague, the doctor mentioned that the parents had lost three other children and suggested in a demeaning tone that these children were probably "buried in the bush." When the physician's statement was repeated in a case conference, the interpreter challenged the physician's interpretation of the family's parenting experience and current reaction to their child's impending death. The interpreter described her reaction.

> The second time I heard that I thought "What's happening here?" Can you imagine the sort of image that creates for an intern? "Indian people just throw their dead out in the bush." I went to see one of the doctors who had been involved in the conversation, he was quite surprised at my reaction. He [the doctor] said "Perhaps you are being too sensitive." However, I've been here long enough to try to be open-minded and understand, but those kinds of statements don't sit well with me, particularly when I'm trying to make people aware of the differences and values and customs. Maybe twenty-five years ago those statements would have been okay. We were ignorant of how the hospitals worked and doctors and nurses were ignorant of our values. However, they must understand that we value life. So do these parents value life. Its a gift to them. However, if there's a sickness or something that happens, it's seen as being meant to happen because of something that had happened to them before and therefore it's acceptable. This explanation just isn't accepted by the medical profession. The medical staff seem to be willing to dismiss them as callous parents rather than to try and find out the way they feel about the situation.

During the final hours of the child's life, the interpreters remained with the parents. The mother wanted to know how the child was doing. The physician apparently answered with a reference to the clinical condition which did not directly acknowledge that the child's death was imminent. The interpreter described the mother's response.

> They never say, "your child is dying," they use a lot of words sometimes you don't understand what they mean. Sometimes I wish they would just come out and say things directly—they don't, it's not the way they do things.

Immediately after the death of the child, the interpreter attempted to organize a series of in-service training sessions in which physicians and nurses could be sensitized to the cultural values governing Native definitions of viability, quality of life, and rituals appropriate for caring for dying patients. She described her experience in these in-service sessions.

> It's very hard to convince medical staff that these things are important, that it's important to know that Native people don't simply bury their dead in the bush. There are ceremonies that are to be performed because life is sacred to these parents and they value life much the same way as a doctor values life.

This case illustrates the problems of interpreting Native and biomedical understandings of terminal prognosis, cause of death, and grief response by members of the family group. The misinterpretation of causal explanations and appropriate approaches to caring and grieving illustrates the tragedy of co-terminus symbols among clients and care providers. The mother's interpretation of the child's illness as punishment for her own transgression (harming an animal) led her to distance herself to prevent further retribution. The clinical staff's interpretation of the mother's behavior caused them to stereotype the family as uncaring. Reciprocally the family interpreted the imposition of a more medicalized regimen on the final hours of the child's life as inappropriate. Finally, Native interpreters regarded the clinical staff's characterization of the family as stereotypic and discriminatory.

MEDIATION OF CULTURAL EXPLANATIONS
OF AUTOPSY

Cultural differences in understandings were also apparent in situations where there was conflict between biomedical and traditional understandings of post-mortem care of the body. One case involved a ten-month old female Ojibway child from a reserve community. The child had a wide range of neurological problems and was eventually referred for diagnostic evaluation to an urban pediatric hospital. The child's illness was finally diagnosed as lucodystophy, and the attending physicians attempted to communicate the child's diagnosis to the parents. They told the parents that lucodystrophy involved progressive degeneration of the brain tissue and that it was genetically transmitted. The physicians also stressed that the condition was inevitably fatal, and that they would primarily be providing life support and palliative care.

During the final stages of the child's illness the medical staff of the pediatric intensive care unit were heavily involved in the clinical management of the child's condition. As the level of medical intervention was increased and respiratory support equipment was used, the grandparents and parents became concerned that the medical staff were providing "experimental care" that would prolong the child's suffering. The next day the parents decided to take the child from hospital and return to the reserve to seek the intervention of a traditional healer. As they were driving back to the reserve community, the child stopped breathing and was admitted to a community hospital, where she was pronounced dead on arrival.

The body of the child was then returned to the pediatric hospital, and the parents and grandparents were contacted by the attending physician for their consent to perform an autopsy. In speaking with the relatives, the medical staff emphasized that autopsies were required in cases where the cause of death was undetermined. The parents refused to consent to the procedure, saying that it conflicted with their spiritual beliefs about the care of the body of the deceased. When it became evident that an autopsy was going to be performed by the hospital, the grandfather, who was a community elder and band council member, called on the band chief to try to intervene to prevent the autopsy. Even the pediatricians, who had cared for the child supported the need for post-mortem examination, despite the fact that death was almost certainly related to the degenerative effects of lucodystrophy. Ultimately, the provincial medical examiner ordered the autopsy, despite the protests of the parents. Interpreters were finally called in when the child's grand-parents returned to the hospital and were informed that an autopsy had been performed as ordered by the provincial medical examiner. The parents and grand-parents reacted emotionally and requested assistance from the community leaders from their reserve. When the band chief and council asked the provincial medical examiner and attending pediatricians for a detailed explanation of why the autopsy was performed without parental consent, a spokesperson for the hospital explained that autopsies were often performed to determine the cause of death, particularly when there was the possibility of it being associated with infectious diseases posing wider community threats. The interpreters and family reacted angrily because they felt the spokesperson had rationalized the decision by intro-ducing considerations of potential threats of infectious disease to the community. They pointed out that there was nothing in the medical history of the case which suggested the presence of communicable disease. Unfortunately, the damage had been done, and rumors spread throughout the Native community that the child had died from an unknown contagious disease. When the child's body was flown back to the reserve, family and community responses at the viewing the body and burial continued to be influenced by the rumor that the child had died from an infectious disease. At the church, community members did not approach the open casket.

Under pressure from the hospital interpreters, the hospital spokesperson finally stated that in fact, infectious disease had not been suspected in this particular case. The band chief then contacted the medical examiner and demanded that existing guidelines for performing autopsies be re-examined. Pediatricians involved with northern health care and Native interpreters proposed that the subject be discussed in a wider forum in which clinicians, representatives of the medical examiner's office and representatives of the Native community could discuss the cultural and medical basis for post-mortem examinations.

The case of the infant with lucodystrophy was one of three incidents in which the biomedical criteria for performing autopsies came into conflict with cultural ideologies about post-mortem care. The medical staff of the pediatric hospital, therefore, decided to convene an in-service training workshop dealing with the general issue of the cultural interpretation of autopsies among Native people. The provincial medical examiner, attending medical and nursing staff, and Native Services workers were invited. The interpreters also invited a woman who was identified as an elder who had special knowledge of Ojibway spiritual beliefs and healing practices.

The meeting opened with a general discussion of conflicting interpretations of the function of an autopsy. The biomedical perspective of the physicians empha-sized the importance of an autopsy for improving the general level of medical knowledge. Native speakers argued that a paramount value in Native culture was the corporeal integrity of the body after death and explained that this value was linked to spiritual understandings about the length of time required for the transi-tion of a person's soul to the afterworld. The deputy medical examiner stated that he felt that there had been an exaggerated response by the Native community. He attempted to dispel what he described as a "popular myth" that autopsies were automatically performed on all patients who died in hospitals. He explained that there was a legal requirement that autopsies be performed in cases of unexplained deaths, accidents, violent deaths, suicides, maternal and infant deaths, cases of suspected clinical malpractice, poisoning and people who died while in prison or legal custody. He emphasized that requirements that autopsies be performed had grown out of traditions in forensic medicine and biomedical research which emphasized that post-mortem investigations were the key to understanding all disease processes.

Another pathologist stressed that a physician's involvement with a patient extended beyond terminal illness to post-mortem examination. He emphasized that physicians who were heavily involved in trying to save a patient's life often requested an autopsy in order to more fully understand why they had "lost the struggle to save the person." The deputy medical examiner emphasized that autopsies in the case of unexplained deaths, violent crimes and suspected clinical mismanagement provided protection for the individual and the community. He stated that he felt Native clients' objections to autopsies must be balanced against the wider community interest in assuring deaths do not occur without determina-tion of negligence or malevolent cause. The deputy medical examiner also stressed that post-mortem examination was also sometimes necessary to control contagious or environmentally caused diseases. Finally he emphasized that autopsies were one of the main ways that scientific medicine learned about disease processes.

Following the deputy medical examiner's remarks, the Director of the Native Services program was asked to provide an overview of the concerns of Native clients about the current policies governing autopsies. She described her personal experience with health professionals who had misinterpreted the approach of

Native clients and communities to dying, grieving and care of the body. In her remarks, the interpreter/advocate contrasted the analytical approach, used in medical and legal determination of the cause of mortality, with Ojibway beliefs about dying and post-mortem care of the deceased. She emphasized that traditional beliefs focussed on the importance of understanding the reasons for a person's death in terms of violation of traditional beliefs or moral transgressions. She pointed out that, like autopsies, traditional approaches to understanding the cause of death also involved identifying events or acts performed by the deceased or members of their family which might have contributed to the person's death. She emphasized that, like doctors, traditional believers, were also concerned with identification of cause of death and stressed that Cree or Ojibway traditions also emphasized environmental influences—influences such as the relationship of the deceased to animals or spirits. The interpreter stated that in contrast to the narrower understanding of causation in biomedical culture, Ojibway beliefs fostered an integrative approach. Funeral rituals provided mechanisms which transformed death into an integrative event for the community. Determination of causation also allowed offending individuals to understand and ritually remedy their offenses.

The interpreter followed her remarks by introducing an elder from the community and asked the woman to describe Ojibway perspectives on the post-mortem care of the body as it influenced Native beliefs about autopsies. The elder began by relating the family's refusal of consent for autopsy to traditional beliefs: "Autopsy is a sensitive issue for traditional people and is very difficult to talk about because it is linked with spiritual concepts such as *ondjine*."

The elder stressed that post-mortem examination conflicted with traditional Ojibway beliefs about the process of dying and movement of the spirit after physical death. She emphasized that traditional believers would be opposed to any procedure which disturbed corporal integrity, including amputation or tissue removal in biopsies. The elder explained that Ojibway people believed the spirit resided in the body for a defined period after death. Procedures which involved opening the body cavity or removal of tissue disrupted the departure of the spirit and thereby engendered the possibility of retribution via *ondjine*.

Following the elder's statement, a pathologist asked whether autopsy procedures could be modified to accommodate traditional beliefs stressing the maintenance of corporal integrity. He suggested that it was very often possible to determine the cause of death from the medical history, blood samples and external physical examination. He asked whether this kind of approach to determining the cause of death might overcome objections raised by traditional believers. The elder replied that prohibitions would apply to any procedure which disturbed the body and therefore that there could be no such thing as a 'non-invasive autopsy.'

Discussion then shifted the question of whether traditional beliefs should be respected in situations in which there was potential wrong-doing or risk to the community. A pediatrician asked whether the function of autopsies to protect the individual and the community could be balanced against considerations of respect for client beliefs or community values. The physician described a hypothetical case of a pediatric patient who had died from apparent insecticide poisoning. The physician asked the elder whether, in a case where an autopsy might be able to detect a threat to the entire community, traditional prohibitions against autopsies might be set aside. The elder demurred, saying that spiritual beliefs governing the disposition of the body after death were absolute. Concepts of the wider security of the community or protection from unknown diseases were not part of the traditional framework of knowledge.

Following the elder's explanation, an oncologist observed that there were important parallels in the ways that Orthodox Jewish families were able to restrict autopsies. The physician stated that as both a scientist and a member of an Orthodox Jewish congregation, he often questioned whether autopsies either contributed to research or individual clinical understanding of causality. He emphasized that in his own experience in pediatrics, autopsies of juvenile cancer patients frequently had minimal value in terms of extending general medical knowledge or benefit in terms of protecting the individual family or wider community. He suggested that in his own experience, determining the need for an autopsy was influenced more by statutory requirements and payment for pathologists. He emphasized that the success of the Orthodox Jewish community in restricting autopsies had been related to their retention of legal council. In pursuing his comparison of Native and Orthodox Jewish teachings about post-mortem dispositions of the body, he emphasized the common belief about the need to preserve the corporal integrity of the body after death. He concluded his statement by expressing his surprise that his medical colleagues would dismiss Native beliefs about post-mortem disposition of the body as mere 'customs' which could be strategically accommodated or circumvented. He asked whether the deputy medical examiner would have considered attempting to persuade an Orthodox Jewish family or their representatives to reverse their refusal to consent to the autopsy. The deputy examiner replied that with the understanding of the prohibitions related to Cree and Ojibway traditional beliefs, he felt that Native clients and community groups could successfully challenge orders for autopsies using the provisions of the Canadian Charter of Rights.

The conference was followed up with continuing informal consultations between interpreter/advocates, clinicians and the medical examiner in later instances in which autopsies were contemplated for Native patients. In some cases the consultation and mediation by the interpreters resulted in family acceptance of the autopsy. In other situations the pathological examination was limited to minimally invasive procedures. However, in several instances families and community groups pursued their opposition to autopsy through legal channels or through going to the media.

DISCUSSION

These case studies demonstrate the very real problem of mediation between Native and biomedical explanations of death, dying and grieving. Examination of work of interpreters in advocacy for Native patients and their families illustrates the problem of reconciling Native beliefs about appropriate care of the dying with the organizational constraints of the hospital and the biomedical culture of the health professional. Case studies of attempts to integrate traditional healers and to develop more sensitive post-mortem care illustrate the profound problems of reconciling alternative approaches to causality and remediation. They bring approaches to care of the dying emphasizing professional and technological control of terminal care into sharp contrast with traditional approaches which stress the need to maintain autonomy, spirituality and continuity.

In the final analysis, the emphasis upon mediation, interpretation and accommodation of alternate systems of understanding may place interpreter advocates in a vulnerable position of brokering fundamentally irreconcilable values. Culturally sensitive support for dying and grieving Native patients and families may require that individuals and communities assert their prerogative to die in their homes and local communities.

Good Stories from There Develop Good Care Here: A Therapeutic Perspective

John A. O'Connor

The following chapter of this volume by John O'Connor, a chaplain in the Chedoke-McMaster Hospitals of Hamilton, Ontario, Canada, is a commentary on the chapters that precede it, on the work that anthropologists do and might do, and on the contrast between the roles of analytical scholar and interventionist clinician. O'Connor searches for, and finds, some utility in what anthropologists do with respect to the study of death and grief but urges them to go further. His chapter is also a commentary on the nature of death and grief in our own North American society.

*   *   *

PREFACE

Richard Kalish's absence from the symposium where the first drafts of these chapters were presented provided a McLuhanish realism to the presentation of the papers. In an ironic way, his influence on the symposium may have been more significant than if he had been there. The death of a co-presenter cannot be reduced to a footnote, distanced on a remote island, or limited to an "In memory of" page. His dying was felt and sensed in those two days. The impact of his death on the authors is reflected in our final drafts for this volume. The comments and interpretations in this chapter are my own, but they have their origins in the voices from the grave (or the graveside) of those who have shared their living and dying with me.

I will not pretend to be an ethnographer. When a speaker at the symposium said that she had attended the "Triple A" meeting, I thought she belonged to a car club.[1] My experience of other cultures is severely limited. I did grow up on a somewhat exotic island in the Atlantic Ocean—Brooklyn, New York. I am the oldest son in an Irish Catholic family. I was a fringe player with most of the sub-cultures of the 60s. I worked for periods of time in the inner city, Bed-Sty and Greenpoint in Brooklyn, South Chicago and a summer in the barrios of East Los Angeles. There my Spanish was only adequate for little children and extremely polite, patient, older persons. Later, I directed a counseling center in the heart of a Mennonite community. After my ordination, I served as pastor to an assimilated German Lutheran congregation. The population I serve now is predominantly W.A.S.P., if not by birth, then by temperament.

I am a practicing clinician and have been for more than twenty years. For over a decade, I have been a chaplain in a tertiary care university hospital. My involvement with people has been because death is nearby, either for themselves or someone they know and, usually, love. Some have been as young as the never born and others as old as centenarians. Some have outlived their deaths while others have died before they lived. Some died so quickly they missed their dying, while for others dying was so long that their living was remembered by no one.

A DREAM

I had fallen asleep
reading a draft of my paper
when I had a dream which woke me up:
A voice message came over my paging unit,
"Chaplain O'Connor, please call home immediately.
There are anthropologists trapped in your basement."

I AM SUPPOSED TO DO WHAT?

My assigned task was to comment on the papers presented at the symposium from the perspective of a North American clinician. From my reading of the anthropologists' chapters two major questions came to mind. First, can chaplains, palliative care workers, physicians and bereavement counsellors find anything of value in these anthropological studies? Second, can the skills and insights

---

[1]At the symposium, I was very naive about anthropology and what to expect from anthropologists. Was I in for a surprise! We were all given working drafts of these articles; sometimes they came only a few days before the meeting. As the authors got up to present issues, questions, problems related to their papers, it was apparent that all the other presenters had read each paper carefully. In health care meetings, this would be considered a first class miracle. The non-defensive style of the presenters encouraged open criticism, as well as open support. It was an enthusiastic and enriching experience. I was so turned on that I enrolled in a course on Interpretive Anthropology. Many issues raised by the course were identical or clearly paralleled those which concern systems therapists.

developed by North American clinicians assist ethnographers in their fieldwork experiences?

In this chapter, I will argue the affirmative for both questions. Anthropologists and clinicians need each other if they are to increase each other's understanding of dying, death, bereavement, mourning and grief. Fundamental to my argument will be questions concerning the similarities and differences of each profession's mandates, the development of key definitions, the relationship between personal necessities and public performances, the health status of dying, tears and pain, and created meanings.

DOES ANYONE KNOW WHAT THE ANTONYM OF SYMBIOSIS IS?

Most anthropologists will have had very little access to the private anguish of individuals dealing with death, while therapists have had overdoses of privacy inside their closed-door and windowless offices. The sharing of what each knows will enhance the care offered by therapists and will permit anthropologists to better understand the societies they study.

Anthropologists in the field and therapists in the office do have much in common. Both groups watch people. Since Malinowski, anthropological field-work has become identified with its methodology, participant observation. Therapists are also participant observers. Both groups pride themselves on how well they observe others, but they have not even glanced at each other. It is time to take this next step.

Anthropologists go overseas to study different peoples. The group which I serve is also comprised of a "different peoples." In an emotional sense, at least, they are members of a refugee population. These persons have been (or have felt) outcast by our modern society because of the trauma of their own dying or the sad memories of another's death. Our society has not been able to hold them in its social support systems. Often, either no kin are around for these people, or the extended network of friends common in our communities is fragmented and unable to provide adequate support. Most people in our society do not want to think seriously—or for long—about what causes the death of a two-year old child. Perhaps the child was riding her tricycle when she was hit by a driver (maybe her grandfather) backing out of her driveway. My world wants to hide these deaths away. It does not want to think about them (except for the spectacular headline). Certainly, people aren't encouraged to experience the accident as if it had happened to their child.

Some of my refugees are people who come because their pain and their grief have not been resolved six months or a year or five years after a death. They are referred to me because they have no place to turn; everyone has emigrated from their stories, leaving them as refugees from their culture's mainstream. They may live, shop and work in the mainstream, but they no longer feel they belong to it.

An understanding of the way other cultures deal with such problems would help therapists better care for their patients. A broader understanding of the psychological refugee would help anthropologists broaden their perspective of how cultures deal with death.

A methodological difference between anthropologists and clinicians is that anthropologists have worked harder than therapists at ridding themselves of the supposition that one global theory can explain every culture. Therapists use previously formulated theoretical frameworks or bits of their own experience to draw conclusions within the first hour of seeing someone. These frameworks often fit theoretical models which assume a 'normal' standard from which all else can be measured. The model often becomes more valuable than the ideas and feelings of the person being observed. This may be because therapists do not have the luxury (you can tell that I have never done fieldwork) of spending a year or two with people. They cannot let their observations sit for a few more years before reaching conclusions. They must act quickly. Unlike anthropologists, therapists do have the luxury of checking out their judgments with the observed.

An attitudinal difference which results from the dissimilarities in method is that anthropologists expect the behaviors and customs they observe to be within a framework of "different, but normal." Therapists are trained to see anything that is different from the methodological ideal as pathology. Clinicians' tasks rest on fixing something that is broken or about to break. Something has to be 'not right' so a clinician can do something about it.

Therapeutically, it should be recognized that uncommonness is not pathology. Therapists with an understanding of anthropology might then realize that their concept of pathology is reductionist when viewed from a broader cultural perspective of human behavior. They would perhaps consider some of their client's supposed pathology to be more 'normal.' This broader viewpoint would help the therapist reframe strategies to assist those who are normal but require care. In turn, anthropologists would serve modern day society better if they considered that some parts of the societies they study may have aspects of pathological behavior within them.

At the symposium, I recognized one of my major working assumptions: people are people. They do not die by denomination or ethnic grouping. There is a commonness to the human responses surrounding a death—a shared humanity. At the level of their personal reactions, there is a familiarity, a homogeneous repertoire shared by all those I have known. I have always known that this belief could get me a heresy trial in many religions; but I did not realize it would upset anthropologists so much. They make their mark by emphasizing difference, too.

Kaufert (Kaufert and O'Neil, Chapter 14) showed a film of a Canadian Cree Indian undergoing heart catheterization. This person is lying awake on an operating room table, his vision, limited by green sheets to a bright light shining on his face. On his leg, through one of his veins, a masked man is inserting a tube with a small tv camera on the end. He will try to weave it through the patient's body to his heart. Kaufert, wanting to highlight cultural differences, made the comment that the procedure was very threatening for Indians. Well, that must make me a Cree because I was tense just watching. This was more than a culturally determined response—it was a human response.

There is a tendency to let our theoretical bias, for either reducing differences (therapists) or highlighting them (anthropologists), assist us to gloss over the expressions of the opposing perspective. The solution to this problem will require us to develop similar approaches to the sameness or difference of a series of events. Perhaps if therapists were less reductionist they would better recognize the 'normalness' of those they see. The anthropological highlights differences which in part is helpful to the clinician but highlighting the 'sameness' would be helpful as well.

Although anthropologists see people in turmoil, their mandate is for nonintervention. While the public relations material for the therapist emphasizes that a person does not have to be sick, dumb, stupid or crazy to seek therapy, the therapist's participation with people is clearly interventional. The goal of therapy is change—in feelings, thoughts, behaviors. Therapy is meant to change something, even if it is only to add one more person who is willing to walk with the client through his pain.

Many of the events in which my co-authors have participated are viewed from a public vantage point. Even the ideal death—alluded to in most of the papers as the one which occurs in old age, with the dying person in control, having healed old relationships and closed out one's duties—is from the perspective of the objective observer and not from the one who is dying. If an eighty-eight-year-old dies, society may comment that he lived a full life; but, for the eighty-eight-year-old it might have been nice to be eighty-nine. And does the spouse who is left see the death's idyllic aspects?

Therapists are a special type of participant observer when they are with people who are dying. Patients give us intimacy, their histories and their secrets. When attending a family in an Intensive Care Unit waiting room, or standing next to a bed while a person dies, one may hear more about a person's intimate thoughts and feelings than their families or neighbors have heard in years.

It follows, then, that what people tell each of us is different. Therapists, whether religious or secular, are thought to be bound by the old seal of confession (a prohibition to act on or repeat what is heard). Our clients assume that what is said will be held in confidence. It is not for publication, not to be shared with others. There is the need to externalize upset, pain, or confusion to someone, to have heard oneself say the unsayable; and so it is shared secretly with us. The other's expectations of us and invitations to us determine what they let us see and hear.

In addition, our expectations of ourselves determine what questions we will ask. As a result our questions must be based on thought and experience—if not our own, then those of others who have had similar experiences. As a therapist, reading and listening to the stories told in those papers, there were so many questions I wanted to ask those people. But the response of almost all of the symposium anthropologists was that my type of questions were not talked about at all or were too private—too personal. The questions would not have been so for a therapist.

And these questions do not have to be too private for anthropologists—because the roots of clinicians in dying and death related fields closely parallel the relationship of an anthropologist and an informant. The informant knows and the anthropologist learns. Dr. Elizabeth Kubler-Ross developed her style of listening, observing and engaging persons when she was at Bellevue Hospital in New York City. She would sit for hours with severely disturbed schizophrenics, not knowing exactly what she was doing. She tried to understand what their worlds were all about by simply being there. These patients were her informants. When she pioneered the area of death and dying, she proceeded in the same way. Dying patients were her teachers.

Kubler-Ross' adoption of anthropological method exploded the West's understandings of a person's responses to dying. At first, and identical to the anthropologists' response, hospital staff would not help her because they thought that dying was "too personal, too private" to be discussed. In her first book, *On Death and Dying* (1969), Kubler-Ross provided a series of observations. Her text had all sorts of ambiguities. The patient's experiences and feelings took precedence over her conceptualizations. She raised her own questions as to whether her observations and theoretical framework were correct (Kubler-Ross, 1969:xi).

> It is not meant to be a textbook on how to manage dying patients, nor is it intended, as a complete study of the psychology of the dying. It is simply an account of a new and challenging opportunity to refocus on the patient as a human being. . . . I am simply telling the stories of my patients who shared their agonies, their expectations, and their frustrations with us.

Anthropologists must question their work in the same way. The stories presented in all of the papers hinted at the potential for a symbiotic relationship between clinical therapy and anthropology, particularly in the area of dying, death and bereavement. This relationship can exist despite the differences in professional mandates. Both professions will benefit from fostering a closer relationship.

DO YOU MIND IF WE ASK YOU A QUESTION?

In order for anthropology to be of maximum value to the clinical therapist and subsequently to mankind, the differences between public and private participant observation must be discussed. In this context, I wish to raise a series of questions to both groups simultaneously because it will take cooperation to find good answers.

What do individuals feel they need to do after a death, and does the society at large facilitate or hamper the resolution of the individual's needs?

Can we expect any social system to be flexible enough to respond to the wide range of normal responses present in bereavement?

Does every society try to limit the acceptable mourning responses to a small, fixed repertoire, so that the nonbereaved do not have to listen or respond to the uniqueness of a particular situation? Do they simply fall back upon rote responses?

Should individuals sublimate what they need to do, feel and say to have the concern and care of others, plus society's judgement that they are acceptable members?

Does the limited choice of mourning responses which a society prescribes save the individual from the disorientation and pain that comes after the death of a loved one?

Are individuals left vulnerable to suffering in our pluralistic society where there are few prescriptions and multiple, self-directed options?

Does there need to be balance between individual needs (autonomy) and what society says is required to be practiced (beneficence) in the mourning process?

An individual must express some things after the death of someone close. The question is, do the cultures that anthropologists study facilitate the resolution of grief any better than the West does? How would the comparison be measured?

What is the failure rate for people who do not survive their grief within your particular cultures? Who are they? How do people of other cultures define a grief failure? Do they measure it by an increased somatization, similar to a psychosomatic model where colitis or asthma are born of unresolved grief? Or is failure measured by emotional distress: by the incidence of unacceptable affect or behavior?

It would be useful to know whether mourning practices are actually helpful in resolving grief and if so, which practices are most helpful. Do some cultures impose an extra burden on the bereaved by expecting them to perform extensive mourning practices, or do these requirements aid in healing? Are the bereaved expressing their grief or just putting on a good show for the neighbors?

Anthropologists have the opportunity to ask these questions and the answers have relevance for the 20th century therapist. Anthropologists ask "too personal, too private" questions because they are scientists and persons with social responsibility. To obtain this information is the task of the anthropologist and to use the information is the task of the clinician. The clinical therapist must offer the anthropologist an appropriate way to ask these questions. But first, the anthropologist must recognize that these questions need to be asked. In most cases, the narrative itself demands the asking of questions.

The posing of these questions has proved critical for the development of the West's understanding of dying and bereavement. I am not trying to turn anthropologists into therapists but rather am suggesting strategies which could be incorporated into an already superior methodological structure. To develop these strategies a standardization of terminology would be helpful.

ARE WE TALKING ABOUT THE SAME THING?

Although it seems that anthropologists and therapists are granted access to different parts of people's experiences, it is only because different questions are asked. If therapists and anthropologists are to try to ask complementary questions they should agree on what certain concepts mean. Neither anthropology nor the therapeutic disciplines share definitions for major terms, including bereavement, grief and mourning. Little critical work is being done anywhere to establish standard usages. Theorists and clinicians tend to use these words from their own personal experiences and the folklore of their disciplines.

I suspect this has something to do both with the complexity of the terms themselves, and with the analysts' sharing of the same events. At the symposium, I suggested some working definitions which offer some clarification. It is critical that these terms be used precisely. The understanding of dying and bereavement as well as the ability to help people cope with the effects of death depend on appreciating these terms as distinct concepts.

> *Bereavement* is the descriptive term for the period of time in which a person who has suffered the death of a relationship is actively dealing with the impact of the death.
>
> *Mourning* represents those public behaviors and ritual expressions of grief which a society deems appropriate and helpful for a person to practice during a bereavement.
>
> *Grief* refers to the process of thoughts, feelings, attitudes and physiological responses within a person during bereavement.

Individual responses to death are numerous. The term 'bereavement' can be compared to the name on the cover of a large restaurant menu. All the expressions of bereavement are like the appetizers, entrees, soups, salads, desserts, side dishes and drinks listed inside. There are many possibilities to get a good and complete meal, to feel full and satisfied. Grief resolution parallels this analogy. People can pick and choose (with varying degrees of freedom and awareness) according to their particular emotional temperament, socio-cultural heritage and prescriptions, their past experiences, the availability of help, and the actual degree of the stress. The selections for eating are limited by the culture of the restaurant (Pizza is great, but not often available if you are in a Chinese rice shop). So too with bereavement, certain behaviors are featured under some conditions and not under others.

Mourning practices permit the people of a particular culture to create shared meanings about why death happens, thus reducing the potential anxiety about the fragility of life—especially one's own life. They are also an attempt to exert control by providing behavioral boundaries for those who are bereaved and they present role descriptions for those who interact with the bereaved. Perceived helplessness and disorganization in the face of death are minimized by mourning practices in which the first social activity is to do something at the expense of emotion. Lieber (Chapter 11) discusses this. He says ". . . a person's death initiates a flurry of activity that proceeds in stages . . . 1) *Organizational* . . . No weeping or other emotional expression is permitted during this first phase." These reorganizational activities get quickly structured as emotion suppressing the counterbeliefs—fate, immortality, resurrection, reincarnation, etc.—created by the society to reestablish control and meaning. Their basic message is: things aren't as bad as they seem.

The above perspectives on death may complement or oppose each other or do both at the same time. Much of the focus for the symposium papers was on mourning and mortuary rituals, not grief. From the public perspective, if the behaviors of the grieving individual do not coincide with the assigned mourning practices of a particular society, the bereaved is perceived as unacceptable or abnormal or dangerous. Ideally, the mourning practices encouraged and developed by a society should facilitate the expression and resolution of a bereaved person's grief. But to do so, they must adequately reflect the nature and quantity of the emotional and physical attachments in the lost relationship. Rituals, religious or secular, are powerful tools for healing and effecting change, but they must address the pertinent aspects of the bereaved's grief. In modern North American society, it is more likely that the mourning rituals prescribed for a particular bereavement are abnormal. (See Ramsden's account (Chapter 3) of his birth culture.)

In this pluralistic society, normalcy is achieved by the reduction of every phase of required mourning to a least common denominator. In effect, this process offers no guidance or support from the larger society to facilitate a structured path or limited behavioral boundaries for the grieving individuals. Mourning is the expectation of society for what is appropriate for a bereaved person. This expectation may or may not coincide with a person's feelings about the death of a loved one. The kinship description of a relationship does not limit the quality, quantity or personal importance of the relationship. When a man dies, we can anticipate the specific mourning rituals of a particular culture for his wife. However, we must ask private questions if we are to know about the private grief of his wife . . . or his nephew.

CAN YOU LISTEN WITH YOUR THIRD EAR?

There was a young man whose uncle had died several months earlier. He had lived with his uncle in his uncle's house. In no way could he get reinvested in life, and he could not return to work. He was sad but could not cry. His friends thought he was depressed. He was becoming more and more isolated. He had been referred to a social worker and then later to a psychiatrist. He would describe experiences of waking up in the middle of the night and find his uncle standing at the foot of the bed. They would talk for long periods of time. In spite of professional help, he was still not doing any better, so he was referred to me. Whenever I am asked to see someone who has been seen by others, I assume that most professionals are as smart as I am and that they have done the usual sorts of things. Therefore I have to be a little unusual. When I walked in to see this young man, and after the initial chatter of all conversations, I said, "This guy was more than an uncle to you, right?" He replied, "Yeah. We were lovers. Nobody knows so I cannot talk about it." I replied, "You can talk with me about him, if you want." For almost fifteen or sixteen years they had hidden this part of their relationship. They had devised an elaborate structure; everybody in his whole world believed that this man was his uncle. Therefore, he could mourn for him only as an uncle; he could not grieve his loss as a lover.

Earlier therapists had seen his grief as abnormal or as a depression[2] or a personality disorder because his mourning seemed inappropriate to his relationship with an 'uncle.' Similarly, Lieber (Chapter 11) points out for Kapingamarangi that such discrepancies between how persons mourn and how society thought they should mourn were cause for suspicion. Lieber says

> A man's sister-in-law was overly sincere in her sobbing, occasioning the anger of both her own and the deceased's relatives. Her uncontrolled sobbing was embarrassing enough, but even worse was the fact that her relation as in-law to the deceased did not warrant that sort of emotion.

We cannot determine the inner reality of persons by what we see in behavior. I did not know that the man in the foregoing vignette was grieving for a lost lover. Something was wrong with the storyteller's story, but I did not know that. At the end of our time together, he asked me, "How did you know we were lovers?" I told him, "Just a guess." There was something in his story that told me that I needed to question, and I could ask. So, too, must the anthropologist find ways of asking.

DOES IT EVER END?

While the anthropologists at the symposium discussed the problem of privacy and personal questions, another difficulty arises from the perspective of therapists. In order to be an effective participant observer, one must recognize that grief is a process. Using the previous story I would like to demonstrate how this is so.

---

[2]In these chapters, there was a tendency to equate grief and depression. The study of grief is a highly complex field. Grief and depression are different phenomena; depression may be more an inability to grieve.

I am no sweetness-and-light therapist offering bargain basement salvation with a cute set of magical, mysterious interventions. In the above example, the time was ripe and full for the key question to be asked and answered. Differences exist between a fresh grief and a grief that has been lived with for a while. Some issues arise at the beginning of the process, others are saved for the end or the resolution of the process. Though the symposium participants were asked to assume that grief is a process, they sometimes failed to address the question of movement through grief. The same story means different things to a person at differing places in the grief process. A sense of timing and an evaluation of "the time" the story is told helps determine how many meanings the story has for the teller.[3]

All the cultures described in these chapters recognize that death has a significance that needs to be dealt with communally both before and after the event. Just as it takes time to establish emotional, intellectual, spiritual, physical bonds between people in a relationship, so too it takes time to remove that bondage after death. The depth of the crisis that death presents to an individual and to a society is directly related to the value placed on a particular life, and life in general, by the individual and the society.

Societies have provided the transition phases necessary for the living and for the dead, as Ramsden has indicated in Chapter 3. It takes a while to become fully human or to develop a relationship; and it takes a while to lose all humanity or to let go of a relationship. Whether societies try to forcibly resolve the loss of a relationship in a short period of time (e.g., the Roman Catholic Funeral is called the Mass of Resurrection) or sustain it in an extended period of time (e.g., the black dress worn by Old Believer widows years after their spouses' death described by Morris in Chapter 7), most societies do provide some transition. Does any society see death as an event that is singular? There seem to be many prescribed steps for the dying and the mourning.

The dying and mourning rituals of a culture try to control and manage the depth and the duration of the crisis presented by death, especially the death of someone in the midst of social power. These rituals try to control the disorganization and the social disruption by using methods similar to those used to control the living while, at the same time, inculcating and supporting the worldview of the society.

A culture's power to prohibit the expression of certain grief responses has an added significance because there are many things grieved for at the death of a particular person. The focus of grief may not be the person who has died but, instead, it may be something symbolically encoded in the relationship—a dream, a virtue, a history. Ramsden recorded Brebeuf's comments about the intensity of mourning that occurred in the secondary burials of the 17th Century Huron

[3]The title of the talk I was supposed to do was "The Meaning of Death." It would have been more appropriate to have called it "The Meanings of a Death."—not only do different people see one death differently, but one person sees the same death differently as they move through a process and a journey of resolution.

Indians. We can speculate that the source of grief might have been the community's loss of its roots in a place it had called home for ten years. Also, in the Counts' Chapter (12), the villagers' grief over the decrepit and blind old woman who died in her fire in Kaliai may have derived from their failure to be involved with this woman. Their indifference had become fixed forever by her death. The Lusi-Kaliai may have been grieving more about their loss of kindness than anything to do with Mary, the blind woman. Anthropologists should start asking what a person's tears are for, as well as analyzing their behaviors.

DO YOU THINK I'M NORMAL?

Another story reveals how my society uses its unwritten prohibitions to shape the way tears are seen or not seen. Societies do have an enormous effect on how stories get told and all story gatherers must recognize this contribution to the final story.

There was a woman in her early fifties. Her husband had a degenerative muscle disease that took about ten years to kill him. He got more disabled with each passing year. She worked near her home; at lunch time, she would go home to see how he was doing. She would do her afternoon's work and return home to take care of him. She did not go out because he could not go out with assistance, even for weekend drives. In reality, her whole life involved nursing her spouse. When he finally died, she lost the jovial personality maintained all those years when she was nursing her husband. People noticed her sadness for she could not get back to work. Every time someone said "Hello" to her she broke into tears.

She was another one of those referrals I got because nobody else had done anything to help her. It was a case of "Aw, what the hell! Try the chaplain." I made the assumption that everybody had done all the 'right' things, for who had not read Kubler-Ross or a similar high priest?

After we talked about her husband for a few minutes, I asked her, "Does your husband's death remind you of anybody else's death?" And she said to me, "Yes. My son died when he was six and my husband never let me talk about it." I wish I had the session on tape because I could not tell from her affective responses, nor by the detail of the description, that I was not right then in an Emergency "quiet room" where they were trying to resuscitate her son. She could tell me what day it was, the time of day. He was on his bike. She saw him from the living room window of their home, hit by a car. The make, model and color, the driver's description and his words all came rushing out. She knew immediately what had happened. He was dead. After the funeral, her husband said that she had to get on with her life. This child's death was to be mentioned no more.

There had been a complete lapse for over twenty years; grief suspended, just put on hold and swallowed. When her husband died nobody remembered about her son. I do not even think she realized there might be a connection. Though her son's death never was mentioned, she was not immobilized by her husband's death, she was grieving the death of her son. Her husband, as well as her family and friends, felt she had grieved enough for her son. Now that her husband had died, somewhere inside of her she could grieve and mourn her son's death according to her needs and not the needs of others.

What price do the bereaved pay to their society in order to have its blessing? Ernest Becker used a quote from Kierkegaard's *Sickness Unto Death* to describe this culturally normal person (Ernest Becker, 1973:79):

> But while one sort of despair plunges wildly into the infinite and loses itself, a second sort permits itself as it was to be defrauded by "the others." By seeing the multitude of men about it, by getting engaged in all sorts of worldly affairs, by becoming wise about how to go in this world, such a man forgets himself. . . . does not dare to believe in himself, finds it too venturesome a thing to be himself, far easier and safer to be like the others, to become an imitation, a number, a cipher in the crowd.

Society can drive grief inside, stopping the process, encapsulating it and not letting it out to be shared with others. Are the cultures which were studied helping to dispel this despair? Do they manage all the varieties and the repertoires that emerge through the grief process without throwing some people out of union or making them "a cipher in the crowd" or, worse, driving them to therapists' offices?

In my opinion, anthropological studies of grief and bereavement ought to be directed to the general public. Individuals who are bereaved have many reactions which they keep secret because they perceive their expression to be unacceptable in our culture. If they do venture to share them, they are met immediately with "shouldn'ts," "can'ts" and "don'ts." This censorship by others has drastic consequences, especially if the others are supported by the society's norms. These silenced bereaved are alone, isolated, and strange.

The bereaved will adapt rituals to meet their personal needs either at the expense of doctrinal or legal regulations. In Chapter 7, Morris footnoted the importance of baptism for the Old Believers. In one incident the parents and a small group may have risked the physical life of the newborn and censure from the hospital to have the baby baptized, so "all those responsible could relax for they had fulfilled their duties." People feel a great need to have death rituals performed. In order to stay In Union, and as part of their faith, the Old Believers felt a personal need to baptize their ill child. If they had permitted others to convince them to follow hospital rules and had not performed the sacrament, they would have always remembered that their child died unbaptized. Their grief would have been compounded.

People will use rituals to make reality more bearable. They do not worry primarily about the timing of things or the legal niceties. As a chaplain, I have baptized children even a day or two after an autopsy. Cognitively, any Christian family knows that a baptism should occur before death; their personal necessity is to have the sacrament performed. In order to stay in union and as part of their faith community, the family does not tell anyone that the baptism took place after the death. But if they allowed others citing rules to refuse them the ritual, they—like the Old Believers—would always remember that their child was not baptized.

Some people who have chosen to be cremated have asked to have their ashes spread over a rose garden. However, when relatives try to place the ashes at the botanical gardens, they discover that this practice is prohibited. You cannot leave grandma with the *floribunda*. But does this restriction stop anyone? People do it. And they pay a price whether they get caught or not. If caught, they pay a fine; if they are not caught, they must keep silent. I have come to think that all the private necessities of grief may require public expression if grief is to be resolved.

IS DYING A DIAGNOSIS?

In North America, we have succeeded in making death a referrable sub-specialty. Ordinary people (such as family and friends) think they need to be thanatologists to understand a person's reactions to a death. One must read The Experts before helping the bereaved. Actually, theories of grief are not that beneficial because they are too restricted. The limiting of acceptable feelings, thoughts, behaviors is inherent in the development of any theory. Whenever I teach about grief I encounter this exclusion. As soon as I say, "Grief is . . . . 'this'" I am aware that grief can also be a 'that,' which is opposite my first 'this.' However, I am trying to say something that makes sense, so I cannot keep contradicting myself. I exclude some aspects of grief from the usual. This, by itself, would not be too bad; but the usual has a way of becoming the normal. Hence, a normal, but infrequent, reaction becomes abnormal and the bereaved who give expression to these infrequent responses are considered sick.

Too much attention has been given in the popular press of the West to dying as an unknown and incomparable part of a person's life. This perspective denies that we are a grieving people and displaces society's problems with living onto a fear of death. Consider Cephalus' answer to Socrates' question about whether old age (substitute dying or mourning) is a hard time of life (Plato, 1968:5):

> By Zeus, I shall tell you just how it looks to me, Socrates, he said. Some of us who are about the same age often meet together and keep up the old proverb. Now then, when they meet, most of the members of our group lament, longing for the pleasures of youth and reminiscing about sex, about drinking bouts, and feasts and all that goes with things of that sort; they take it hard as though they were deprived of something very important and had lived well but are now not even alive . . .
>
> But Socrates, in my opinion these men do not put their fingers on the cause. For if this was the cause, I too would have suffered these same things insofar as they depend on old age and so would everyone else who has come to this point in life. . . .
> But of these things and those that concern relatives, there is one certain cause: not old age, Socrates, but the character of human beings. If they are balanced and good

tempered, even old age is moderately troublesome; if they are not, then both age, Socrates, and youth alike turn out to be hard for that sort.

People die as they lived; they retain their responsibilities. Dying and grief are no longer normal parts of living in our society, but have become diseases which some people get, and, what then naturally follows, some other people offer to cure them. The major coping mechanisms which people have employed (freely or forced) to manage their lives will be the same ones they choose to use to confront death. Anybody who says knowing grief theory is more important than knowing who a person is, is wrong. Persons employ their limited coping strategies to manage both their lives and deaths.

People in other cultures do the same with mourning and mortuary practices. Ramsden notes in Chapter 3 that:

> Since perceptions of the nature of death are societally constructed, and necessarily embody notions of the nature of life and of the afterlife, mortuary customs probably do subsume all of the traditional issues mentioned above. A notion of what death is cannot be separated from a notion of what life is, and it necessarily implies some concept of what follows death, even if that concept is that nothing follows death. It is also probably impossible to separate a perception of death from a perception of society, insofar as it is probably impossible to dream up a notion of *anything* that is entirely independent on one's experience of social relations.

Similar comment is made in Chapter 7 by Morris in discussing the funerals of Old Believers: "The funeral service reflects many aspects of their religious beliefs, rituals and internalized understandings." If there is a consistent approach to both life and death, how can that be compatible with the assumption of many cultures that having foreknowledge is being forearmed. A typical comment is Badone's observation (Chapter 13) that 'good death' is the one that comes forewarned."

This is not true in practice for North America. The dissociation of dying from living gives the impression that dying will give you life skills which you did not have while you were living. I wonder how much validity this notion of a change in personality in the face of death has anywhere. Some of the glib stuff that happens in palliative care where some overly well intentioned helper is going to redeem a person's whole life in the two weeks before he or she dies is part of this infection. The lie goes like this: if people know they're going to die,[4] then they'll correct, enhance, enjoy, cherish, etc., their relationships with their kids, their spouses, life, whatever. If they cannot do these things while they are living, they probably will not be able to do them while they are dying.

It takes a lot of energy to change almost anything about yourself. Forget personality changes! Just the energy expended trying to beat a cigarette, stay on a diet, or have a new year's resolution last more than a month is quite draining. Do

---

[4] I probably should have added 'soon' here because which one of us isn't going to die.

you think that you will be able to make life changes around relationships when some disease is drawing energy from you?

The saddest words I hear from people are, "All my life I wanted to (insert anything), but now I'm never going to be able to do it." Many times I've been asked, "How can you stay involved with death and dying all the time?" Well, it helps to be a little crazy; but the dying and grieving teach you about living. Life is precious and surprising. If you want to do something, then do it; you cannot count on being around tomorrow. Why do we worry so much about the distant future, whether we will get tenure or retire early? It must be a sacred myth. Living is full of ironies, and there are no limited warranties; and dying—especially our own—has a way of destroying our assumptions about how our lives will unfold. When one is aware that death may intervene, there can be an added pressure on relationships here and now—to make them creative, intimate, cleaner or more supportive—because life is a fragile, uncertain gift. While you still have the energy and time (maybe) to do something about what or who is really important in your life, let life's transitoriness shake you for awhile (not for long). From the grief of death you may have the chance to reevaluate "the whole tenor and motivation of your life."[5] But it is painful to change at any time.

IS THIS GOING TO HURT?

One theme hidden in the chapters, but which is present universally in my experience, is pain. It was momentarily contemplated sadly by Sarah Preston (Preston and Preston, Chapter 9) in her account of the funeral of Malcolm Diamond and frighteningly anticipated in Badone's account of Marie-Thérèse's pain (Chapter 13). Yet it was not analyzed. A pain is present which is pure and full, even before cognitions necessary for suffering are formed. The experience of pain which surrounds a death may be the only cultural universal in the field of death and bereavement and not the finding of a particular pattern.

There are many reasons for pain's absence in these chapters; a few are technical, most are painful. Few writers are skilled enough in literary techniques to convey emotions with words. Also, anthropologists half-wishing to have the objective distance of scientists, do not reflect on the affective nature of their relationships with people. In addition, the contributors to this volume are for the most part North Americans whose own cultural heritage encourages the avoidance of pain. (See Ramsden, Chapter 3.)

Therapists also distance themselves from pain. We have rationalized it, even theorized its necessity for us to do our jobs. Sociologists Glaser and Strauss (1975)

---

[5]Many of the ideas expressed in this paragraph come from a great teacher, and my favorite unpublished author, Ken Beal. Of course, denial is truly a gift of some god. What I know and witness in the rest of humanity I can blissfully escape ever applying to myself. For example, the symposium was held in May 1988 and the revised draft was due weeks ago. I know that I still have time, but I am not so sure about Ken.

saw professionals relating to the dying on three levels: impersonal, interpersonal and intrapersonal. This range of relatedness stretches from the dehumanizing—and not painful for caregivers—"cancer in room 3" to the intimacy where the other's experiences, including pain, blend identically with the clinician's personal story. If caregivers always keep their protective distance from the dying or bereaved, then, those persons who have not become deaf and dumb observers will give us what caregivers have given them. Centuries ago a Latin poet, Horace, expressed it concisely, "If you wish to draw tears from me, you must first feel pain yourself." I will weave a story to help you feel this pain:

> At 6:10 one Friday night when I was at home, my pager went off: beep-beep-beep-beep-5-6-9-3. It was the Intensive Care Unit and I called, "Hi. It's John. You looking for me?"
> "We've got a three-year-old coming in. Hit by a car earlier. Not going to do real well . . ."
> "Ok. I'll be in . . . in twenty minutes."

On Saturday night, we said he was dead, though he probably was dead earlier. Later, his organs went all over the province; and his parents went home together for the first time in months. It was already a second marriage for both. His son from his first marriage died at eight months from SIDS. Her thirteen-year-old from her first marriage was watching the three-year-old, watching him get hit by a truck which did not stop. Together they had a daughter who had open heart surgery. She had been born with mongoloid deficits. The thirteen-year-old and I sang "Happy Birthday" to her brother, not because it was his birthday, but because he was never going to have another birthday. She was slow, too; but she was right.

In between, on Friday night late, a nine-year-old boy was hit by a car. He was playing a superman with a wand. He had seen it on cartoons. His mom called his father, though he had been charged with assaulting their older daughter. The father had not seen his son for six months. His new wife was there and no one could stand being in the same room with the others, except for the fact that the boy might die. He might even make it, but nobody could promise that he would ever be the same. The father told the mother, "You haven't let me see him for six months and now I see him on his deathbed. It's your fault. You shouldn't have let him out at night."

Early Saturday morning, there was a head-on collision—two cars, two deaths (both drivers). In one car was the driver's wife and their eleven-year-old son. The wife was taken to one hospital and the son to another. She had most of her bones broken. He had a head injury (not bad by trauma standards) and a broken pelvis. When the boy first came in, we christened him John Doe. In a while, we learned his story and his name. He was talking, but not understanding. We called his grandparents. They would come in on Saturday night and Sunday morning. They would have trouble getting flights.

He did not know his father had died. He did not know until Monday afternoon. I had just gone back to get some sleep. I already had worked more hours than I get paid for and it was only Monday; but, he finally asked where his parents were. The staff in the ICU must have felt that I could disguise the word 'dead,' so that he would not be hurt by the news. I still have not found another way to say 'dead,' but people think I can:

> "Hi," I said to the boy using his name, "I'm John. I've been talking to you since you came in. Do you remember that you were in a car accident?"
>
> "No," he whispered.
>
> "Well, you were on your way to a hockey tournament . . . You've had a tough time. Your pelvis is broken and you took a shot to your head . . . You are going to have to stay in bed for a long time."
>
> "I want to get up. Can you get me a wheelchair? I want to see the hospital . . ."
>
> "Can't do that for awhile. But when you can I'll give you the grand tour . . . All your grandparents are here. They are worried about you."
>
> "Oh, thank you. . . . Where are my parents?"
>
> "I've got some sad news for you . . . Your father died right away in the car crash . . ."
>
> "I'm glad he didn't have a painful death . . . And my mother?"
>
> "She's at a different hospital. She is going to be alright, but she has alot of broken bones. We are going to bring her over here in the next few days."
>
> "That's good. Can I have a drink."
>
> "Right now you can't drink anything. It would make you feel sicker."
>
> "Can I talk to my mom?"
>
> "Sure. I'll arrange it.

They talked and he told her he was okay. Well, there was nothing okay about it. And I was not okay. I cried. And, he did not remember. I had to tell him again the next day.

My words cannot capture the overwhelming pervasiveness of the pain. They may in fact only capture some of my pain or the pain I shared with them. Their pain is: something of the pain of hell; the pain of emotional paralysis; the pain that prevents concentration on words or sounds or feelings; the pain that blocks awareness of the sunshine, the wind. Nor did I write of the facial expressions, the touching, the silences, the sadness of the staff as they imagined how their own children would be told of their deaths—or the craziness. When the first boy came into Emergency, his aunt was his nurse. The second boy was beaten by his father, but he had convinced his mother to drop the charges. The third boy's father thought hockey was getting too violent.

DO YOU REALLY WANT TO LISTEN?

The major reason for the difficulty in conveying the reality of pain is that most people avoid pain in themselves and the awareness of it in others. Staff turnover in critical care areas is high. Deaths constantly confront health care people with pain and destroy their illusions that there is some order and justice in the world. Most of us would like to think, and in fact do, that if we can do the right things (avoid sin, smoke and saturated fats) and say the right things (prayers and the words taught in assertiveness training), we might not live forever but we will not die before we are ready (which may be the same as the former). Are there societies that welcome the sharing of this pain? Or are others like our own society? Are expressions of pain ritualized into familiar forms so others need pay no attention to the individuality of the individual's pain?

The extreme avoidance of anything painful in North America means that a lot of peoples are better off than we are. The societies that my anthropology colleagues have written about have ways of restructuring a role for people to come back into society. There is a place for them. Their society makes a place, or it forces them into a place, or it may assist them into a place. Our society has abdicated most of the responsibility it had for the mourning practices of individuals. My society imposes no community rituals for either the dying or the mourning and grieving. Kaufert and O'Neil (Chapter 14) notes this *laissez-faire* attitude of Canadian society:

> In urban hospitals, the organizational structure of the ward and professional control of terminal care further isolates the patient from family and community support networks. It also interferes with rituals which integrate the family's experience of dying and grieving into the life of the community.

Everyone in society must wait for the invitation of the bereaved who determine what mourning practices will be observed by the community. Even the pastor of their church needs an invitation to do the funeral, and ironically, the invitation usually is extended by the mortician for the family.

The shift in responsibility has been sanctioned by our society: funeral homes are now customer service, not community service, industries. We assign further responsibility for comforting the bereaved to the bereaved themselves. It is much easier that way on those who are not bereaved. Self-help groups which used to be restricted to the outcasts of society—alcoholics, drug addicts—are now formed to help the new outcasts—widow to widow programs or bereaved families associations. All this is done with good intentions and the assumptions that only the afflicted can understand the problems of others so afflicted.

The young widow has no place to be; she gets transformed into a symbol. Nobody wants her. She does not know how to restructure a new life for herself and we do not have the place for her. We do not want her in our neighborhood where we must see, not a bereaved friend, but a painful symbol. We have forced mourning into being more and more of a private experience.

When a prominent woman—well known for her grace and concern for others—died, many people in the community were surprised by her death. She kept her disease a secret because she knew that once people see you as dying they forget everything else about who you are. Many of her acquaintances did not go to the church service, not because they were not her denomination nor because they did not have the time off, but because they thought that they did not know her well enough to attend her funeral; after all, a funeral is for families or very close friends.

Of those people who did go to the church, most did not go to the cemetery because they thought the graveside service was more private, more just for family. It required a degree of kinship. Of those people at the cemetery, probably only half went back to the home.

We in the West have a mythology of privacy which says that we are closer to our family than to our friends, so no place is made for mourning our friends. Because of this mythology, people are reluctant to become like family to widows, widowers, or bereaved parents. And because we are not family we have no role in structuring mourning, though we may have more grief over the loss of our friend than over some of our relatives. When someone dies who is an influence on our own lives as well as on the community, neither we nor the community know how to behave, how to be mourners.

This dismissal of the larger community from active participation in mourning is unlike the practice in many of the societies reported in this volume, especially the two traditional Russian communities (Chapter 7). According to Morris, for Old Believers, "Death is a 'village' affair, and when it occurs, all turn their attention to it and rather rapidly do what they consider necessary to lay the body to rest and to acknowledge the event among all the living present." The person who attends a Molokan funeral, "plays a personal part in the event, and feels a responsibility and an obligation to attend, even though the travel distance might be quite far."

HAVEN'T I SEEN YOU BEFORE?

My analysis of the chapters has convinced me that if anthropologists and clinical therapists were to share their experiences the result would be a powerful symbiotic relationship between the two professions. As I read of the customs of peoples of whom I knew nothing, I realized that I *had* seen exotic responses in my work at McMaster. However, the responses I had seen were not supported by mortuary rituals or mourning practices. People did what they did because they felt they had to do it. As I read the stories in the chapters, I would say to myself, "This is just like so and so. Are they really that different?" I do not think so. Much of the information presented has clinical parallels in the stories told in secret to clinicians. For example:

Temporary Burials

In Chapter 3 Ramsden argues that Huron Indians took some time to see their deceased as "fully dead." He states:

> I would predict that the 'temporary' state of being 'just dead' might be reflected in a temporary, primary burial, situated so that the deceased's soul had access to the activities of the living. Following this I would predict a more 'permanent' burial, in which the body is permanently and irretrievably disposed of, in a special location removed from the living.

Like the "just dead" of the Hurons, when people here are cremated, their bereaved cannot decide where to put the remains. At first, they leave the ashes with the funeral home until a decision is reached. Sometimes—more frequently if there have been multiple marriages—families are unable to reach a decision. Then the ashes are split: some will go to one family grave, the rest will get spread on a favorite lake.

Or the remains are placed in an urn which assumes a prominent place (on the coffee table) with the bereaved's household for a while. It will eventually be moved from this center of discussion to the basement, a closet or a burial spot. Shortly after death, the deceased—like the ashes—retains a decision-making role in the family. This power continues in a symbolic union with the urn until both parts of the deceased are moved from the center of activities for the living.

Temporary Weddings

In Chapter 8, Wellenkamp recounted the *pakendek*, a simple marriage ceremony performed between the surviving spouse and another person who is also widowed:

> Following the ceremony, the couple stays together for a few nights, during which time they are permitted but not required to have sexual relations. After this, if the couple so desires, they may continue to live together as husband and wife. Otherwise, a simple divorce ceremony is performed.

There is a surprisingly similar practice in the West, but it lacks the formalities of a public ritual. Widows and widowers often find themselves in brief sexual encounters after the death of a spouse. These are usually short-lived and serve the purpose of stating, mostly to themselves, that they have further separated from their commitments to their former spouse. They are still desirable members of the larger society. It is the act of sex that becomes their private ritual passage rather than a public wedding ceremony, as with the Toraja.

The Desire for Revenge

The Counts (Chapter 12) said, "Lusi-Kaliai grief is almost always a mixture of sorrow with anger and a desire for revenge." In North America, surgeons seldom are shot when somebody dies on an operating table, but lawsuits for malpractice have become commonplace. Occasionally, when I have told a family that their child or father has died, I have been punched. Parents of a child killed by a drunk driver are very descriptive of what they are going to do if they ever get that person. The commitment that such people invest in organizations such as MADD or joining the fight against cancer can be seen as an attempt at revenge. The act of making donations to a society dedicated to the elimination of the disease that killed a loved one is a symbolic form of revenge against the enemy more that it is a contribution to the deceased's life or ideals.

Indirect Communication

Wellenkamp's reference in Chapter 8 to the Toraja's use of fallen leaves is familiar in the West. She wrote, "Although the death is not formally acknowledged . . . One way of alluding to the death is to say, 'A leaf has fallen in the village' . . ." A popular children's book about death uses a leaf which falls as the protagonists. Doctors are infamous for roundabout communication. For example:

> It is two o'clock in the morning and they call a family to say that their mother has taken a turn for the worse; but there is no need to hurry.
> A patient has been given to understand that he is doing well, until relatives that he has not seen in twenty years just happen to stop by. They just happen to be driving through from Newfoundland.
> If I go into a room and introduce myself as a chaplain, some people think that there is a hidden message, "There's something wrong with me, Mr. Death is here." Others ask me, "I am not dying, am I?"

Communication With the Dead

Among others, the Weigands in Chapter 5 focused on the ongoing communication with the dead among the Huichol Indians. The Weigands say: "The presence of these ancestors among the living is real, and their physical death does not impinge upon their continued social life and functions." In North America, caressing and talking to the dead at a funeral home or graveside could not be considered unusual. After the death of his spouse, a man who is usually considered very sane kept a vigil at the funeral home for two nights with the deceased sitting up in the opposite chair. They had a wonderful discussion all night long about their relationship. This was not a unique experience. It is just not the type that is shared publicly.

IN THE END

Grief behavior that is manifested privately in some places and publicly elsewhere can be understood accurately only through the collaboration of clinicians and anthropologists. Everyone tries to create meaning about life and death—individually and societally. If one can understand anything or give a meaning to it, some measure of control has been achieved over it.

The driving impulse to explain chance, accident, or chaos is unyielding whether it is fueled by guilt or fear or love. Even if bereaved sacrifice themselves in the process, convict themselves of culpability in the death, or attribute responsibility to sorcery, or medical malpractice—they will not leave a death without some meaning. The dying and their mourners do create personal, idiosyncratic meanings as they move from the initial pain. These created truths help them place the death into the broader framework of their worldview. The difficulty in North America is that we have become too individualistic. Mourners can not be supported by a mainstream of the culture because there is not one. This is not a contradiction of my earlier statement that individual responses to bereavement should not be constrained by social mores. It is a very different thing to give someone the right to do something and to support those same people while they are exercising that right.

I am so tired of saying "I do not know" or "I have not got an answer for you" to the questions which I am asked by the dying or the bereaved. The last comforting phrase that I still could utter was used not by me but by a student chaplain whom I had convinced of its power. This chaplain was sitting with a Ukrainian grandmother whose daughter had delivered stillborn twins minutes before. The chaplain wanted to offer some words of comfort to alleviate her pain, so he told her that God shared our tears and God wept with us. The old woman through her broken English said, "So what good is a God who weeps?" Instead of helping to lighten her pain, it raised another question to which I must answer, "I don't know." However, the anxious struggle to help others (and ourselves) by offering some comfort, some meaning, will not be satisfied until the event whose truth we explain becomes painless. As the bereaved, the clinician and anthropologist move further from the moment of death, they and society can create more comforting truths. But in the midst of pain, any true words are hard to find.

When I look into Ramsden's mirror (Chapter 3) what I see is that I cannot see beyond. My test for what constitutes truth and what does not, or what one can say or not say in the face of death is fairly crude. Many things make sense in a classroom or book or from a pulpit. We think they help us understand the meaning of life. To those of my students from health care or theology who think they know the truths concerning these things, I give this situation:

> A six-year-old boy is going home from school for lunch, crossing with his nine-year-old brother and with the green light. A drunk driver comes through the intersection, cannot stop, and runs over the younger brother; and does not stop. No one can locate their mother or father, so the nine-year-old comes in as the only family for his six-year-old brother. You are with the nine-year-old across the hall as doctors and nurses try to resuscitate his brother. You can both hear when the heart monitor does not go beep anymore. A nine-year-old boy knows what the silence means but cannot comprehend anything more, so he asks you, "Why?" And you say, ...

If you can find an answer to say out loud with him looking in your eyes, then it is a good one. Remember it; it may even be a partial truth. At the very least, you should have been the one to write this chapter. I doubt that even together we will find answers. Although I am sure that if we ask the difficult questions of ourselves and those we observe, we will help the dying and the bereaved and ourselves live better with the questions.

CHAPTER
16

Conclusions: Coping with the Final Tragedy

David R. Counts
and
Dorothy A. Counts

Grief and death are experiences shared by all humanity and, so far as we know, *homo sapiens* is the only species that lives in the anticipation of death. We are the only ones who have beliefs that give meaning to death. Only we have rules instructing us how to die and how to cope with our loss when death strikes those we care for. Although these are common human experiences, there is remarkable variety in the ways that people understand and experience death and grief. The chapters in this volume demonstrate this variety and provide insight into human resourcefulness and ingenuity as people cope with death, the final tragedy.

DEATH

Death is necessarily the starting point for any discussion of grief and mourning. While it is not the only experience that causes human grief, death is usually a powerful trigger for the personal, private, and sometimes violent emotions of grief among those close to the dead person. Death also calls into play the customs of mourning that structure the public expression of grief. Even though the focus of this volume is grief and mourning, most chapters deal with the nature and understanding of death.

The perspectives on death held by many of the societies discussed in this volume are shaped by the fact that most death is premature. In preindustrialized societies only about 10 percent of the population lives past the age of sixty (Weiss, 1981: 55-56). Members of such societies do not usually die of the degenerative diseases of old age. Rather, most people die of infectious disease, trauma, childhood illness, and childbirth. As Simmons noted more than forty years ago, people in preindustrialized societies more commonly associate death with youth and vitality than with old age and decrepitude (1945: 217). In these societies ". . . life has been more often snuffed out suddenly than left to flicker out by degrees" (Simmons, 1945: 217). Even though their expectations of death may differ from those held by most North Americans, many of the peoples in this volume have an understanding of death that is similar to the one held by Western clinicians. Russian Old Believers, for example, view death as process, not event (Chapter 7). For the Maori (Chapter 4), the stages of death begin while the individual is still conscious and are complete only a year or so after the corpse is buried. In fact, many of the peoples of the South Pacific consider death to be a transforming, sometimes reversible process with boundaries on either side of the end of the body's vital signs (Counts and Counts, 1985a: 2).

In contrast, laymen in Western society generally assume that death is a non-reversible, unitary event and that life and death are opposed categories (see Ramsden's Chapter 3). Before modern technological advances it was simple to test for death. If there were no breath and no pulse, then death had occurred. Now the issue is more complex. Bodies attached to machines can live without either brain or heart function. Death does not even affect all organs simultaneously. Some vital parts may be dead while others still live. This has a number of implications. One is that the life/death transition is a process that can be prolonged almost indefinitely. Another is that although it may be possible to control the timing of death, the control often does not reside with the dying individual. Rather it may lie in the hands of technicians who ignore—may even be *bound* by society's laws to ignore—the wishes of the dying person. Because of the ethical complications implicit in this state of affairs, authorities have reconsidered the definition of death, and there is debate over whether it is a process or an event (see the debate in Korein [1978] and between Robert Morison and Leon Kass in *Science* [1971]).

Bodily death is everywhere more complicated than its simple physical manifestation. A society's perception of the dying process is complex because, ultimately, this perception is a question of culture, ideology, and cosmology. As Ramsden argues in Chapter 3, the nature of death is socially constructed and necessarily embodies notions of the nature of life and of the afterlife. A society's comprehension of what death is cannot be separated from its notion of what life is. Further, a society's understanding of death mirrors its understanding of life. In this vein there are a number of themes linking life, death and grief that run through the chapters of the volume.

Cultural Motifs

One theme is that the ethos of a society, the central cluster of values that directs its members how to live will also likely tell them how to die. As the papers in this volume demonstrate, the central motif of a culture provides guidelines for dying, both for persons facing their own deaths and for those who face the deaths of others. O'Connor (Chapter 15) stresses that his experience in North American society is that people die in the same way that they have lived. The strengths they use in managing life will be the same ones that enable them to manage death. This is true in other societies too. For example, in Chapter 9 the Prestons report that the Cree believe that people should meet death as they meet life—with equanimity, competence, reticence and self-reliance. Mead (Chapter 4) demonstrates how their legends provide modern Maori with models of behavior, including how to meet death. Wellenkamp (Chapter 8) finds that the response of the Toraja toward death is consistent with their general attitude toward misfortune. The ideal Toraja response "is a combination of resignation, attempting not to think about one's misery, and adherence to the traditional belief that by continuing to carry out one's spiritual obligations, one will eventually recoup one's losses." In contrast, the Counts argue that when death strikes among Lusi-Kaliai it brings anger and desire for revenge, and that those who die in their prime carry those same emotions into death with them.

People must also use the strategies they employ in facing life and their own deaths in coping with the deaths of their fellows. Cree recast the emotion of grief into equanimity. In Tanacross (Chapter 10), grief becomes joy. Sufi (Chapter 6) transform it into tranquility. Lusi-Kaliai (Chapter 12) and Huichole (Chapter 5) often express grief as anger and rage.

Alice's Mirror

A second theme in these chapters is a focus of Ramsden's chapter:

> The ways in which a society divides up or constructs a person's life are also the ways in which it constructs or divides up a person's career after death, but as a mirror or reverse image. Thus, while perceptions of the nature of life and the nature of death may vary widely, the one will consistently be reflected in the other.

Ramsden argues that a people's belief about the nature of life is reflected in their belief about the type of existence that follows death. Ramsden's reasoning applies to many societies other than the Huron. See, for example, Morris' chapter on Old Believers, the Counts on Kaliai, Wellenkamp on the Toraja of Indonesia, Badone on the people of rural Brittany, and Mead on the New Zealand Maori. Also note that the Huichol make explicit use of the metaphor of a mirror to describe the land of the dead where conditions are the reverse of those in the land of the living. Ramsden's analysis also adds depth to the concepts of "good" and "bad" death. In many of the societies in this volume, persons whose dying takes them through the full transition from life to death—however the society defines that transition— have a good death. Persons who are catapulted prematurely from full participation in life without going through the prescribed transition from it are unable to complete the journey to full death. The spirits of those who die a bad death are unable to proceed to the existence of the dead. Among the Lusi-Kaliai, suicides are unable to enter the spirit village and they cannot return to life. Therefore they lurk on the fringes of existence, malevolent and dangerous, the familiars of sorcerers. The ghosts of Huichole who die of sorcery seek vengeance for their deaths and may even murder their own relatives if they feel that their survivors are not properly avenging them (Chapter 5). According to Huichol myth, the spirit may continue to animate the dead body, refusing to die until the death is avenged and it is released to join the world of the ancestors. The Old Believer who dies in a drunken state is considered to be like a dog, the most unclean of animals, and is unforgivably tainted (Chapter 7). He is buried wherever the family can arrange a place, at best along the margin of the cemetery. There is no ceremony and no prayers are said.

Physical Body vs. Social Persona

The most common theme concerning death in these chapters is the distinction made by many societies between the physical body and the social persona. Not only are these different aspects of the individual thought of as separate, they may have different lifespans: the social life and death of a person need not be coterminous with his or her physical life and death. The continuation of relations between the living and ghosts or spirits of the dead is an example of social life continuing after physical life has ended. North Americans often dismiss belief in ghosts as "superstition," although it is a common experience in the West for newly bereaved persons to hallucinate the dead (Eisenbruch, 1984a: 287-288).

In many of the societies in this volume, the spirits of the dead continue to affect the living. For instance, Badone's friends in La Feuillée (Chapter 13) visit the graves of their loved ones and discuss matters with them; the helpful dead of the Cree (Chapter 9) bring animals to their relatives; spirits of long dead Kapinga (Chapter 11) protect their kinsmen by driving off malevolent spirits; Huron (Chapter 3) burials were arranged so that the living and the dead could have easy access to each other and continue social relations not disrupted by death; death transformed the Sufi shaikh (Chapter 6) into a universal being accessible to all his followers and also permitted him to remain directly involved in the growth of his group of adherents. Lusi-Kaliai ghosts may in their loneliness, grief, and anger call some of the living to join them (Chapter 12 and Counts and Counts, 1989: 289-90). Huichol (Chapter 5) regard ancestors who are purified and therefore eligible for veneration, to be "living" *ancestor humans*, in continuity with, rather than separate from *living humans*. These ancestor humans have an ongoing relationship with the living that, the Weigands emphasize, is an important part of Huichol social organization, religion, and ceremonial life.

Belief in ghosts is widespread in pre-industrial society, even wider than the selection of chapters in this volume suggests. Blauner links the prevalence of such beliefs to the frequency with which death occurs during the middle years, when people are at their peak of activity and social involvement. Death at this point in the life cycle leaves much "unfinished business" (1966: 39). He suggests that ghosts are the reification of this unfinished business. Their presence allows the living to continue the relationship that was broken off in an untimely manner (Blauner, 1966: 39). Data from most of our chapters support Blauner's argument.

Social Death

More than two decades ago, Glaser and Strauss observed that persons may experience social death before physical death (1965). As Riley notes, Glaser and Strauss were focussing on the dying person's awareness of impending death and on how this awareness might affect relations between the dying and the living (1983: 193). The chapters in this volume extend this idea. Our data may be best understood if we consider physical and social life to exist along a continuum that ends in both social and physical death, as in Figure 1.

Social life/death and physical life/death may not coincide at either end of the life course. Physical life may, and often does, start before social life. Ramsden's analysis of the burial of Huron infants, for example, is that the children were not fully (that is, *socially*) alive (Chapter 3). Morris (Chapter 7) reports that the children of Russian Old Believers who die without the benefit of baptism are buried on the margins of the cemetery, but not with those who are excommunicated. They believe that unbaptized children will be in the presence of God, but will not be able to see His face.

Although not a topic that arises in the chapters of this volume, it is tempting and, we think, illuminating to extend this idea to the fierce controversy going on currently in North American society over abortion. One aspect of the conflict is disagreement about whether the social life of a fetus, and hence society's interest in protection of it, begins at the same time as physical life or at some later time. At one end of the continuum are those who, arguing that social life is coincident with conception, oppose abortion under any circumstances: at the other end are those who argue that any feotus *in utero* is not a *child*—that is, is not a social person—and thus it cannot *ipso facto* have any legal status. There being no child, but only a "pregnancy," the proponents of this belief argue that the woman may elect to terminate the condition.

At the other end of the life cycle, the senile, the decrepit, or those who are isolated may experience social death long before their bodies die. Anthropologists have also reported a variety of evidence for culturally defined social death. These include the neglect of the critically ill (Heider, 1970: 229-230), premature burial (Van Baal, 1966: 171), and the failure to bury a corpse (Panoff, 1968). In these instances, the loss of the animating spirit, or the self occurs while the body is still vital. The *person* is, however, socially dead. As Leenhardt (1979) suggests, no apparent significance is attached to the body once it ceases to be a container for the spirit. The living body may be treated as though it were a corpse, the husk may

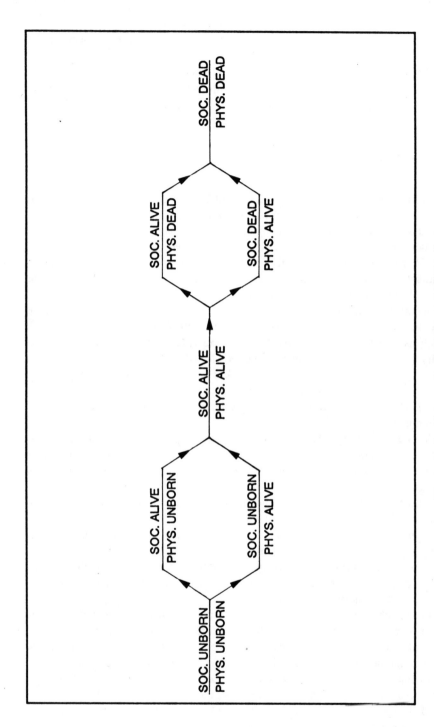

Figure 1. Continuum of social/physical life/death.

282

be buried while it is still breathing or, as in the Maenge case reported by Panoff, the body may be only a long-empty shell that is not worth the bother of interment.

The Lusi-Kaliai formally express the notion that social death occurs before physical death (Chapter 12). There an elderly man participated in the mortuary exchanges held to mark his social death. Examples are also found in other chapters. Leiber notes (Chapter 11) that Kapinga who are socially isolated in old age will adopt senile behavior as an expression of social death. Badone's aged Breton friends (Chapter 13) regard old folk's homes as the "antechambers of death."

Elderly persons are not the only victims of social death. The phenomenon sometimes known as "voodoo death," in which members of a society isolate and treat as already dead one of their members who has been cursed, is an example of this form of social death (Eastwell, 1982). Another is the situation of those Huichole who are socially dead, but physically still alive (Chapter 5). These individuals, usually males, have been exiled for violent behavior, incest, bestiality, sorcery, or ceremonial violations beyond the pale of acceptability. The Weigands note that the other villagers view these persons' passage from the community of the living with relief, even though they continue to inspire fear among their survivors.

Another type of social death takes place when the deceased is forgotten, when future generations no longer remember one's name or accomplishments. The peasants of rural Brittany consider this to be a *second* death and, as Badone observes, people often fear this type of death—evidenced by the neglected grave—more than physical death itself. They attempt to avoid it by taking themselves and the remains of their relatives to the place where their ancestors are buried. Indeed, the desire to avoid this "second death" seems to be widespread and may drive the urgency that people of many cultures feel to return to the place where they were born in order to die. A similar case in this volume is provided by Ramsden. His analysis is that when a Huron village was moved and the bones of many persons were mixed and cast into an ossuary, this represented a second death and the final destruction of the individual personae.

A third type of social death occurs when a person who is of symbolic stature dies. The death of an individual who is the symbolic focus of community or a way of life is felt as a personal loss by those for whom the symbol has meaning, even though they may never have known the human being. Waugh (Chapter 6) discusses the grief of people at the death of their shaikh, who represented both religion and way of life, even though many knew him only at a distance. We are also reminded of the outpourings of sorrow at the deaths of John Kennedy, Martin Luther King, John Lennon, Emperor Hirohito, and the Ayatollah Khomeni. These men were larger than their individual identities. People grieved their deaths because these men symbolized qualities—such as youth, hope, national pride, morality—that were at the core of the cultural ethos of the society and gave life purpose for its members. The death of the individual became, therefore, a metaphor for the loss of these core qualities and was agonizing for many of the society's members.

The end of a way of life—the death of a society—is, for the people living through it, a *final* social death, and one that people mourn as it happens. Badone (Chapter 13) describes the feelings of elderly people in a rural European village which has been abandoned by the young. As these people see their friends die and await their own deaths, they also anticipate that the knowledge and values that have given their lives meaning will be forgotten. They experience the end of their culture and the loss of all that they are. This type of social death combines isolation and eradication from memory and is perhaps the most difficult of all to endure.

GRIEF

The preceding section has focussed on the kinds and meanings of death as a prelude to the consideration of grief.

Anthropologists have written extensively about the public ceremonies and rituals by which the people of other cultures respond to death. There have, however, been few studies of the meaning death has for the people of other cultures or of their personal experience of grief (Rosenblatt, Walsh, and Jackson, 1976; Rosaldo, 1984). As Rosaldo notes, most anthropological studies of death conflate ritual process with the process of mourning. This approach avoids the emotion of grief, for even the most careful analysis of the language and symbols of a funeral ritual "could reveal precious little about the lived experience of bereavement" (Rosaldo, 1984: 189). One of the goals of this volume is to understand how people in other cultures experience death and grief and what the experiences mean to them. It is critical to distinguish between the emotions that people feel in the face of death and the things they do to express those emotions. To do this, we must define our terms. *Grief* is "the feelings of sorrow, anger, guilt and confusion that can arise when you have suffered a loss or are bereaved" (Kalish, 1985: 181). It is one of "the passions that animate human conduct" (Rosaldo, 1984: 192).[1] *Mourning* is "the overt expression of grief and bereavement" (Kalish, 1985: 182): it is the culturally defined behavior that expresses grief. Grief is the emotional reaction to the death of a loved one that may impel a bereaved man to kill a fellow human being and cut off his head as an act of mourning (Rosaldo, 1984).

The powerful emotion we call grief manifests itself by physiological changes in the grieving individual. These changes—described by Zeller in her chapter—

---

[1] An important counter-example to Rosaldo's generally pertinent observation is the work of Loring Danforth, cited in Badone's Chapter 13. The title of his excellent study *The Death Rituals of Rural Greece* (1982) is misleading, for it is much concerned with the experience of personal grief.

include variable levels of heart rate, body temperature, plasma cortisol, and adrenal catecholamine. Grieving individuals withdraw socially, are lethargic, lose their appetites, experience sleep disturbance and depression. Although Zeller's chapter is most concerned with it, the interplay between physiology and emotions in the grieving process is dealt with in several of the chapters in this volume. Indeed, this interplay is so pervasive in human experience that it may be, as Averill argues, biological in origin (Averill, 1968).

According to Averill, grief is found in other animals including birds and, because it has an evolutionary function, may be universal among non-human primates as well as among human beings (1968). According to this argument, grief conveys an adaptive advantage because primates are gregarious animals who live in groups and depend for their survival on their social relationships with others. The emotional state of grief which arises from separation is physiologically and psychologically stressful. This stress is particularly pronounced when the separation breaks a dependent relationship such as parent/child, mated pair, or even a relation of mutually supportive friendship. Thus efforts to avoid the stress of separation will foster group cohesion. The ensuing mutual support and protection will be highly advantageous to group survival.

Although we cannot know the thoughts or inner state of other animals, we can compare the behavior of humans and other primates who have suffered the death of an infant or the loss of a close companion. Such a comparison strongly suggests that humans are not the only ones to suffer grief. In this volume Zeller compares the physiological changes in behavior that monkeys and apes undergo following the loss of a mate, parent, or offspring with changes in human beings in similar crises. She concludes that "the similarities in physiology, behavior, and probable adaptive function are very marked." The question of whether grief is biologically based and evolutionarily adaptive is an important one. If it is so, human beings in all societies will have a common physical and emotional experience at the death of a loved one (see Eisenbruch, 1984a: 284-287 for a discussion of this point).

Most cultures seem to tolerate a wide range of responses to death and recognize that behavior that might be bizarre or pathological under other circumstances is a normal expression of bereavement. For example, hallucinating or making contact with the dead is recognized as being a common experience in urban industrialized settings (Eisenbruch, 1984a: 287-288), as well as in other societies (see chapters by Counts, Badone, Lieber, Waugh). The variety of individual responses to grief is reflected in an equally wide variety of public expressions of bereavement. In some societies, mourners may inflict damage on themselves or others or destroy their property. For example it is normal for the Dani to cut off the fingers of little girls who are closely related to a person who has died (Heider, 1979: 124-125). In contrast, in Java even close relatives are usually detached and do not weep or otherwise show grief, even though only minutes may have passed since a death (Siegal, 1986: 257-258; Geertz, 1957).

We are, then, dealing with two things. First, we recognize a powerful emotional state that affects nearly all human beings at one time or another and that likely crosses species lines to be experienced by other primates and, perhaps, other animals. Second, we recognize a uniquely human phenomenon: people make rules that *interpret* the physiological response to loss and *define* the behavior that is appropriate for expressing the powerful emotions of grief. We will return to this in our discussion of mourning behavior and social control. In a volume such as this, where the focus is on cultural variation, we must pay far more attention to the latter of these two points.

There is evidence in this volume that grief is a powerful emotional state, but it is underlying evidence, largely asserted rather than demonstrated. The focus of most of the chapters is not on whether there is strong emotional reaction to death, for that, like other universal physiological processes—aging and the attainment of sexual maturity for example—is *assumed*. Instead, the chapters call our attention to the fact that the range of emotions that constitute grief—the feelings of loss, the anger, the sorrow, the self-destructive depression—may be given diverse emphases in different societies. That is, cultures will vary in what is considered to be an appropriate expression of the emotions of grief by bereaved individuals. Nevertheless, each society must respond to, control, channel or transform the emotional storm that death unleashes.

While there is much variation in the way that the peoples in this volume respond to death and handle grief, one distinction is particularly striking and deserving of further research. In societies where most death is regarded as a *natural* part of life, grief is perceived differently than it is in societies where death is routinely considered to be an *unnatural* occurrence. It is not that societies fall into two opposed categories. Rather, cultural notions of the place of death in the life course vary along a continuum. At one pole death is rarely a "natural" event. At the other end of the continuum death is accepted as a whim of fate or as the inevitable natural outcome of the life cycle. In societies where death is accepted as natural the *emotion of grief* is likely to be highly dangerous. It threatens not just the bereaved individual but society itself. In such societies the expression of grief is likely to be tightly controlled. An examination of the contrasting ends of the continuum is in order.

Grief and Unnatural Death

Among the Huichol, the Maori and the Lusi-Kaliai nearly all death—even suicide or a death following the lingering illness of an elderly person—is thought to result from human malevolence. It is evidence of witchcraft or sorcery, sometimes practiced at the behest of the victim's own relatives. Under these circumstances death is always considered to be premature and provides profound and powerful evidence of a breakdown in basic social relationships. For this reason it carries the potential for disintegration of the community. *Death* is most dangerous in these societies although grief, too, may pose hazards. If anger and the desire for vengeance are dominant aspects of grief, or if intense grief is seen as a state that enhances vulnerability to death, then it endangers bereaved individuals. Among the Huichol, for example, the distance between life and death is shortest during intense grief, and it is possible for a person to die of grief (Chapter 5).

Sometimes the dead themselves participate in the "grief work," for until they are avenged they may be unable to complete the process of dying and join the other spirits of the dead in the spirit world. These unincorporated ghosts become the dangerous dead. Van Gennep's (1960) description of the fate of suicides and others for whom funeral rites are not performed is also applicable to the ghosts of some of those who die prematurely. According to Van Gennep they are

> . . . condemned to a pitiable existence, since they are never able to enter the world of the dead or to become incorporated in the society established there. These are the most dangerous dead. They would like to be reincorporated into the world of the living, and since they cannot be, they behave like hostile strangers toward it (Van Gennep, 1960: 160).

Van Gennep's analysis is consistent with the findings in this volume. Among the Lusi-Kaliai (Chapter 12), for instance, neither suicides nor persons whose premature deaths have been unavenged are able to participate fully in spirit society. They cannot sever their ties to the living and are in a condition that is a mixture of anger, loneliness, and the desire for revenge—a state which is similar to the grief that is felt by their bereaved kin.

In spite of the danger of uncontrolled anger, people in societies where death is unnatural do not consider it pathological to express the rage in their grief. Instead, "grief work" includes assessing guilt and exacting retribution. People attempt to establish responsibility for death so that anger may be directed at the appropriate target, and they understand that the only way to assuage the anguish of bereavement may be to bring about another death. Since grief may lead to more death, people in such societies recognize that the uninhibited or uncontrolled expression of grief is potentially dangerous. Nevertheless, while they may attempt to bound and channel it they do not fear it, nor do they try to suppress it.

Grief and Natural Death

In contrast, in a number of societies (Toraja, Chapter 8; Cree, Chapters 9 and 14; Kapinga, Chapter 11), death is a natural part of the life cycle, an act of fate (or of God) that is usually beyond human control. It is, to borrow a metaphor used by the Toraja, as inevitable as the falling leaves. Life is like a thread and death comes when the thread runs out. Even deaths that are caused by malevolent humans are, ultimately, destined to occur when they do. The people responsible may be only the agents of fate. In these societies, the uninhibited expression of strong emotions, particularly the powerful and sometimes violent emotions that follow death, is dangerous both for individuals and for society. Survivors who give vent to their anguish are often seen to be behaving pathologically. They risk madness, possession, or death. Or, perhaps even worse, their behavior may prevent the spirit of the dead from completing the transformation into death and incorporation into the spirit world. Such spirits may linger and, out of pity or loneliness, attempt to draw others into death. Consequently, both the spirit of the dead and the grief that holds it near are potential problems for society, and uncontrolled emotion may beget more death.

In societies where people are reticent about expressing emotion and grief is dangerous, "grief work" focuses on providing the bereaved with publicly structured procedures for managing and eliminating their emotion. The Tanacross (Chapter 10), for instance, objectify grief through singing, dancing, oratory, and distributing gifts which metaphorically cover the deceased with love. The goal of the potlatch for mourning is to transform grief into joy and to reaffirm the community of the living.

The response to death in modern societies where people often die of old age shares qualities with societies where death is natural as well as with those where it often is attributed to human agent. Marshall (1989) observes that when death becomes predictably placed in old age it is more likely to be viewed as natural and does not require explanation (see Ramsden's discussion of British-Canadian society and Badone on death in Brittany for discussions that support Marshall's proposition). We suggest that a corollary of Marshall's point is that in modern societies premature, unexpected, unpredictable death has become anomalous. In other words, people in Western society share the assumption made by some of the societies in this volume that premature death is not part of the life cycle and, therefore, requires explanation (see the chapter by O'Connor). Frequently this explanation involves a search for a culpable party and triggers the anger and desire for revenge that is characteristic of grief in societies where death is usually seen as the result of human malevolence. Public reaction to "trigger-happy policemen" and drunk drivers, the frequency of malpractice suits against allegedly incompetent or careless physicians, and community hostility toward people found to be carriers of the AIDS virus illustrate the desire in Western society to place blame for untimely death.

In other words, anger and rage in response to death is not limited to societies where death is usually premature and where people assume that it is caused by a malevolent human agent. As the chapters by Kaufert and O'Neil and by O'Connor demonstrate, both bereaved relatives and professional clinicians commonly react angrily to death. When hospital workers think that the relatives of a dying person are behaving inappropriately they may react with considerable anger. Kaufert and O'Neil discuss the response of nursing and medical staff to a mother's withdrawal from her dying infant. This conflict, though founded on profound cultural misunderstanding, is a good example of this kind of anger.

As O'Connor's chapter illustrates, health care professionals who deal constantly with death need a way to distance themselves from its pain and anguish. Sometimes they achieve this by resorting to the enforcement of bureaucratic rules. Kaufert and O'Neil provide powerful illustrations of how such enforcement may work to the detriment of dying patients and their families when hospital rules directly contravene the cultural rules of dying persons and their attendants. As they show, even the reticent Cree may find their grief compounded by anger when "senseless" rules require autopsy or limit the number of visitors who may say farewell to a dying relative.

MOURNING

Mourning rituals constitute the public face of grief. They provide the forum for the expression of grief's emotion and channel and mold grief into acceptable forms. It is important to distinguish between the public role-playing that goes on when people mourn and the perhaps biologically-based, individual, emotional grief that people feel in the aftermath of a death.

The contributors to this volume report a variety of emotional and ritual responses to death. One of the questions arising from consideration of this variety has become a focus of this volume: "Do people feel the emotions they express?" and its reciprocal, "Do people express the emotions they feel?" These questions have also been raised by a number of scholars including Huntington and Metcalf (1979: 24-44), Rosaldo (1984: 186-187) and Eisenbruch (1984a: 288-291). As early as 1922 Radcliffe-Brown noted that public performance may not reflect actual emotion. He recounted that the Andaman Islanders engage in two kinds of weeping—reciprocal (social) and solitary—and argued that public mourning display is not necessarily a response to grief. Instead society may prescribe mourning behavior that involves the entire community. There are for example, a number of occasions when people weep together: after death when friends and relatives embrace the corpse, at the end of mourning, and when bones are removed from a grave. He says, "In certain circumstances men and women are required by custom to embrace one another and weep, and if they neglected to do so it would be an offence condemned by all right-thinking persons" (1922: 239). He continues:

> Not in any of the above-mentioned instances is the weeping simply a spontaneous expression of feeling. It is always a rite the proper performance of which is demanded by custom . . . they are all customary actions to which the sentiment of obligation attaches, which it is the duty of persons to perform on certain definite occasions (Radcliffe-Brown, 1922: 239, 245-246).

One common criticism of Western society is that its rules negatively sanction the expression of intense emotion and either prevent or limit expression of the sorrow, anger, guilt and despair associated with grief. For example, Gorer has eloquently argued that this is true of British society (1965). He maintains that the British treat death, corruption, and decay with disgust, as though they were pornographic. He says, "one mourns in private as one undresses or relieves oneself in private, so as not to offend others" (1965: 113). Consequently the majority of British people have not accepted rituals or adequate guidance in how to deal with death or come to terms with grief. The result is maladaptive behavior that includes a preoccupation with death and cruelty which may be expressed in a number of ways: fascination with horror films and comics and the brutality of Nazi concentration camps, either callousness or squeamishness about death; and increased vandalism and mutilation of property for its own sake, without the motives of revenge or hope of personal gain. Although they do not go as far as Gorer, the chapters by O'Connor and Ramsden develop this same point for Canadian society.

As we have already seen—and as the chapters by Lieber, Wellenkamp, Mead, the Prestons, Simeone, and Morris demonstrate—many societies besides mainstream North America attempt to exercise tight control over the expression of grief and to channel it through mourning ceremonies. This is accomplished in a variety of ways. Some societies emphasize emotional restraint and equanimity as expressions of self-reliance and autonomy (Cree). Sometimes people believe intense emotion has a detrimental effect on one's own health and on the maintenance of smooth interpersonal relations (Toraja). Others think that uninhibited emotion is dangerous both to the individual and to society (Kapinga, Tanacross). It may be that the society teaches that it is unseemly or disgraceful to lose control (Toraja, Canadian), or that only the immediate kin are given license to show intense grief by excessive weeping (Russian Old Believers). Some societies distinguish between weeping as private expression of grief and wailing or keening as public performance and encourage public performance instead of private display (Toraja, Kapinga, Maori). Sometimes private sorrow becomes submerged in the public and politically charged aspects of the mortuary ceremony where, through song and competitive speech-making, people review past wrongs, settle scores, and either resolve old disputes or begin new ones that may continue long after the funeral (Kapinga, Maori, Tanacross). Finally, public expressions of grief may be transformed through song into demonstrations of joy, celebration, and community (Sufi, Tanacross). Thus strong negative and potentially destructive emotions become powerful positive and sustaining ones that reaffirm social bonds and the basic values of the culture.

The data in this volume lead us to agree with Reid (1979) that through their mourning customs, societies attempt to accomplish the following goals:

1. permit bereaved persons to resolve their grief, thereby preventing pathological responses to death. As O'Connor's chapter makes clear, pathological grief is an open-ended term that must be defined anew for each culture. In general, however, it is behavior that the society defines as being abnormal and related to the loss caused by death (Reid, 1979: 322). In her

discussion of mourning processes among the Yolngu of Australia, Reid suggests the kinds of maladaptive behavior that mourning customs should forestall.

These [episodes of pathological behavior] are marked by absent or suppressed grief, distorted or chronic grief, decompensation into recognizable medical disease, conspicuous or deleterious alterations in relationships to others, furious hostility against others, lasting loss of patterns of social interaction, behavior detrimental to the individual's (or to his dependents') social and economic existence, agitated depression and suicidal feelings (Reid, 1979: 321).

2. Mourning practices should help people to express and cope with their grief rather than imposing another burden by requiring them to perform in ways that are uncomfortable or stressful. They should facilitate the reintegration of bereaved persons into society and aid them in assuming any new role— widow, orphan, childless person—that results from the death.
3. They should enable the society to readjust to the loss of one of its members.
4. Finally, mourning ceremonies should expedite the integration of the dead person into his or her new role, as the particular society understands it. Usually mourning rituals enable the spirit to enter the world of the dead, thereby permitting society and its bereaved members and the spirit of the dead to let each other go. They may, however, facilitate the transformation of the deceased and reintegrate the spirit into the society of the living in a new role, as Waugh reports for the Sufi.

Whatever form mourning rituals assume, and the possibilities are many and wondrous as the practices reported in these chapters demonstrate, they represent attempts by societies to accomplish these goals. If they do not, then they may add to the ordeal of the dying and their grieving survivors and make an already difficult time even more burdensome.

References Cited

ACCIAIOLI, G.
n.d.   Networks and nets: Principles and processes in Bugis migra-
            tion strategies to Lake Lindu, Central Sulawesi. Unpublished
            manuscript.
AGUIRRE BELTRÁN, G.
1967   *Regiones de Rufugio*. Instituto Nacional Indigensita, #46,
            Mexico.
ARIES, P.
1974   *Western Attitudes towards Death from the Middle Ages to the
            Present*. Baltimore, Johns Hopkins University Press.
ASQUITH, P.
1984   The inevitability and utility of anthropomorphism in description
            of primate behavior. In *The Meaning of Primate Signals*, R. Harre
            and V. Reynolds, eds., pp. 138-176, Cambridge University Press,
            Cambridge.
AVERILL, R. J.
1968   Grief: Its nature and significance, *Psychological Bulletin 70*:
            721-748.
BADONE, E.
1987a   Changing Breton responses to death, *Omega: Journal of Death
            and Dying 18*:77-83.
1987b   Death omens in a Breton memorate, *Folklore: Journal of the
            Folklore Society (London) 98*:99-104.
1989   *The Appointed Hour: Death, World View and Social Change
            in Brittany*. Berkeley, University of California Press.
BALDWIN, D. V.
1985   Neonatal interactions in pig-tailed macaque (*M. nemistrina*)
            dyads. Influence on rearing success, infant weight change and
            behavioral response to reunion with mother, *Primates 26*(1):
            45-56.
BARROW, T.
1972   *Art and Life in Polynesia*. A. H. Wellington and A.W. Reed,
            (eds.).

BARTROP, R. W., LAZARUS, L., LUCKHURST, E., KILOH, L. G., and PENNY, R.
1977   Depressed lymphocyte functions after bereavement, *Lancet* *1*(B):834-836.

BATESON, G.
1977   *Steps to an Ecology of Mind*. New York, Bantam Books.

BECKER, E.
1973   *The Denial of Death*. New York, The Free Press.

BEHAR, R.
1986   *Santa Maria del Monte: The Presence of the Past in a Spanish Village*. Princeton, Princeton University Press.

BENEDICT, R.
1934   *Patterns of Culture*. Boston, Houghton Mifflin.

BENÍTEZ, F.
1968   *Los Huicholes*. Biblioteca ERA, Mexico.

BERMAN, C. M.
1983   Effect of being orphaned: A detailed case. In *Primate Social Relationships*, R. A. Hinde, ed., pp. 79-81, Massachusetts, London, Blackwell.

BEST, E.
1941   *The Maori*. Wellington, The Polynesian Society.

BEUCHET, J.
1982   Regards sur le peuplement des communes bretonnes, *Octant: Cahiers Statistiques de la Bretagne 11*:5-20.

BILLINGTON, J. H.
1966   *The Icon and the Axe: An Interpretive History of Russian Culture*. New York, Alfred A. Knopf.

BINFORD, L. R.
1971   Mortuary practices: Their study and their potential. In *Approaches to the Social Dimensions of Mortuary Practices*, J. A. Brown, ed., pp. 6-29, Society for American Archaeology, Memoir 25.

BLAUNER, R.
1966   Death and social structure. In *Death and Identity*, R. Fulton, ed., pp. 35-59, Bowie, Maryland, Charles Press (originally published in *Psychiatry 29*:378-394).

BLOCH, M., and PERRY, J.
1982   *Death and the Regeneration of Life*. Cambridge University Press.

BLYTHE, J., BRIZINSKI, P., and PRESTON, S.
1985   *I Was Never Idle: Women and Work. . . .* TASO Report No. 21, McMaster University.

BOWLBY, J.
1973   *Separation, Attachment and Loss*. New York, Basic Books.

1981   *Attachment and Loss*, Vol. III *Loss: Sadness and Depression.* New York, Penguin Books.

BOX, H. O.
1984   *Primate Behaviour and Social Ecology.* London, Chapman and Hall.

BRANDES, S.
1981   Gender distinctions in Monteros mortuary ritual, *Ethnology* 20:177-190.

CAINE, N. C., and REITE, M.
1981   The effect of peer contact upon physiological response to maternal separation, *American Journal of Primatology 1*:271-276.

CAIRNS, R. B.
1977   Beyond social attachment: The dynamics of interactional development. In *Attachment Behavior*, J. Alloway, P. Oliver and L. Krames, eds., pp. 1-24, New York, Plenum.

CAMBRY, J.
1979   *Voyage dans le Finistère, Geneva and Paris.* Slatkine Reprints. (first printed 1836).

CANNADINE, D.
1981   War and death, grief and mourning in modern Britain. In Mirrors of Mortality, J. Whaley, ed., pp. 187-242, New York, St. Martin's Press.

CARRASCO, D.
1981   City as symbol in Aztec thought: The clues from the Codex Mendoza. In *History of Religions*, 20(3):199-223.
1982   *Quetzalcoatl and the Irony of Empire.* Chicago, University of Chicago Press.

CARROLL, V.
1977   Communities and non-communities: The Nukuoro on Ponape. In *Exiles and Migrants in Oceania*, M. D. Lieber, ed., Association for Social Anthropology in Oceania Monograph Series, no. 5, pp. 68-79, Honolulu, University Press of Hawaii.

CHAPMAN, R., ET AL., EDS.
1981   *The Archaeology of Death.* New York, Cambridge University Press.

CHAUSSY, M., EMEILLAT, R., and MESSAGER, G.
1976   *Monographie Communale: La Feuillée.* Angers, Ecole Supérieur d'Agriculture.

CODNER, M. A. and NADLER, R. D.
1984   Mother-infant separation and reunion in the great apes, *Primates* 25(2):204-217.

COE, C. L., and LEVINE, S.
1981   Normal responses to mother infant separation in non-human primates. In *Anxiety: New Research and Changing Concepts*, D. F. Klein and J. Rabkin, eds., pp. 155-177, New York, Raven Press.

COE, C. L., WIENER, S. G., ROSENKER, L. T., and LEVINE, S.
1985   Endocrine and immune responses to separation and maternal loss
            in non-human primates. In *The Psychobiology of Attachment and
            Separation*, M. Reite and T. Field, eds., pp. 163-199, Orlando,
            Academic Press.
COLE, M.
1986   Great apes—more human than we think, *Animal Keepers Forum*,
            December, pp. 394-396.
COUNTS, D., and COUNTS, D.
1974   The Kaliai lupunga: Disputing in the public forum. In *Contention
            and Dispute: Aspects of Law and Social Control in Melanesia*,
            A. L. Epstein, ed., pp. 113-151, Canberra, ANU Press.
COUNTS, D. R.
1976-77   The good death in Kaliai: Preparation for death in western New
            Britain, *Omega* 7:367-372 (Reprinted in *Death and Dying: Views
            from Many Cultures*, R. Kalish, ed., Amityville, New York,
            Baywood Publishing Co., 1979).
COUNTS, D. R., and COUNTS, D. A.
1983-84   Aspects of dying in northwest New Britain. In Special Section:
            Dying in Cross-Cultural Perspective, P. Stephenson, ed., *Omega*
            14:101-112.
1989   Complementarity in medical treatment in a West New Britain
            society. In *A Continuing Trial of Treatment: Medical Plural-
            ism in Papua New Guinea*, S. Frankel and G. Lewis,
            eds., pp. 277-294, Dordrecht, Holland, Kluwer Academic
            Publishers.
COUNTS, D. A.
1980a   Akro and Gagandewa: A Melanesian myth, *The Journal of the
            Polynesian Society 89*:33-65.
1980b   Fighting back is not the way: Suicide and the women of Kaliai,
            American Ethnologist 7:332-351.
1983   Near-death and out-of-body experiences in a Melanesian
            society, *Anabiosis—The Journal for Near-Death Studies 3*:115-
            135.
1984   Revenge suicide by Lusi women: An expression of power. In
            Rethinking Women's Roles: Perspectives from the Pacific,
            D. O'Brien and S. Tiffany, eds., pp. 71-93, Berkeley, University
            of California Press.
1985a   Sweeping men and harmless women: Responsibility and gender
            identity in later life. In *Aging in the Third World: Part II*,
            Publication No. 23. J. Sokolovsky, ed., Studies in Third World
            Societies, pp. 1-26, Williamsburg, Virginia, College of William
            and Mary.

1985b   Tamparonga: The 'big women' of Kaliai (Papua New Guinea). In *In Her Prime*, J. K. Brown and V. Kerns, eds., pp. 49-64, South Hadley, Massachusetts, Bergin & Garvey.

1987   Female suicide and wife abuse: A cross-cultural perspective, *Suicide and Life Threatening Behavior* 17:194-204.

1988   Ambiguity and interpretation of suicide: Female death in Papua New Guinea. In *Why Women Kill Themselves*, D. Lester, ed., pp. 87-110, Springfield, Illinois, Charles C. Thomas.

COUNTS, D. A., and COUNTS, D. R.
1985a   Introduction: Linking concepts aging and gender, aging and death. In *Aging and Its Transformations: Moving toward Death in Pacific Societies*, D. A. Counts and D. R. Counts, eds., Association for Social Anthropology in Oceania Series, no. 10, pp. 1-24, Lanham, Maryland, University Press of America.

1985b   I'm not dead yet! aging and death: Process and experience in Kaliai. In *Aging and Its Transformations: Moving toward Death in Pacific Societies*, D. A. Counts and D. R. Counts, eds., Association for Social Anthropology in Oceania Series, no. 10, pp. 145-146, Lanham, Maryland, University Press of America.

CROIX, A., and ROUDAUT, F.
1984   *Les Bretons, la Mort et Dieu. De 1600 à Nos Jours.* Paris, Messidor—Temps Actuels.

CRUMRINE, N. R., and WEIGAND, P. C., eds.
1987   *Ejidos and Regions of Refuge in Northwestern Mexico.* University of Arizona Press Anthropological Papers, #46, Tucson.

DANFORTH, L.
1982   *The Death Rituals of Rural Greece.* Princeton, Princeton University Press.

DARWIN, C.
1872   *The Expression of the Emotions in Man and Animals.* (reprinted in 1965), Chicago, University of Chicago Press.

DE LAGUNA, F.
1975   Matrilineal kin groups in northwestern North America. In *Proceedings: Northern Athapaskan Conference, 1971*, Vol. 1, A. McFadyen Clark, ed., pp. 19-145, Canadian Ethnology Service Paper No. 27, Ottawa, National Museum of Man Mercury Series, National Museums of Canada.

DOLHINOW, P.
1980   An experimental study of mother loss in the Indian langur monkey (*Presbytis entellus*), *Folia Primatologica* 33:77-128.

DOLHINOW, P., and DE MAY, M. G.
1982   Adoption: The importance of infant choice, *Journal of Human Evolution, 11*:391-420.

DOLHINOW, P., and KRUSKO, N.
1984   Langur monkey females and infants. In *Female Primates: Studies by Women Primatologists*, M. Small, ed., pp. 37-57, New York, Alan R. Liss Inc.
DOLHINOW, P., and MURPHY, G.
1983   Langur monkey mother loss: Profile analysis with multivariate analysis of variance for separation subjects and controls, *Folia Primatologica 40*:181-196.
DU BOIS, C.
1944   *The People of Alor: A Social Psychological Study of an East Indian Culture.* Minneapolis, University of Minnesota Press.
DU TOIT, B. M.
1979   Faith, pharmacopoeia and ritual, *Journal of Asian and African Studies 14*(3-4):283-286.
EASTWELL, H. D.
1982   Voodoo death and the mechanism for the dispatch of the dying in East Arnhem, Australia, *American Anthropologist 84*:5-17.
EISENBRUCH, M.
1984a   Cross-cultural aspects of bereavement: A conceptual framework for comparative analysis, *Culture, Medicine and Psychiatry 8*: 283-309.
1984b   Cross-Cultural aspects of bereavement II: Ethnic and cultural variations in the development of bereavement practices, *Culture, Medicine and Psychiatry 8*:315-347.
EMORY, K. P.
1965   *Kapingamarangi: Social and Religious Life of a Polynesian Atoll*, Bernice P. Bishop Museum Bulletin 228, Honolulu, Bernice Bishop Museum Press.
EPSTEIN, A. L.
1984   *The Experience of Shame in Melanesia: An Essay in the Anthropology of Affect*, Occasional Paper No. 40, London, Royal Anthropological Institute of Great Britain and Ireland.
ERIKSON, E.
1964   *Insight and Responsibility.* New York, W. W. Norton & Co.
EVANS-PRITCHARD, E. E.
1937   *Witchcraft, Oracles and Magic among the Azande.* Oxford, Clarendon Press.
FABIAN, J.
1973   How others die—reflections on the anthropology of death. In *Death and American Experience*, A. Mach, ed., pp. 177-201, New York, Shocken Books.

FÁBILA, A.
1959   *Los Huicholes de Jalisco*. Instituto Nacional Indigenista, Mexico.
FIKES, J. C.
1985   Huichol Indian Identity and Adaptation, Ph.D. Dissertation, University of Michigan, Department of Anthropology, Ann Arbor.
1988   Personal communication, April.
FITZGERALD, W. R.
1979   The Hood site: Longhouse burials in an historic Neutral village, *Ontario Archaeology 32*:43-60.
FOSSEY, D.
1983   *Gorillas in the Mist*. Boston, Houghton Mifflin Co.
FOUTS, R. A., HIRSH, A. D., and FOUTS, D. H.
1982   Cultural transmission of a human language in a chimpanzee mother-infant relationship. In *Child Nurturance: Studies of Development in Non-Human Primates, 3*, H. E. Fitzgerald, J. A. Mullens, and P.Gage, eds., pp.159-193, New York, Plenum Press.
GEERTZ, C.
1957   Ritual and social change: A Javanese example, *American Anthropologist 59*:32-54.
1973   *The Interpretation of Cultures*. New York, Basic Books.
1976   *The Religion of Java*. Chicago, University of Chicago Press.
GIGUERE, G.-E.
1972   *Oeuvres de Champlain*, Montreal, Editions du Jour.
GLASER, B. G., and STRAUS, A.
1965   *Awareness of Dying*. Chicago, Aldine Publishing Co.
1968   *Time for Dying*. Chicago, Aldine Publishing Co.
GOFFMAN, E.
1961   *Asylums: Essays on the Social Situation of Mental Patients and Other Inmates*. Garden City, New York, Anchor Books.
GOODALL, J.
1986   *The Chimpanzees of Gombe*. Cambridge, Massachusetts, Belknap Press of Harvard University Press.
GORER, G.
1965   *Death, Grief and Mourning in Contemporary Britain*. London, The Cresset Press.
GUBERNICK, D. J.
1981   Parent and infant attachment in mammals. In *Parental Care in Mammals*, D. J. Gubernick and P. H. Klopfer, eds., pp. 243-305, New York, Plenum Press.
GUEDON, M. F.
1974   *People of Tetlin Why Are You Singing?* Paper No. 9 National Museum of Man Mercury Series, Ethnology Division, Ottawa.

HALE, M. S.
1987   Grief—somatic symptom. In *Principles of Thanatology*, A. H. Kutscher, A. C. Carr, L. G. Kutscher, eds., pp. 211-243, New York, Columbia University Press.
HALLOWELL, A. I.
1936   The passing of the Midewiwin in the Lake Winnipeg region, *American Anthropologist 38*:32-51.
1955   *Culture and Experience*. Philadelphia, University of Pennsylvania.
HANDELMAN, D.
1983   Inside-out, outside-in: Concealment and revelation in Newfoundland Christmas mumming. In *Text, Play, and Story: The Construction and Reconstruction of Self and Society*, E. M. Bruner, ed., pp. 247-277, Proceedings of the AES. Washington, DC, American Ethnological Society.
HASEGAWA, T., and HIRAIWA, M.
1980   Social interactions of orphans observed in a free ranging troop of Japanese monkeys, *Folia Primatologica 33*:129-158.
HENNESSY, M. B., KAPLAN, J. N., MENDOZA, S. P., LOWE, E. L., and LEVINE, S.
1979   Separation distress and attachment in surrogate reared squirrel monkeys, *Physiology and Behavior 23*:1017-1023.
HEIDER, K.
1970   *The Dugum Dani: A Papuan Culture in the Highlands of West New Guinea*. Viking Fund Publications in Anthropology No. 49, New York, Wenner Gren Foundation for Anthropological Research.
HERTZ, R.
1960   *Death and the Right Hand*. (translation of the 1907 Essay, by Rodney and Claudia Needham), New York, Free Press and Aberdeen University Press.
HINDE, R. A., and SPENCER-BOOTH, Y.
1970   Individual differences in the response of rhesus monkeys to a period of separation from their mothers, *Journal of Child Psychology and Psychiatry 2*:159-176.
HOEBEL, E. A.
1964   *The Law of Primitive Man: A Study in Comparative Legal Dynamics*. Cambridge, Harvard University Press.
HOLLAN, D. W.
1988a   Pockets full of mistakes: The personal consequences of religious change in a Toraja village, *Oceania 58*:275-289.
1988b   Staying "cool" in Toraja: Informal strategies for the management of anger and hostility in a nonviolent society, *Ethos 16*(1):52-72.

1989 The personal use of dream beliefs in the Toraja highlands, *Ethos* *17*(2):166-186.

1990 Indignant suicide in the Pacific: An example from the Toraja highlands of Indonesia, *Culture, Medicine & Psychiatry 14*:365-379.

HOMANS, P.

1987 The uses and limits of psychobiography as an approach to popular culture: The case of the "Western." In *The Biographical Process*, F. E. Reynolds, D. Capps, eds., pp. 297-316, The Hague, Mouton.

HOSKINS, J. A.

1987 Complementarity in this world and the next: Gender and agency in Kodi mortuary ceremonies. In *Dealing with Inequality: Analysing Gender Relations in Melanesia and Beyond*, M. Strathern, ed., pp. 174-206, New York, Cambridge University Press.

HUNTINGTON, R., and METCALF, P.

1979 *Celebrations of Death: The Anthropology of Mortuary Ritual.* New York, Cambridge University Press.

INSEE

1980 *Annuaire statistique régional—Bretagne.* Rennes, Le Colbert.

JACKSON, E.

1963 *For the Living.* Des Moines, Iowa, Channel Press.

JAY, P.

1963 Maternal infant relations in langurs. In *Maternal Behavior in Mammals*, H. L. Rheingold, ed., pp. 282-304, New York, John Wiley and Sons.

JORDAN, T. C.

1982 *Texas Graveyards: A Cultural Legacy.* Austin, University of Texas Press.

KAISER, D. H.

1988 *Death and Dying in Early Modern Russia.* Occasional Paper #228 of the Kennan Institute for Advanced Russian Studies.

KALISH, R. A.

1985 *Death, Grief and Caring Relationships.* Monterrey, California, Brooks/Cole Publishing Co.

KAN, S.

1983 Words that heal the soul: Analysis of the Tlingit potlatch oratory, *Arctic Anthropology 20*(2):47-59.

1986 The 19th-century Tlingit potlatch; A new perspective, *American Ethnologist 13*(2):191-212.

KAPCHES, M.

1976 The interment of infants of the Ontario Iroquois, *Ontario Archaeology 27*:29-39.

KASS, L. R.
1971   Death as an event: a commentary on Robert Morison, *Science* *173*:698-702.
KAUFERT, J., KOOLAGE, W., KAUFERT, P., and O'NEIL, J.
1984   The use of 'trouble case' examples in teaching the impact of sociocultural and political factors in clinical communication, *Medical Anthropology 8*(1):36-45.
KAUFERT, J., and KOOLAGE, W.
1984   Role conflict among culture brokers: The experience of Native Canadian medical interpreters, *Social Science and Medicine 18*: 283-286.
KAUFERT, J., O'NEIL, J., and KOOLAGE, W.
1985   Cultural brokerage and advocacy in urban hospitals: The impact of native language interpreters, *Sante, Culture, Health 3*(2)2-9.
KAUFMAN, I. C.
1977   Developmental considerations of anxiety and depression: Psychobiological studies of monkeys. In *Psychoanalysis and Contemporary Science*, T. Shapiro, ed., pp. 317-363, New York, International Universities Press.
KIDD, K. E.
1953   The excavation and identification of a Huron ossuary, *American Antiquity 18*(4):359-379.
KIECOLT-GLASER, J . K., GARNER, W., SPEICHER, C., PENN, G. M., HOLIDAY, J., and GLASER, R.
1984   Psychological modifiers of immunocompetence in medical students, *Psychosomatic Medicine 46*:7-14.
KIEV, A.
1964   The study of folk psychiatry, In *Magic, Faith and Healing*, A. Kiev, ed., pp. 6-13, Glencoe, Illinois, The Free Press.
KNIGHT, D., and MELBYE, J.
1983   Burial patterns at the Ball site, *Ontario Archaeology 40*:37-48.
KOREIN, J., ed.
1978   Brain Death: Interrelated Medical and Social Issues. Annals of the New York Academy of Sciences, Vol. *315*, New York.
KUBLER-ROSS, E.
1969   *On Death and Dying*. New York, Macmillan Co.
LAMBO, T. A.
1964   Patterns of psychiatric care in developing African countries. In *Magic, Faith and Healing*, A. Kiev, ed., Glencoe, Illinois, The Free Press.
LE BRAZ, A.
1928   *La Légende de la Mort Chez les Bretons Armoricains*. 5th ed., (2 volumes), Paris, Honoré Champion.

LEE, P. C.
1983   Effects of the loss of the mother on social development. In *Primate Social Relationships*, R. A. Hinde, ed., pp. 73-79, London, Blackwell.

LEENHARDT, M.
1979   *Do Kamo: Person and Myth in the Melanesian World*, B. M. Gulati, trans. (first published in French in 1947), Chicago, University of Chicago Press.

DE LEYVA, A.
1579   *Descripción hecha por el ilustre Señor Antonio de Leyva, Alcalde Mayor por S.M. del Pueblo de Ameca*, Ediciones Colegio Internacional, 1976, Guadalajara, pp. 1-92.

LIEBER, M.
1970   Adoption on Kapingamarangi. In *Adoption in Eastern Oceania*, V. Carroll, ed., Association for Social Anthropology in Oceania Monograph Series, no. 1, pp. 158-205, Honolulu, University of Hawaii Press.

1974   Land tenure on Kapingamarangi. In *Land Tenure in Oceania*, H. P. Lunsgaarde, ed., pp. 70-99, Association for Social Anthropology in Oceania Monograph Series, no. 2, Honolulu, University Press of Hawaii.

1984   Strange feast: Negotiating identities on Ponape, *Journal of the Polynesian Society 93*:141-189.

LIFTON, R. J.
1979   *The Broken Connection: On Death and the Continuity of Life*. New York, Simon and Schuster.

LINDEN, E.
1985   *Silent Partners*. New York, Times Books Random House

LINDENBAUM, S.
1979   *Kuru Sorcery: Disease and Danger in the New Guinea Highlands*. Palo Alto, California, Mayfield Publishing Co.

LOFLAND, L.
1985   The social shaping of emotion: The case of grief, *Symbolic Interaction 8*(2):171-190.

LUMHOLTZ, C.
1973   *Unknown Mexico*, vol. 2, (reprint edition of Scribner 1903), Glorieta, New Mexico, Rio Grande Press.

MALINOWSKI, B.
1954   *Magic, Science and Religion*. Garden City, New York, Doubleday.

MANDELBAUM, D. G.
1976   Social uses of funeral rites. In *Death and Identity*, R. Fulton, ed., pp. 344-363, Bowie, Maryland, Charles Press.

MAPLE, T. L., and HOFF, M. P.
1982   *Gorilla Behavior*. New York, Van Nostrand Reinhold Co.
MARSHALL, V. W.
1989   Do we have, or want, a theory of aging and dying? Paper
            presented at Fourteenth International Congress of Gerontology,
            Acapulco, Mexico, June 1989.
MC GINNIS, L. M.
1980   Maternal separation studies in children and non-human primates.
            In *Maternal Influences and Early Behavior*, R. W. Bell and
            W. P. Smotherman, eds., pp. 311-335, New York, Spectrum
            Publishing.
MC KINNEY, W. T.
1985   Separation and depression: Biological markers. In *The Psycho-
            biology of Attachment and Separation*, M. Reite and T. Field,
            eds., pp. 201-222, Orlando, Academic Press.
MELBYE, J.
1983   The people of the Ball site, *Ontario Archaeology 40:* 15-36
MENDOZA, S. P., and MASON, W. A.
1986a   Contrasting response to intruders and to involuntary separation
            by monogamous and polygynous new world monkeys, *Physi-
            ology and Behavior 38*:795-801.
1986b   Parenting within a monogamous society. In *Primate On-
            togeny, Cognition, and Social Behaviour*, J. G. Else and P. C.
            Lee, eds., pp. 255-266, New York, Cambridge University
            Press.
MERZ, E.
1978   Male-male interactions with dead infants in *macaca sylvanus,
            Primates 19*(4):749-754.
METCALF, P.
1982   *A Borneo Journey into Death: Berawan Eschatology from its
            Rituals.* Philadelphia, Pennsylvania, University of Pennsylvania
            Press.
MC KENNAN, R. A.
1959   *The Upper Tanana Indians*. New Haven, Yale University Publi-
            cations in Anthropology, no. 59.
MOLTO, E., SPENCE, M. W.,
and FOX, W. A.
1986   The Van Dordt site: A case study in salvage osteology, *Canadian
            Review of Physical Anthropology 5*(2):49-61.
MORISON, R. S.
1971   Death: Process or event?, *Science 173*:694-698.
1974   Death: Process or event? In *Death Inside Out*, P. Steinfels
            and R. Veatch, eds., pp. 63-70, New York, Harper and Row.

MINEKA, S.
1982   Depression and helplessness in primates. In *Child Nurturance. Studies of Development in Non-Human Primates, 3*, H. E. Fitzgerald, J. A. Mullens and P. Gage, eds., pp. 197-242, New York, Plenum Press.

MOHNOT, S. M.
1980   Behavioural changes in Hanuman Langur infant after mother's death, *Zoologischer Anzeiger 205*:67-75.

MORRIS, R. A.
Forthcoming *Old Russian Ways: Cultural Variations among Three Russian Groups in Oregon.* New York, AMS Press.

MYERHOFF, B.
1974   *Peyote Hunt: The Sacred Journey of the Huichol Indians.* New York, Cornell University Press.

MYERS, F. W.
1961   *Human Personality and its Survival of Bodily Death.* New Hyde Park, New York, University Books, Inc.

NICHOLSON, H .
1971   Religion in Pre-Hispanic Central Mexico. In *Handbook of Middle American Indians*, vol. 10, pp. 395-446, Austin, University of Texas Press.

NOOY-PALM, H.   ·
1979   *The Sa'dan Toraja: A Study of Their Social Life and Religion*, Vol. I, *Organization, Symbols and Beliefs.* The Hague, Martinus Nijhoff.

1986   *The Sa'dan Toraja: A Study of Their Social Life and Religion*, Vol. II, *Rituals of the East and West.* Cinnaminson, New Jersey, Foris Publications.

O'NEIL, J. D.
1988   Referrals to traditional healers: The role of medical interpreters. In *Health Care Issues in Northern Canada*, D. Young, ed., pp. 29-38, Edmonton, Boreal Institute Press.

OBEYESEKERE, G.
1985   Depression, Buddhism, and the work of culture in Sri Lanka. In *Culture and Depression: Studies in the Anthropology and Cross-Cultural Psychiatry of Affect and Disorder*, A. Kleinman and B. Good, eds., pp. 134-152, Berkeley, University of California Press.

OPPENHEIM, R. S.
1973   *Maori Death Customs.* Wellington, A. H. and A. W. Read.

ORTEGA, J.
1944   *Maravillosa Reducción y Conquista de la Provincia de San Joseph del Gran Nayar.* Mexico, Editorial Layac.

PALGI, P., and ABRAMOVITCH, H.
1984   Death: A cross-cultural perspective. In *Annual Review of Anthropology 13*, B. Siegel, ed., pp. 385-417, Palo Alto, Annual Reviews.

PANOFF, M.
1968   The notion of double-self among the Maenge, *Journal of the Polynesian Society 77*:275-295.

PATTERSON, P.
1985   *Koko's Kitten*. New York, Scholastic Inc.

PINA-CABRAL, J. de
1980   Cults of death in northwestern Portugal, *Journal of the Anthropological Society of Oxford 11*(1):1-14.

PLATO
1968   *Republic 1*. A. Bloom, trans. New York, Basic Books.

PRAMOEDYA, A. T.
1975   *A Heap of Ashes*. St. Lucia, University of Queensland Press.

PRESTON, R. J.
1975   *Cree Narrative: Expressing the Personal Meaning of Events*. National Museum of Man, Mercury Paper in Ethnology, No. 30.
1976   Reticence and self-expression: A study of style in social relationships. In *Papers of the Seventh Algonquian Conference*, W. Cowan, ed., pp. 450-494, Carleton University.
1980   The witigo: Algonquian knowledge and Whiteman knowledge. In *Manlike Monsters on Trial: Early Records and Modern Evidence*, M. Ames and M. Halpin, eds., pp. 111-131, University of British Columbia Press.
n.d.   Interference and its consequences: An East Cree variant of deviance? In *Deviance in Cross-Cultural Perspective*, R. Brymer and D. Counts, eds., Special issue of *Anthropologica*, in preparation.

PREUSS, K.
1982   *Mitos y Cuentos Nahuas de la Sierra Madre Occidental*. Mexico, Instituto Nacional Indigenista.

PUSEY, A. E.
1983   Mother-offspring relationships in chimpanzees after weaning, *Animal Behaviour 3*(2):363-377.

RADCLIFFE-BROWN, A. R.
1922   *The Andaman Islanders*. Glencoe, Illinois, The Free Press.
(reprinted
in 1948)

RAHMAN, F.
1970   Revival and reform in Islam. In *The Cambridge History of Islam*, (2 vols.), P. M. Hold, A. K. S. Lambton, B. Lewis,

eds., Vol, 2, pp. 638-645, Cambridge, Cambridge University Press.

RAMSDEM, P. G., and SAUNDERS, S. R.
1986   An in-house infant burial at the Benson site, *Ontario Archaeology 46*:21-26.

RASMUSSEN, K. L. R., and REITE, M.
1982   Loss induced depression in an adult macaque monkey, *American Journal of Psychiatry 139*(5):679-681.

REES, W. D.
1971   The hallucinations of widowhood, *British Medical Journal 4*: 37-41.

REID, J.
1979   A time to live, a time to grieve: Patterns and processes of mourning among the Yolngu of Australia, *Culture, Medicine and Psychiatry 3*:319-346.

REITE, M., and CAPITANO, J. P.
1985   On the nature of social separation and social attachment. In *The Psychobiology of Attachment and Separation*, M. Reite and T. Field, eds., pp. 233-255, Orlando, Academic Press.

REITE, M., HARBECK, R., and HOFFMAN, A.
1981   Altered cellular immune response following peer separation, *Life Science 29*:1133-1136.

REITE, M., SEILER, C., and SHORT, R.
1978   Loss of your mother is more than a loss of a mother, *American Journal of Psychiatry 135A*:370-371.

REITE, M., SHORT, R., SEILER, C., and PAULEY, J. D.
1981   Attachment, loss, and depression, *Journal of Child Psychology and Psychiatry and Related Disciplines 22*:141-169.

REITE, M., and SNYDER, D. S.
1982   Physiology of maternal separation in a bonnet macaque infant, *American Journal of Primatology 2*:115-120.

REYNOLDS, V.
1971   *The Apes*. New York, Harper and Row.

RHINE, R. J., NORTON, G. W., ROENTGEN, W. J., and KLEIN, H. D.
1980   Brief survival of free-ranging baboon infants (*Papio Cynocephalus*) after separation from their mothers, *International Journal of Primatology 1*(4):401-409.

RILEY, J.
1983   Dying and the meanings of death, *Annual Review of Sociology, 9*:191-216.

RIVERS, W. H. R.
1926   *Psychology and Ethnology*. London, Kegan Paul.

ROSALDO, R.
1984   Grief and a headhunter's rage: On the cultural force of emotions. In *Text, Play and Story: The Construction and Reconstruction of Self and Society*, E. M. Bruner, ed., pp. 178-195, Proceedings of the AES, Washington, DC, American Ethnological Society.

ROSENBLATT, P. C., WALSH, P. R., and JACKSON, D. A.
1976   *Grief and Mourning in Cross-Cultural Perspective.* New Haven, Human Relations Area Files Press.

ROSENBLUM, K. A., and PLIMPTON, E. H.
1981   The infant's effort to cope with separation. In *The Uncommon Child*, M. Lewis and L. A. Rosenblum, eds., pp. 225-257, New York, Plenum Press.

ROWELL, T.
1972   *The Social Behaviours of Monkeys.* Harmondsworth, Penguin.

SAAVADRA, A. A. de
1899   Información Rendida por el P. Antonio Arias y Saavaedra, acerca del Estado de la Sierra del Nayarit, en el Siglo XVII. In *Colección de Documentos Inéditos*, A. Santoscoy, ed., Nayarit, J. M. Yguiniz, Guadalajara.

SAHAGÙN, FR. BERNARDINA DE
1981   *Florentine Codex*, Book #2, *The Ceremonies*, A. J. O. Anderson and C. Dibble, eds., School of American Research and the University of Utah Press.

SAUNDERS, S. R.
1986   The Mackenzie site human skeletal material, *Ontario Archaeology 45*:9-26.

SCALETTA, N. M.
1985   Death by sorcery: The social dynamics of dying in Bariai, West New Britain. In *Aging and Its Transformation: Moving Toward Death in Pacific Societies*, D. A. Counts and D. R. Counts, eds., Association of Social Anthropology in Oceania Monograph Series, no. 10, pp. 223-248, Lanham, Maryland, University Press of America.

SCHEFF, T. J.
1977   The distancing of emotion in ritual, *Current Anthropology 18*(3):483-505.

SCHWARTZMAN, J.
1975   The addict, abstinence and the family, *The American Journal of Psychiatry 132*:84-87.

SHROPSHIRE, J. W.
1970   A burial at Wasaga Beach, Ontario, *Ontario Archaeology 15*: 16-20.

SIEGEL, J. T.
1986   *Solo in the New Order: Language and Hierarchy in an Indonesian City.* Princeton, Princeton University Press.
SIMMONS, L. W.
1945   *The Role of the Aged in Primitive Society.* New Haven, Yale University Press.
SMUTS, B. M.
1985   *Sex and Friendship in Baboons.* New York, Aldine.
SNYDER, D. H., GRAHAM, G. E., BOWEN, J. A., and REITE, M.
1984   Peer separation in infant chimpanzees, *Primates 25*(1): 78-88.
SPENCE, M. W., PIHL, R. H., and MOLTO, J. E.
1984   Hunter-gatherer social group identification: A case study from Middle Woodland Southern Ontario. In *Frontiers and Boundaries in Prehistory*, S. DeAtley and F. Findlow, eds., pp. 117-142, British Archaeological Reports, International Series.
SPENCER-BOOTH, Y., and HINDE, R. A.
1971   Effects of brief separations from their mothers during infancy on behaviour of rhesus monkeys 6-24 months later, *Journal of Child Psychology and Psychiatry 12*:157-172.
SPIRO, M. E.
1984   Some reflections on cultural determinism and relativism with special reference to emotion and reason. In *Culture Theory: Essays on Mind, Self, and Emotion*, R. A. Shweder and R. A. Levine, eds., pp. 212-346, New York, Cambridge University Press.
STRAUSS, A., FAGERHAUGH, S., SUCZEK, B., and WIENER, C.
1968   *The Social Organization of Medical Work.* Chicago, University of Chicago Press.
SUOMI, S. J.
1982   Abnormal behavior and primate models of psychopathology. In *Primate Behavior*, J. L. Forbes and J. E. King, eds., pp. 171-21, New York, Academic Press.
1983   Models of depression in primates, *Psychological Medicine 13*(4): 465-468.
AL-TAFTAZANI, A. W.
1985   *at-Tasawwuf al-Islamiya 71*:41-42.
TAINTER, J.
1978   Mortuary practices and the study of prehistoric social systems. In *Advances in Archaeological Method and Theory*, vol. 1, M. Schiffer, ed., pp. 106-141, New York, Academic Press.

TELEKI, G.
1973   Group responses to the accidental death of a chimpanzee in Gombe National Park, Tanzania, *Folia Primatologica 201*:81-94.

TEMERLIN, M. K.
1975   *Lucy: Growing Up Human.* Palo Alto, California, Science and Behavior Books, Inc., Palo Alto, California.

TEUTING, P., and KOSLOW, S. H.
1966   *Special Report on Depression Research.* Washington, D.C., National Institute of Mental Health.

THÍERRY, B., and ANDERSON, J. R.
1986   Adoption in anthropoid primates, *International Journal of Primatology 5*(2):191-216.

THUNBERG, U.
1981   Clinical perspectives in the sick and dying child. In *The Uncommon Child*, M. Lewis and L. A. Rosenblum, eds., pp. 173-191, New York, Plenum Press.

THWAITES, R. G., ed.
1896-1901   *The Jesuit Relations and Allied Documents.* Cleveland, The Burrows Brothers Company.

TOOKER, E.
1964   *An Ethnography of the Huron Indians 1615-1649.* Bureau of American Ethnology Bulletin 190, Washington.

TRIGGER, B. G.
1976   *The Children of Aataentsic*, (two vols.), Montreal and London, McGill-Queen's University Press.

TRIMINGHAM, J. S.
1965   *Islam in the Sudan.* London, Frank Cass & Co.

UCKO, P. J.
1969   Ethnography and archaeological interpretation of funerary remains, *World Archaeology 1*:262-277.

VAN BAAL
1966   *Dema: Description and Analysis of Marind-Anim Culture (South New Guinea).* The Hague, Martinus Nijhoff.

VAN GENNEP, A.
1960   *The Rites of Passage.* M. B. Vizedom and G. L. Caffee trans. Chicago, University of Chicago Press.

VAN LAWICK-GOODALL, J.
1971   *In the Shadow of Man.* Boston, Houghton Mifflin Co.

VOGT, J. L., and HENNESSY, M. B.
1982   Infant separation in monkeys: Studies on social figures other than their mother. In *Child Nurturance: Studies of Development in*

Non Human Primates, 3, H. E. Fitzgerald, J. A. Mullens and P. Gage, eds., pp. 109-133, New York, Plenum Press.

VOLKAN, V. D.
1972   The linking objects of pathological mourners, *Archives of General Psychiatry* 27:215-221.
1981   *Linking Objects and Linking Phenomena: A Study of the Forms, Symptoms, Metapsychology, and Therapy of Complicated Mourning*. New York, International Universities Press.
1987   Severe reactions to bereavement and special professional care. In *Principles of Thanatology*, A. H. Kutscher, A. C. Carr, L. G. Kutscher, eds., pp. 245-274, New York, Columbia University Press.

VOLKMAN, T. A.
1979   The arts of dying in Sulawesi, *Asia* 2(2):24-31.
1985   *Feasts of Honor: Ritual and Change in the Toraja Highlands*. Urbana, University of Illinois Press.

VOLL, J. O.
1980   Hadith scholars and tariqahs: An Ulama group in the 18th century Haramayn and their impact in the Islamic world, *Journal of Asian and African Studies* 15(3-4):265-273.

DE WAAL, F. M. B.
1982   *Chimpanzee Politics*. London, Jonathan Cape Ltd.

WAUGH, E. H.
1989   *The Munshidin of Egypt: Their World and Their Song*, Columbia, South Carolina, University of South Carolina Press.
Forthcoming 'All knower of secrets, acknowledge my pleadings with your face:' Reflections on the interaction of saint and singer in Egyptian dhikr. In *Saints in Islam,* G. Smith and C. Ernest, eds., Princeton, Princeton University Press.

WEIGAND, P. C., and SPENCE, M.
1982   The obsidian mining complex at La Joya, Jalisco. In *Mining and Mining Techniques in Ancient Mesoamerica*, special issue of *Anthropology*, VI:175-188, P. C. Weigand and G. Gwynne, eds.
1972   *Co-operative Labor Groups in Subsistence Activities among the Huichol Indians,* Mesoamerican Studies #7, Carbondale, Southern Illinois University Museum.
1985a   Considerations on the archaeology and ethnohistory of the Mexicaneros, Tequales, Coras, Huicholes, and Caxcanes of Nayarit, Jalisco, and Zacatecas. In *Contributions to the Archaeology and Ethnohistory of Greater Mesoamerica*, W. J. Folan, ed., pp. 126-187, Carbondale, Southern Illinois University Press.

1985b   Evidence for complex societies during the Western Meso-american Classic period. In *The Archaeology of West and Northwest Mesoamerica*, M. Foster and P. C. Weigand, eds., pp. 47-91, Boulder, Westview, Praeger.

WEINER, A. B.
1985   Inalienable wealth, *American Ethnologist 12*:210-227.

WEISS, K. M.
1981   Evolutionary perspectives on human agina. In *Other Ways of Growing Old*, P. Amoss and S. Harrell, ed., pp. 25-58, Palo Alto, California, Stanford University Press.

WELLENKAMP, J. C.
1984   A Psychocultural Study of Loss and Death among the Toraja, Ph.D. dissertation, University of California, San Diego.
1988a   Order and disorder in Toraja thought and ritual, *Ethnology 27*(3): 311-326.
1988b   Notions of grief and catharsis among the Toraja, *American Ethnologist 15*(3):486-500.

WIKAN, U.
1987   Public grace and private fears: Gaiety, offense and sorcery in northern Bali, *Ethos 15*(4):337-365.

WILLIAMS, H. W.
1957   *A Dictionary of the Maori Language*, 6th ed. Wellington, Government Printer.

WILLIAMSON, R.
1978   Preliminary report on human interment patterns of the Draper Site, *Canadian Journal of Archaeology 2*:117-121.

VON WINNING, H., and HAMMER, O.
1972   *Anecdotal Sculpture of Ancient West Mexico*. Los Angeles, Ethnic Arts Council of Los Angeles.

WRIGHT, J. K.
1966   *Human Nature in Geography*. Cambridge, Cambridge University Press

WRONG, G. M.
1968   *The Long Voyage to the Country of the Hurons*. (by G. Sagard, facsimile edition, 1939). New York, Greenwood Press.

YERKES-BLANCHARD, R.
1977   Home safe with chimpanzees, Part 2. In *Progress in Ape Research*, G. H. Bourne, ed., pp. 7-13, New York, Academic Press.

YERKES, R.
1925   *Almost Human*. New York, The Century Co.

ZELLER, A. C.
1985   Understanding anthropomorphism. Paper presented at American Society of Primatologists Meetings, Niagara Falls, New York.

ZELINSKY, W.
1975   Unearthly delights: Cemetery names and the map of the changing American afterworld. In *Geographies of the Mind*, D. Lowenthal and M. Bowden, eds., pp. 171-195, New York, Oxford University Press.

ZENKOVSKY, S. A.
1970   *Russia's Old Believers: Spiritual Movements of the Seventeenth Century* (in Russian). Munich, Wilhelm Fink Verlag.

ZINGG, R.
1938   *The Huichols: Primitive Artists*. Denver, University of Denver Contributions to Ethnography, #1.

ZOLA, I. K.
1973   Medicine as an institution of social control: The medicalizing of society, *Sociological Review 29*(4):487-504.

Contributors

ELLEN BADONE is an Assistant Professor of Anthropology and Religious Studies at McMaster University in Hamilton, Ontario. She received her doctorate in Anthropology at the University of California, Berkeley, in 1985. Her fieldwork in Brittany has focussed on death and dying, as well as on non-biomedical healing practices. Ellen Badone's publications include *The Appointed Hour: Death, Worldview and Social Change in Brittany* (University of California Press, 1989), and an edited volume *Religious Orthodoxy and Popular Faith in European Society* (Princeton University Press, 1990).

DAVID R. COUNTS is Professor and Chair in the Department of Anthropology of McMaster University, Hamilton, Canada, where he has taught since 1968. Most of his research has been conducted jointly with Dorothy Counts in West New Britain Province of Papua New Guinea. Topics of research and publication have ranged from linguistics to development, aging, and death. He and Dorothy have recently begun a study of nomadic North American retirees who live in their recreational vehicles.

DOROTHY A. COUNTS is Professor and Chair in the Department of Anthropology of The University of Waterloo, Waterloo, Canada, where she has taught since 1968. With David Counts, she has been carrying out field research in West New Britain Province of Papua New Guinea since 1966 on topics that have included development, cargo cults, aging, suicide and domestic violence as well as death and dying. With her husband, she has recently begun a study of retiree "RV Nomads" in North America.

JOSEPH M. KAUFERT is an applied medical anthropologist and Professor in the Departments of Anthropology and Social and Preventive Medicine in the University of Manitoba. His doctoral work was done at Northwestern University in Anthropology and Political Science and he taught as far afield and the University of Ghana before moving to Manitoba. He is particularly interested in intercultural problems of health care delivery.

MICHAEL D. LIEBER is Associate Professor of Anthropology at the University of Illinois, Chicago, Ill., and he has taught anthropology at the Community College of Micronesia. He has been working at understanding Kapinga people on their own atoll, Kapingamarangi, and on Pohnpei, where many are resettled, since 1965. Chief among his interests are the anthropology of personhood and the understanding of resettled communities.

HIRINI MOKO MEAD is Professor of Maori Studies in the Victoria University of Wellington, NZ. After a successful career as a rural teacher in Maori schools and a writer of children's stories about Maori, he returned to university, taking BA and MA Honours degrees at Auckland University, and the Ph.D. at Southern Illinois University. Before accepting the position of Head of Maori Studies at Victoria University, he taught at Auckland University, and at the University of British Columbia and McMaster University in Canada. As both as Maori elder and an anthropologist, he is well-known for his part in developing the *Te Maori* exhibition of Maori Art that toured internationally in the 1980s.

RICHARD A. MORRIS completed his doctorate in Anthropology at the University of Oregon in 1981. He has carried out extensive research among Russian religious isolates in both the Western United States and the Soviet Union. Since the completion of his chapter in this book he has returned for further research in the USSR and currently resides near his Molokan and Old Believer friends in Oregon. He is a research anthropologist affiliated with the Russian and East European Studies Center of the University of Oregon.

JOHN A. O'CONNOR is the Director, Chaplaincy Services, Chedoke-McMaster Hospitals and an Assistant Professor, Department of Family Medicine, McMaster University. The last time he checked he was still an ordained Lutheran pastor. He is a Teaching Supervisor with the Canadian Association for Pastoral Education and a Clinical Member/Approved Supervisor with American Association for Marriage and Family Therapy. He has had extensive involvement with the development of Do Not Resuscitate Orders and Organ Donation Policies. His greatest pleasure and sense of accomplishment come from his two children, Kristin and John, who are both adolescents and still like him. His leisure activities include coaching soccer and pursuing a part-time Ph.D. in Religious Studies.

JOHN D. O'NEIL is an assistant professor in the Departments of Anthropology and Social and Preventive Medicine in the University of Manitoba. Trained in Anthropology at the University of California, San Francisco, he completed his Ph.D. in 1983. With Joseph Kaufert, he has been working in applied medical anthropology in a hospital setting where native patients must deal with a Euro-canadian medical culture.

RICHARD J. PRESTON is Professor of Anthropology at McMaster University, Hamilton, Ont. where he has taught since 1971. Educated at the University of North Carolina, he and Sarah Preston have been sojourners among the Cree of James Bay, Quebec, many times since 1963.

SARAH C. PRESTON was for many years a participant in Richard's research among the Cree of James Bay, Quebec. Since completion of an MA in anthropology, she has pursued her own research among Cree women. She teaches part-time in the Department of Religious Studies at McMaster University.

PETER RAMSDEN was born in Kent, England, and moved with his family to Canada at the age of 11. His interest in archaeology was kindled while attending St. Michael's College School in Toronto, and he went on to obtain a B.A. in

Anthropology at the University of Toronto. After getting an M.A. in Archaeology at the University of Calgary, he returned to the University of Toronto, receiving a Ph.D. in Anthropology in 1975. He has held teaching positions at the University of Western Ontario, Wilfrid Laurier University and McMaster University, where he is now Associate Professor of anthropology. His archaeological research has taken him all over Southern Ontario, to the central Canadian Arctic, and most recently to Ireland.

WILLIAM E. SIMEONE received his B.A. in European history at the University of Alaska, Fairbanks, in 1974 and then became a construction worker on the Trans-Alaska pipeline. In 1984 he received an M.A. in anthropology at McMaster University where he has just completed his Ph.D. dissertation on History, Identity and the Northern Athabaskan Potlatch. Currently Simeone is working on a research project investigating the impact of the Exxon-Valdez oil spill on Native Alaskans.

EARLE H. WAUGH is professor of Religious Studies at the University of Alberta. He studied History of Religions under Mircea Eliade at the University of Chicago and has specialized in Islamic religious tradition in his publications. His four edited books include two dealing with Islam in North America; his most recent book is *The Munshidin of Egypt: Their World and Their Song*, South Carolina, 1989. He is currently Chair of Canadian Studies at the University of Alberta.

CELIA GARCÍA DE WEIGAND, MLAS (State University of New York, 1984), was born in Jalisco, Mexico. She has had a life-time interest in Native American cultures, especially their arts and crafts. She has accomplished years of field work in various areas of Mexico. Her monograph, *Huichol Indian Beadwork: Techniques and Designs 1820-1980,* was published in 1990. She has four articles published on various aspects of Huichol arts and crafts.

PHIL C. WEIGAND, Ph.D. (Southern Illinois University, 1970), was born in Nebraska. His interests are the archaeology, ethnohistory, and ethnography of Western and Northwestern Mesoamerica, where he has spent most of his professional career. He is currently a 'Profesor de Investigaciones' at the Colegio de Michoacán (Zamora, Michoacán, México) and a research archaeologist for the Museum of Northern Arizona. He has published 2 monographs and 14 articles on various aspects of Huichol culture, aside from those in archaeology. A book, *Los Huicholes en su Contexto Nayarita,* is in press.

JANE WELLENKAMP is a psychological anthropologist who received her Ph.D. from the University of California, San Diego. She has been at UCLA since 1985. Her primary research interests are grief and mourning, culture and emotions, rites of passage, and the ethnography of insular Southeast Asia. She is also a Senior Public Administration Analyst for a Comprehensive Child Development Program (CCDP) project in Venice, California.

DR. ANNE C. ZELLER received her Ph.D. from the University of Toronto in 1978. Her research experience includes research on human and chimpanzee chromosomes between 1971 and 1973, field research on Barbary macaques in

Morocco and Gibraltar in 1973, field research on communication in Barbary macaques in 1978, the study of Japanese macaque facial gestures in 1980, field trips to Nevis in 1981 to study vervet monkeys, to Florida in 1985 to study crab-eating macaques, and to Indonesia in 1988 to study adult-infant interaction in long-tailed macaques. She has written widely on a variety of topics including facial gestures in Barbary macaques, the use of film in primate research, the ethics of primate research, the controversy over sign language in apes, the role of children in Hominid evolution, the history of communication research in primates, deviant behavior in primates, cognition in primate communication, Arctic hysteria in the Salem witch trials, and spouse abuse in Canadian novels.

Index